CULT TV THE COMEDIES

CULT TV THE COMEDIES

THE ULTIMATE CRITICAL GUIDE

JON E. LEWIS AND PENNY STEMPEL

First published in Great Britain in 1998 by
PAVILION BOOKS LIMITED
London House, Great Eastern Wharf
Parkgate Road, London SW11 4NQ

Designed by Nigel Partridge

A CIP catalogue record for this book is available from the British Library.

ISBN 1 86205 245 X

Set in Trade Gothic
Printed in Spain by Book Print

2 4 6 8 10 9 7 5 3 1

This book can be ordered direct from the publisher. Please contact the Marketing Department. But try your bookshop first.

CONTENTS

User's Guide 8

Introduction 9

Entries from A to Z 12

Acknowledgments 245

Index 246

Jon E. Lewis is a writer and a critic. He has written for *Time Out* and the *Independent*, and is the author of numerous books on popular culture, including the bestselling *Cult TV*. His other books include several *Mammoth Book of... Anthologies* and the forthcoming encyclopaedic *Ultimate TV Guide*.

Penny Stempel has worked in film and television as both a director and a producer, and lectures in Media Studies. She was TV critic of *Venue* magazine and is the co-author of the forthcoming *Ultimate TV Guide*.

Basil: Oh, prawn, that was it. When you said *prawn,* I thought you said *war.* Oh, the war! Oh yes, completely slipped my mind, yes, I'd forgotten all about it. Hitler, Himmler, and all that lot, oh yes, completely forgotten it, just like that *(snaps his fingers).* Sorry, what was it again?

2nd German: *(with some menace)* A prawn cocktail...

Basil: Oh, yes Eva Prawn... and Goebbels too, he's another one I can hardly remember at all.

1st German: And *ein* ickled herring!

Basil: Herman Goering, yes, yes... and von Ribbentrop, that was another one...

1st German: And four cold meat salads, please.

Basil: Certainly, well, I'll just get your *hors d'oeuvres... hors d'oeuvres* vich must be obeyed at all times without question... Sorry! Sorry!

Polly: Mr Fawlty, will you please call your wife immediately?

Basil: I can't, I've got too much to do. Listen... *(he whispers through his teeth)* Don't mention the war... *I* mentioned it once, but I think I got away with it...

Basil: What's the matter?

2nd German: It's alright.

Basil: Is there something wrong?

2nd German: Will you stop talking about the war?

Basil: Me? You started it!

2nd German: We did not start it.

Basil: Yes you did, you invaded Poland...

KEY TO ENTRY CREDITS

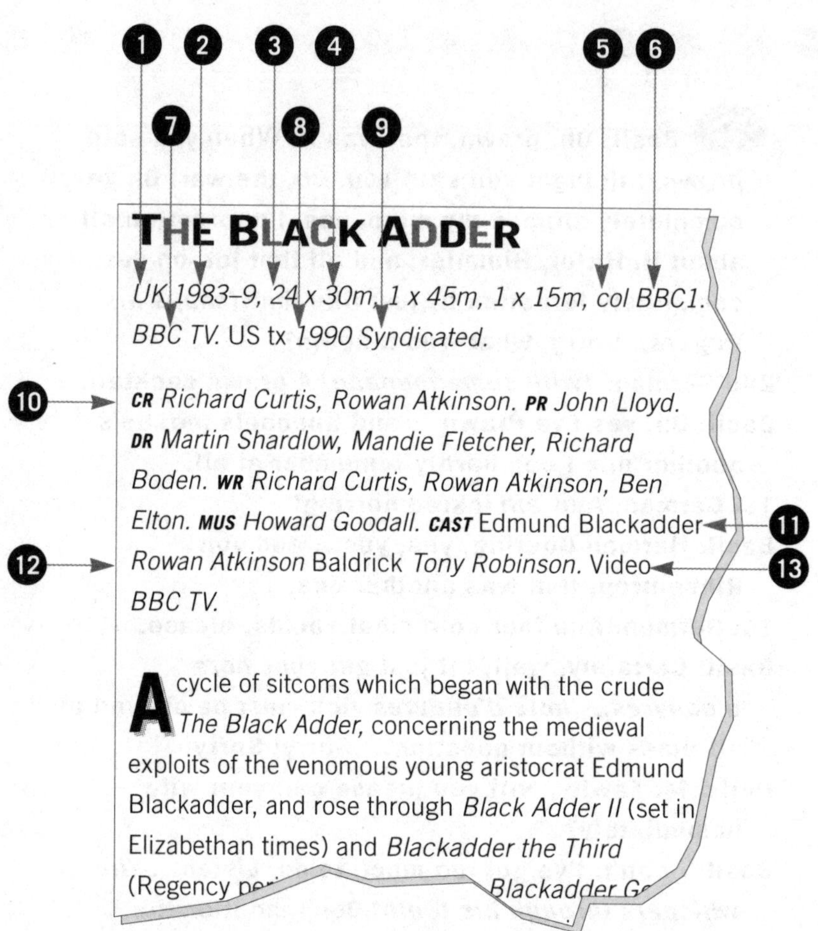

1
2
3
4
5
6
7
8
9
THE BLACK ADDER
UK 1983–9, 24 x 30m, 1 x 45m, 1 x 15m, col BBC1.
BBC TV. US tx 1990 Syndicated.
10
CR Richard Curtis, Rowan Atkinson. PR John Lloyd.
DR Martin Shardlow, Mandie Fletcher, Richard
Boden. WR Richard Curtis, Rowan Atkinson, Ben
Elton. MUS Howard Goodall. CAST Edmund Blackadder
11
12
Rowan Atkinson Baldrick Tony Robinson. Video
13
BBC TV.
A cycle of sitcoms which began with the crude
The Black Adder, concerning the medieval
exploits of the venomous young aristocrat Edmund
Blackadder, and rose through Black Adder II (set in
Elizabethan times) and Blackadder the Third
(Regency per
Blackadder G

1 Country of origin
2 Year(s) of transmission
3 Number of episodes
4 Programme length
5 Colour or black and white
6 Transmission channel in country of origin
7 Production company/companies
8 Transmission date(s) in secondary country
9 Transmission channel in secondary country
10 ***CR:*** creator(s), ***EXEC PR:*** executive producer(s), ***PR:*** producer(s), ***DR:*** director(s), ***WR:*** writer(s), ***MUS:*** composer(s)
11 Character(s)
12 Actor(s)/Actress(es)
13 Video availability

INTRODUCTION

And now for something completely different... In its 27th June 1923 edition, *The Times* of London carried a small ad: 'Seeing by wireless. Inventor of apparatus wishes to hear from someone who will assist (not financially) in making working model. Write Box S. 686.' The inventor behind the box was John Logie Baird who, three years later, demonstrated 'television' for the first time. Ten years further on, Baird, the British Broadcasting Corporation and EMI-Marconi founded the world's first regular 'high-definition' television service. The TV Age had begun.

They had the technology, the only one problem remained – what to put on Baird's tube of delight? Initially, the BBC – under the high-minded rule of Lord Reith – concentrated on news and 'worthy' programmes, but gradually it begin to dawn on even the walls of the Corporation that man and woman cannot live on seriousness alone – they need to enjoy themselves. Even better, they need to partake of that peculiarly human activity: laughing. In the USA, the situation was different for the simple reason that commercial TV stations, desperate to seek out the mass audience, had aimed for the audience's funny bone from the start.

Oh, Mr Grant...

But UK or USA, the first comedies to arrive on the TV were derived from three fountainheads – radio (with some shows, such as *Amos 'n' Andy* transferring to the new medium almost intact), film and, especially, music hall/vaudeville. The new TV audience wanted funny sights a plenty and got them in such 'vaudeo' slapstick programmes as Milton Berle's *Texaco Star Theatre* and *The Abbott and Costello Show.* Audience desire for high visual content also ensured that the initial TV situation comedies – humorous shows involving recurring characters in a defined setting – also traded heavily on pratfalls and physical comedy.

The greatest hit of the 1950s, *I Love Lucy,* being

perhaps the exemplar. (Of the first wave of TV comedy, *The Jack Benny Show* was the odd programme out, since it depended on Benny's verbal wit; at the same time, it was absolutely typical in that it was built around a star personality). Since people get the TV they deserve, the fifties and early sixties saw a rash of cosy sitcoms, invariably centred on the family: *Bachelor Father, The Dick Van Dyke Show, The Adventures of Ozzie and Harriet, The Beverly Hillbillies, The Andy Griffith Show.* The 'Hi Honey, I'm Home' show, as the family sitcom became dubbed, was less dominant in Britain, however, where post-war disillusion set in early, and a distinctly black vein of sitcom humour emerged in *Hancock's Half Hour* in 1956, to be continued by that show's principal writers, Alan Galton and Ray Simpson, in *Steptoe and Son* in 1962. The other main form of TV humour, the vaudeville-derived skit and gag show, also took an early turn away from complacency in Britain, first with ex-Goon Michael Bentine's *It's a Square World,* then with the political satire of *That Was The Week That Was.* As the sixties rocked and rebelled, so did the airwaves, with such topical, even directly political, shows as *The Smothers Brothers Comedy Hour* and *Rowan and Martin's Laugh-In* becoming mega-hits. Unconcerned with politics, but deeply subverting the rules of TV comedy, was 1969's surrealistic and anarchic *Monty Python's Flying Circus.* One of a handful of programmes to move the boundaries of TV humour, *Python* even dropped such traditional joke elements as the punch line (Graham Chapman's colonel arriving mid-sketch to proclaim that 'this sketch is becoming too silly – stop it'), and was always busy in the use of *ostranie*

Schwing!

– the drawing of attention to artifice – for humorous effect, routinely parodying other shows and the portentousness of BBC announcements, replacing the latter with fakes ('Now on BBC television, a choice of viewing. On BBC2, a discussion on censorship between the Bishop of Woolwich and a nude man. And on BBC1, me telling you this').

TV comedy innovation continued into the early 70s with *The Mary Tyler Moore Show* (the first hit comedy featuring a woman who was single by choice) and the anti-war ethos of *M*A*S*H.* By mid-decade, however, the pendulum had swung back to domestic conservatism, a trend reinforced in America by the introduction of 8.00–9.00pm 'family viewing' and a reaction to the realism of such comedies as *All In the Family* (the US take on *Till Death Us Do Part).* In Britain, it was the age of *The Good Life* and a comedy orbit that hardly moved outside Suburbia. Of course, *The Good Life* was funny, but most of the comedy shows which issued forth from the TV production companies were not, their tired titles *(Holding the Fort, Thicker Than Water)* a Brobdingnagian clue to their equally tired content.

Then in 1982 came *The Young Ones,* a sitcom which pushed the boundaries of convention (surrealist interludes, rock bands performing mid-show), taste (lashings of cartoon violence) and inaugurated the coming of alternative comedy, a wave of non-racist/sexist humour which would continue through *The Comic Strip, Red Dwarf,* and

Saturday Live/Friday Night Live, a show which (like its US original) took one stream of TV comedy back to its fountainhead: the theatre stand-up. *Vic Reeves' Big Night Out* only confirmed the fact.

As the eighties progressed into the nineties, so it became obvious that TV humour was splitting its sides, so to speak, to form many trends. The small screen is often but a mirror to the faces which looked into it. And those who looked into the small screen in the nineties were atomised, divorced and dysfunctional, with the kids viewing in one room and their parent(s) in another.

Did we laugh? You bet your bottom dollar. The whole family might not gather around the glowing tube to watch the same show (well they do in the USA if it's *Seinfeld),* but television – especially television comedy – is what family remnants talk about, peer groups talk about and what strangers find to talk about. It's the glue which binds whole portions of society together.

Titter ye not

And here's the funny thing. The most fashionable form of the late-nineties sitcom, the goofy singles show *(Ellen, Seinfeld)* is just as much a traditional family sitcom – if you care to look at it – as those of the Eisenhower fifties. Relatives have simply been replaced by a family of friends, *Friends* itself being a case in point. The inalienable truth of the sitcom is that no single person must face things alone. The same might go for life itself.

Of the thousands of pure comedy shows which have been produced, a select number have reached an exulted status. These are the shows whose catchphrases are repeated in the school yard, whose characters become peer and national institutions, whose fans organise viewing parties, whose fans weep tears of sadness when their time on the tube is ended (until resurrected for immortality on satellite and cable). These are the cult comedies. Leaf through the following pages for the full monty on everything from *Abbott and Costello* to *The Young Ones.* A catalogue of the series and the stars who entranced the viewing world for fifty years is there for the reading.

And the laughing.

THE ABBOTT AND COSTELLO SHOW

USA 1952–3, 52 x 30m, bw Syndicated. TCA Corp.

CR *Bud Abbott and Lou Costello.* **PR** *Pat Costello, Alex Gottlieb.* **DR** *Jean Yarborough.* **WR** *Bud Abbott and Lou Costello, Clyde Bruckman.* **CAST** Bud Abbott *himself* Lou Costello *himself* Sid Fields *himself* Hillary Brooke *herself* Mike the Cop *Gordon Jones* Stinky *Joe Besser* Mr Bacciagalupe *Joe Kirk.*

With their Hollywood career in decline, slapstick stars Bud Abbott (born William Abbott) and Lou Costello (Louis Cristillo) tested the new medium of TV, first as hosts of *The Colgate Comedy Hour*, then with this half-hour sitcom for syndication. The storyline – such as it was – had the duo as unemployed, apartment-sharing actors constantly concocting schemes to make easy money or dodge bills, particularly the rent owed to landlord Mr Fields. Usually, however, episodes unravelled into a collection of unrelated jokes and knock-abouts, almost all of them recycled direct from Abbott and Costello's old movies.

Audiences lapped it up. Endlessly rerun, the show became one of the most successful in the history of syndicated TV, doing much to fill the coffers of Costello – the short, funny one – who owned the show.

Also seen was Costello's girlfriend Hillary, a bullying tenant called Stinky (always dressed in the clothes of a little boy), Mike the Cop, and Abbott and Costello's pet chimp, Bingo. Towards the end of the series, there was a perceptible rise in quality, as director Jean Yarborough insisted on tighter plots, and a new gag writer, Clyde Bruckman, was drafted in, Abbott and Costello having used up their own patented stock of humour. In 1966 a cartoon version of *Abbott and Costello* was syndicated by Hanna-Barbera. Abbott provided his own voice, but that of Costello (who had died in 1959 at the age of fifty-two) was supplied by Stan Irwin.

ABSOLUTELY

UK 1989–93, 24 x 30m, col C4. Absolutely Productions.

PR *David Tyler, Alan Nixon.* **DR** *Various, including Graham C Williams.* **WR** *Morwenna Banks, Jack Docherty, Moray Hunter, Gordon Kennedy, John Sparkes.* **CAST** *Morwenna Banks, Jack Docherty, Moray Hunter, Gordon Kennedy, John Sparkes.*

Anarchic sketch show, dubbed the >*Monty Python* of latter televisual times, courtesy of the Scottish school of alternative comedy. Although it ran the gamut of skit-programme possibilities, from animation (*pace Python*) to spoofed-up songs, its particular pleasure was its regular gallery of invented characters: Little Girl, rabid nationalist McGlashen, the Stoneybridge town council, melodious Mr Muzak, anorak Calum Gilhooley, disaster-prone DIY expert Denzil and scatalogical Frank Hovis (these last two creations performed by lone Welsh team-member John Sparkes), Hovis being an expert on the curing of chapped anuses. The characters Donald McDiarmid and George McDiarmid, even enjoyed their own spin-off series, *mr don and mr george*. Most of the *Absolutely* performers moved ever up the showbiz ladder, though Gordon Kennedy progressed downwards to co-host *The National Lottery Live.*

Absolutely Fabulous

UK 1992–6, 20 x 30m, col BBC2/BBC1. BBC TV. US tx *1994 Comedy Central.*

CR *Jennifer Saunders.* ***PR*** *Jon Plowman, Janice Thomas.* ***DR*** *Bob Spiers.* ***WR*** *Jennifer Saunders.* ***MUS*** *Julie Driscoll and Adrian Edmondson ('This Wheel's on Fire' theme vocals; lyrics by Bob Dylan and Rick Danko).* ***CAST*** Edina Monsoon *Jennifer Saunders* Patsy Stone *Joanna Lumley* Saffron Monsoon *Julia Sawalha* Mother *June Whitfield* Bubble *Jane Horrocks.* Video *BBC.*

Hugely popular sitcom set in the trendy world of the nineties fashion industry, developed from a >*French and Saunders* sketch in which Jennifer Saunders played a baseball-capped parent berated by her conservative daughter (Dawn French) for playing hip-hop too loudly. For the series, Saunders took the part of Edina Monsoon – rumoured to reference Saunders' sometime PR, Lynne Franks – a late-thirtysomething sixties leftover with her own PR/fashion business, who behaved badly (drugs, Bollinger champagne, cigarettes, men, fashion-following) with bouffanted pal Patsy (Joanna Lumley, *New Avengers, Sapphire and Steel*), a *Cosmo*-type fashion writer. Looking on aghast at the antics of the two 'dahlings' were Edina's sensible daughter Saffron (Julia Sawalha from *Press Gang*) and her mother (played by MOR comic actress June Whitfield, >*Terry and June*). Bubbles (RSC actress Jane Horrocks) was Edina's vacant PA. Also seen was Adrian Edmondson (>*Comic Strip,* >*Bottom,* and husband of Saunders in real life) as restaurant critic Hamish. Direction was by veteran Bob Spiers (whose CV constitutes a virtual TV's Greatest Hits catalogue, including segments of >*Dad's Army,* >*The Goodies,* >*Are You Being Served?*), while comedian Ruby Wax (>*Girls on Top*) served as script editor.

Oh, sweetie

Saunders' first solo project after her years with *The Comic Strip, Girls on Top* and *French and Saunders,* the politically incorrect, slay-every-sacred-nineties-cow (dieting, cosmetic surgery, crystals) *Ab Fab* was an immediate hit, securing two BAFTAs for its first season (Best Comedy, and Best Light Entertainment Performer for Lumley's turn as the dipso, nymphomaniacal Patsy) and BBC2's highest ratings for 1992. Although performances continued to be of high calibre, the second series – transmitted on BBC1 – was short on comedy, long on guest appearances (Germaine Greer, Suzi Quatro, Lulu even) and Edina's spouting of 'Darling!', though the episode in which the kitchen at 34 Claremont Avenue, London, burned down ('Birth') had its moments, as Edina tried to dress for the occasion (Edina to schoolgirl Saffron: 'It's OK for you, you've got a uniform to wear') and restyle the room with the 'Irish Crofter's Look'. A third and final series marked a return to form, by which time *Ab*

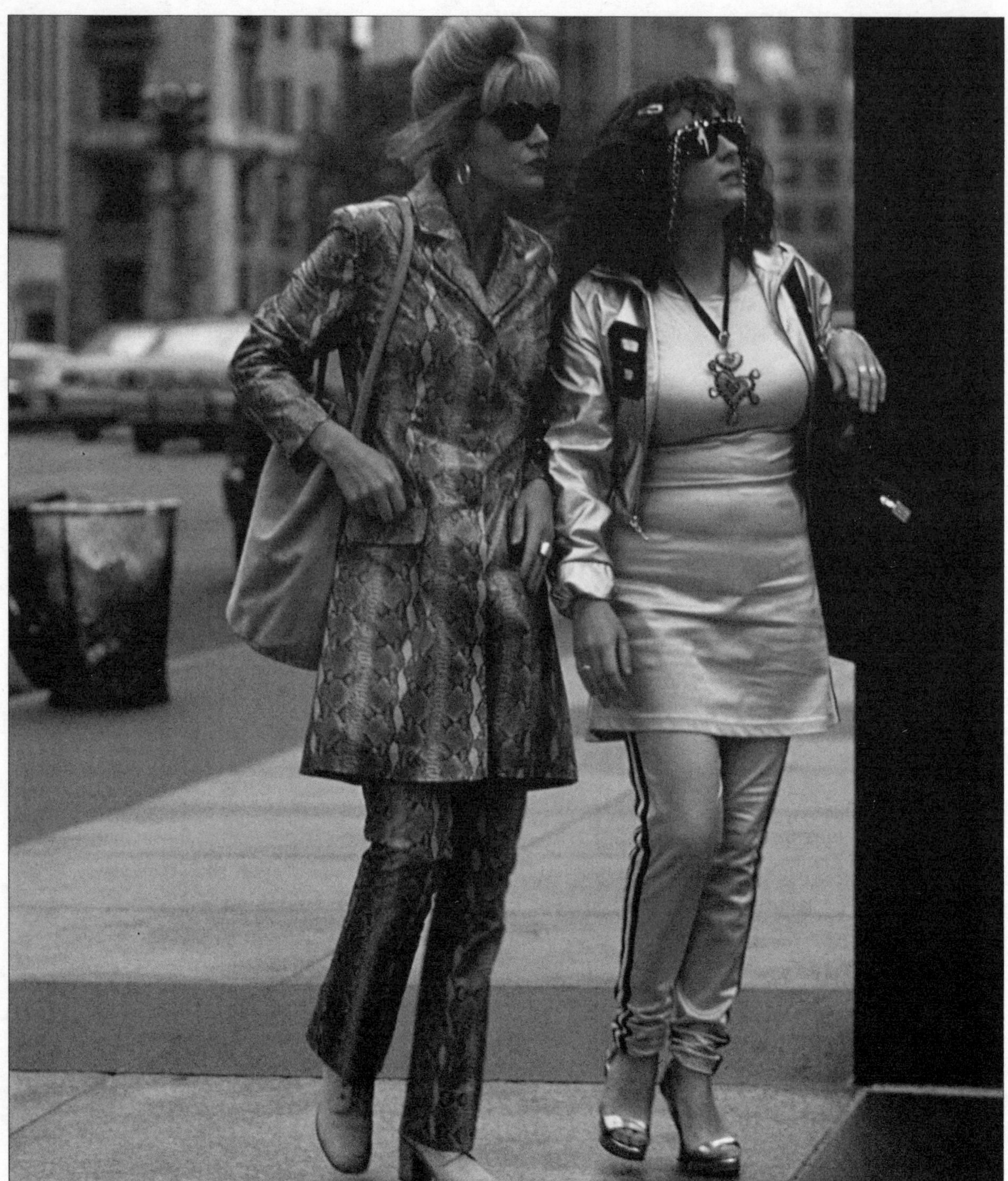

Fab had become a huge seller around the world, being screened in, among other countries, South Africa, Iceland, Australia and Poland. A rapturous response in the USA led to Roseanne Barr buying the rights for a Stateside version, which floundered when the ABC network wanted to remove the characters' drunkenness and swearing. 'Oh, sweetie…

A one-off *Ab Fab* special was released in 1996, in which Edina and Patsy contemplated the setting up of a cable TV station, but got distracted by a chance to go on the piste at Val d'Isère.

THE ADDAMS FAMILY

USA 1964–6, 64 x 30m, bw ABC. Filmways. UK tx *1966–8 ITV.*

CR *Charles Addams, David Levy.* **EXEC PR** *David Levy.* **PR** *David Levy, Nat Perrin.* **DR** *Various, including Sidney Lanfield, Nat Perrin, Sidney Soklon, Jerry Hopper, Arthur Hiller, Jean Yarborough.* **WR** *Various, including Hannibal Coons, Preston Ward, George Tibbles, Carol Henning, Jameson Brewer, Harry Winkler, Keith Fowler, Phil Leslie.* **MUS** *Vic Mizzy.* **CAST** Morticia Frump Addams *Carolyn Jones* Gomez Addams *John Astin* Uncle Fester Frump *Jackie Coogan* Lurch/Thing *Ted Cassidy* Grandmama Addams *Blossom Rock* Pugsley Addams *Ken Weatherwax* Wednesday Addams *Lisa Loring* Cousin Itt *Felix Silla (voice: Tony Magro).* Video *Polygram.*

◀◀◀ *'Oh, sweetie…' Joanna Lumley and Jennifer Saunders yet again indulge in a spot of shopping in* Absolutely Fabulous.

» ***They're creepy and they're kooky, their life is kinda spooky…*** **«**

Spoof freak show, developed from Charles Addams' famous *New Yorker* cartoon strip. Heads of the eponymous and altogether 'ookie family' were Latino lawyer Gomez (seldom seen without a gangster suit and Castro-sized cigar) and his tantalising black-haired wife Morticia. Their ramshackle mansion on North Cemetery Ridge was filled with strange *objets d'art* and *du mort* (including a stuffed fish with a protruding human leg), as well as ghoulish, bald-headed Uncle Fester (who lit light bulbs by placing them in his mouth), haggish Grandmama, and Gomez and Morticia's perverse spawn, daughter Wednesday and son Pugsley. Household tasks were performed by the gaunt family retainer, Lurch ('You rang?'), and the disembodied hand-in-a-box, Thing. Making up the distended Addams family was hirsute Cousin Itt. Episodes began with a sombre family group adding percussive finger clicks to the show's theme tune.

Much of the appeal of *The Addams Family* lay in the simmering sexual attraction between Gomez and Morticia, and, as with rival CBS show >*The Munsters,* in its black comic inversion of normality. Thus Morticia snipped the blooms off stalks before arranging flowers in a vase, thrilled with her

You rang?

The 'altogether ookie' members of The Addams Family.

Morticia went to a named Hollywood actress. The only one to apply was Carolyn Jones (sometime wife of TV mega-producer Aaron Spelling), an Oscar nominee for a bit part in the 1956 feature *Bachelor Party*. Former child star Jackie Coogan (who had played, aged four, the title role of Charlie Chaplin's 1921 film *The Kid*) was cast as Fester.

Moderately successful on its initial ABC run, ranking twenty-third in the Nielsen ratings, *The Addams Family* proved durable enough to spawn a 1973 Hanna-Barbera animated version, broadcast on NBC, in which the Addams Family roamed America in a creepy camper (the voice cast included a young Jodie Foster as Pugsley), and a 1977 reunion TVM, *Hallowe'en with the New Addams Family*. A feature film *The Addams Family,* starring Anjelica Huston and Raul Julia, was a huge box-office success for Paramount Pictures in 1991, taking a first weekend gross of $24.1 million. It in turn was followed by *Addams Family Values,* 1993, and a 1998 TVM, *Addams Family Reunion*.

husband to the thought of torture (to please Gomez, she drilled his teeth until she hit the nerve), and sent Pugsley to a psychiatrist when she saw him help an old woman across the road.

The outlandishness of *The Addams Family* made it the virtual TV definition of the breaking sixties counter-culture. To ensure a wide audience, however, a nervous ABC insisted that the part of

As if to prove you can't keep a good freak show down, in 1992 Hanna-Barbera reanimated *The Addams Family* as a Saturday morning serial for ABC network. Of the original cast, only John Astin (also >*I'm Dickens, He's Fenster, Operation Petticoat, Tazmania,* and director of segments on such TV shows as *CHiPS* and *Macmillan and Wife*) lent his voice.

The Adventures of Ozzie and Harriet

USA 1952–66, 435 x 25m, bw/col ABC. ABC/ Stage 5.

CR *Ozzie Nelson.* **PR** *Ozzie Nelson, Robert Angus, Bill Lewis, Leo Penn.* **DR** *Various, including Ozzie Nelson, Leo Penn.* **WR** *Various, including Ozzie Nelson.* **CAST** Ozzie Nelson *himself* Harriet Hilliard Nelson *herself* Eric 'Ricky' Nelson *himself* Dave Nelson *himself* Kris Nelson (Rick's wife) *herself* June Nelson (Dave's wife) *herself* 'Thorny' Thornberry *Don DeFore* Joe Randolph *Lyle Talbot* Clara Randolph *Mary Jane Croft* Darby *Parley Baer* Doc Williams *Frank Cady* Wally *Skip Young.*

Long-running family sitcom, the gimmick of which was that the principal actors were, er, a family themselves. They were: middle-class bandleader Ozzie Nelson, his wife (and band chanteuse) Harriet, and their sons Ricky and David. By the end of the run, Ricky (who had gone from a boyish eleven to a husband of twenty-five) had parlayed his small-screen career into one as a fifties rock'n'roller, helped by a 1957 episode in which he sang Fats Domino's 'I'm Walkin'.' This, with a B-side of 'A Teenager's Romance', became a million seller. Like a number of other classic fifties sitcoms, *Ozzie and Harriet* began life on radio, while its route to TV land was eased by a 1951 feature film entitled *Here Come the Nelsons.* In 1973, the Nelson parents returned with a sequel to the TV *Adventures* in which they took in two college girls as boarders and surrogate daughters. It was called, with no great originality, *Ozzie's Girls.*

The Adventures of Pete and Pete

USA 1993–6, Approx 30 x 1/10/30m, col Nickelodeon. Nickelodeon.

CR *Will McRobb and Chris Viscardi.* **DR** *Katerine Dieckman, Alison MacLean.* **WR** *Will McRobb and Chris Viscardi.* **MUS** *Polaris (theme), Miracle Legion et al.* **CAST** Little Pete Wrigley *Danny Tamberelli* Big Pete Wrigley/Narrator *Mike Maronna* Mom (Joyce Wrigley) *Judy Grafe* Dad (Don Wrigley) *Hardy Rawls* Ellen Hickle *Alison Fanelli* Artie *Toby Huss* Mr Mecklenberg *Iggy Pop.* Video *Nickelodeon.*

Sitcom chronicling the excellent – if plain odd – misadventures of two brothers (both named Pete) and their friends from Westville, USA. Knowingly heavy on music and celebrities (guests included rapper LL Cool J, rockers Michael Stipe from REM and Iggy Pop, and actors Bebe 'Cheers' Neuwirth and Steve 'Reservoir Dogs' Buscemi), the *Adventures* started as one-minute promos for Nickelodeon cable channel, before becoming specials, and then a weekly series. Also seen was Mom (who had a metal plate in her head, useful as a radio antenna), the relatively normal Dad, older Pete's friend Ellen, and Artie, the Strongest Man in the World.

Classic episodes included 'The Burping Room' (in which, after excessive belching, younger Pete is forced by Dad to conduct all belching in a specially designed room); 'X-Ray Man' (in which younger Pete gets X-ray vision, forcing Ellen to wear a lead smock); 'What We Did on our Summer Vacation'; and 'Staremaster'.

THE ADVENTURES OF TUGBOAT ANNIE

Canada 39 x 30m, bw. Normandie. US tx *1957 Syndicated.* UK tx *1958 ITV.*

PR *Anthony Veiller.* **CAST** Annie Brennan *Minerva Urecal* Captain Horatio Bullwinkle *Walter Sande* Murdoch McArdle *Stan Francis.*

Much-publicised but short-lived TV exercise in screwball comedy, featuring Minerva Urecal as widow Annie Brennan, foghorn-voiced skipper of the *Narcissus,* a tug based in the Pacific Northwest of America. Brennan's main preoccupation was one-upwomanship over rival skipper Horatio Bullwinkle but, in standard sex-comedy fashion, circumstances invariably required the antagonists to misadventure together.

The character of Tugboat Annie first appeared in the short stories of Norman Reilly Raine, before progressing to cinema in 1933 to be played by Marie Dressler (opposite Wallace Beery's drunken Bullwinkle). Although the Canadian company Normandie bought the TV rights in 1954, casting and technical problems quagmired the production and the series did not air until 1957. Sometimes transmitted as *Tugboat Annie.*

A J WENTWORTH, BA

UK 1982, 6 x 25m, col ITV. Thames TV.

PR *Michael Mills.* **DR** *Michael Mills.* **WR** *Basil Boothroyd.* **CAST** A J Wentworth, BA *Arthur Lowe* Matron *Marion Mathie* Reverend R G Saunders (Headmaster) *Harry Andrews* Rawlinson *Ronnie Stevens* Mason *Marcus Evans.*

The last screen work of narcoleptic actor Arthur Lowe *(Coronation Street, Pardon the Expression, >Dad's Army, Potter)*, in which he played a pompous but benign maths master at a 1940s prep school, Burgrove. Obsessed with the honour of the school, Wentworth was also frequently preoccupied by such diverting details as the rising cost of pen nibs, the tactics of arch-enemy matron and the antics of Form 3A, particularly the dreaded mason. Adapted by Basil Boothroyd from the short stories of *Punch* writer H F Ellis.

ALAS SMITH AND JONES

UK 1982–7, 43+ x 30m, 1 x 60m, col BBC2. A Talkback Production.

CR *Mel Smith, Griff Rhys Jones.* **PR** *Martin Shardlow, John Kilby, Jimmy Mulville, Jamie Rix,* **DR** *Various, including Robin Carr, John Kilby.* **WR** *Various, including Mel Smith, Griff Rhys Jones, Clive Anderson, Jimmy Mulville, Rory McGrath, Rob Grant, Doug Naylor, Colin Bostock-Smith.* **CAST** *Mel Smith, Griff Rhys Jones, Clive Mantle.*

Originally the half of *>Not the Nine O'Clock News* that none could name, Mel Smith (son of a betting shop owner) and Griff Rhys Jones (son of a doctor) spun their friendship into a double-act skit show that became a mainstay of BBC comedy in the 1980s. Their head-to-head sketches, between a continually bemused Jones and a know-all Smith,

Well then, where is this woman when you're...? Don't know, might be anywhere... probably shopping.

were minimalist classics (if lifted unacknowledged from >*Not Only... But Also*), as was their sperm donor routine ('Well then, where is this woman when you're...?'/ 'Don't know, might be anywhere... probably shopping'). A 1988 Christmas special was released as *Alas Sage and Onion*.

In 1988 the duo produced *The World According to Smith and Jones* for LWT, returning to the BBC for *Smith and Jones in Small Doses* and *Smith and Jones* (BBC1 1990–5). Although the latter was in the same format as *Alas*, it tilted increasingly at alternative comedy's usual suspects – police, politicians, TV ads (this despite the fact that Smith and Jones' own TV production company made many of them) – and quality declined. An attempt to revive *Alas* itself was made in 1998.

Over the years, those to be found toiling in Smith and Jones' the backroom have included Rob Grant and Doug Naylor (>*Red Dwarf*) and Clive Anderson (*Whose Line Is It Anyway?*).

Alexei Sayle's Stuff

UK 1988–91, 18 x 30m, col BBC2. BBC TV.

PR *Marcus Mortimer, Jon Plowman.* **DR** *Marcus Mortimer, Bob Spiers.* **WR** *Various, including Alexei Sayle, Andrew Marshall, David Renwick.* **CAST** *Alexei Sayle, Angus Deayton, Tony Millan, Felicity Montagu, Harriet Thorpe, Jan Raven.*

After an ill-conceived sojourn (alongside Chris Tarrant and Lenny Henry) on ITV's lamentably crude *OTT* show, bulbous Jewish comic Alexei Sayle developed in the direction of alternative comedy TV via guest appearances on >*The Young Ones* and >*The Comic Strip Presents,* notably the latter's film segment 'Didn't You Kill My Brother?'. This solo show, created by Sayle, followed, mixing mock-reflective monologues with (*pace* nearly every other late eighties sketch series) parodies of TV itself. But *Stuff* also had an edge of wry observational absurdism – sample: a nationwide film critics' strike, with the Army called in to pen all columns, even providing an emergency Barry Norman – that garnered plaudits and the 1989 Emmy Award for Best Foreign Comedy Show. It was followed by the *All-New Alexei Sayle Show* (two series for BBC2) which, title aside, was more of the same *Stuff*. Those aiding and abetting Sayle on screen included Angus Deayton (>*KYTV*, >*One Foot in the Grave, Have I Got News for You*) and Jan Raven.

ALF

USA 1986–96, 102 x 30m, 2 x 60m, col NBC. Lorimar. UK tx *1987– ITV.*

CR *Paul Fusco, Tom Patchett.* **EXEC PR** *Bernie Brillstein, Tom Patchett.* **PR** *Tom Patchett.* **DR** *Various, including Paul Bonerz, Nancy Heydorn, Tom Patchett, Paul Fusco, Tony Csiki.* **WR** *Various, including Paul Fusco, Tom Patchett, Bob and Howard Bendetson.* **CAST** Willie Tanner *Max Wright* Kate Tanner *Anne Schedeen* Lynn Tanner *Andrea Elson* Brian Tanner *Benji Gregory* Trevor Ochmonek

John LaMotta Raquel Ochmonek *Liz Sheridan* Eric Tanner *Charles Nickerson* Neal Tanner *J M J Bullock* Dorothy Halligan *Anne Meara.*

In which a small, hairy 229-year old Alien Life Form (hence the title) called Gordon Shumway from planet Melmac crashes his spaceship through the garage roof of archetypal suburban American family, the Tanners. Unlike fellow alien abbreviation ET, ALF stayed, moved in with the Tanners – whom he then proceeded mercilessly to satirize. It might be complained that the device of employing an extraterrestrial lodger to comment on human foibles is almost as old as TV sitcom time, dating back to >*My Favorite Martian* (via >*Mork and Mindy*), but *ALF* did it to bitingly funny effect. The family-time episodes also related ALF's evasion of the government's Alien Task Force and his various unpleasant hobbies, prime among them cat-snacking (to the standard fast exit of the Tanner's pet feline). Sometime magician Paul Fusco, the show's creator, provided the puppet ALF with his voice, while three-foot midget Michu Meszaros donned fur for the walkabout scenes. Selling to over fifty countries around the world, the show spun off a 1987 cartoon prequel (detailing Shumway's life on Melmac, produced by Bernie Brillstein, Andy Heyward and future kiddie showmeister Haim Saban) and a merchandising bonanza. There was also a big-screen version, *ALF: The Movie.*

ALF's spaceship, for those who care to know, was a Phlegm 220 model.

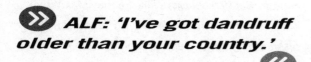

ALF: 'I've got dandruff older than your country.'

Kiss my grits

ALICE

USA 1976–85, 209 x 30m, col CBS. Warner TV. UK tx *1984–6 C4.*

CR *Robert Gretchell.* **EXEC PR** *Bob Carroll Jr, Madelyn Davis.* **PR** *Various, including David Susskind, William P D'Angelo, Ray Allen, Harvey Bullock.* **MUS** *Linda Lavin ('There's a New Girl in Town' theme vocals).* **CAST** Alice Hyatt *Linda Lavin* Mel Sharples *Vic Tayback* Flo Castleberry *Polly Holiday* Vera Gorman *Beth Howland* Tommy Hyatt *Alfred Lutler/Philip Mikeon* Belle Du Pre *Dianne Ladd* Chloe *Ruth Buzzi* Earl Hicks *Dave Madden.*

This spin-off from the 1974 movie *Alice Doesn't Live Here Any More* (directed by Martin Scorsese) starred Linda Lavin (formerly >*Barney Miller*) as the singing single mom of the title who heads towards a new life in California, only to become stranded *en route* as a waitress in Mel's Diner in Phoenix Arizona. Also bussing tables was diffident Vera and big-mouthed Flo ('Kiss my grits'), the latter eventually moving off to Houston and a sitcom of her own, *Flo.* To offset the loss of Flo, waitress Belle was added to the cast, the character being played by Dianne Ladd, who had, confusingly, portrayed the character of Flo in the movie version. The show was a solid top ten hit for much of its run, a success due in large measure to the coterie of regular diner characters at Mel's, who became so intimately known that to watch an episode was like a VR trip to the neighbourhood hostelry.

ALL GAS AND GAITERS

UK 1967–71, 32 x 30m, bw BBC1. BBC TV.

CR *Edwin Apps and Pauline Devaney.* **PR** *Stuart Allen, John Howard Davies.* **WR** *Edwin Apps and Pauline Devaney.* **CAST** Reverend Mervyn Noote *Derek Nimmo* Bishop *William Mervyn* Archdeacon *Robertson Hare* Dean *Ernest Clark/John Barron.*

Much-loved British sixties 'charactercom' which trespassed on previously hallowed ground by poking (affectionate) fun at the clergy. Derived from a *Comedy Playhouse* presentation, 'The Bishop Rides Again', it featured a trio of incompetent incumbents – the Bishop, the Archdeacon, the Chaplain Noote – of fictitious St Ogg's Cathedral, who were the bane of the severely unamused Dean. Derek Nimmo took his verbose, bumbling, be-cassocked character on to >*Oh Brother!* and its sequel *Oh Father!*

Created by the husband-and-wife writing team of Edwin Apps and Pauline Devaney.

▲▲▲ *The main cast of* All in the Family, *CBS's make-over of* Till Death Us Do Part.

ALL IN THE FAMILY

USA 1971–91, 160 x 30m, col CBS. Tandem Productions/Yorkin-Lear. UK tx *1971–5 BBC1/BBC2.*

CR *Norman Lear, Bud Yorkin.* **PR** *Norman Lear.* **DR** *Various, including John Rich, Michael Ross, Paul Bogart.* **WR** *Various, including Norman Lear.* **MUS** *Strouse and Adams ('Those Were the Days' theme lyrics and music), Carroll O'Connor and Jean Stapleton (theme vocals).* **CAST** Archie Bunker *Carroll O'Connor* Edith Bunker *Jean Stapleton* Gloria Stivic *Sally Struthers* Mike Stivic *Rob Reiner* Joey *Jason and Justin Draeger* Lionel Jefferson *Mike Evan* Louise Jefferson *Isabel Sanford* Henry Jefferson *Mel Stewart* George Jefferson *Sherman Hemsley* Irene Lorenzo *Betty Garrett* Frank Lorenzo *Vincent Gadenia* Barney Hefner *Allan Melvin* Teresa Betancourt *Liz Torres* Stephanie Mills *Danielle Brisebois* Harry Snowden *Jason Wingreen* Murray Klein *Martin Balsam* Veronica Rooney *Anne Meara* Mr Van Ranseleer *Bill Quinn.*

Transplantation of British sitcom >*Till Death Us Do Part* from London to Queens, New York. Initially developed for ABC (who rejected two pilots), the show was eventually taken up by CBS, whose president, Robert Wood, was consciously seeking a small-screen package that reflected the controversies of contemporary US society.

All in the Family had them in droves, as well as an abrasive style completely at odds with the synthetic 'Hi, Honey, I'm home' television comedies of the time.

Like its British model, *All in the Family* was built on the clashes between a working-class bigot and his daughter and son-in-law, here dock foreman Archie Bunker of the Prendergast Tool and Die Company, determined offspring Gloria and her Polish-American sociology student spouse, Mike Stivic ('Meathead'). Other targets of Bunker's ire were his ethnic neighbours in Houser Street: the Italian Lorenzos, the black Jeffersons. Throughout, Bunker's dim-witted wife Edith ('Dingbat') long suffered.

For five consecutive years *All in the Family* was the highest-rated series on US TV, garnering audiences of around 50 million per episode, winning the Outstanding Comedy Emmy in 1971, 1972 and 1973. It also spun off two other successful shows, *The Jeffersons* and >*Maude* (the latter based around Edith's liberal cousin, played by a pre->*Golden Girls* Bea Arthur). When *All in the Family* began to fade in the ratings, it was dramatically restructured, with Archie taking shares in a bar, Edith dying of a stroke (actress Jean Stapleton had tired of the part), and Gloria and Mike moving to California with son Joey. It opened the 1979–80 season as *Archie Bunker's Place* and continued under this title until 1991, by which time 'Bunker' had entered the American lexicon as a term for a blue-collar reactionary, Archie's chair – one of seventies TV's icons – had been gifted to the Smithsonian, and *All in the Family* had decisively changed the course of US situation comedy towards realism and mature themes. Actor Rob Reiner (son of comedian Carl, of *Caesar's Hour* and >*The Dick Van Dyke Show* fame), meanwhile, left his meathead persona behind to direct such Hollywood movies as *This Is Spinal Tap* (also writer), *When Harry Met Sally* and *A Few Good Men.*

'ALLO, 'ALLO

UK 1982–94, 86 x 30m, 1 x 60m, col BBC1. BBC TV. US tx *1987 Syndicated.*

CR *David Croft, Jeremy Lloyd.* **PR** *David Croft, Mike Stephens, John B Hobbs.* **DR** *Various, including David Croft, Mike Stephens, Sue Longstaff.* **WR** *Various, including David Croft, Jeremy Lloyd, Paul Adam.* **CAST** René Artois *Gordon Kaye* Edith *Carmen Silvera* Yvette *Vicki Michelle* Maria *Francesca Gonshaw* Lieutenant Gruber *Guy Siner* Mme Fanny *Rose Hill* Flying Officer Fairfax *John D Collins* Flying Officer Carstairs *Nicholas Frankau* Colonel Von Strohm *Richard Marner* General Von Klinkerhoffen *Hilary Minster* Captain Hans Geering *Sam Kelly* Helga *Kim Hartman* M Leclerc *Jack Haig/ Derek Royle/Robin Parkinson* Herr Otto Flick *Richard Gibson/ David Janson* Von Smallhausen *John Louis*

▶▶▶ *René fraternizes with friend and foe in* 'Allo, 'Allo.

Mansi Alfonse *Kenneth Connor* Crabtree *Arthur Bostrom* Bertorelli *Gavin Richards, Roger Kitter* Mimi le Bonque *Sue Hodge*.

Good moaning

Spoof version of stiff-upper-lip Second World War Resistance drama Secret Army, laden – like Croft and Lloyd's earlier >Are You Being Served? – with slapstick, innuendo and caricature characters. 'Leesten very carefooly, I weel say zees ernly wernce...' Almost every episode of the farce, which was set in the Occupied French town of Nouvion, had a cleavage joke (most famously Yvette's attempt to sell ice-cream in a vibrating truck), a scene in which café owner René was caught in flagrante with a waitress by his grim-faced wife Edith, or a development in the convoluted saga of the priceless painting of 'The Fallen Madonna with the Big Boobies'. Other running gags included René's reluctance to help the Resistance, the fumbling attempts to use the secret radio hidden beneath his mother-in-law's chamber-pot, and the preposterous French of British secret agent Officer Crabtree ('Good moaning').

Politically correct *`Allo, `Allo* was not, and unease over the material caused Jewish actor Sam Kelly, who played Wehrmacht officer Hans Geering, to refuse to say 'Heil Hitler!', substituting 'Klomp!' instead. Yet accusations of racism were easily countered: in the small world of Nouvion absolutely everybody – French, Germans, British – was a pantomime joke. The final series bowed out with the war drawing to an end and naughty Nazis Colonel Von Strohm and Lieutenant Gruber heading for the Spanish border dressed as flamenco dancers. As with everything about *`Allo, `Allo*, it was done in the worst possible taste, but to knock-about perfection.

Co-creators Croft and Lloyd have a string of TV credits between them. Actor-writer Jeremy Lloyd came up through the TV comedy mill on such shows as >*Dickie Henderson* and >*Rowan and Martin's Laugh-In* (in which he also appeared), before penning *Are You Being Served?* The TV credits of David Croft (son of musical comedy star Anne Croft) include >*Dad's Army*, >*It Ain't Half Hot, Mum* and >*Hi-De-Hi!* Notable not least for his spotting and reuse of comic actors (Gordon Kaye had previously appeared in *Are You Being Served?* and *It Ain't Half Hot, Mum*, while Carmen Silvera was Captain Mainwaring's fling in an early episode of *Dad's Army*), Croft is holder of British TV's highest accolade, the Desmond Davies Award. In 1979 Croft was awarded the Order of the British Empire for services to the small screen.

AMOS'N'ANDY

USA 1951–5, 78 x 30m, bw CBS. CBS. UK tx *1954 BBC.*

CR *Freeman Gosden, Charles Correll.* **PR** *Freeman Gosden, Charles Correll.* **DR** *Various, including Charles Barton.* **WR** *Various, including Freeman Gosden, Charles Correll.* **MUS** *Gaetano Braga ('Angels Serenade' theme song).* **CAST** Andrew Hogg Brown *Spencer Williams Jr* George 'Kingfish' Stevens *Tim Moore* Amos Jones *Alvin Childress*

Sapphire Stevens *Ernestine Wade* Mama *Amanda Randolph* Algonquin J Calhoun *Johnny Lee* Madame Queen *Lillian Randolph* Lightnin' *Horace Stewart (aka Nick O'Demus).*

TV version of popular American radio series about a black Chicago conman, George 'Kingfish' Stevens and his endlessly gullible prey, Andy Brown ('the big dummy'). Both were members of a Freemasons-like organization, and any qualms on Brown's part were quieted by Kingfish's appeal to Lodge loyalty: 'Holy mackerel (a catchline invented by a New Orleans DJ, and later to be recycled by Robin in *Batman*), Andy! We's all got to stick together in dis heah thing… remember, we is brothers in that great fraternity, the Mystic Knights of the Sea.' The Amos of the title was actually a minor character, a hard-working philosophical driver for the Fresh Air Taxi Cab Company who doubled as narrator. Also seen were Sapphire, Kingfish's wife, her mama, Andy's girlfriend Madame Queen and Lightnin', the slow-moving Lodge janitor.

The series drew big audiences during its CBS run, and for a decade of reruns on local US stations. It ceased airing in 1966, not for want of viewers but because African-American pressure groups, led by the NAACP, objected to its racist stereotyping of black people (as 'inferior, lazy, dumb and dishonest'). When Blatz Beer withdrew sponsorship and Kenya banned it, CBS responded to the protest by withdrawing *Amos'n'Andy* from sale. Produced by Freeman Gosden and Charles Correll, the white actors who created and starred in the radio version (and were thus blacked up for the small screen), the show merits a mention in the annals of TV technology for being the first to be broadcast with a canned-laughter soundtrack.

THE ANDY GRIFFITH SHOW

USA 1960–8, 249 x 30m, bw/col CBS. Mayberry Productions.

PR *Sheldon Leonard, Aaron Ruben.* **DR** *Various, including Richard Crenna, Earl Bellamy, Howard Morris, Bob Sweeney, Alan Rafkin.* **MUS** *Earle H Hagen.* **CAST** Andy Taylor *Andy Griffith* Opie Taylor *Ronny Howard* Aunt Bee Taylor *Frances Bavier* Barney Fife *Don Knotts* Ellie Walker *Elinor Donahue* Gomer Pyle *Jim Nabors* Clara Edwards *Hope Summers* Goober Pyle *George Lindsey* Floyd Lawson *Howard McNear* Howard Sprague *Jack Dodson* Otis Campbell *Hal Smith.* Video *United American Video.*

Feel-good countrified sitcom concerning a small-town sheriff, Andy Taylor of Mayberry, North Carolina. Since Mayberry was an almost crime-free zone, most of Taylor's job consisted of dispensing gentle philosophical advice to the oddball (but pleasantly oddball) townspeople and helping them with their problems. The inept, malapropping Barney Fife was Taylor's deputy (and cousin); other prominent Mayberry folk included Andy's son Opie, Andy's Aunt Bee, Gomer Pyle, the naïve pump boy

Fly a quail through here and every one of them would point.

at Wally's gasoline station, and the spaced-out barber, Floyd.

The show was spun off from an episode of *The Danny Thomas Show,* in which Thomas was arrested in a small North Carolina town, and ran for a phenomenal 249 episodes, its success (along with the similarly rustic >*Beverly Hillbillies*) spawning a number of lookalikes. *The Andy Griffith Show* itself bore a spin-offspring: >*Gomer Pyle, USMC.* Co-star Don Knotts, meanwhile, earned his own variety slot in 1965, *The Don Knotts Show.* When Griffith himself left the series in a storyline which had him marrying schoolteacher Helen Crump and moving away, CBS concocted a successful successor in *Mayberry RFD* (1968–71), with Ken Berry in the lead as councilman Sam Jones. This was eventually axed because CBS, concerned at its audience demographics (which were skewed to the rural Midwest and West of the USA), felled all shows 'with trees in'. Certainly *The Andy Griffith Show*'s sometimes rustic humour (eg Barney Fife: 'Fly a quail through here and every one of them would point' – illustrating his assertion that all female guests at Mrs Wiley's party were dogs) was not always to the taste of East Coast sophisticates.

Another case for Mayberry's finest in hick sitcom The Andy Griffith Show.

In syndication, *The Andy Griffith Show* was titled *Andy of Mayberry* (and has not been off the air since entering syndication a quarter of a century ago). A *New Andy Griffith Show* (1971), in which Griffith played the mayor of a small Southern town, lasted a single season, but a 1986 TV movie, reuniting the show's original cast, *Return to Mayberry,* was the highest-rated film on US TV for the 1985–6 season.

ARE YOU BEING SERVED?

UK 1972–84, 69 x 30m, col BBC1. BBC TV. US tx *1984–5 PBS.*

CR *Jeremy Lloyd and David Croft.* **PR** *David Croft.* **DR** *David Croft, Jeremy Lloyd, Ray Butt, Bob Spiers, Bernard Thompson.* **WR** *Jeremy Lloyd and David Croft.* **CAST** Mrs Betty Slocombe *Mollie Sugden* Mr Wilberforce Clayborne Humphries *John Inman* Captain Peacock *Frank Thornton* Mr Grainger *Arthur Brough*

Mr James Lucas *Trevor Bannister* Mr Rumbold *Nicholas Smith* Mr Harman *Arthur English* Young Mr Grace *Harold Bennett* Mr Goldberg *Alfie Bass* Bert Spooner *Mike Berry* Mr Tebbs *James Hayter* Miss Brahms *Wendy Richard.* Video *BBC.*

The doors of Grace Brothers department store first opened for business as part of BBC's *Comedy Playhouse*, launching the sales staff of Ladies and Gentlemen's Ready-to-Wear on an eleven-year career of bargain-basement jokes, (customers stuck in lifts, double entendres such as 'We'd like to complain about the state of our drawers – they're disgusting'). As with David Croft's earlier shows, which included >*Dad's Army* and >*Hi-De-Hi!*, the atmosphere was quaintly old-fashioned. John Inman's portrayal of camp, mincing menswear assistant Mr Humphries, who volunteered to measure an inside leg with alacrity and a cry of 'I'm free!', made him a household name. (Initially the target of gay protests in the USA, Inman, a former window dresser for Austin Reed, eventually became a homosexual icon.) Also appearing were Wendy Richard (later Pauline Fowler in soap *EastEnders*) as tottering blonde Miss Brahms, Frank Thornton as pompous floorwalker Captain Peacock, Trevor Bannister as junior assistant Mr Lucas and Harold Bennett as the geriatric dolly-bird-chasing owner, Young Mr Grace ('You've all done very well'). It fell, though, to Mollie Sugden (*That's My Boy, My Husband and I*) as the lacquered, lilac-eyeshadowed Mrs Slocombe to deliver the show's most risqué lines, which involved the activities of her 'pussy'.

In America, the show had a successful run on PBS, although a US version entitled *Beane's of Boston* failed to attract customers. A film of *Are You Being Served?* was released by EMI in 1977, and three years later John Inman headed a 1980 Australian TV version for Lyle McCabe Productions.

In 1992 most of the characters from *Are You Being Served?* were revived by Croft and Lloyd for a spin-off, *Grace and Favour,* which set them in a rundown country hotel, Millstone Manor, bought by Young Mr Grace with the store's pension fund. The humour, however, remained the same.

I'm free

THE ARMY GAME

UK 1957–61, 157 x 30m, bw ITV. Granada TV.

CR *Sid Colin.* **PR** *Peter Eton, Graeme McDonald.* **DR** *Milo Lewis, Max Morgan-Witts, Gordon Flemyng, Graeme McDonald.* **WR** *Various, including Sid Colin, Lew Schwarz, Barry Took and Marty Feldman, John Antrobus, Larry Stephens.* **MUS** *Pat Napper (theme lyric).* **CAST** Cpl Springer *Michael Medwin* Pte 'Excused Boots' Bisley *Alfie Bass* Pte 'Cupcake' Cook *Norman Rossington/Keith Banks* Pte 'Popeye' Popplewell *Bernard Bresslaw* Pte 'Professor' Hatchett *Charles Hawtrey/Keith Smith* Sgt Major Bullimore *William Hartnell* Major Upshot-Bagley *Geoffrey Sumner/Jack Allen* CSM Claude Snudge *Bill Fraser* Major Geoffrey Duckworth *CB Poultney* Ernest 'Moosh' Merryweather *Mario Fabrizi* Pte 'Chubby' Catchpole *Dick Emery.*

Phenomenally popular British sitcom, modelled on the 1956 film *Private's Progress*. Set in Hut 29 of Nether Hopping transit camp and surplus ordnance depot, it featured a group of peacetime conscripts determined to avoid every military duty, with Corporal Springer their Bilkoesque leader. Bellowing Sergeant Major Bullimore (geddit?) was charged with the maintenance of their discipline, while upper-class twit Major Upshot-Bagley was camp commandant. Mostly broadcast live, the show spawned a top five pop hit with its theme tune in 1958 and, in the same year, the spin-off movie *I Only Arsked,* after the catchphrase of dense Private 'Popeye' Popplewell.

A slow drain of thespian talent – Charles Hawtrey, Bernard Bresslaw, William Hartnell (later to become *Dr Who*) and Michael Medwin (later >*Shoestring*) were among the first to go – proved the show's undoing. Notable later players included Bill Fraser as CSM Claude Snudge ('I'll be leaving you now, sah!') and Dick Emery as Private 'Chubby' Catchpole (whose stock line, 'Hello, honky tonks', the actor took into his later solo show). Those working in the writers' room included Barry Took and Marty Feldman. When, in 1960, producer Peter Eton decided to transfer the characters of Bootsie and Snudge into another series, *Bootsie and Snudge in Civvy Street, The Army Game* was dismissed from the schedules. Thirty years on, its innocent, unsophisticated humour makes for dated viewing.

Hello, honky tonks!

At Last the 1948 Show

UK 1967, 12 x 30m, bw ITV. Rediffusion.

CR *David Frost.* **EXEC PR** *David Frost.* **DR** *Ian Fordyce.* **WR** *Marty Feldman, John Cleese, Graham Chapman, Tim Brooke-Taylor.* **CAST** *Marty Feldman, John Cleese, Graham Chapman, Tim Brooke-Taylor, Aimi Macdonald, Mary Maude, Barry Cryer, Christine Rodgers.*

Innovative gag and sketch show, derived from executive producer David Frost's >*Frost Report*. Taking its title from an in-programme joke about how long indecisive TV executives had left the show on the shelves, *At Last the 1948 Show* brought together the madcap scribing and performing talents of (among others) John Cleese, Graham Chapman, Marty Feldman and Tim Brooke-Taylor, with a result that was off-the-wall and anarchic, the only link between the items being Aimi Macdonald's baby-voiced commentary. Classic skits included: an accident-prone John Cleese applying for life insurance; Tim Brooke-Taylor as a madman who believed he was a rabbit, only to be persuaded by unsympathetic psychiatrist Cleese that he was actually a dog; and Brooke-Taylor as a cowboy wishing to go the 'pretty way' to Dead Man's Gulch. The final episode played out with a routine in which Brooke-Taylor, Cleese, Chapman and Feldman tried to outdo each other in the awful poverty of their upbringing.

In its surreal silliness *At Last the 1948 Show* prefigured both >*Monty Python's Flying Circus* (to which Cleese and Chapman graduated, even taking some *At Last* jokes directly with them) and >*The*

Goodies (who would number among them Brooke-Taylor). One of the defining moments in the rise of the new wave of sixties comedians.

▲▲▲ *Oz and Barry in deep water in Dick Clement and Ian La Frenais'* Auf Wiedersehen, Pet. *The show was brought to a premature end by the drink-and-drugs death of actor Gary Holton.*

AUF WIEDERSEHEN, PET

UK 1983–6, 26 x 60m, col ITV. Witzend/Central TV.

CR *Dick Clement and Ian La Frenais (from an idea by Franc Roddam).* **EXEC PR** *Allan McKeown.* **DR** *Roger Bamford, Baz Taylor, Anthony Garner.* **WR** *Dick Clement and Ian La Frenais, Bernie Cooper, Francis Megahy.* **MUS** *Ian La Frenais, Joe Fagin ('That's Livin' Alright' theme).* **CAST** Denis *Tim Healy* Neville *Kevin Whately* Oz *Jimmy Nail* Wayne *Gary Holton* Bomber *Pat Roach* Barry *Timothy Spall* Moxey *Christopher Fairbank* Dagmar *Brigitte Khan* Ulrich *Peter Birch* Magowan *Michael Elphick* Ally Fraser *Bill Paterson* Brenda *Julia Tobin.*

A show that could have been called >*The Likely Lads* go to Germany. Created, like that classic serial, by Dick Clement and Ian La Frenais, *Auf Wiedersehen, Pet* related the misadventures of three Geordies – philosophical Denis, anxious Neville and slobbish Oz – obliged by local unemployment in Tyneside to seek work on a Düsseldorf building site. They were joined *en route* by Cockney casanova Wayne, Bristolian ex-boxer Bomber, boring Brummie Barry and pock-faced Liverpudlian arsonist Moxey. Although the series acutely reflected early eighties concerns about unemployment, it was ultimately a study in Britishness, with the confines of the Düsseldorf accommodation hut – in which most of the action took place – acting as a sort of comic intensifier. Its success (13.4 million viewers by February 1984) ingrained the *Auf Wiedersehen* characters in the UK psyche as few since >*Dad's Army*, with the bigoted, dirty underpants-wearing Oz (former nightclub singer and ex-convict Jimmy Nail) foremost among them. In the second season, 'The Magnificent Seven' went to work – not exactly willingly – for Tyneside gangster Ally Fraser, first on his Derbyshire pile, then on his villa on Spain's Costa del Crime. During filming, however, actor Gary Holton died of a drink-and-drugs cocktail, his demise removing a vital screen presence (despite some adroit use of a double, which made Wayne seemingly a part of every episode). In recognition of Holton's contribution, the rest of the cast refused a third series, provisionally set in Moscow. Most, however, have since progressed to other things, with Spall (>*Frank Stubbs Promotes, Outside Edge*), Whately (*Inspector Morse*), Healy (*Boys from the Bush, Common as Muck*) and Nail (*Spender, Crocodile Shoes*) now staples of the British small screen.

The series was based on an idea by expatriate bricklayer Franc Roddam. Among the classic episodes are: 'The Girls They Left Behind' (in which Oz is accidentally transported back to England with a coachload of soccer fans); 'Last Rites' (smuggling porn videos in a coffin – later cremated); 'The Return of the Seven'; 'Hasta La Vista' (a pathetic Oz bids goodbye to a son lost through his own negligence); 'Quo Vadis' (the finale, with the gang pursued by Spanish coastguards to Morocco).

Bachelor Father

USA 1957–62, 157 x 25m, bw CBS. Universal.

PR *Everett Freeman, Robert Sparks, Harry Ackerman.* **DR** *Various, including Earl Bellamy, John Newland, Stanley Z Cherry, Greg Garrison.* **MUS** *Conrad Salinger, John Williams.* **CAST** Bentley Gregg *John Forsythe* Kelly Gregg *Noreen Corcoran* Peter Tong *Sammee Tong* Ginger Farrell/Mitchell *Bernadette Withers* Howard Meechim *Jimmy Boyd* Cal Mitchell *Del Moore* Adelaide Mitchell *Evelyn Scott* Cousin Charlie Fong *Victor Sen Yung* Vickie (secretary) *Alice Backus* Kitty Devereaux (secretary) *Shirley Mitchell* Kitty Marsh *Sue Anne Langdon* Suzanne Collins (secretary) *Jeanne Bal* Connie (secretary) *Sally Mansfield* Warren Dawson *Aaron Kincaid.*

Smooth John Forsythe (aka John Lincoln Freund) starred as a Hollywood lawyer and ladies' man who becomes guardian to his thirteen-year-old orphaned niece. Typical storylines involved niece Kelly trying to find Uncle Bentley a wife, or his incompetence in teenager management. There was, of course, a lovable dog too (Jasper). Oriental house-boy Peter inscrutably (of course) kept the Gregg mansion functioning amid the mayhem.

Moderately likeable sitcom, one which established the single parent, actual or surrogate, as a sitcom staple (the unfortunate Vice President Dan Quayle's assertion that >*Murphy Brown* was a dangerously novel TV portrayal of single parenting thus being nearly forty years off the mark). Funnily enough, one episode of *Bachelor Father* featured an unknown Linda Evans in the guest cast, with whom Forsythe would later star (after stints on *The John Forsythe Hour* and as the voice of Charlie in *Charlie's Angels*) in *Dynasty*. Another notable tyro appearance was that of Mary Tyler Moore (>*The Mary Tyler Moore Show*) in the episodes, 'Bentley and the Big Board' and 'Bentley and the Combo'.

BAGDAD CAFÉ

USA 1990–1, 15 x 30m, col CBS. Zeb Braun Productions/New World Television. UK tx *1991 C4.*

EXEC PR *Zev Braun, Mort Lachman.* **DR** *Various, including Paul Bogart.* **WR** *Mort Lachman, Sy Rosen.* **MUS** *Bob Telson ('Calling You' theme).* **CAST** Brenda *Whoopi Goldberg* Jasmine Zweibel *Jean Stapleton* Junie *Scott Lawrence* Debbie *Monica Calhoun* Sal *Cleavon Little* Rudy *James Gammon* Dewey Kunkle *Sam Whipple* Sheriff Wayne Highsmith *William Shockley.*

Percy Adlon's 1988 German art-house movie of the same name (but aka *Out of Rosenheim*), transmogrified into an American sitcom.

Ex-mortuary beautician Whoopi Goldberg portrayed Brenda, the cynical boss of a rundown diner-motel in the middle of California's Mojave desert, whose employee list grew by one when warm-hearted fiftysomething tourist (triple Emmy-winner Jean Stapleton, Mrs Archie Bunker in >*All in the Family*) signed on as maid after having abandoned her husband. The two women's chalk-and-cheese friendship was the main laughter dish of the show. Brenda's family – errant and usually absent husband Sal (Cleavon Little from *Blazing Saddles*), aspiring pianist and temporary diner cook son Junie, troublesome teen daughter Debbie (Monica Calhoun reprising her movie role) – and diner regular Rudy also featured. When Junie quit to find his fortune in the second season, nervous Dewey Kunkle took over in the fleapit's kitchen.

A pilot episode, 'Bagdad Café', was transmitted in March 1989.

BARNEY MILLER

USA 1975–82, 168 x 25m, col ABC. Columbia TV. UK tx *1982 ITV.*

CR *Danny Arnold, Theodore J Flicker.* **PR** *Danny Arnold, Chris Hayward.* **DR** *Various, including John Rich, Tony Sheehan, Robert Day, Danny Arnold, Noam Pitlik, Theodore J Flicker, Lee Bernhardi, Hal Linden.* **WR** *Various, including Danny Arnold, Chris Hayward, Reinhold Weege, Bob Colleary, Jordan Moffat, Nat Mauldin, Tony Sheehan, Jeff Stein,*

SQUAD ROO
DETECT
DET. DELUCCA
DET. WILSON
DET. PINCUS
DET. SMITH
STAND BY
DET. ROE
DET. NORTH
SGT. DIBBY

Frank Dungan. **MUS** *Jack Elliott, Ally Fergusson.* **CAST** Capt Barney Miller *Hal Linden* Det Sgt Phil Fish *Abe Vigoda* Det Sgt Chano Amenguale *Gregory Sierra* Det Sgt Stan Wojciehowicz *Maxwell Gail* Det Sgt Nick Yemena *Jack Soo* Det Sgt Ron Harris *Ron Glass* Insp Frank Luger *James Gregory* Det Sgt Arthur Dietrich *Steve Landesburg* Off Carl Levitt *Ron Carey* Elizabeth Miller *Abby Dalton (pilot)/Barbara Barrie* Det Janice Wentworth *Linda Lavin* Lieut Scanlon *George Murdock* Det Maria Battista *June Gable.*

Eventually to be awarded the 1981 Emmy for Best Comedy, *Barney Miller* almost never got made. It had two strikes against it: it featured a Jewish policeman, which US network bosses considered 'too ethnic'; worse, its humour was sophisticated and wrily mocked such prime-time taboos as homosexuality, teenage pregnancy and arson. Pestered by co-creators Danny Arnold (>*Bewitched*) and Theodore Flicker into a pilot, 'The Life and Times of Barney Miller', ABC then binned the project, to near-audible sighs of relief. It was only resurrected to please hot director John Rich, whom ABC was desperate to recruit. Rich's price was that ABC commissioned a season of a cop comedy made by his friend Danny Arnold – *Barney Miller.*

Shot on videotape instead of film (a parsimony insisted on by ABC), the show achieved its famed downbeat look by altering the lighting for each scene, as is done in movie-making. Almost all the action took place within a single set, the chaotic, rubbish-strewn squadroom of New York's 12th Precinct (Greenwich Village). To play the varied parade of 12th Precinct cops, Arnold hired in a fine ensemble cast, headed by Hal Linden (aka big band singer Harold Lipschitz) as the compassionate Barney Miller, and Abe Vigoda (Tessio in *The Godfather*) as the weak-bladdered Phil Fish, eventually spun off to his own show, *Fish.* Frequently, however, *Barney Miller* episodes were made good by the guest cast who acted the human flotsam and jetsam who passed through the station house: mad bombers, gay purse snatchers, prostitutes, teenage burglars, even a werewolf. All, no matter how deviant or disadvantaged, were treated with respect. Perhaps along with only >*M*A*S*H* and >*Taxi* for company, *Barney Miller* was one of the great statements of humanism in late seventies sitcom.

After eight seasons, the crew and cast decided to close the New York cop shop for the simple reason that they were running out of topics to deflate and wanted to bow out with artistic standards intact. In the last episode, a three-parter called 'Landmark', the station house was declared a site of historic significance (it had supposedly been the campaign HQ of Theodore Roosevelt), and the Twelfth was disbanded. The jail cell door and duty roster board used on the show were presented to the Smithsonian Institution, the director of which declared them to be 'part of American culture'. And so they were.

In addition to the 1981 Comedy Emmy, *Barney Miller* also won a 1979 Comedy Writing Emmy for Bob Colleary's 'The Photographer'.

◀◀◀ *Dismissed as 'too ethnic' by network bosses, the Emmy-winning* Barney Miller *almost never got made.*

BEAVIS & BUTT-HEAD

USA 1993–7, Approx 186 x 10/30m, 1 x 60m, col MTV. MTV Networks. UK tx *1993–7 MTV.*

CR *Mike Judge.* **EXEC PR** *Abby Terhule.* **PR** *Various, including John Andrews, Kristofer Brown, Christina Norman.* **WR** *Various, including Mike Judge, Sam Johnson, Chris Marcil, David Felton, Tracy Grandstaff, Joe Stillman, Chris Kreski, Glenn Eichler, Geoff Whelan.* **CAST** *(voices)* Beavis/Butt-head/Tom Anderson/Principal McVicker *Mike Judge* Daria/Cassandra/Lolita *Tracy Grandstaff* Stewart *Adam Welch* Mr Graham *Guy Maxtone-Graham.*

'It's just this funny awkward moment in life when you want to be supermacho and show everyone you're not a kid any more. You wear serious, badass death-rock T-shirts, but you've got to put rubber bands on your braces.'
MIKE JUDGE, BEAVIS & BUTT-HEAD CREATOR

Beavis and Butt-head were two ugly, pubescent cartoon males variously regarded as 'the first truly modern attempt at TV' *(Time)* or 'the latest link in the Darwinian descent of the American adolescent' *(New York Times).* Moronically stupid, anally and genitally fixated, Beavis (Metallica T-shirt, distended lower jaw) and Butt-head (AC/DC T-shirt, short upper lip) spent half of their thirty-minute show critiquing pop videos, with a philosophy of aesthetics that was disarmingly simple: thrash metal (accompanied by the playing of frantic air guitar), 'chicks' with 'thingees' and death were 'cool'. Everything else 'sucked'. They were particularly remorseless about the manhood of high-voiced heavy metal hopefuls ('wusses'), and cruelly pricked pop pretensions, once memorably claiming that singer Edie Brickell looked like she was 'pinching a loaf'. The vaguest *double entendre* ('He said come...') would set off a breathy stuttering chorus of 'huh-huh, huh-huh, huh-huh'.

Away from the couch, the glue-sniffing duo wandered a suburban, parentless wasteland of shopping malls and monster truck rallies, embarking on sordid adventures that sometimes proved controversial. Among other outrages, they deep-fried a rat, killed a grasshopper with a chainsaw, put a vomit-coated poodle in a washing machine, and sprayed MEGADETH on the side of a teacher's house. In one episode they shot down an aircraft but failed to call the emergency services after becoming distracted by a bout of flatulence. To no great surprise, the duo were soon targeted by morally concerned parents, whose campaign – led by Americans for Responsible Television – against *B&B* peaked in 1993, when the activities of a five-year-old pyromaniac were blamed on Beavis and

Huh-huh, huh-huh... Cartoon bad boys, Beavis and Butt-head.

Butt-head's pronouncement that 'Fire is cool'.

Beavis & Butt-head was the creation of Mike Judge, an American born (in 1963) in Ecuador. A sometime musician and physics student at the University of California at San Diego, Judge based the characters of Beavis and Butt-head on 'people I knew in junior high school and kids I just see everywhere', developing them for the small screen with the help of a $300 animation kit. The humour of the show, which was written mostly by Judge and *National Lampoon* alumni Sam Johnson and Chris Marcil, had a noticeably subversive as well as puerile bent; in one episode, the metal-heads did a school report on the *Challenger* disaster, destroying a toy rocket in science class, an act which tastelessly but effectively burlesqued government and NASA propaganda. Notable guest stars over the show's run included David Letterman, in the spoof segment 'Late Night with Butt-head'.

Although *B&B* sent up the MTV generation of 'blank heads', the show ironically enough debuted on MTV's *Liquid Television* series in September 1992 with 'Frog Baseball' (in which, as the title indicated, the boys used an amphibian instead of a ball). Beavis and Butt-head got their own show just three months later, with MTV rushing sixty-five episodes into production. Running conspicuously counter to MTV's self-conscious political correctness, *B&B* became the station's most popular show, earning over $15 million in advertising revenue in 1994 alone. As is the way of all TV hits, the show eventually graduated to a major cinema feature, the ultimate sign of cultural acceptance and commercial success. This was the 1996 *Beavis and Butt-head Do America*. It was followed by *Beavis and Butt-head 2: Another Movie* in 1998. There was also a TV spin-off in >*Daria*, featuring Beavis and Butt-head's sardonic classmate of that name. Mike Judge himself went on to more highbrow pastures with >*King of the Hill*.

THE BENNY HILL SHOW

UK 1969–89, 99 x 30m, col ITV. Thames TV. US tx *1979–82 Syndicated.*

PR *Various, including John Robbins, Mark Stuart, Dennis Kirkland, Keith Beckett, John Street.* **DR** *Various, including John Robbins.* **WR** *Various, including Benny Hill.* **MUS** *Ronnie Aldrich Orchestra, The Ladybirds (theme vocals).* **CAST** *Benny Hill, plus others, including Henry McGee, Bob Todd, Felicity Buirski, Patricia Hayes, Nicholas Parsons, Bella Emberg.*

The first British comedian to be made by the medium of TV, Alfred Hawthorne 'Benny' Hill (born 1925, the son of a surgical appliance fitter) enjoyed years of fortune with the BBC before transferring his *The Benny Hill Show* to ITV in 1969, where it enjoyed even greater success. The eighteen series (plus numerous specials) were full of slapstick visual gags and corny jokes – and sexism. The standard model Hill skit invariably required Hill, whatever the persona assumed (from jittery bridegroom to woolly-chaps-wearing cowpoke), to be surrounded by scantily clad women. A trademark scene involved the lascivious comedian being pursued across the screen by a bevy of 'Hill's Angels'. Stock Hill characters included Captain Fred Scuttle, the Firemen's Choir and Professor Marvel. Henry McGee, Jack Wright (the small bald 'slaphead') and Nicholas Parsons were among the most prominent of Hill's stooges. The show was cancelled in 1989, after mounting criticism, although Hill continued making programmes for overseas sale until his death in April 1992. In the USA, where Hill was one of the few British comedians to hit the jackpot, his shows developed a devoted audience following syndication in 1979.

Though she might now wish to forget it, >*Frasier* star Jane Leeves was one of those who bared almost all as a Hill's Angel.

BENSON

USA 1979–86, 60 x 30m, col ABC. Witt Thomas Productions/Columbia Pictures TV. UK tx *1981–4 ITV.*

CR *Susan Harris, Paul Junger Witt, Tony Thomas.* **EXEC PR** *Rob Dames, Bob Fraser.* **DR** *Various, including John Rich, Peter Baldwin, Jay Sandrich, Bob Fraser, Hilton Smack.* **WR** *Various, including Susan Harris, Ron Silver.* **CAST** Benson DuBois *Robert Guillaume* Governor James Gatling *James Noble* Katie Gatling *Missy Gold* Gretchen Kraus *Inga Swenson* Marcy Hill *Caroline McWilliams* James Taylor *Lewis J Stadlen* Clayton Endicott III *Rene Auberjonois.*

A spin-off from >*Soap* in which the back-talking black butler Benson DuBois was sent to take charge of the household of widowed State Governor

Robert Guillaume as the black, back-talking butler in Soap *spin-off,* Benson.

James Gatling. This was almost as lunatic an establishment as *chez* Tate. Aside from the incompetent Gatling, prominent residents included the Governor's precocious daughter Katie, his secretary Marcy, the formidable – and incomprehensible – German housekeeper Gretchen Kraus, and aide John Taylor (later replaced as bag carrier by Clayton Endicott III, played by Rene Auberjonois, eventually to beam up to *Star Trek: Deep Space Nine* as Odo). Over the course of the sixty-plus episodes, Benson rose inexorably from lowly buttling to become Lieutenant Governor, in the ultimate episode even challenging Gatling for the governorship itself. In the process actor Robert Guillaume became something of a role model for a generation of Afro-Americans. He first achieved fame as a star of the cult blaxploitation pic, *Superfly TNT*. After *Benson* he revisited the wackier edges of sitcomdom in the Californian police spoof, *Pacific Station*.

Not at all at home on the range... the city slicking Best family try life on the ol' frontier in ABC's spoof oater, Best of the West.

Best of the West

USA 1981–2, 22 x 25m, col ABC. Weinberger-Daniels/PAR-TV.

CR *Earl Pomerantz.* **PR** *Earl Pomerantz, James Burrows, Ronald E Frazier, David Lloyd.* **DR** *Various, including Howard Storm, Stan Daniels, James Burrows.* **MUS** *Roger Steinman.* **CAST** Sam Best *Joel Higgins* Elvira Best *Carlene Watkins* Daniel Best *Meeno Beluce* Parker Tillman *Leonard Frey* Jerome 'Doc' Kullens *Tom Ewell* The Calico Kid *Christopher Lloyd* Lamont Devereux *Andy Griffith.*

Spoof Western. After service in the Civil War, Sam Best heads West to the frontier town of Copper Creek, accompanied by refined southern belle wife Elvira and city-raised kid Daniel ('I want you to understand, Dad, I'm *never* going outside'). When Best accidentally defeats the local gunfighter, the Calico Kid (Christopher Lloyd, >*Taxi,* the *Back to the Future* movies), he is elected Marshal and duly charged with keepin' law'n'order among the ultra-caricatured townsfolk: alcoholic Doc Kullens, no-good saloon owner Parker Tillman, raucous mountain-woman Laney Gibbs and all.

THE BEVERLY HILLBILLIES

USA 1962–71, 216 x 25m, bw/col CBS. Filmways Pictures. UK tx *1964–70 ITV.*

CR *Paul Henning.* **EXEC PR** *Martin Ransohoff.* **PR** *Paul Henning, Joseph DePew, Aaron Ruben, Al Simon, Mark Tuttle.* **DR** *Various, including Joseph de Pew, Richard Thorpe, Richard Whorf.* **WR** *Various, including Paul Henning.* **MUS** *Jerry Scoggins (theme), Lester Flatt, Earl Scruggs.* **CAST** Jed Clampett *Buddy Ebsen* Granny (Daisy Moses) *Irene Ryan* Elly May Clampett *Donna Douglas* Jethro Bodine *Max Baer, Jr* Milburn Drysdale *Raymond Bailey* Margaret Drysdale *Harriet MacGibbon* Jane Hathaway *Nancy Kulp* Pearl Bodine *Bea Benaderet* Flo Shafer *Kathleen Freeman* Janet Treago *Sharon Tate.*

▶▶ *One of US TV's greatest sitcom hits,* The Beverly Hillbillies *was axed because its audience was too old and too rural.*

Classic US sitcom charting the adventures of the crazy Clampett family, who found oil on their backwoods Ozark ranch and then decamped to Beverly Hills in their boneshaker car to live the high life. Alas, the enterprise was doomed; although they bought every mod con that $25 million could buy, they were not always sure what to do with them. Granny Clampett even had difficulty in differentiating the washer from the TV. The other members of the Clampett clan were level-headed patriarch Jed, dim-witted Cousin Jethro and animal-loving Elly May, wearer of the tightest blue jeans west of the Ozarks. Elderly cousin Pearl Bodine

featured for the first seasons, before being spun off to >*Petticoat Junction*. Also seen were the Clampetts' banker and next-door neighbour, Milburn Drysdale, and his socially prominent wife, Margaret. (In one ignominious, if classic, episode her pampered poodle gave birth to pups fathered by Jed's old coondog, Duke.)

At the show's best, when scripts raised themselves to match performances, *The Beverly Hillbillies* was an attack on materialism; at its worst, it merely ridiculed rural folks. It was universally lambasted by critics, but became the fastest hit in US small-screen history, shooting to the top of the Nielsens within four months. It stayed there for nearly two years. Along with >*The Andy Griffith Show, The Beverly Hillbillies* was responsible for inventing a new sub-genre of TV humour, the 'rustic sitcom'; later manifestations included, as well as *Petticoat Junction,* >*Green Acres.*

Buddy Ebsen, star of *Beverly Hillbillies and* former song-and-dance man had previously featured in *Davy Crockett* and later starred in detective show *Barnaby Jones*. Max Baer, Jr, who played Cousin Jethro, was the son of the former world heavyweight boxing champion, Max Baer. Actress Sharon Tate, later infamously to be murdered by the Charles Manson gang, appeared as Janet Treago, the bank secretary. In 1981 *Beverly Hillbillies* creator Paul Henning produced *The Return of the Beverly Hillbillies,* with Imogene Coca replacing the late Irene Ryan as Granny. A 1993 movie, *The Beverly Hillbillies,* based on the TV series, starred Dabney Coleman, Erica Eleniak *(Baywatch)* and Cloris Leachman. Penelope Spheeris directed Ian Bryce's production for 20th Century Fox.

BEWITCHED

USA 1964–72, 254 x 30m, col ABC. Screen Gems. UK tx *1964–72 BBC1.*

CR *Sol Saks.* **EXEC PR** *Harry Ackerman.* **PR** *William Asher.* **DR** *William Asher, Alan Rafkin, Sidney Miller, Ida Lupino, David McDearmon, Sherman Marks, Joseph Pevney, William D Russell, E W Swackhamer, Howard Morris, Jerry Davis, R Robert Rosenbaum, Alan Jay Factor, Paul Davis, Richard Kinon.* **WR** *Sol Saks, Barbara Avedon, Danny Arnold, Jerry Davis, Bernard Slade, Paul David and John L Greene, Fred Freeman and Lawrence J Cohen, Jack Sher, Roland Wolpert, Herman Groves, Tom and Frank Waldman, Earl Barrett, Richard and Mary Sale, Joanne Lee, Ken Englund, Richard Baer, Ted Snerdeman and Jane Klove, Ruth Brooks Flippen, Mort R Lewis, Paul Wayne, Howard Leeds, Ron Friedman, Lee Erwin, James Henerson, Syd Zelinka, Doug Tibbles, David V Robinson, Ed Jurist, David Braverman and Bob Marcus, Coslough Johnson, Jerry Devine and Izzy Elinson.* **MUS** *Howard Greenfield and Jack Keller (theme), Warren Barker.* **CAST** Samantha Stephens/ Serena *Elizabeth Montgomery* Darrin Stephens *Dick York (1964–9)/Dick Sargent (1969–72)* Endora *Agnes Moorehead* Maurice *Maurice Evans* Larry Tate *David White* Louise Tate *Irene Vernon (1964–6)/ Kasey Rogers (1966–72)* Tabitha Stephens *Heide and Laura Gentry (1966)/Erin and Diane Murphy (1966–72)* Adam Stephens *David and Greg Lawrence* Abner Kravitz *George Tobias* Gladys Kravitz *Alice Pearce (1964–6)/Sandra Gould (1966–72)* Aunt Clara *Marion Lorne* Uncle Arthur *Paul Lynde* Esmeralda *Alice Ghostley* Dr Bombay *Bernard Fox.* Video *C-VIS/BMG.*

With just a twitch of her nose she got he housework done... Samantha, Darrin and baby Tabitha in the spell-binding Bewitched.

Long-running sitcom starring Elizabeth Montgomery (daughter of Robert) as Samantha Stephens, a white witch who had only to twitch her nose cutely to get the dusting done. Dick York (later Dick Sargent) played her hapless, merely mortal husband Darrin, an accountant at New York ad agency McMann and Tate. To please hubbie, Samantha tried to curb her supernatural powers, but invariably failed, causing big comic trouble for Darrin (and the bemusement of nosy neighbours, the Kravitzes) before order was restored. Oscar nominee Agnes Moorehead took the role of Samantha's mean, meddlesome mother Endora, who used Darrin – or 'Durwood' as she insisted on calling him – as the butt of her ill humour, turning him variously into a goat, a donkey or whatever took her fancy. Also seen was Sam's father Maurice, her Aunt Clara and Uncle Arthur, and Darrin's boss Larry Tate. There was also Sam's mischievous lookalike cousin, Serena (played by Montgomery). The population of show hexes increased by two when Sam gave birth to Tabitha and Adam, the former achieving the distinction of being the only offspring born to a sitcom mother to be given a series on her own: *Tabitha* (1977–8), in which she featured as a young adult (played by Lisa Hartman) working for TV station KXLA.

Bewitched, bewitched, you've got me in your spell.
Bewitched, bewitched, you know your craft so well.
Before I knew what you were doing I looked in your eyes.
That brand of woo that you've been brew-in' took me by surprise...

Not all the stars of the show appeared before the camera. Much of *Bewitched*'s success – which was considerable, it being ABC's biggest hit up to that time – lay in the hands of special effects man Dick Albain. It was Albain who invented Samantha's 'magic' self-operating vacuum cleaner and made objects fly around the rooms. (The first was a remote controlled device, the latter achieved by a hidden network of wires.) Some effects were more prosaically achieved: Samantha's cleaning of the kitchen by witchcraft required Montgomery to raise her arms, say 'whoosh' – and stand stock still, while the crew swept and dusted, the footage of them then being edited out.

Although it left the air in 1972, the show continues to be a staple filler of daytime schedules the world over. Its politics seem uncomfortably dated, with Darrin's insistence on a 'wife's place' being at home, but most else holds up well, particularly the performances of Moorehead and the demurely sexy Montgomery. A piece of TV magic. As it were.

Some *Bewitched* trivia: Montgomery was married to the show's producer-director, William Asher; a pre-celebrity Raquel Welch is to be seen as a stewardess in the 1964 episode, 'Witch or Wife'; although the show was nominated for numerous Emmys, it only won two, a Best Supporting Actress in a Comedy award for Alice Pearce, and the same award for Marion Lorne; Tammy Grimes was originally slated to play Samantha, but turned it down for *The Tammy Grimes Show* – which lasted six months; the Stephens' address was 1164 Morning Glory Circle, Westport, Connecticut. Samantha and Darrin once appeared in >*The Flintstones,* as the Stone Age couple's new neighbours.

THE BLACK ADDER

UK 1983–9, 24 x 30m, 1 x 45m, 1 x 15m, col BBC1. BBC TV. US tx *1990 Syndicated.*

CR *Richard Curtis, Rowan Atkinson.* **PR** *John Lloyd.* **DR** *Martin Shardlow, Mandie Fletcher, Richard Boden.* **WR** *Richard Curtis, Rowan Atkinson, Ben Elton.* **MUS** *Howard Goodall.* **CAST** Edmund Blackadder *Rowan Atkinson* Baldrick *Tony Robinson.* Video *BBC TV.*

A cycle of sitcoms which began with the crude *The Black Adder,* concerning the medieval exploits of the venomous young aristocrat Edmund Blackadder, and rose through *Black Adder II* (set in Elizabethan times) and *Blackadder the Third* (Regency period) to the sublime *Blackadder Goes Forth* (the First World War). Accompanying Blackadder (rubber-faced Rowan Atkinson from >*Not the Nine O'Clock News*) on his ophidian odyssey was foul-smelling retainer Baldrick (Tony Robinson, after Timothy Spall turned down the part), seemingly having 'dung for brains'.

When the first series emptied the BBC coffers, new head man Michael Grade reached for the axe, but writer Richard Curtis (>*Not the Nine O'Clock News,* later >*The Vicar of Dibley* and the movie *Four Weddings and a Funeral*) and new partner Ben Elton (from >*Friday Night Live*) produced, in veritable Blackadder professor-of-cunning fashion,

Black Adder, Black Adder
He rides a pitch black steed
Black Adder, Black Adder
He's very bad indeed...

scripts for a second series with all the expensive bits removed. Curtis and Elton also decided to trim back on the gurning and slapstick on which the premier season had relied, and instead nursed a wondrous mix of schoolboy japes ('The enemy is thinner on the ground opposite your trenches, Blackadder.' 'Could be my batman's socks, sir'), convoluted wordplay, historical parody and lampooning of exactly the sort of costume dramas the BBC itself loves to make.

Supporting the performances of Atkinson (later >*Mr Bean, The Thin Blue Line*) and Robinson

Edmund Blackadder and his faithful – if foul-smelling – retainer Baldrick in the Richard Curtis/Ben Elton sitcom, The Black Adder.

(*Maid Marian and Her Merry Men*), who played their parts with rare sitcom verve and comic timing, was a regular cast of Tim McInnerny (Lord Percy in *The Black Adder* and *Black Adder II,* Captain Darling in *Blackadder Goes Forth*), Hugh Laurie (Prince Regent in *Blackadder the Third,* Lt George Colthurst St Barley in *Forth*) and Stephen Fry (Lord Melchett in *Black Adder II,* the General in *Forth*). Others who provided sterling thespian work included Patsy Byrne (Nursie in *II*) and Miranda Richardson (Queenie in *II*).

Two specials were also produced in 1988: *Blackadder: The Cavalier Years* (15 minutes, script by Curtis and Elton) and *Blackadder's Christmas Carol* (45 minutes, with Atkinson as Ebenezer Blackadder, script by Curtis and Elton). The series took its bow in 1989 with an uncompromisingly bleak, anti-war scene in which Blackadder, by now a thoroughly subtle and sympathetic character, and his pals went 'over the top' to assault German trenches on the Western Front in 1917. The eighties were not a great decade for the British sitcom – proved, not least, by declining viewing figures – but *Blackadder* was a shining peak of achievement.

The series episodes were: *The Black Adder*: The Foretelling/Born to be King/The Archbishop/The Queen of Spain's Beard/Witchsmeller Pursuivant/ The Black Seal. *Black Adder II*: Bells/Head/Potato/ Money/Beer/Chains. *Blackadder the Third*: Dish and Dishonesty/Ink and Incapability/Nob and Nobility/Sense and Senility/Amy and Amiability/Duel and Duality. *Blackadder Goes Forth*: Captain Cook/ Corporal Punishment/Major Star/Private Plane/ General Hospital/Goodbyee.

BLESS THIS HOUSE

UK 1971–6, 65 x 30m, col ITV. Thames TV.

CR *Vince Powell and Harry Driver.* ***PR*** *William G Stewart.* ***DR*** *William G Stewart.* ***WR*** *Various, including Vince Powell and Harry Driver, Carla Lane, Myra Taylor, Dave Freeman, Bernie Sharp, Adele Rose.* ***MUS*** *Geoff Love.* ***CAST*** Sid Abbott *Sid James* Jean Abbott *Diana Coupland* Mike Abbott *Robin Stewart* Sally Abbott *Sally Geeson* Trevor *Anthony Jackson* Betty *Patsy Rowlands.*

Quintessential British domestic comedy of the seventies, the main themes of which were 'The Generation Gap' (the title of the first episode) and the battle of the sexes. Sid Abbott was a sales rep for a stationery firm, a man who listed his pleasures alphabetically as 'Ale, Birds and Chelsea [football club]'. He was much exasperated by his permissive, workshy, ex-art college son Mike, and teenage schoolgirl daughter Sally (played by Sally Geeson, sister of movie actress Judy). Meanwhile, wife Jean long suffered. Their neighbours in Birch Avenue, Putney, London, were meddlesome Trevor and his caricature nagging wife, Betty.

The series, which topped the BARB ratings in 1973 and 1974, marked the last starring venture on the small screen of veteran alcoholic actor Sid James (>*George and the Dragon,* >*Hancock, Taxi, Citizen James,* >*Carry On Laughing*). Born Solly Cohen in South Africa in 1913, James died of a heart attack on 26 April 1976, which was allegedly caused by unrequited love for Barbara Windsor, his co-star in the *Carry On* film cycle. Created by Vince Powell and Harry Driver, and

▲▲▲ *Veteran comic actor Sid James – star of the* Carry On *movies and possessor of the world's dirtiest laugh – in* Bless This House.

produced by future host of *Fifteen to One* daytime quiz show, William G Stewart. Carla Lane (later >*Liver Birds*, >*Butterflies*) cut her scripting teeth on the show.

A spin-off feature film was released by Peter Rogers Productions in 1972, directed by Gerald Thomas (of the *Carry On* movies) and with Terry Scott and June Whitfield (>*Terry and June*) as the Abbotts' new neighbours.

BLOSSOM

USA 1991–5, Approx 90 x 30m, col NBC. A Witt-Thomas Production/Buena Vista Pictures/ Touchstone Television. UK tx *1991– C4.*

CR *Don Reo.* ***EXEC PR*** *Paul Witt, Tony Thomas, Don Reo, Judith D Allison, Allan Katz, Gene Reynolds.* ***PR*** *Various, including Jonathan Schmock, Susan Seeger, Josh Goldstein, John Ziffren.* ***DR*** *Bill Bixby, Zane Busby, Gil Junger, Allan Katz, Ted Wass, John Whitesell.* ***WR*** *Various, including Judith D Allison, Dan Cohen, Brian Herskowitz, Racelle Rosett Schaefer, Don Reo.* ***MUS*** *Frank Denson.*

CAST Blossom Russo *Mayim Bialik* Nick Russo (father) *Ted Wass* Joseph Russo (brother) *Joey Lawrence* Anthony Russo (brother) *Michael Stoyanov* Vinnie *David Lascher* Six LeMeure *Jenna Van Oy.*

Touted as the sitcom successor to American eighties hits >*Cheers* and >*The Cosby Show, Blossom* related the growing-up misadventures of the eponymous teenage girl in an all-male (and totally dysfunctional) household. In the standard manner of TV shows with a mainly pre-adult audience, it tackled issues – sex, drugs and first periods – with alacrity, even simultaneously. One classic episode found Blossom's ambulance-driving, substance-abusing brother Anthony waking up after a drinking spree in Las Vegas to find himself married to a black girl he had no recollection of ever meeting. Guest celebrities included TV sitcom legends Estelle Getty (>*Golden Girls*), Rhea Perlman (>*Cheers*), ALF (>*ALF*), and musicians Little Richard and Sonny Bono, these celebs usually appearing in Blossom's fantasies to proffer comedic advice to her current problem. Show directors included Bill Bixby, better known for his before-the-camera appearance as Dr Bruce Banner in *The Incredible Hulk*. A two-hour TV movie, *Blossom in Paris,* aired in 1993.

THE BOB NEWHART SHOW

USA 1972–8, 142 x 30m, col CBS. MTM.

CR *David Davis, Lorenzo Music.* ***EXEC PR*** *David Davis, Lorenzo Music.* ***PR*** *Tom Patchett, Jay Tarses.* ***DR*** *Various, including Peter Bonerz, Alan Myerson, Alan Rafkin, Dick Martin.* ***WR*** *Various, including David Davis, Lorenzo Music.* ***CAST*** Robert Hartley *Bob Newhart* Emily Hartley *Suzanne Pleshette* Howard Borden *Bill Daily* Jerry Robinson *Peter Bonerz* Carol Kester Bondurant (secretary) *Marcia Wallace* Ellen Hartley *Pat Finley* Elliot Carlin *Jack Riley* Miss Larson *Penny Marshall* Mr Gianelli *Noam Pitlik* Mrs Bakerman *Florida Friebus* Margaret Hoover *Patricia Smith* Dr Bernie Tupperman *Larry Gelman* Michelle Nardo *Renee Lippin* Mr Peterson *John Fiedler.*

Comic raconteur Bob Newhart's first TV series (also called *The Bob Newhart Show*), was a short-lived variety affair, 1961–2, which failed to showcase his talents. Assorted stints on other variety shows and in movies followed before >*The Mary Tyler Moore Show* staffers and former >*The Smothers Brothers* writers, David Davis and Lorenzo Music, tailored this sitcom concept (both Davis and Music had supplied Newhart with jokes for his radio and nightclub shows), in which Newhart played practising Chicago psychologist Robert Hartley, whose patients and friends (notably bachelor orthodontist Jerry and airline pilot neighbour Howard) were a collection of basket cases. Accomplished at sorting out the problems of others, Hartley was less successful with his own, to the bemusement of his schoolteacher wife Emily.

After a slow start, the show performed strongly, reaching number twelve in the Nielsens for 1973–4. The success was not surprising; as the producers declared, their product had 'class and charm and wit'. It also played direct to Newhart's comic strengths; his precise comic timing, his famed deadpan persona, and the low-key portrayal of the sane man surrounded by lovable zanies. However, despite its success, the show was always overshadowed by its stable mate, *The Mary Tyler Moore Show,* and failed to win a single Emmy. *Newhart* directors included Dick Martin from >*Rowan and Martin's Laugh-in* while Penny Marshall (later >*Laverne and Shirley*) made her first screen appearance in *Newhart,* later securing a regular role as Miss Larson.

Four years after the close of the show, Newhart returned in *Newhart* (1982–90), playing Dick Loudon, a writer of 'How-to' books who moves to Vermont to restore and manage a colonial inn (and be the sane one amid the oddballs). The last episode ended with Newhart waking up next to Emily (Suzanne Pleshette), his wife in *The Bob Newhart Show,* to find that the Vermont interlude had been just a dream... It could only happen on TV.

Newhart has also starred in the comedies *Bob* (1992–3) and *George and Leo* (1997).

The Bottle Boys

UK 1984–5, 13 x 30m, col ITV. LWT.

CR *Vince Powell.* **PR** *Stuart Allen.* **DR** *Stuart Allen.* **WR** *Vince Powell.* **CAST** Dave Deacon *Robin Asquith* Stan Evans *Richard Davies* Sharon Armstrong *Eve Ferrett.*

Low-brow, high-innuendo escapades of an amorous milkman, Dave Deacon of Dawson's Dairy. Starred Robin Asquith from the trashy *Confessions of...* films.

Bottom

UK 1991–5, 18 x 30m, col BBC2. BBC TV.

CR *Rik Mayall, Adrian Edmondson.* **PR** *Ed Bye.* **DR** *Ed Bye.* **WR** *Rik Mayall and Adrian Edmondson.* **CAST** Richie Rich *Rik Mayall* Eddie Hitler *Adrian Edmondson* Spudgun *Steven O'Donnell* Dave Hedgehog *Christopher Ryan* Dick Head *Lee Cornes.* Video *BBC.*

Originally to be called *Your Bottom* (to allow viewers the tantalizing prospect of declaring, 'I saw your bottom on TV last night'), *Bottom* was the story of two sex-starved bachelors who lived in an unsavoury Hammersmith bedsit where, in time-honoured TV comedy fashion, they sat and sniped at each other.

Conceived, written and starring Rik Mayall and Adrian Edmondson, the show heavily reprised their >*The Young Ones* characters: Mayall's Richie Rich being snivelling and virginal, Edmondson's Eddie Hitler being headbangingly violent. If the characters were revivals, *Bottom* lacked the parent show's originality and surrealism. Its title did not lie: *Bottom* was the sitcom of scatology: farting, dirty socks, festering food, vomiting, vile male habits.

However, the show had its moments, mostly in the duo's woefully inadequate attempts to impress women ('I wish someone would sleep with me, I mean stay awake with me'). According to director Ed Bye, most of its devoted following were young empathizing males aged between fifteen and twenty.

Adrian Edmondson (husband of Jennifer Saunders from >*French and Saunders,* >*Absolutely Fabulous*) and Rik Mayall first performed together

Their minds were on lower things... Richie (left) and Eddie try seducing a blonde (Helen Lederer) in Bottom.

as 20th Century Coyote at Manchester University in 1976, before becoming regular performers together at London's Comedy Store. They have starred on television in >*The Comic Strip Presents*, >*Saturday Live* and >*Filthy Rich and Catflap*. Mayall has also starred as odious politician Alan B'Stard in >*The New Statesman* and in the series of short dramas *Rik Mayall Presents*.

THE BRADY BUNCH

USA 1969–74, 117 x 25m, col ABC. Paramount TV.
UK tx *1970–3 ITV.*

CR *Sherwood Schwartz.* **PR** *Various, including Sherwood Schwartz, Howard Leeds.* **DR** *Various, including John Rich, Hal Cooper, David Alexander, Jack Arnold, Robert Reed, Lloyd Schwartz, Leslie H Martinson, Jerry London, Earl Bellamy, Russ Mayberry, Oscar Rudolph.* **WR** *Various, including Sherwood Schwartz, Brad Radnitz, Ben Starr, Elroy Schwartz, Tam Spavia, Michael Morris, Skip*

Webster, Harry Winkler. ***MUS*** *Frank de Vol.* ***CAST*** Mike Brady *Robert Reed* Carol Brady *Florence Henderson* Alice Nelson *Ann B Davis* Marcia Brady *Maureen McCormick* Jan Brady *Eve Plumb* Cindy Brady *Susan Olsen* Greg Brady *Barry Williams* Peter Brady *Christopher Knight* Bobby Brady *Mike Lookinland.*

The last of the great 'Hi, Honey, I'm home' domestic comedies, *The Brady Bunch* was the tale of two Los Angeles families, those of Mike and Carol, amalgamated by marriage. Full of smiling, white-teethed children in hokey battles for the bathroom/phone, a shaggy dog (Tiger), and good-natured, ultra-respectable middle-class parents (Mike was an architect), it had a feel-good factor of 10/10. A five-year run followed. Typical storylines were Marcia having braces fitted, Greg trying out for the high school football team, girlfriend/boyfriend

The last of the great Hi-honey-I'm-home sitcoms was ABC's The Brady Bunch.

trouble, a camping trip to the Grand Canyon.

The show also spun off an animated *The Brady Kids*. The Bradys ('the family that won't go away') returned in a live-action sequel, *The Brady Bunch Hour* (1977), in which the Bradys became a TV variety act, then *The Brady Girls Get Married* (1981), then *The Brady Brides* (1981), and finally *The Bradys* (1990). By this time collective madness had descended on the producers, for the last of these viewed like soap opera, with Bobby Brady paralized in a car crash. Even the Bradys found that one somewhat difficult to smile at.

THE BRITTAS EMPIRE

UK 1991–7, 52 x 30m, col BBC1. BBC TV.

CR *Richard Fegen and Andrew Norriss.* **PR** *Mike Stephens.* **DR** *Various, including Mike Stephens, Christine Gernon.* **WR** *Various, including Richard Fegen and Andrew Norriss, Tony Millan and Mike Walling, Terry Kyan, Paul Smith, Ian Davidson, Peter Vincent.* **CAST** Gordon Wellsley Brittas *Chris Barrie* Helen Brittas *Pippa Haywood* Laura Lancing *Julia St John* Carole Parkinson *Harriet Thorpe* Colin Weatherby *Michael Burns* Tim Whistler *Russell Porter* Linda Perkins *Jill Greenacre* Gavin Featherleigh *Tim Marriott* Julie *Judy Flynn* Angie *Andree Bernard* Penny Bidmead *Anouschka Menzies.*

Semper Omnibus Facultas

After playing the nerdish Rimmer in sci-fi spoof >*Red Dwarf,* Chris Barrie (formerly an assistant in the sports department at Harrods, and supplying such voices for >*Spitting Image* as Prince Charles and Ronald Reagan) played Gordon Brittas, the nerdish manager of Whitbury Newtown Leisure Centre, in this sitcom from the team of Richard Fegen and Andrew Norriss *(Chance in A Million, The Labours of Erica, Ffizz).* Possessed by the Jinx-touch, every improvement the pompous, whiney-voiced, over-zealous Brittas – the very TV examplar of petty officialdom – planned for his personal fiefdom ended in comic disaster, usually of epic proportions. (In one episode, 'The Assassin', his misguided endeavours filled an entire hospital intensive care unit, which, as his neurotic, pill-popping wife Helen was obliged to point out was 'a good score, even for Gordon'.) Those working under Brittas included sensible assistant Laura, receptionist Carole, incompetent maintenance man (and Brittas idolizer) Colin Weatherby, secretary Julie, and the fitness/sports coaches Tim, Gavin and Linda. Despite his mega-bumbling, Brittas was once appointed European Commissioner for Sport, before returning to the Centre (motto: Semper Omnibus Facultas) for more mayhem. A spin-off series, *Get Fit with Brittas* (produced by Paul Reizin), was released in 1997.

In its positing of an incompetent in charge of others, *The Brittas Empire* mined a traditional vein of TV humour (eg >*Dad's Army* and >*Are You Being Served?*). Yet it also had an element of absurdism (Carole's keeping of her children in a cupboard behind the desk, Brittas's quasi-bionic indestructibility, including his rebuilding by surgeons in Zurich), which gave it an appeal to younger viewers. At a stretch the show could also be viewed as a critique of the managerial class which expanded in the Thatcherite eighties. A show for all the couch.

BUTTERFLIES

UK 1978–82, 36 x 30m, col BBC2. BBC TV.

CR *Carla Lane.* **PR** *Gareth Gwenlan, Sydney Lotterby.* **DR** *Various, including Mandie Fletcher, Gareth Gwenlan, John B Hobbs.* **WR** *Carla Lane.* **CAST** Ria Parkinson *Wendy Craig* Ben Parkinson *Geoffrey Palmer* Adam Parkinson *Nicholas Lyndhurst* Russell Parkinson *Andrew Hall* Leonard Dunn *Bruce Montague* Ruby (cleaner) *Joyce Windsor* Thomas *Michael Ripper.*

Carla Lane (>*The Liver Birds*) comedy in which bored middle-class, mid-life crisis-facing Ria Parkinson began to tire of her nineteen-year marriage to dentist Ben and motherdom to thankless teenage offspring Russell and Adam. A platonic but guilt-laden affair with smooth businessman Leonard followed. Meanwhile, the eternally depressive Ben ('I don't like singing. I don't do a lot of it because there isn't much to sing about') added to his butterfly collection, and tried to instil in his 'chick'-crazy sons, with their 'groovy' talk and their Mini (with rooftop Union Jack), a sense of conformist duty.

I don't like singing. I don't do a lot of it because there isn't much to sing about.

Whimsical but also bleak, the show pushed at the edges of seventies domestic comedy, even containing voice-overs and an experimental dream sequence. BBC2's highest-rated show for much of its run, it benefited from faultless performances, especially that of the lugubrious Geoffrey Palmer (>*The Fall and Rise of Reginald Perrin*, >*Fairly Secret Army, Executive Stress, As Time Goes By*) as Ben, and an uncharacteristically soulful Wendy Craig (>*Not in Front of the Children* et al) as Ria. Nicholas Lyndhurst, former children's presenter of *Our Show,* soon parlayed his role as Adam into that of Rodney in >*Only Fools and Horses.* Further down the cast list, Milton Johns and Wendy Williams did memorable turns as the Parkinsons' timid neighbours, trapped on their drive by the Parkinsons' frantic vehicular goings-on.

The title theme was a reworking of the Dolly Parton song, 'Love is Like a Butterfly'. The series was syndicated in the US, although a 1979 ABC pilot for an American version (with Jennifer Warren as Ria Parkinson) flunked.

CAR 54, WHERE ARE YOU?

USA 1961–3, 60 x 25m, bw NBC. Eupolis.

CR *Nat Hiken.* **PR** *Nat Hiken.* **DR** *Nat Hiken, Stanley Prager.* **WR** *Various, including Nat Hiken.* **CAST** Off Gunther Toody *Joe E Ross* Off Francis Muldoon *Fred Gwynne* Lucille Toody *Beatrice Pons* Capt

Martin Block *Paul Reed* Off Leo Schnauser *Al Lewis* Off Anderson *Nipsey Russell* Off O'Hara *Albert Henderson* Off Kissel *Bruce Kirby.*

Nat Hiken's follow-up to >*The Phil Silvers Show* (aka *Bilko*) was a lunatic comedy about a pair of inept police officers who shared the patrol vehicle of the title. Set in the mythical New York 53rd Bronx Precinct remarkably free from major felonies, it starred Fred Gwynne (an occasional *Bilko* guest actor) as the tall, dim Francis Muldoon and Joe E Ross (Mess Sergeant Ritzik in *Bilko*) as his short and even dimmer partner, Gunther Toody. The close comedic connection between *Bilko* and *Car 54* was only emphasized by the presence of actress Beatrice Pons, who played Ross's nagging wife/foil in both. Shot on location, the show, despite some gold-standard scripts, lasted only two seasons; it did, however, give Gwynne the exposure which secured his casting as Herman in >*The Munsters*. In this he was joined by fellow *Car 54* alumnus Al Lewis who played officer Schnauser.

A 1994 *Car 54* movie based on the series (which resurrected Lewis and Nipsey Russell from the original cast) isn't worth describing.

◀◀◀ *Fred Gwynne (left) and Joe E Ross in the lunatic cop comedy,* Car 54, Where Are You?

CAROLINE IN THE CITY

USA 1995–, 49 x 30m, col NBC. CBS Entertainment Productions/Barron:Pennette Productions/Three Sisters Entertainment. UK tx *1995– C4.*

CR *Fred Barron.* **EXEC PR** *Fred Barron, Marco Pennette, David Nichols.* **PR** *Faye Oshima Belyeu, Bill Prady, Billy Masters, Brian Hargrove, Jack Kenny, Lester Lewis.* **DR** *Various, including James Burrows, Will Mackenzie, Arlene Sanford, Joshua Baerwald, Tom Cherones, Pamela Fryman.* **WR** *Various, including Amy Cohen, Bill Prady, Ellen Idelson, Rob Lotterstein, Dottie Dartland, Fred Barron, Marco Pennette, Jennifer Glickman.* **MUS** *Jonathan Wolff.* **CAST** Caroline Duffy *Lea Thompson* Del Cassidy *Eric Lutes* Richard Karinsky *Malcolm Gets* Annie Spadaro *Amy Pietz* Remo *Tom La Grua* Charlie *Andrew Lauer.*

T*he Mary Tyler Moore Show* for the nineties. Lea Thompson (former ballet dancer and star of the *Back to the Future* movies) played Caroline Duffy, a well-groomed single working gal adrift in the metropolis (New York City). Although she was phenomenally successful as a newspaper cartoonist, her romantic life was a mess; in one sequence, she even resorted to throwing fruit on the street in an effort to meet men. There were, however, a couple of suitors, in the shapes of buffoonish ex-boyfriend Del and brooding cartoon colourist Richard (with whom it started to get serious). Annie was the mandatory comic next-door neighbour, incontinent with advice for Duffy on all aspects of dating. Still, no matter how tumultuous was la Duffy's existence, it all made good material for her weekly biographical comic strip, 'Caroline in the City'.

Savvy, slick, squeaky clean and difficult to dislike, the show had an obvious appeal in the late-twentieth-century world of troubled singles. It even managed to knock >*Friends* from the top of the US ratings. One disconcerting habit was the introduction of characters from other sitcoms as guests; in one episode Chandler (Matthew Perry) from >*Friends* turned up in *Caroline,* and in another it was Niles (David Hyde Pierce) and Daphne (Jane Leeves) from >*Frasier*.

For the record, Duffy's cat was called Salty.

CARROTT'S LIB

UK 1982–4, 17 x 30m, col BBC1. BBC TV.

PR *Paul Jackson, Geoff Posner.* **WR** *Various, including Jasper Carrott, Rob Grant and Doug Naylor, Duncan Campbell, Ian Hislop.* **CAST** *Jasper Carrott, Emma Thompson, Chris Barrie, Debby Bishop, Steve Frost, Nick Wilton, Kay Stonham, Nick Maloney.*

After a TV career remarkable only for its unremarkableness, Birmingham comic and folk singer Jasper Carrott (real name: Robert Davies) noticed that the comedic times were a-changin' and used the opportunity to reinvent himself as an alternative humourist in *Carrott's Lib*. Strange to say, it worked.

While *Carrott's Lib* included Carrott's stock-in-trade, observational humour about everyday life, it also introduced bug-eyed diatribes (*Sun*-reading Robin Reliant drivers coming in for particular ire) and sharp political satirising (pinkish type). Between the rants and musings were sketches, the performers including such showbiz tyros as Emma Thompson and Chris Barrie (later >*Red Dwarf,* >*Brittas Empire*). Much of the material was self-penned, but Ian Hislop, Rob Grant and Doug Naylor (the latter duo soon to team up for >*Red Dwarf*) also contributed.

A follow-up series in 1987, *Carrott Confidential,* marked a failure of nerve, with Carrott relying on such gagmen of yesteryear as Barry Cryer for the titters, before Carrott refound the alternative vein in the 1990 *Canned Carrott*. With Carrott up on his high chair, most of the skitting fell to Steve Punt and Hugh Dennis of the >*Mary Whitehouse Experience,* but it was Carrott's running cop spoof with Robert Powell that endeared most, even becoming a show in its own right: *The Detectives*.

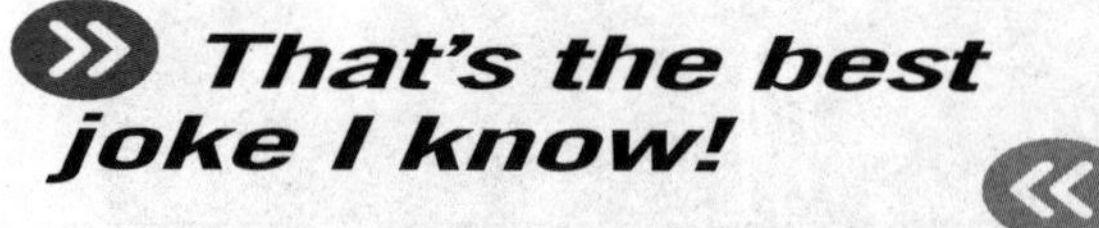
That's the best joke I know!

Hampton Court?' 'No, I always walk like this'.

Carry On Laughing

UK 1975, 6 x 30m, col ITV. ATV.

CR *Gerald Thomas.* **EXEC PR** *Peter Rogers.* **PR** *Gerald Thomas.* **DR** *Alan Tarrant.* **WR** *Various, including Lee Schwarz, Barry Cryer, Dick Vosburgh.* **CAST** *Various, including Barbara Windsor, Sid James, Jack Douglas, Bernard Bresslaw, Joan Sims, Kenneth Connor.* Video *ITC.*

An attempt to transfer the *Carry On* film series to TV, with a series of specially written half-hour pieces, variously spoofs of TV shows ('And in My Lady's Chamber' sent up period soap *Upstairs, Downstairs*) or historical romps ('Under the Round Table'). Where the latitude offered by small-screen production might have encouraged exploration, however, it only produced laziness. The jokes included such antediluvian specimen double entendres as 'Anyone for a little crumpet?' and (even) 'Hampton Court?'/'No, I always walk like this.'

Worth catching, though, for an appearance by thespian Simon Callow, in one of his earliest outings, playing a sailor in the episode 'Orgy and Bess'.

Anyone for a little crumpet?

Cheers

USA 1982–93, 273 x 25m, 1 x 90m, col NBC. A Charles Burrows Charles Production/Paramount TV. UK tx *1983–93 C4.*

CR *Les Charles, Glen Charles, James Burrows.* **EXEC PR** *Various, including James Burrows, Les Charles, Glen Charles.* **PR** *Various, including Ken Levine, Heide Perlman.* **DR** *Various, including James Burrows, Andy Ackerman, Tom Moore, John Ratzenberger.* **WR** *Various, including James Burrows, Les Charles, Glen Charles, Heide Perlman, Sam Simon, David Lee, Ken Levine, David Isaacs.* **MUS** *Judy Hart Angelo and Gary Portnoy ('Where Everybody Knows Your Name' theme).* **CAST** Sam Malone *Ted Danson* Diane Chambers *Shelley Long* Ernie 'Coach' Pantuso *Nicholas Colasanto* Norm Petersen *George Wendt* Cliff Clavin *John Ratzenberger* Carla Tortelli/LeBec *Rhea Perlman* Frasier Crane *Kelsey Grammer* Woodrow Tiberius Boyd ('Woody') *Woody Harrelson* Rebecca Howe *Kirstie Alley* Lilith Sternin Crane *Bebe Neuwirth* Eddie LeBec *Jay Thomas* Robin Colcord *Roger Rees* Kelly Gaines/Boyd *Jackie Swanson* Harry Gittes *Harry Anderson* John Allen Hill *Keene Curtis* Evan Drake *Tom Skerritt.* Video *Columbia.*

Sometimes you want to go
Where everybody knows your name,
And they're always glad you came,
You want to be where you can see,
Our troubles are all the same,
You want to go where everybody
knows your name...

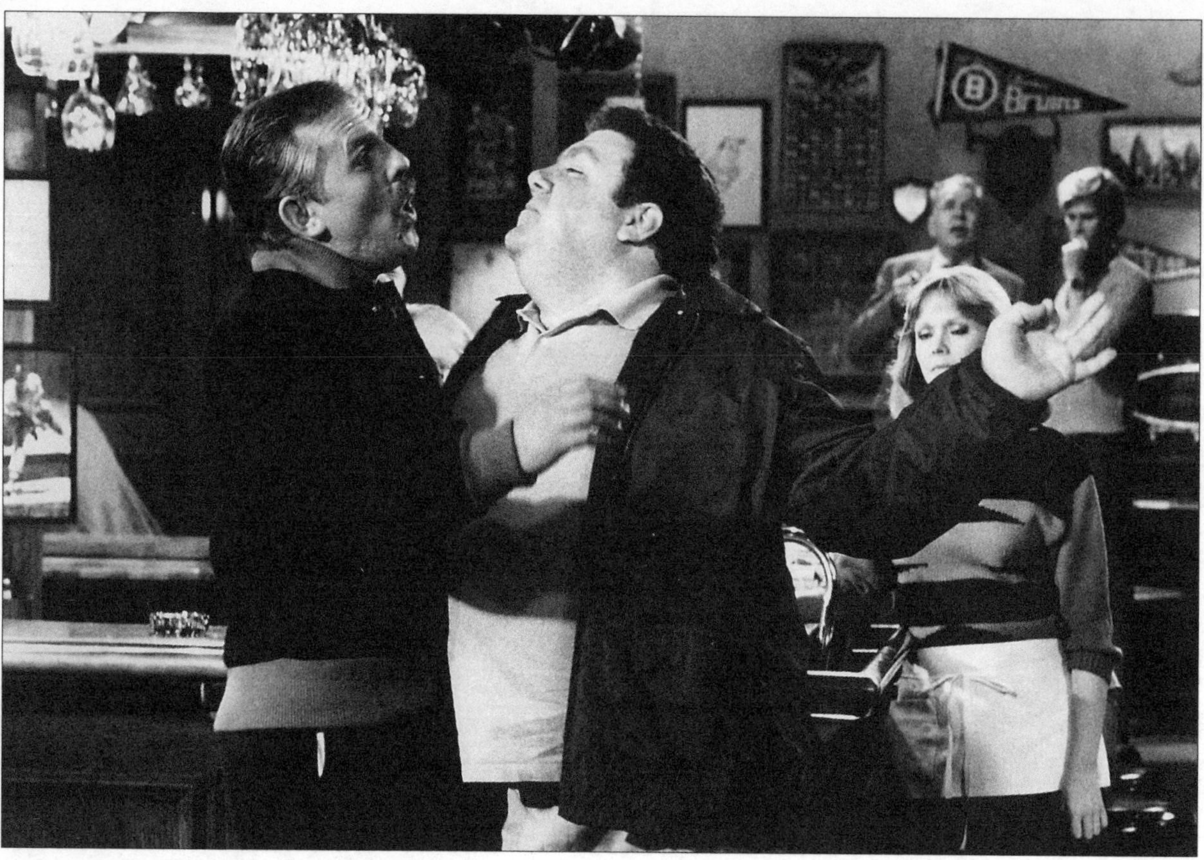

Cliffie and Norm in the 'barcom' Cheers, *a hit till it quit.*

Set in the Boston bar of the title (est. 1895), this single-set show was one of the most popular and critically acclaimed comedies of recent decades. The regulars were womanizing owner Sam 'Mayday' Malone, a reformed alcoholic and one-time relief pitcher for the Red Sox, dense barman Ernie 'Coach' Pantuso, promiscuous acid-tongued waitress Carla Tortelli (Rhea Perlman, wife of Danny De Vito and sister of *Cheers* producer Heide Perlman), corpulent barfly Norm (who always entered to a holler of 'NORM!'), prim English Lit graduate Diane, and anally retentive mailman Cliff Clavin, a veritable fountain of trivia. The storylines of the first seasons were dominated by Sam and Diane's love/hate relationship; eventually she left him to marry pompous psychologist Frasier Crane. However, unable to forget Sam, she jilted Frasier and returned to bussing tables at Cheers. Then Coach died (as had actor Nicholas Colasanto, who was also one of US TV's principal directors). His place was taken by Woodrow Tiberius Boyd ('Woody'), a farmboy of frightening simpleness from Hanover, Indiana. At around the same time the dejected Frasier pulled up a stool at the bar, and later married the acerbic, night-creaturish Lilith (who once asked the bar where she could sleep, to which Carla replied memorably, 'I've got an attic you can hang upside down in').

In 1987 Diane left the bar to write a novel, and a saddened Sam sold the business to a large corporation and set off to sail the world. But his yacht sank and he had to slink back to Cheers to beg a job off the new manager, gold-digging Rebecca Howe. Meanwhile, Carla married hockey player Eddie LeBec (who was subsequently killed in an ice rink accident) and had two more children, making her the mother of eight. Though Sam set out to seduce Rebecca, and she had to fight her attraction to him, ultimately she was more interested in rich corporate raider Robin Colcord – until he ended up in jail. Eventually Sam regained control of the bar, making the supercilious Rebecca *his* underling. Subsequent storylines included Woody's marriage to Kelly Gaines (an occasion which produced a rare *Cheers* episode in physical comedy), Lilith's sojourn with an eccentric scientist in an underground pod, the revelation that Sam wore a hairpiece, and the culmination of the bar's long rivalry with Gary's Old Time Tavern, when the *Cheers* gang finally got one over on the smug Gary.

Although it was replete with brilliant one-line gags, the wit of *Cheers* came from its characters, who were types but not stereotypes. 'How's life in the fast lane?' Sam asked Norm. 'Don't ask me, Sammy,' replied Norm, 'I can't find the on ramp.' Such jokes were all the better for the fact that the characters were not portrayed with the cloying sentimentality of much sitcom; on the contrary, they were almost painfully inadequate. As conman Harry 'The Hat' Gittes put it to the bar staff and patrons of Cheers: 'How would we know we were winners if we didn't have you guys?' It is testament to the sublime quality of the show that only one of the main cast, Shelley Long, ever quit to do other things (although Danson, Alley and Harrelson combined *Cheers* with active movie careers). The guest list included Christopher Lloyd, Fred Dryer (who he? – the actor originally slated to play Sam Malone), and John Cleese in an Emmy-winning performance as a deranged marriage guidance counsellor, Dr Simon Finch-Royce, in the segment 'Simon Says'.

The final episode, 'One for the Road' (in which Diane returned to the bar), aired in America in May 1993, gained an audience of 150 million, making it the most-watched show in TV history. It had also become the most expensive, costing $65 million for twenty-six episodes. (Much of the cost went on cast salaries; Danson alone earned $450,000 per episode.) *Cheers*' final tally of Emmy Awards was twenty-seven, just two fewer than the record held by >*The Mary Tyler Moore Show*.

Among the classic episodes are: Simon Says/One for the Road/Coachie Makes Three/The Two Faces of Norm/Where Have All the Floorboards Gone?/ Indoor Fun with Sammy and Robby/One Hugs, the Other Doesn't/Cliffie's Big Score/I Do, Adieu/Woody Interruptus/Showdown/Death Takes a Holiday on Ice/Grease/'I' On Sports.

There were two spin-offs: the short-lived *The Tortellis* and the hugely successful >*Frasier*.

Cheers was created by >*Taxi* writers James Burrows, Les Charles and Glen Charles. The Cheers bar is based on a real Boston tavern, the Bull and Finch.

'Power to the people!' Robert Lindsay as Citizen Smith.

CITIZEN SMITH

UK 1977–80, 30 x 30m, col BBC1. BBC TV.

CR *John Sullivan.* **PR** *Dennis Main Wilson.* **DR** *Ray Butt.* **WR** *John Sullivan.* **CAST** Walter Henry 'Wolfie' Smith *Robert Lindsay* Shirley *Cheryl Hall* Ken Mills *Mike Grady* Charlie Johnson *Peter Vaughan/Tony Steedman/ Artro Morris* Mrs Johnson *Hilda Braid* Tucker *Tony Millan* Anthony 'Speed' King *George Sweeney* Harry Fenning *Stephen Greif* Ronnie Lynch *David Garfield.* Video *BBC.*

Sitcom by sometime BBC scene-shifter John Sullivan that parodied the Marxist Left, in the shambolic shape of the fictional Tooting Popular Front. Leader of the suburban guerrilla army was busker Wolfie Smith (Robert Lindsay from >*Get Some In*), an Afghan-coated Che Guevara wannabe. Weedy Buddhist sidekick Ken, fecund Tucker and greaser Speed filled out the ranks. Shirley was Wolfie's long-suffering record shop girlfriend (played by Lindsay's real-life wife, Cheryl Hall), whose conservative parents, Mr Johnson (the frightening Peter Vaughan, later >*Porridge, Our Friends in the North*) and dim Mrs J – who was constantly malaproping 'Wolfie' into 'Foxie' – eventually became the leader maximo and Ken's landlords.

A socialist Walter Mitty Wolfie may have been, but his occasional victories over the narrow-minded adult world made him one of seventies British comedy's most engaging creations. His proselytizing was also tempered by a bent to con artistry, the comic possibilities of which Sullivan magnified into his greatest creation, Del Boy Trotter of >*Only Fools and Horses,* the latter even taking its title from a *Citizen Smith* episode.

Classic episodes are headed by 'The Glorious Day' (season three), when Wolfie and comrades found an abandoned tank and decided to invade Parliament. Alas, their long-dreamed-of desire to stand the class enemy 'up against the wall... bop-bop-bop' never came to fruition. Also: 'The Party's Over', in which the TPF sabotaged the punch at a nob's bash, and 'The Hostage', in which they mistakenly kidnapped local gangster Harry Fenning instead of the local MP.

The show was developed from a 1977 pilot, screened as part of *Comedy Special.*

'Power to the People!'

THE COMIC STRIP PRESENTS...

UK 1983–93, 21 x 45/60m, 15 x c30m, col C4/BBC2. Filmworks/Comic Strip.

CR *Peter Richardson.* **EXEC PR** *Michael White, Peter Richardson.* **PR** *Michael White, Lolli Kimpton, Nira Park.* **DR** *Various, including Peter Richardson, Keith Allen, Paul Bartell, Robbie Coltrane, Stephen Frears, Bob Spiers, Adrian Edmondson, Pete Richens.* **WR** *Various, including Peter Richardson, Pete Richens, Adrian Edmondson, Dawn French, Jennifer Saunders, Nigel Planer, Alexei Sayle, Pauline Melville, Roland Rivron, David Stafford, Barry Dennen, Robbie Coltrane, Morag Fullerton.* **MUS** *Jeff Beck, Simon Brint, Kate Bush, Chrissie Hynde, Steve Nieve.* **CAST** *Peter Richardson, Adrian Edmondson, Rik Mayall, Nigel Planer, Jennifer Saunders, Dawn French, Alexei Sayle, Daniel Peacock, Keith Allen, Nosher Powell, Sara Stockridge, Gary Beadle, Doon Mackian, Robbie Coltrane.*

The transfer to TV of Peter Richardson's Soho-based 'The Comic Strip' club, as overseen by impresario Michael White. The first small-screen piece was 'Five Go Mad in Dorset', transmitted on Channel 4's opening night in 1982, which ruthlessly spoofed Enid Blyton and was finished to perfection with a cameo by soap star Ronald Allen *(Crossroads)* as dubious Uncle Quentin ('I'm a screaming homosexual, you little prigs'). Post-modernist parody proved the mainstay of the ensuing *Comic Strip* series, with targets ranging from the music industry ('The Bad News Tour') to TV ('The Bullshitters', a lampoon of the ultra macho crime show, *The Professionals*). Most favoured of all, though, were film genres ('Slags', 'A Fistful of Travellers' Cheques', 'The Yob'), Richardson's preoccupation with cinema eventually leading to the *Comic Strip* apogee, 'The Strike' (1988), an over-dramatic Hollywood-style version of the British 1984–5 miners' dispute, with Richardson as Al Pacino playing Arthur Scargill, Jennifer Saunders as Meryl Streep playing Scargill's wife. Alexei Sayle was the committed leftist writer whose work was distorted for lucre. The *faux* Hollywood make-overs continued in 'GLC', with Robbie Coltrane as Charles Bronson playing Ken Livingstone, the Greater London Council leader.

By this time (1990), *The Comic Strip* had decamped from C4 to BBC2. Although Richardson and Co. would produce fifteen 'films' for the Corporation, these tended to be reheats of previous themes. Few lodged in folkloric memory, apart from 'The Crying Game', the story of gay footballer Roy Brush and his hounding by *The Scum* newspaper. Yet as *The Comic Strip*'s own star waned, those of its individual members waxed large, in shows such as >*The Young Ones*, >*Alexei Sayle's Stuff*, >*French and Saunders*, >*Bottom* and a score more. Its own merit aside, *The Comic Strip* deserves notice in the cult TV annals for being the veritable fountainhead of small-screen British alternative comedy.

Stephen Frears (later *My Beautiful Laundrette*, *The Grifters*), quick-flic specialist Paul Bartell (*Death Race 2000*), and Richardson himself were among those sharing the director's chair, with Richardson also helming *The Comic Strip*'s three cinematic releases, *The Supergrass* (1985), *Eat the Rich* (1987) and *The Pope Must Die* (1991).

In 1998 many of the cast were reunited for a special, in which four salesmen found themselves on a nightmare journey to a sales conference.

The episodes were: Season 1: Five Go Mad in Dorset/War/The Beat Generation/Bad News Tour/Summer School. Season 2: Five Go Mad on Mescalin/Dirty Movie/Susie/A Fistful of Travellers' Cheques/Gino: Full Story and Pics/Eddie Monsoon, a Life/Slags/The Bullshitters: Roll Out the Gunbarrel. Season 3: Consuela/Private Enterprise. Season 4: The Strike/More Bad News/Mr Jolly Lives Next Door/The Yob/Didn't You Kill My Brother?/ Funseekers. Season 5: South Atlantic Raiders I/ South Atlantic Raiders II: Argie Bargie/GLC: The Carnage Continues/Oxford/Spaghetti Hoops/Les Dogs. Season 6: Red Nose of Courage/The Crying Game/ Wild Turkey (Christmas 1992 special). Season 7: Detectives on the Verge of a Nervous Breakdown/Space Virgins from Planet Sex/Queen of the Wild Frontier/Gregory: Diary of a Nutcase/ Demonella/Jealousy. Plus 1998 reunion special: Four Men in a Car.

The Cosby Show

USA 1984–93, 196 x 25m, 4 x 60m, col NBC. A Carsey-Werner Production in Association with Bill Cosby. UK tx *1985–94 C4.*

CR *Ed Weinberger, Michael Leeson, William H Cosby, Jr, EdD.* **EXEC PR** *Marcy Carsey, Tom Werner.* **PR** *Various, including John Markus, Terri Guarnieri, Matt Williams.* **DR** *Various, including Jay Sandrich, Tony Singletary.* **WR** *Various, including Ed Weinberger, Michael Leeson, John Markus, Chris Auer, Gary Knot, Bill Cosby, Earl Pomerantz, Matt Williams, Bernie Kukoff and Ehrich Van Lowe.* **MUS** *Stu Gardner and Bill Cosby (theme).* **CAST** Dr Heathcliff 'Cliff' Huxtable *Bill Cosby* Clair Huxtable *Phylicia Rashad (née Ayers Allen)* Denise Huxtable Kendall *Lisa Bonet* Sondra Huxtable Tibideaux *Sabrina LeBeauf* Vanessa Huxtable *Tempestt Bledsoe* Theodore Huxtable *Malcolm Jamal-Warner* Rudy Huxtable *Keshia Knight Pulliam* Pam Tucker *Erika Alexander* Russell Huxtable (Cliff's father) *Earle Hyman* Anna Huxtable (Cliff's mother) *Clarice Taylor* Martin Kendall *Joseph C Phillips* Elvin Tibideaux *Geoffrey Owens.*

◀◀◀ *William H Cosby, star of* The Cosby Show.

Although Bill Cosby *(I Spy, The Bill Cosby Show, The New Bill Cosby Show, Captain Kangaroo, Fat Albert and the Cosby Kids)* had been a TV item for nearly two decades, few gave this comedy of domestic drolleries much hope of success; it was a 'domcom' at a time when the form was held to be in decline and, worse, it was about a black family. Whites, it was feared, would turn off. This wisdom did not last *The Cosby Show*'s first season. By 1985 and its second season it had risen to number one in the Nielsens and stayed there for four years running, a record only ever surpassed by >*All in the Family*.

What audiences watched were poignant and gently amusing moments (episodes were frequently plotless) in the life of the middle-class Huxtables, headed by caring Cliff (Cosby's most sensitive performance to date), an obstetrician, and wife Clair, a lawyer (played by Phylicia Rashad, née Phylicia Ayers-Allen, sister of Debbie Allen of *Fame* and wife of NBC sportscaster Ahmad Rashad). Sharing their NY home at 10 Stigwood Avenue, Brooklyn Heights, were offspring Denise, Theo, Vanessa, Rudy and Sondra, all of them high achievers.

The show was a conscious crusade by Cosby to enlighten, providing a role model parade for blacks and instruction in anti-racism for whites (as Cosby put it: 'The Huxtables were set up to counter some of the minstrel shows Hollywood had set up'). Above all, though, the show was a lesson for everybody on how to bring up baby (i.e. with tolerance and love). Significantly, in early episodes Cosby styled himself William H Cosby Jr, Doctor of Education. *The Cosby Show* won four Emmys: Outstanding Comedy Series, 1985; Outstanding Writing in a Comedy, 1985; Outstanding Guest Performer in a Comedy Series (Roscoe Lee Browne, 1986); and Outstanding Directing in a Comedy Series (Jay Sandrich, 1986). It also made 'the Cos' one of the richest men in showbiz – though even with the benefit of an extended last episode in 1993, Cosby/Cliff was unable to fix the hall chimes.

A 1987 spin-off, *A Different World,* related Denise Huxtable's experiences on leaving the family brownstone for Hillman College.

Four years after the close of *The Cosby Show,* Cosby and Rashad were reunited in *Cosby,* concerning a retired airline executive and his sorely-tried wife. It was based on the British sitcom >*One Foot in the Grave.*

CRAPSTON VILLAS

UK 1990–5, Approx 19 x 30m, col C4. Spitting Image Productions.

CR *Sarah Anne Kennedy.* **PR** *Richard Bennett.* **DR** *Sarah Anne Kennedy.* **WR** *Sarah Anne Kennedy.* **CAST** *(voices) Jane Horrocks, Steven Steen, Alison Steadman, Liz Smith.*

Animated soap opera from the >*Spitting Image* team. Set in mythical London SE69 (a jibe at soap *EastEnders*), where the featured characters shared a crumbling Victorian villa. In slug-ridden Flat B lived down-trodden Sophie, her 'resting' film-maker boyfriend Jonathon (complete with pretentious goatee), and cutsie actress lodger Floss (who saw life in SE69 as 'just like being in a documentary'). In Flat C was single mother Marge Stenson, her teenage son and poppet-from-hell daughter Samantha. Robbie and Larry were the gay couple in Flat D. Fatso was the cat. Enid the granny.

Grotesque in both its scatalogical humour and its unnervingly accurate characterization; it would have been funny if it wasn't so real. Jane Horrocks (from >*Absolutely Fabulous*) and Alison Steadman were among the famous lending their voices.

THE CRITIC

USA 1994, 23 x 30m, col ABC/Fox. Gracie Films/ Columbia Pictures Television/Film Roman Production. UK tx *1995 Bravo.*

CR *Mike Reiss, Al Jean.* **EXEC PR** *James L Brooks, Al Jean, Mike Reiss, Phil Roman.* **PR** *Various, including Richard Sakai, Richard Raynis, Steve Tompkins.* **DR** *Various, including Bret Haaland, Lauren McMulen, Rich Moore, Dan Jeup.* **MUS** *Hans Zimmer (theme), Alf Hauser.* **CAST** *(voices)* Jay Sherman *Jon Lovitz* Duke Phillips *Charles Napier* Doris *Doris Grau* Jeremy Hawke *Maurice La Marche* Marty Sherman *Christine Cavanaugh* Margo *Nancy Cartwright* Franklin *Gerritt Graham* Eleanor *Judith Ivey* Alice Tompkins *Park Overall* Penny Tompkins *Russi Taylor* Vlada *Nick Jameson.*

The success of >*The Simpsons* caused much pitching of 'toon' ideas at US networks. *The Critic* – from the producers of *The Simpsons* – was one of the few to make it on to the airwaves.

Its title character was unattractive Manhattan film critic Jay Sherman (any resemblance to reviewer Roger Ebert was of course, um, coincidental), host of the little-watched cable show 'Coming Attractions'. Here he pilloried the latest releases, none of which could meet his impossibly high standards ('It stinks!'). As well as jibing nicely at the movie crit brigade, *The Critic* also parodied the movies themselves and cable TV (not least in the shape of Sherman's megalomaniacal media mogul boss), and even found time to follow Sherman's disastrous personal life. Guest voices included Billy Crystal, Adam West, Dan Castellaneta and Rod Steiger.

A thumbs up for this one.

CYBILL

USA 1995–8, 82 x 30m, col CBS. YBL/River Siren Productions/Carsey-Werner Productions/Chuck Lorre Productions/Jay Daniel Productions. UK tx *1995– C4.*

CR *Cybill Shepherd.* ***EXEC PR*** *Marcy Carsey, Caryn Mandabach, Cybill Shepherd, Chuck Lorre, Jay Daniel.* ***PR*** *Various, including Bob Meyer.* ***DR*** *Various, including Jonathan Weiss, Tom Moore, Robert Berlinger, Andy Weyman.* ***WR*** *Various, including Joey Murphy and John Pardee.* ***CAST*** Cybill Sheridan *Cybill Shepherd* Ira Woodbine *Alan Rosenberg* Jeff Robbins *Tom Wopat* Maryann Thorpe *Christine Baranski* Zoey Woodbine *Alicia Witt* Rachel Blanders *Deedee Pfeiffer* Sean *Jay Paulson* Claire *Paula Cole* Kevin *Peter Krause.*

After a period of conspicuous absence from the small screen, Cybill Shepherd *(>Moonlighting)* did a Roseanne Barr and based a sitcom around herself. In the resultant *Cybill* she played a bit-parting Hollywood actress (victim of vampires, that sort of thing) with fortysomething ageing worries and two daughters, conservative Rachel and sarcastic Zoey (played by Alicia Witt, who made her screen debut at seven in *Dune,* and is the daughter of the woman with the world's longest hair). There was also a duo of intrusive ex-husbands, dunder-headed stuntman Jeff Robbins (a wondrously cast Tom Wopat from *The Dukes of Hazzard*) and neurotic novelist Ira Woodbine. Cybill's best friend was the hard-drinking Maryann (an Emmy-winning performance by Christine Baranski).

If *Cybill* never broke new ground, it was likeable enough, with savvy swipes at Hollywood and a stockpile of smart one-liners. (Stuntman Jeff: 'There's this great scene where I jump from a speeding train with my head on fire.' Cybill: 'Well, nobody's head burns like yours.') Morgan Fairchild, Paula Abdul, Jonathan Frakes, and Shepherd's real-life ex-husband, Peter Bogdanovich (who had long, long before directed her in the best of movies, *The Last Picture Show,* and the worst of movies, *At Long Last Love*) were among those on the obligatory roster of stellar guests.

Stuntman Jeff: 'There's this great scene where I jump from a speeding train with my head on fire.' Cybill: 'Well, nobody's head burns like yours.'

DAD'S ARMY

UK 1968–77, 80 x 30m, col BBC1. BBC TV.

CR *Jimmy Perry, David Croft.* ***PR*** *David Croft.* ***DR*** *David Croft, Bob Spiers, Harold Snoad.* ***WR*** *Jimmy Perry, David Croft.* ***MUS*** *Ivor Novello (theme music), Jimmy Perry (theme lyrics), Bud Flanagan (theme vocal).* ***CAST*** Captain Mainwaring *Arthur Lowe* Sergeant Wilson *John Le Mesurier* Corporal Jones *Clive Dunn* Private Frazer *John Laurie* Private Pike *Ian Lavender* Private Walker *James Beck* ARP Warden Hodges *Bill Pertwee* Verger Yeatman *Edward Sinclair* The Vicar *Frank Williams* Mavis Pike *Janet Davies* Private Sponge *Colin Bean* Mrs Fox *Pamela Cundell.* Video *BBC.*

It was their finest half-hour. Based by writer Jimmy Perry on his youthful experiences with the local defence corps, this archetypal English TV comedy gently and nostalgically followed the misadventures of a Home Guard platoon in the fictional South Coast town of Walmington-on-Sea during the Second World War. Initially the show was rejected by the BBC for fear it would denigrate the wartime heroes. This gloriously missed the point; the Walmington platoon, led by pompous bank manager Captain Mainwaring, may have been bumbling amateurs, but there was never any doubt that, if the feared 'Narzi paratroopers' had landed, they would have fought bravely to a man.

Much of the humour of the show came from the mixing of the social classes that war occasioned (epitomized by Mainwaring's outranking of the public school educated Sergeant Wilson), and from the inspired characters. Under Mainwaring ('Right then. Pay attention, men') served the diffident Wilson ('Is that really wise, sir?'), the eternally volunteering Corporal Jones ('Don't panic!'/'They don't like it up 'em'), spivvy Private Walker (whose shiftiness was captured perfectly in the end credits, as he sneaked a 'gasper' on duty), the wild-eyed coffin maker Private Fraser ('We're doomed I say. Doomed'), young Mummy's boy Pike, and ageing incontinent Private Godfrey ('Do you think I might be excused, sir?'). The ARP warden, Hodges (who addressed Mainwaring as 'Napoleon'), the vicar and the verger were constant irritations to the platoon, endlessly competing with them for use of the church hall. Perhaps the quintessential moment of

▼▼ *'They don't like it up 'em' – Arthur Lowe (centre) leads the cast of* Dad's Army *into TV legend.*

Don't panic!

Dad's Army, when its sense of Englishness, its debt to Ealing film comedy, its characterization and performances all came together, was the episode 'The Deadly Attachment', in which the platoon captured a German submarine officer (Philip Madoc), who haughtily demanded the name of the Home Guardsman who mocked him. 'Don't tell him, Pike,' shouted Mainwaring.

So identified did the cast become with their *Dad's Army* roles that their other achievements are frequently overlooked. Arthur Lowe had previously starred in *Coronation Street* and *Pardon the Expression,* and would later lead *Potter* and >*A J Wentworth, BA,* while the distracted John Le Mesurier (of whom BBC comedy head Michael Mills once remarked, 'he suffers so beautifully') had previously starred in >*George and the Dragon* as well as a reel of cinema films. (First married to *Carry On* and >*Sykes* actress Hattie Jacques, Le Mesurier's air of good breeding hid an irreverent nature; he once famously smoked a cannabis joint at a BAFTA Awards ceremony.) Arnold Ridley OBE had thirty-eight plays to his name, including the West End classic, *The Ghost Train.*

Filmed on location at Thetford, Norfolk, *Dad's Army* recruited a small army of guest actors, many of whom – Don Estelle, Jack Haig, Donald Hewitt, Michael Knowles, Carmen Silvera (Mainwaring's fling) and Wendy Richard (Walker's girlfriend) – would be economically recycled by producer (and ex-Royal Artillery major) David Croft in future shows such as >*Are You Being Served?,* >*'Allo, 'Allo,* >*It Ain't Half Hot, Mum* and >*Hi-De-Hi!.*

Classic episodes include: 'The Deadly Attachment', 'The Gorilla' and 'The Day the Balloon Went Up'. The series won the BAFTA for Best Comedy in 1971. Columbia Pictures released a spin-off feature film in the same year. There were also stage and radio versions.

Although the last original episode was filmed in 1971, the show remains timelessly popular, for it was Perry and Croft's great genius to create in *Dad's Army* a sublime picture of the English as they like to see themselves.

DARIA

USA 1997–, 19 x 30m, col MTV. MTV. UK tx *1997– MTV.*

CR *Glenn Eichler.* **EXEC PR** *Glenn Eichler.* **PR** *Susie Lewis Lynn.* **CAST** *(voices)* Daria Morgendorffer *Tracy Grandstaff* Jane Lane/Quinn Morgendorffer *Wendy Hoopes* Trent Lane *Alvaro J Gonzalez* Jake Morgendorffer *Julian Rebolledo.*

Spin-off from >*Beavis & Butt-head* in which the boys' smart, sardonic and unpopular eponymous friend (she of the specs and ironic post on the school newspaper as fashion reporter),

Art teacher: 'Good work, Daria... You've really created the illusion of depth!'

Daria: 'I'm thinking of going into politics.'

moves to the posh suburbs to be smart, sardonic and unpopular at Lawndale High. Typical unteen hobbies: watching TV show 'Sick Sad World' and... writing. She was the daughter of hyperactive lawyer Helen and stressed businessman Jake, and older sister of the beautiful and popular Quinn (with whom she was engaged in a mutual pact of dislike). Jane Lane was Daria's best friend and fellow teen cynic and observer of the ridiculous behaviour of the world.

Actress-writer Tracy Grandstaff, who supplied the teen cynic's voice in *B&B,* carried the job over to the new animation.

DAVE ALLEN AT LARGE

UK 1971–5, 50 x 35m, col BBC2. BBC TV. US tx *1975 Syndicated.*

PR *Peter Whitemore.* **WR** *Dave Allen, Austin Steele, Peter Vincent.* **CAST** *Dave Allen, with Paul McDowell, Ralph Watson, Jacqueline Clark, Robert East, Ronnie Brody.*

Rambling monologues from Irish sit-down (on a stool) comic, with nine-and-a-half nicotine-stained fingers and a perpetual whiskey glass. Interspersing the rants were filmed sketches. Much the most favoured of Allen's targets were sex, religion and bureaucracy, his risqué comedic thrusts – often skilfully done – were much appreciated by a TV audience tired of conservatism on the small screen. A virtuoso interlude in which Allen anagrammed the names of famous politicians ('Rev Ian Paisley' became 'Vile IRA Pansy') remains an undimmed classic, even if long ago locked in the vaults of TV land.

Born David Tynan O'Mahoney, Dave Allen ('Anal Delve') began his TV career with Val Doonican, graduating to his first solo series, *The Dave Allen Show,* in 1969. Others followed, for both the ITV and BBC networks, but *At Large* was the creative high tide.

THE DAY TODAY

UK 1994, 14 x 30m, col BBC2. Talk Back.

CR *Christopher Morris, Armando Iannucci.* **EXEC PR** *Peter Fincham.* **PR** *Armando Iannucci.* **DR** *Andrew Gilman.* **WR** *Christopher Morris, Armando Iannucci.* **CAST** *Christopher Morris, Patrick Marber, Rebecca Front, Steve Coogan, Doon Mackichan, David Schneider.*

TV news satire, similar to >*Drop the Dead Donkey* and >*KYTV* of the same era, but infinitely more savage in its exposure of media manipulation and the degrading of newscasting standards. In this it proved award-winningly successful, despite a tendency in moments of laziness to fall back on the standard ploy of alternative shows, a dose of >*Monty Python* surrealism, eg the headline 'Dismantled Pope Found Sliding Along Road'. Among the featured newzak folk were decapitated weatherman Sylvester Stuart, economics correspondent Peter O'Hanraha'hanrahan (Patrick Marber), business affairs reporter Collaterlie Sisters (Doon Mackichan, >*The Comic Strip Presents*), Christopher Morris (played by Christopher Morris) as argumentative Paxman-like anchor, and Pringle-clad sportscaster Alan Partridge (Steve Coogan) – soon to enjoy a spoof show of his own, >*Knowing Me, Knowing You... with Alan Partridge*. A pre-famous Minnie Driver could be glimpsed as an Italian TV presenter.

Designing Women

USA 1986–93, 163 x 30m, col CBS. Bloodworth: Thomason Mozark Productions/Columbia Pictures Television/CPT Holdings. UK tx *1993–6 Sky 1.*

CR *Linda Bloodworth-Thomason.* **EXEC PR** *Harry Thomason, Linda Bloodworth-Thomason, Pamela Norris, Douglas Johnson, Tommy Thompson, Norma Safford Vela.* **DR** *Various, including Jack Shea, Ellen Falcon, Arlene Sanford, Harry Thomason, David Steinberg, David Trainer.* **WR** *Various, including Linda Bloodworth-Thomason, Pamela Norris.* **CAST** Suzanne Sugarbaker *Delta Burke* Julia Sugarbaker *Dixie Carter* Charlene Frazier Stillfield *Jean Smart* Mary Jo Shively *Annie Potts* Anthony Bouvier *Meshach Taylor* Carlene Frazier Dobber *Jan Hooks* Allison Sugarbaker *Julia Duffy* Bernice Clifton *Alice Ghostley* Bonnie Jean ('BJ') Poteet *Judith Ivey* Etienne Toussant Bouvier *Sheryl Lee Ralph* Bill Stillfield *Douglas Barr* Claudia Shively *Priscilla Weems.*

Created by writer Linda Bloodworth-Thomason (an Arkansas friend of Bill and Hillary Clinton, no less), this comedy about a quartet of Southern belles working for an Atlanta interior design firm débuted in fall of 1986 to respectable ratings. For reasons best known to themselves, however, CBS then moved the show to a death slot and ratings plummeted. *Designing Women* went into 'hiatus'.

However, in a virtual re-run of the *Cagney and Lacey* saga, viewers (predominantly women, and led by Viewers for Quality Television) campaigned for *Designing Women*'s return. And got it, the show later reaching the top ten of the Nielsens.

The original drawling decorator foursome who worked at Sugarbakers were employees Mary Jo Shively (single mother) and Charlene Frazier (utterly conventional), and the two Sugarbaker sisters who employed them, Julia (liberal professional) and Suzanne (sex mad and dumb: 'I'm gonna turn the TV off – it's only the news and I saw that yesterday'). Essentially, though, the Sugarbaker four were archetypes used to explore the problems of modern women, which the show did humorously well. The sole man in the hen coop was Anthony Bouvier (Meshach Taylor), a camp black ex-convict who served as their assistant. (Eventually, Anthony made the grade as partner, thus neatly puncturing viewer notions that the Deep South was run entirely by rednecks.)

There were several cast changes, the most important being the departure of former Miss Florida, Delta Burke, who played Suzanne. Burke went to fat and was fired – somewhat tarnishing the show's image as a feminist sitcom beacon. (Burke later starred in the short-lived 1992 sitcom, *Delta*.) She was replaced by Julia Duffy as Cousin Allison

I'm gonna turn the TV off – it's only the news and I saw that yesterday

Sugarbaker. Duffy lasted a single year, to be replaced by Tony-winner Judith Ivey as B J Poteet, a Texan widow who became the part owner of Sugarbakers. As Ivey went in through the Sugarbakers door, so Annie Potts, who played Mary Jo (and previously the record store owner in *Pretty in Pink*), went out. By the end of the 1992 season only Dixie Carter and Taylor were left from the original cast, and the show was clearly floundering in its attempt to restore the original balance of characters, even shifting the epicentre of the humour away from the Sugarbaker belles to Bouvier and wacky client Bernice Clifton. It was cancelled in May 1993. The show's co-executive producer was Linda Bloodworth-Thomason's husband, Harry Thomason.

A spin-off, *Women of the House,* aired in 1991.

DESMOND'S

UK 1989–94, 65 x 30m, col C4. Humphrey Barclay Productions. US tx *1990– Black Entertainment Television.*

CR *Trix Worrell.* **PR** *Humphrey Barclay, Charlie Hanson.* **DR** *Various, including Trix Worrell, Charlie Hanson, Nic Phillips, Liddy Oldroyd, Mandie Fletcher, David Askey, Ian McLean.* **WR** *Trix Worrell, Joan Hooley.* **CAST** Desmond Ambrose *Norman Beaton* Shirley Ambrose *Carmen Munroe* Porkpie *Ram John Holder* Matthew *Christopher Asante/Gyearbuor Asante* Sean *Justin Pickett* Gloria *Kim Walker* Lee *Robbie Gee* Tony *Dominic Keating* Michael Ambrose *Kim Walker* Louise *Lisa Georghan* Mandy *Matilda Thorpe* Beverley *Joan Ann Maynard.*

Not Britain's first all-black sitcom (that honour belongs to *The Fosters,* LWT 1976–7), nor its second (>*No Problem!*), but certainly its most successful. Norman Beaton, who had starred in *The Fosters,* played the testy yet tolerant Desmond Ambrose, proprietor of a barber-shop in Peckham, South London that served as the social scene for his family and assorted locals – and gave the occasional haircut. Carmen Munroe – also of *The Fosters* – played Desmond's long-suffering wife, Shirley. The other main characters included the Ambrose offspring, Michael, Sean and Gloria, and regular customers/friends, usually of a philosophising bent – lollipop man Porkpie, Matthew, Lee (Robbie 'Buck' Gee, *The Real McCoy*), Tony and Louise.

Most of the humour was spun from the intergenerational conflict between the values of young black characters who grew up in Britain and an older generation from the West Indies. Some predictable scripts were triumphed over by charismatic performances, and the show ran to five seasons, earned Beaton an appearance on >*The Cosby Show* (as a cricket-loving West Indian doctor) and sold around the world. In the USA, it attracted millions on the Black Entertainment Television cable network. It also spawned a spin-off, *Porkpie,* following that character and his fabulous, million-pound lottery win. Like *Desmond's* itself, it was created and written by Trix Worrell.

The Dick Van Dyke Show

USA 1961–5, 156 x 30m, bw CBS. Calvada Productions/T & L Productions. UK tx *1963–6 BBC1.*

CR *Carl Reiner.* **EXEC PR** *Sheldon Leonard, Carl Reiner, Danny Thomas.* **PR** *Carl Reiner, Ronald Jacobs.* **DR** *Various, including Carl Reiner, John Rich, Jerry Paris, Robert Butler, Stanley Z Cherry, Claudio Guzman.* **WR** *Various, including Carl Reiner, Bill Persky, Sam Denoff.* **MUS** *Earle H Hagen.* **CAST** Rob Simpson Petrie *Dick Van Dyke* Laura Petrie (née Meeker) *Mary Tyler Moore* Ritchie Petrie *Larry Matthews* Alan Brady *Carl Reiner* Jerry Helper *Jerry Paris* Millie Helper *Ann Morgan Guilbert* Buddy Sorrell *Morey Amsterdam* Sally Rogers *Rose Marie* Mel Cooley *Richard Deacon.*

▲▲▲ *One of the most sophisticated sitcoms ever to hit the tube,* The Dick Van Dyke Show *followed the lives of TV comedy writer Rob Petrie and his wife Laura.*

Classic sixties sitcom about Rob Petrie, the head TV comedy writer for the fictional *The Alan Brady Show*. For the most part, the plots involved shenanigans at the office, where Petrie worked with man-eating Sally Rogers and Buddy Sorrell (plus pompous balding producer, Melvin Cooley), and at his home in the New York suburb of New Rochelle. There Petrie worked with his perky wife, the former dancer Laura, and son Ritchie. Jerry and Millie Helper were the next-door neighbours.

Originally creator Carl Reiner (who had previously worked on *Your Show of Shows*) intended to play the lead part of Petrie himself, but was persuaded to stand down by veteran TV executive producer Sheldon Leonard (although Reiner got to play the often heard but rarely seen Alan Brady). In his stead Sheldon cast, after initially slating Johnny Carson, one-time game show host and Broadway actor Dick Van Dyke. Sixty actresses were interviewed before the unknown Mary Tyler Moore (whose most substantial roles hitherto had been the secretary – seen only from the hips down – in *Richard Diamond, Private Eye* and the 'Happy Hotpoint Elf' in TV commercials that aired during >*The Adventures of Ozzie and Harriet*) was cast as Petrie's wife Laura.

As if to prove the truth of Sheldon's axiom 'the higher the quality of the show, the longer it will take to catch on with the general public', *DVDS* took two seasons to become a hit (and then needed to be scheduled to follow >*The Beverly Hillbillies* on Wednesday nights), but was never out of the ratings top twenty thereafter. The show's slow start was partly caused by the obstruction of CBS chief Jim Aubrey ('The Smiling Cobra'), who took a perverse dislike to *DVDS* and had to be pressurised into airing it by sponsors Proctor and Gamble. Famously liberal in its world view, the show was financed initially by money from the Kennedy clan, via John F Kennedy's brother-in-law, the Rat Pack actor Peter Lawford. As if to underline the show's embodiment of the Kennedy Age, Moore even looked like Jackie Kennedy.

Among the fifteen Awards bestowed by the Television Academy on *The Dick Van Dyke Show,* a watershed in the development of adult comedy for the sophistication of its scripts, were Emmys for Outstanding Comedy Series in 1963, 1964 and 1966. Van Dyke and Moore also both received individual acting Emmys for their performances. The show came to an end in 1966 when Van Dyke, the 'male Julie Andrews' as he called himself, left to pursue movie work full time. He returned to TV in 1971, however, with *The New Dick Van Dyke Show,* playing Dick Preston, the host of a TV chat show. Meanwhile, Mary Tyler Moore went on to star in her own phenomenally successful >*Mary Tyler Moore Show,* also set in TV land.

Episodes of *The Dick Van Dyke Show* are repeated to this day, its timeless appeal helped by the show having been filmed originally without any slang expressions.

DIFF'RENT STROKES

USA 1978–86, 184 x 30m, col NBC/ABC. Embassy Pictures Corp/TAT Productions.

CR *Jeff Harris, Bernie Kukoff.* **PR** *Budd Grossman, Howard Leeds, John Maxwell Anderson.* **DR** *Leslie H Martinson.* **MUS** *Alan Thicke.* **CAST** Arnold Jackson/ Drummond *Gary Coleman* Willis Jackson/ Drummond *Todd Bridges* Philip Drummond *Conrad Bain* Kimberley Bain *Dana Plato* Mrs Garrett *Charlotte Rae* Charlene DuPrey *Janet Jackson.*

Interracial sitcom which premised the adoption of two black Harlem orphans, Arnold (Gary Coleman) and Willis Jackson, by a white Park Avenue millionaire, Philip Drummond. Developed by NBC executive Fred Silverman as a vehicle for the precocious eight-year-old Coleman (he of the extraordinary savvy self-confidence and comic timing), the show sought to bridge the racial divide in the American audience. It did so, but at the cost of much criticism from black organizations that Coleman was just the grinning wire-headed piccaninny from TV and films of yesteryear.

Tragically, renal disease and a subsequent

kidney transplant stunted actor Coleman's growth and caused his face to look aged, giving his performance a diverting oddness. He also starred in *The Gary Coleman Show,* a Hanna-Barbera cartoon (1982–3), in which he voiced a mischievous angel, Andy Lebeau.

In the days before she became poptastically famous, Janet Jackson appeared in *Diff'rent Strokes* as Willis' girlfriend. Among the show's guest stars were Muhammad Ali and Forest Whitaker.

There were two spin-offs, *The Facts of Life* and *Hello Larry.*

DOCTOR IN THE HOUSE

UK 1969–70, 26 x 30m, col ITV. LWT.

CR *Frank Muir.* ***PR*** *Humphrey Barclay.* ***DR*** *Various, including Bill Turner, David Askey.* ***WR*** *Various, including John Cleese, Graham Chapman, Bill Oddie, Graeme Garden, Jonathan Lynn.*
CAST Michael Upton *Barry Evans* Duncan Waring *Robin Nedwell* Dick Stuart-Clark *Geoffrey Davies* Paul Collier *George Layton* Huw Evans *Martin Shaw* Prof Geoffrey Loftus *Ernest Clark* The Dean *Ralph Michael* Danny Hooley *Jonathan Lynn* Dave Briddock *Simon Cuff.*

Medical sitcom which pleased in small doses. Loosely derived for TV from the novel by Richard Gordon, at the instigation of the then head of comedy at LWT, Frank Muir, it updated the story to feature a fresh intake of students at famed St Swithin's teaching hospital. Prominent amongst the tyro quacks were Michael Upton (Barry Evans, later >*Mind Your Language*), Duncan Waring, Paul Collier (George Layton, >*It Ain't Half Hot, Mum*), and upper-class Dick Stuart-Clark. Leery, beery antics ensued in a style not a whole ward away from *Carry On Doctor.* Professor Loftus and the Dean were the stock figures of aghast authority.

Funnily enough, despite its MORism the show was largely scripted by writers associated with zany edge-of-late-sixties comedy – the Cambridge contemporaries John Cleese, Graham Chapman, Bill Oddie, Graeme Garden and Jonathan Lynn (who also appeared on screen as mad Irish medic Danny Hooley). A sequel, *Doctor at Large* (ITV, 1971), however, allowed Cleese a try-out situation about a rude hotelier that would eventually transmogrify into >*Fawlty Towers.*

After *Doctor at Large* – which saw Upton et al newly qualified and joined in the department of incompetence by puritan kill-joy Bingham (Richard O'Sullivan, later >*Man About the House*) – the *Doctor* series began to issue from LWT with apparent incontinence: *Doctor in Charge* (ITV, 1972–3), *Doctor at Sea* (ITV, 1974), *Doctor on the Go* (ITV, 1975–7), and even the antipodean-set *Doctor Down Under* (ITV, 1980). By this time, only Waring and Stuart-Clark were left from the original cast of TV characters. But there was still more *Doctor*ing to come: in 1983 a film version of *Doctor in the House* segued clips from the *Doctor* shows thus far, and in 1991 the BBC produced a revival, *Doctor at the Top* (BBC1, 1991), which saw Waring, Collier and Stuart-Clark twenty years on and the holders of (improbably enough) high office at St Swithin's. Alas, all the sequels did was to demonstrate the law of diminishing comic returns.

DR KATZ, PROFESSIONAL THERAPIST

USA 1995–, 41 x 30m, col Comedy Central. HBO Downtown Productions/Tom Snyder Productions/ Popular Arts Entertainment. UK tx *1995 Paramount.*

CR *Jonathan Katz, Tom Snyder.* **EXEC PR** *Tom Snyder, Tim Braine, Nancy Geller.* **PR** *Jonathan Katz, Julianne Shapiro, H Jon Benjamin, Tom Snyder, Loren Bouchard, Karen LeBlanc, Anette LeBlanc Cates, Will LeBow.* **MUS** *Tom Snyder and Shapiro Music.* **CAST** *(voices)* Dr Katz *Jonathan Katz* Ben *H Jon Benjamin* Laura *Laura Silverman* Stanley *Will LeBow* Julie *Julianne Shapiro.*

Stand-up comedian Jonathan Katz voiced cartoon therapist 'Dr Katz', whose caseload (neurotic patients, usually impersonated by other comedians) was not helped by having a contemptuous nail-filing secretary, Laura, and a 23-year-old slacker son, Ben. Off duty, Dr Katz (who was, natch, not quite sorted in the department of life himself) liked to pontificate with friend Stan and bartender Julie at 'Jacky's 33'.

A loony toon for the middle- to highbrow market, the show was acerbically funny and scripted with casual brilliance. It was produced using computer-generated SquiggleVision, which made the drawn lines shake distinctively, some thought irritatingly.

>> ***Dr Katz: 'Ray, Ray, Ray. What are we going to do with you, laddy boy?'***
Ray: 'Fix me.' <<

Before going into series production in 1995, the show was preceded by seven one-minute pieces in 1994. Among the guest voices were Ray Romano, Rita Rudner, Garry Shandling and Winona Ryder.

DOOGIE HOWSER, MD

USA 1989–93, 60 x 30m, col ABC. Steven Bochco Productions. UK tx *1990–3 BBC1.*

CR *Steven Bochco, David E. Kelley.* **PR** *Steven Bochco.* **DR** *Various, including Paul Newman, Bill D'elia, Kris Tabori, Steven Cragg, Joan Darling, Matia Karrell, Eric Laneuville.* **MUS** *Mike Post.* **CAST** Dr Douglas 'Doogie' Howser *Neil Patrick Harris* Dr David Howser (father) *James B Sikking* Katherine O'Brien Howser (mother) *Belinda Montgomery* Vinnie Delpino *Max Casella* Nurse Cauly Spaulding *Kathryn Lang* Dr Benjamin Canfield *Lawrence Pressman* Dr Jack McGuire *Mitchell Anderson* Wanda Plenn *Lisa Dean Ryan* Raymond Alexander *Markus Redmond* Nurse Faber *Robyn Lively.*

Implausible but diverting sitcom featuring a boy genius who becomes a fully qualified doctor at fourteen. The fresh-faced one practised – to the jaw-dropping panic of patients – at the Eastman Medical Center in Los Angeles, but was constantly torn between serious career professionalism and wanting to have typical teen fun with his buddy Vinnie.

The show was developed by Steven Bochco as part of his ten-pilot contract with ABC network, and co-created with David Kelley, with whom Bochco later teamed up for *LA Law*.

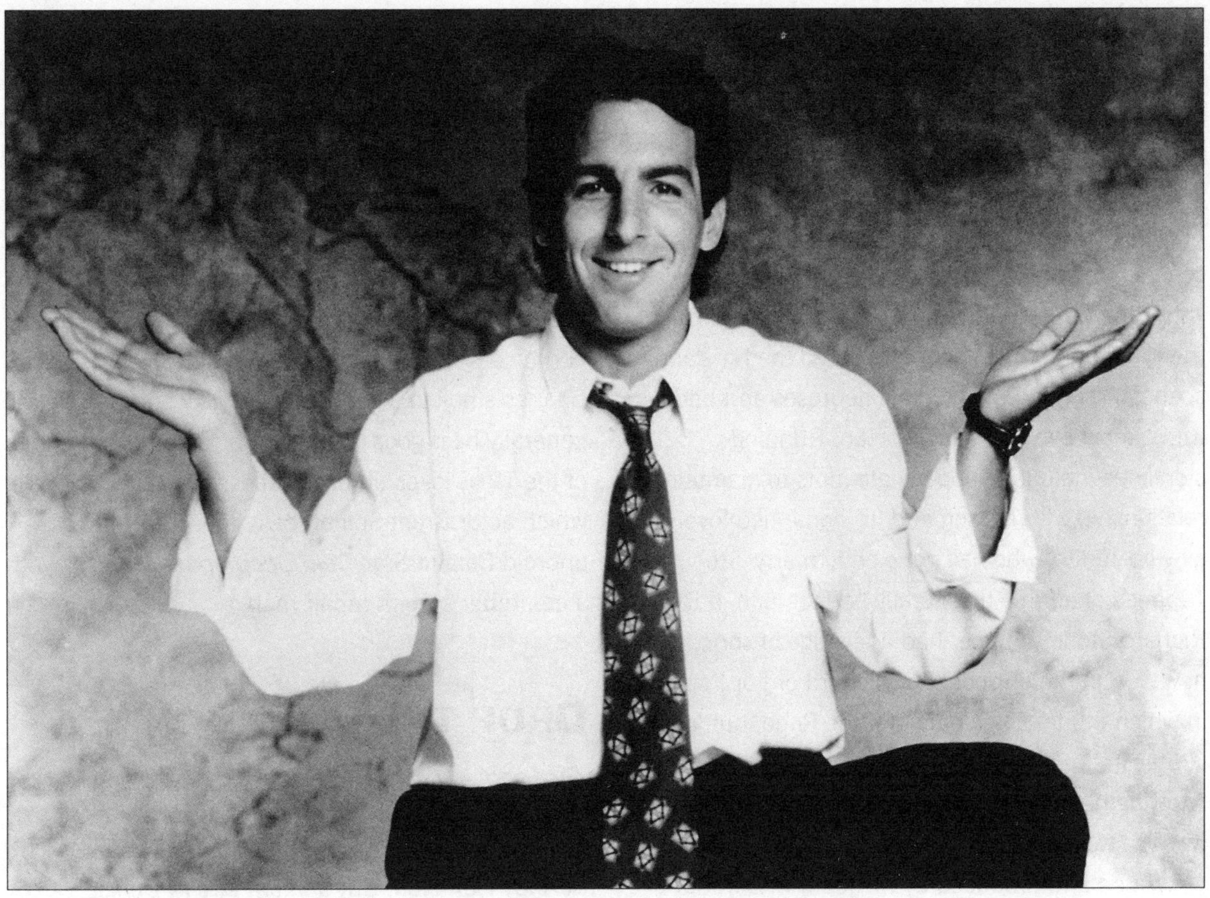

DREAM ON

USA 1990–6, 100 x 30m, col Home Box Office. Kevin S Bright Productions/MCA Television Entertainment. UK tx *1991– C4.*

CR *David Crane, Marta Kauffman.* **EXEC PR** *Kevin S Bright, John Landis.* **PR** *Robb Idels, David Crane, Marta Kauffman.* **DR** *Various, including John Landis, Eric Laneuville, Betty Thomas, Rob Thompson, Anson Williams, Stephen Engel, Lisa Gottlieb, Jerry London, Arlene Sanford, Mel Smith, Peter Baldwin, Debra Hill, Nick Marck, Michael McKean, Bethan Rooney, Kevin Bright.* **WR** *Various, including David Crane, Marta Kauffman, Jeff Greenstein, Jeff Strauss, Stephen Engel, Andrew Gordon and Eileen Conn.* **MUS** *Michael Skloff.* **CAST** Martin Tupper *Brian Benben* Judith Tupper/Stone *Wendie Malick* Toby Pedalbee *Denny Dillon* Jeremy Tupper (son) *Chris Demetral* Eddie Charles *Jeff Joseph (1990)/Dorien Wilson* Gibby Fiske *Michael McKean.*

▲▲▲ *Brian Benben starred in HBO's 'adult comedy'* Dream On *about a thirtysomething sex-obsessed single white male in New York.*

Made-for-cable American 'adult comedy' (ie spiced with naked embonpoint), which also circulated the airwaves in a syndicated version *sans* nudity. Brian Benben played sex-mad NY book editor Martin Tupper, a TV child of the fifties who became a newly divorced guy of the nineties. With scant sympathy from his secretary at Whitestone's, Toby, and dubious advice from womanizing best friend Eddie Charles, Tupper entered the NY dating scene and ended up in comic neuroses and bed with almost every passing woman. Running storylines included Tupper's attempts to maintain a relationship with his son and his continued love for ex-wife Judith, who had gone on to marry – to Tupper's chagrin – the literally perfect man in Dr Richard Stone. (Tupper had a revenge of sorts, however, in the episode 'For Richard or For Poorer' in which Stone took a bullet for the Pope, but lost a kidney in the process; Tupper donated one of his, knowing henceforth that a part of Stone's greatness would always be his.)

Written and produced by the team who would later create >*Friends,* the show's main gimmick was to illustrate Tupper's every thought with a clip from archive black-and-white TV shows, *GE Theatre* and *Alcoa Premiere* being favourites. The device wasn't new – Woody Allen had used it in the 1972 movie *Play It Again Sam* – and co-executive producer John Landis (better known for his helming of such films as *An American Werewolf in London* and *The Blues Brothers*) only adopted it as a lucrative means of utilizing MCA's unsyndicatable back catalogue, but it was often wittily done. When Tupper heard the news that his wife wanted a divorce, the screen cut to footage of Lee Marvin delivering a knock-out blow; when a young college co-ed tried to seduce the 36-year-old Tupper, handsome Hollywood star Cornel Wilde popped up to assure him, 'Age has nothing to do with it, it's performance that counts.'

The cable version had its tacky moments (a threesome with Eddie Charles in 'Come and Knock on Our Door' being the exemplar), and a mite of controversy around a scene in which Tupper and Charles smoked a joint, but the risky adult formula generally held good. The show also contained one of the TV in-jokes of the nineties, in a scene in which actor Brent Spiner, best known as the android Data in *Star Trek: Deep Space Nine,* played a computer system repair man.

DROP THE DEAD DONKEY

UK 1990–8, 66 x 30m, col C4. Hat Trick. US tx *1992– Comedy Central.*

CR *Andy Hamilton, Guy Jenkin.* **EXEC PR** *Denise O'Donoghue.* **PR** *Andy Hamilton, Guy Jenkin.* **DR** *Liddy Oldroyd.* **WR** *Andy Hamilton, Guy Jenkin, Ian Brown, Nick Revell, Malcolm Williamson.* **CAST** Gus Hedges *Robert Duncan* George Dent *Jeff Rawle* Alex Pates *Haydn Gwynne* Damien Day *Stephen Tomkinson* Dave Charnley *Neil Pearson* Henry Davenport *David Swift* Sally Smedley *Victoria Wicks* Joy Merryweather *Susannah Doyle* Helen Cooper *Ingrid Lacey.*

Are we cooking with napalm? Good.

Gus Hedges, Globelink News Executive

In the beginning this behind-the-scenes sitcom set in a TV newsroom was heavily topical in its humour, with a steady stream of up-to-the-minute one-liners about real events (scripts being written twenty-four hours before broadcast). As the seasons passed, however, the current events gags were much reduced in number (from around twenty-five to around twelve per episode) and the humour came to centre on the memorable caricatures who were the staff of Sir Royston Merchant's Globelink TV. These were: Gus Hedges, the craven, virginal, jargon-spouting chief executive ('Could we interlock brain spaces in my office?'); Alex, his acerbic prime mover, later replaced by lesbian Helen; Damien (Stephen Tomkinson, later *Ballykissangel*), the amoral, thrusting cub reporter; Henry, the dissolute news anchorman who was constantly at war with the snobbish but dim newsreader, Sally Smedley; George, the be-cardiganed, hypochondriac, divorced senior news

The dysfunctional staff of the TV newsroom sitcom Drop the Dead Donkey. *It starred, from left to right, Susanah Doyle, Jeff Rawle, David Swift, Robert Duncan, Victoria Wicks, Stephen Tomkinson, Ingrid Lacey and Neil Pearson.*

editor; Dave Charnley (played by Neil Pearson, later the cop show *Between the Lines*), the indefatigable tottyholic – although according to Alex, in the aftermath of a classic drunken office Christmas party episode, he possessed 'a small penis and the sexual prowess of a panda'; and Joy, the permanently angry PA.

Transmuted into what was essentially a conventional comedy – with the added plus of an alarmingly true depiction of the backbiting in office life – the show became a massive international hit, selling to countries as diverse as Turkey and Iceland. It was also accorded two International Emmys and BAFTAs for Best Comedy Series, among other honours. The show was the creation of Guy Jenkin and Andy Hamilton (formerly the producer of >*Who Dares Wins* and a writer for >*Spitting Image*).

DUCKMAN

USA 1994–7, 70 x 30m, col USA Network. Paramount Pictures. UK tx *1995– BBC2.*

EXEC PR *Jeff Reno, Ron Osborn.* **PR** *Gabor Csupo, Sherry Gunther, Arlene Klasky, Gene Laufenberg, Michael Markowitz, David Misch.* **DR** *Various, including Raymie Musquiz, John Eng, Jeff McGrath, Norton Virgien.* **WR** *Various, including Jeff Reno, Ron Osborn, Ron Lux, Bill Canterbury, Bernie Keating, Michael Markowitz.* **MUS** *Scott Wilk, Todd Yvega, Frank Zappa.* **CAST** *(voices)* Eric Tiberius Duckman *Jason Alexander* Cornfed Pig *Gregg Berger* Ajax *Dweezil Zappa* Mambo *E G Daily* Charles *Dana Hill/Pat Musick* Aunt Bernice *Nancy Travis.*

Animated misadventures of an irascible wise-quacking detective duck (with the appearance of 'a urine-coloured feather duster') who, along with porcine partner Cornfed Pig, ran a private dick agency. However, the duo's cases seldom ran along ordinary lines: in one episode alone, Duckman went on the run from the IRS aboard a Harley (shades of *Easy Rider*), joined a hippie commune, drank hallucinogenic potion and burnt his bra – all in under thirty minutes. In another episode, the detective drake staged a coup in South America against pay toilets. Befitting the show's subtitle, 'Private Dick/Family Man', Duckman's home life also figured centrally, his brood being composed of Siamese-twin sons who loathed him, a frighteningly stupid teenager, Ajax ('Stand away from the door, son, then pull'), and exercise fetishist sister-in-law Bernice.

If the show was an obvious spoof of *film noir* and the TV 'domcom', its weird artwork and weirder hardboiled humour gave it the sharp edge of social satire (and was thus completely in keeping with Duckman's origins in Everett Dick's underground cartoon strip). Jason Alexander – from >*Seinfeld* – voiced the venal Duckman with obvious relish, while Dweezil (son of Frank) Zappa was the voice of Ajax. The guest star voices were headed by David Duchovny, Brian Keith (from sixties sitcoms *The Brian Keith Show* and >*Family Affair*, and the sublime Sam Peckinpah TV oater *The Westerner*) as Duckman's father, Burt Reynolds, Ice-T, Coolio and Leonard Nimoy.

Seemingly uneasy at the show's bizarrerie, Paramount pulled the plug after seventy shows (the last episode being the cliffhanging 'Four Weddings

What the hell you starin' at?

Inconceivable'), though lampooning Paramount's own products, such as *Star Trek* ('Where No Duckman Has Gone Before'), might be said to be a classic case of pecking the hand that feeds you. Duckman, however, later bobbed back on the Internet as an MSN talkshow host.

ELLEN

USA 1994–8, 109 x 25m, 1 x 60m, col ABC. The Black-Marlens Company/Touchstone TV. UK tx *1994– C4.*

CR *Neal Marlens, Carol Black, David Rosenthal.* **EXEC PR** *Eileen Heisler, DeAnne Heline, Vic Kaplan, Mark Driscoll, Daval Savel.* **PR** *Various, including Tracy Newman, Jonathan Stark, Lisa Debenedictis, Daryl Rowland, Ellen DeGeneres.* **DR** *Various, including Robby Benson, Tom Cherones, Gil Junger, Gail Mancuso, Lorraine Sevre-Richmond.* **MUS** *W G Snuffy Walden.* **CAST** EllenMorgan *Ellen DeGeneres* 'Coffee' Joe Farrell *David Anthony Higgins* Paige Clark *Joely Fisher* Audrey Penney *Clea Lewis* Adam Green *Ayre Gross* Spence Kovak *Jeremy Piven* Anita *Maggie Jakobson* Holly *Holly Fisher.*

Kooky >*Seinfeld*/>*Caroline in the City*/>*Friends*-type sitcom about mixed-up single people. Stand-up comic Ellen DeGeneres starred as an LA bookshop/coffeeshop manager, queenpin to a group of goofy chums – ambitious Paige, irritating 'Coffee' Joe, lecherous Adam and whiny airhead Audrey – who tolerated her idiosyncrasies (babbling and bumbling in her handling of people) as she tolerated theirs. Filmed in feel-good warm lighting

▶▶▶ *Ellen DeGeneres (right), star of kooky sitcom* Ellen, *aka* These Friends of Mine.

reminiscent of shampoo advertisements, it did OK in plumbing the corners of relationship paranoias and exhibited the occasional flash of inspired surrealism (including a mind-catching weird satire on car consumerism). Those who loved it loved it, but probably not as much as some other sitcoms.

In 1997 *Ellen* made the news headlines when DeGeneres announced 'I'm gay', and that she was in a relationship with actress Anne Heche (the main squeeze of Steve Martin, a fact likely to test his sense of humour). Department store J C Penney and car giant Chrysler withdrew their advertising from the show, and ABC affiliates in the Midwest dropped it from their schedules. ABC responded with a star-studded special (including Demi Moore, kd lang, Oprah Winfrey), 'Ellen: The Episode', in which the sitcom Ellen was introduced to sapphic ways by Laura Dern. The show was axed in 1998.

EMPTY NEST

USA 1988–95, 170 x 30m, col NBC. Witt-Thomas-Harris/Touchstone Productions. UK tx *1989–92.*

CR *Susan Harris.* **EXEC PR** *Susan Harris, Paul Junger Witt, Regina Stewart Larsen, Tony Thomas, Bob Tischler.* **PR** *Various, including Pat Dougherty, David Richardson, Peter Callay, Dennis Snee, Steven Sullivan, Ursula Ziegler.* **DR** *Various, including Hal Cooper, Stephen Zuckerman, Renny Temple, Dinah Manoff.* **WR** *Various, including Dennis Snee, Paolo Poeti (aka Paul B Price), Steven Sullivan, Ursula Ziegler.* **MUS** *John Bettes, George Aliceson Tipton.* **CAST** Dr Harry Weston *Richard Mulligan* Carol Weston *Dinah Manoff* Barbara Weston *Kirsty McNicol* Nurse *LaVerne Todd* Charley Dietz *David Leisure* Sophia Petrillo *Estelle Getty.*

A knock-on from Susan Harris's >*The Golden Girls* and set in the Miami matrons' own neighbourhood. Richard Mulligan from >*Soap* starred as widowed paediatrician Harry Weston, whose daughters – neurotic Carol and undercover cop Barbara – had flown the nest. But only to return. Paternal anxiety and misunderstanding ensued, while Weston sought to deal with the mature female suitors who appeared at his door and lascivious neighbour Charley. A sympathetic ear was lent by dog Dreyfuss. Nothing if not economical, Harris used the show to launch another sitcom, >*Nurses.*

EVENING SHADE

USA 1990–4, 98 x 30m, col CBS. CBS Entertainment Productions/Bloodworth-Thomason/Mozark. UK tx *1992–4 C4.*

PR *Tommy Thompson and Don Rhymer.* **DR** *Various, including Burt Reynolds, John Ratzenberger, Robby Benson, James Hampton.* **CAST** Wood Newton *Burt Reynolds* Ava Evans Newton *Marilu Henner* Taylor Newton *Jay R Ferguson* Molly Newton *Melissa Martin/Candace Hutson* Will Newton *Jacob Parker* Evan Evans *Hal Holbrook* Dr Harlan Elldridge *Charles Durning* Frieda Evans *Elizabeth Ashley* Herman Stiles *Michael Jeter* Fontana Beausoleil *Linda Gehringer* Ponder Blue *Ossie Davis.*

Laid-back ensemble sitcom which marked Burt Reynolds' return to the medium that made him (he came up playing in fifties oaters *Gunsmoke* and *Riverboat*). Here Reynolds starred as a former American football hero, Wood Newton, who goes back to his hometown in Arkansas to become the High School coach. The team hadn't won a game in two years – and Newton's coaching did nothing to change this. His family consisted of wife Ava (Marilu Henner from >*Taxi*), who had career ambitions and eventually became local Prosecuting Attorney, baby daughter Emily, teen son Taylor, and Molly and Will. Ava's father, Evan, owned the local paper, the *Evening Shade Argus*. Other regulars included Ponder Blue, the musing narrator who doubled as restaurateur at Ponder Blue's Barbecue Villa, stripper Fontana Beausoleil (who was being dated by Evan), Ava's straight-talking Aunt Frieda, gimpy maths teacher Herman Stiles, and town physician Harlan Elldridge.

Almost hypnotic (at its best) in its easy charm and sense of rural small-town place rare in nineties sitcomland (you have to go back to the era of >*The Andy Griffith Show* for anything comparable), it went high in the ratings, and Reynolds himself picked up a 1991 Emmy for Best Comedy Actor for the series. Unfortunately, the revelation that Reynolds was engaged in an extra-marital affair was deemed by the network to be a ratings liability, and the show was pulled.

Those sharing the directing duties included Reynolds himself, plus John Ratzenberger, better known as Cliff Clavin in >*Cheers*. *Evening Shade* came from the Arkansas team of Linda Bloodworth-Thomason and Harry Thomason (>*Designing Women*).

FAIRLY SECRET ARMY

UK 1984–6, 12 x 30m, col C4. Video Arts.

CR *David Nobbs.* **PR** *Peter Robinson.* **DR** *Robert Young, Roy Ward Baker.* **WR** *David Nobbs.* **CAST** Major Harry Kitchener Wellington Truscott *Geoffrey Palmer* Nancy *Diana Fletcher* Sgt-Major Throttle *Michael Robbins* Doris Entwhistle *Liz Fraser* Stubby Collins *Ray Winstone* Beamish *Jeremy Child.*

Sitcom veteran Geoffrey Palmer (>*Butterflies, Last Song, As Time Goes By*) played retired army major Harry Kitchener Wellington Truscott, a right-wing fanatic who believed the country to be overrun by 'right-on feminists, do gooders and left-wing anarchist sympathisers.' Accordingly, he founded a private army – alas for him, composed of half-brained fascists and no-brained toffs – to whip the British nation back into shape. Actors Michael Robbins (>*On the Buses*), Liz Frazer and Ray Winstone were among those cast with inspiration.

The character of Truscott was fairly heavily derived from the military-minded Jimmy played by Palmer in David Nobbs' earlier >*The Fall and Rise of Reginald Perrin.*

THE FALL AND RISE OF REGINALD PERRIN

UK 1976–9, 21 x 30m, col BBC1. BBC TV. US tx *Syndicated 1978.*

CR *David Nobbs.* **PR** *John Howard Davies, Gareth Gwenlan.* **DR** *Gareth Gwenlan.* **WR** *David Nobbs.* **MUS** *Ronnie Hazlehurst.* **CAST** Reginald Iolanthe

Perrin *Leonard Rossiter* Elizabeth Perrin *Pauline Yates* CJ *John Barron* Joan Greengross *Sue Nicholls* Doc Morrisey *John Horsley* Tony Webster *Trevor Adams* David Harris-Jones *Bruce Bould* Prue Harris-Jones *Theresa Watson* Jimmy *Geoffrey Palmer* Linda *Sally-Jane Spencer* Tom *Tim Preece/Leslie Schofield* McBlane *Joseph Brady.*

Inspired serial satire on middle everything (age, class, England), adapted by David Nobbs from his novel, *The Death of Reginald Perrin.*

After twenty years as an executive for Sunshine Desserts, Reginald Iolanthe Perrin (Leonard Rossiter, >*Rising Damp*) walks out on his monotonous life and fakes a seaside suicide. After a spell as a pig farmer, he then assumes the persona of Martin Welbourne, remarries wife Elizabeth and starts a company called Grot. This sells everything totally useless (son-in-law Tom's abysmal wines, square footballs) at inflated prices. As a sly critique of consumerism Grot fails abysmally, becoming instead a capitalist success, and Reggie enters the ranks of tycoonery. When Sunshine Desserts collapses, Reggie employs all his old colleagues (boss CJ, secretary Joan, sycophantic juniors Tony 'Super' Webster and David 'Great' Harris-Jones), which seems a pleasant revenge until these incompetents all develop the Midas touch. Worse, Reggie realises that he has simply recreated his former life. At the end of season two, Reggie et al stage a counterfeit suicide, returning for a season in which Reggie founds a community for stressed executives. This also has room for an impenetrable Scottish cook, McBlane, and Reggie's militaristic brother-in-law Jimmy (played by Geoffrey Palmer, who virtually reprised the character in >*Fairly Secret Army*), the latter always on the scrounge for food with the apology, 'Bit of a cock-up on the catering front'. (The show also donated another catchphrase to the English lexicon: CJ's 'I didn't get where I am today...').

Peculiarly cynical and cerebral for a late seventies British sitcom, *Fall and Rise* avoided dry-as-dustness through the vital performance of Rossiter, who took a sitcom creation and made something tragi-comically great out of it: the patron saint of the suburban commuter on the 7.50 from Purley Oaks. (Rossiter's turn as Perrin also managed to camouflage the show's tendency to repeat a distinctly small store of jokes.) It travelled well, going into syndication in the USA in 1978, and eventually gave birth to a US version, *Reggie* (starring Richard Mulligan from >*Soap,* Barbara Barrie, Dianne Kay, Timothy Stack, Chip Zien, Jean Smart and a pre-*Thirtysomething* Timothy Busfield), and was broadcast by ABC in 1983.

Against all sanity, the BBC made a sequel to *Fall and Rise* in 1996, with the scenario that Reggie had been killed by an insurance hoarding (Rossiter himself had died in 1984), leaving his cronies to perform absurd tasks in the hope of receiving large amounts of lucre from his will. Devoid of Reggie and the show's original context, the characters and jokes were just dead ciphers walking around bemused.

I didn't get where I am today...

FAMILY AFFAIR

USA 1966–71, 138 x 30m, col CBS. Don Fedderson Productions. UK tx *1969 ITV.*

CR *Edmund Hartmann and Don Fedderson.* **PR** *Don Fedderson.* **DR** *Various, including James Sheldon, William D Russell, Charles Barton.* **CAST** Bill Davis *Brian Keith* Mr Giles French *Sebastian Cabot* Jody *Johnnie Whitaker* Buffy *Anissa Jones* Cissy *Kathy Garver* Niles French (French's brother) *John Williams* Emily Turner *Nancy Walker.*

American character actor Brian Keith (born Robert Keith Jr) took his first plunge into sitcomland with this archetypal 'heart show', in which he played Bill Davis, a playboy Manhattan millionaire who became the foster father to his orphaned nephew and twin nieces. Such a kindness, however, was much to the initial dismay of his disdainful and obsessively tidy butler, French. But, of course, all eventually lived in tolerant harmony.

An obvious rehash of CBS's own >*Bachelor Father,* the hit show went through 138 episodes in the USA, only a smattering of which were shown in the UK. Keith himself carried over his screen-warming, gruff-but-kind persona – via Sam Peckinpah's oater series *The Westerner* – to sitcom *The Little People* (1972–4, NBC), in which he played Hawaii paediatrician Sean Jamieson, the show eventually being retitled *The Brian Keith Show.* The actor later cropped up in the abysmal thriller series, *The Zoo Gang.*

Guest stars included Myrna Loy, Jackie Coogan, Ida Lupino and Dana Andrews.

FAMILY TIES

USA 1982–9, 181 x 30m, 1 x 60m, col NBC. UBU Productions/Paramount TV. UK tx *1985–9 C4.*

CR *Gary David Goldberg.* **EXEC PR** *Gary David Goldberg.* **DR** *Various, including Debbie Allen, John Pasquin, Lee Shallat, Alan Bergman, Tony Mordente, Sam Weisman.* **WR** *Various, including Gary David Goldberg, Ruth Bennett, Alan Uger.* **MUS** *Jeff Barry and Tom Scott (theme), J A C Redford.* **CAST** Elyse Keaton *Meredith Baxter-Birney* Steve Keaton *Michael Gross* Alex P Keaton *Michael J Fox* Mallory Keaton *Justine Bateman* Jennifer Keaton *Tina Yothers* Andrew Keaton *Brian Bonsall.*

The show responsible for launching the career of the diminutive Michael J Fox. Fox played Alex P Keaton, the arch-conservative teenage son of former flower children Elyse and Steve Keaton, who were continuing to espouse liberal values in the cold climate of the eighties. The pilot episode, in which Alex attended a restricted country club with his socialite girlfriend, set the tone. The other Keaton progeny – none of them the hippie type – were fashion-plate Mallory and cutsie Jennifer, later joined by baby Andrew.

While the show's main vein of humour was the generation gap, it also parodied Reaganite values: Fox's besuited, monetarism-espousing Alex was intended as a ridiculous figure but, like Gordon Gecko in *Wall Street,* ironically became a hero. Tom Hanks appeared in some early episodes as Elyse's embezzling brother, Ned. Johnny Mathis and Deniece Williams crooned the 'Without Us' theme. In the final episode, a one-hour special, 'Alex Does

Live Here Anymore', Alex appropriately enough joined a Wall Street firm.

Reputedly President Ronald Reagan's favourite TV show.

THE FAST SHOW

UK 1995–7, 32 x 30m, col BBC2. BBC TV.

CR *Paul Whitehouse, Charles Higson.* **PR** *Paul Whitehouse, Charles Higson.* **DR** *Mark Mylod, Sid Robertson.* **WR** *Various, including Paul Whitehouse, Charles Higson, Simon Day, Caroline Aherne.*

Furiously inventive and pacy comedy skit show (averaging a machine-gun-like twenty-five sketches per thirty-minute episode), helpfully apolitical, and fuelled by cleverly repetitive, playground-friendly catchphrases and *Viz*-like creations. The Fat Sweaty Cops, Arthur 'Where's Me Washboard?' Atkins, tongue-tied toff Ralph and Irish gardener Ted, coughing Bob Fleming, the Alcoholics and jinxed geriatric Unlucky Alf were among the most famous characters. (These may have all been gross caricatures, but they were caricatures with depth; there was something almost moving in repressed Ralph's unexpressed but powerful emotions for the monosyllabic Ted.)

Creators Paul Whitehouse (ex-plasterer) and Charlie Higson (ex-rock band, the Higsons) had previously scripted for Harry Enfield – even inventing his famous >*Saturday Live* creations Stavros and Loadsamoney – as well as appearing in his >*Harry Enfield's Television Show* and its various incarnations. Whitehouse and Higson had first met as students at the University of East Anglia. As well as penning seventy per cent of *The Fast Show* material, Whitehouse and Higson led the performers, who included Caroline Aherne from >*The Mrs Merton Show. The Fast Show* re-established the art of comic-sketch timing, in contrast to the self-indulgency shown by such contemporaries gone to flab as >*French and Saunders.*

Brilliant!... and now for some (more) catchphrases: Scorchio/Does my bum look big in this?/We're off-roaders/Ooh! Suits you, sir/I'm a geezer. I'll nick anything/Get yer knickers on and make a cup of tea/Relieved *and* gutted, I think/ Roy... you sack of shit/Meal for one... live alone, do you? [check-out girl]/... which was nice.

◀◀◀ *Brilliant! Paul Whitehouse and Charlie Higson's* The Fast Show.

FATHER DEAR FATHER

UK 1968–73, 36 x 30m, col ITV. Thames TV. US tx *1977 Syndicated.*

CR *Johnnie Mortimer and Brian Cooke.* **PR** *William G Stewart.* **DR** *Various, including William G Stewart.* **WR** *Johnnie Mortimer and Brian Cooke.* **CAST** Patrick Glover *Patrick Cargill* Anna Glover *Natasha Pyne* Karen Glover *Ann Holloway* Matilda 'Nanny' Harris *Noel Dyson* Barbara Glover/Mossman *Ursula Howells* Mrs Glover (mother) *Joyce Carey* Georgie (literary agent) *Sally Beazley/Dawn Addams* Bill Mossman *Patrick Holt/Tony Britton* Tim Tanner *Jeremy Child* Howard *Richard O'Sullivan.*

Sitcom starring Patrick Cargill as Patrick Glover, a suave divorced writer of pulp thrillers, whose romantic assignations and attempts to work were farcically interrupted by his mother, his agent, his ex-wife Barbara, her lover (Bill, his ex-best friend), his housekeeper and his two teenage daughters. The latter blonde sixties twosome, who wore skirts up to *there,* were a particular bane to the crusty, cravat-wearing author-father. A St Bernard named H G Wells acted as Glover's sole male confidant. In the later seasons, daughter Anna married Tim Tanner, and daughter Karen found a boyfriend in the eager-puppy shape of Howard (Richard O'Sullivan). The show was produced by William G

▲▲▲ *Daughters Ann and Karen (who wore skirts up to* there*) with novelist pater Patrick in* Father, Dear Father.

Stewart, later to turn up before the camera as the presenter of *Fifteen-to-One*.

This mildly likeable comedy was the dream TV machine for the suave Cargill, a former Army officer, whose previous screen roles had included Number 2 in *The Prisoner* and the doctor in the classic blood donor sketch in >*Hancock's Half-Hour*. The show was sufficiently popular to spin off a 1971 film of the same name, and then an Australian TV version in 1977, with Glover leaving urbane Kensington for Down Under, to care for a couple of inherited nieces. Of the original cast only Noel Dyson, as the fussing housekeeper ('Nanny'), joined him. Almost simultaneously with this, Cargill starred in the LWT sitcom *The Many Wives of Patrick,* in which he played a character highly similar to Glover, one Patrick Woodford, a much-divorced antiques dealer.

FATHER KNOWS BEST

USA 1954–62, 191 x 25m, bw CBS/NBC. Rodney-Young Productions. UK tx *1956– ITV.*

PR *Eugene B Rodney, Robert Young.* **DR** *Various, including William D Russell, Peter Tewksbury.* **MUS** *Irving Friedman, Joseph Weiss.* **CAST** Jim Anderson *Robert Young* Margaret Young *Jane Wyatt* Betty Anderson *Elinor Donahue* Bud Anderson *Billy Gray* Kathy 'Kitten' Anderson *Lauren Chapin* Miss Thomas *Sarah Selby.*

Lightly comic events in the idyllic life of the American family Anderson. The epitome of the 'Hi, Honey, I'm home' family sitcoms of the affluent Eisenhower fifties, *Father Knows Best* transferred to TV after a successful radio run. Somewhat unusually, the show played on all three main US networks, including the reruns on ABC. The show was set in the Midwest town of Springfield, where Jim Anderson worked for the General Insurance Company, returning home each day to deal with mini-crises which had arisen during his absence.

Star Robert Young, a Hollywood front man from the thirties and forties, later led the medical soap, *Marcus Welby MD.*

FATHER TED

UK 1995–8, 19 x 30m, 1 x 40m, col C4. Hat Trick.

CR *Graham Linehan and Arthur Matthews.* **PR** *Lissa Evans, Geoffrey Perkins.* **DR** *Declan Lowney.* **MUS** *Neil Hanlon.* **WR** *Graham Linehan and Arthur Matthews.* **CAST** Father Ted Crilly *Dermot Morgan* Father Dougal McGuire *Ardal O'Hanlon* Father Jack Hackett *Frank Kelly* Mrs Doyle *Pauline McLynn.*

Superior clerical caper following the misadventures of an unholy trinity of priests – relatively sensible Ted, permanently inebriated Jack ('Drinks! Gurrls! Feck!'), transcendentally dim Dougal – living on God-forsaken Craggy Island, somewhere off the west coast of Eire. Dithering old Mrs Doyle was the housekeeper. Blessed, as it were, with outstanding performances, it also had a heavenly absurdity: Mrs Doyle's bad back was cured after tripping over a hamster's bicycle and falling down the stairs (the hamster later rode off...), while minor character Father Duff repeatedly died and reappeared. There was no internal logic whatsoever. Innocently, almost childishly daft, the show was deluged with awards, although it took a repeat of the first season for some to see the joke.

Star Dermot Morgan was the most influential Irish humourist since Dave Allen (>*Dave Allen at Large*), who, before moving to Britain, had created

>> ***Father Ted: 'What was it that he [Father Jack] used to say about the needy? He had a term for them.'***
>
> ***Father Dougal: 'A shower of bastards.'*** <<

an infamous and iconoclastic radio show (favourite targets: politics and the Church), *Scrap Saturday*. Ironically enough, the show – which was street-emptyingly popular in Ireland – was itself scrapped by RTE, reputedly because of political and clerical pressure. Shortly after the filming of the third series of *Father Ted*, Morgan died of a heart attack. He was forty-five.

▼▼ Father Ted *was blessed with unimprovable surreal humour.*

FAWLTY TOWERS

UK 1975–9, 12 x 30m, col BBC2. BBC TV. US tx *1976–9 PBS.*

CR *John Cleese and Connie Booth.* **PR** *John Howard Davies, Douglas Argent.* **DR** *Bob Spiers.* **WR** *John Cleese and Connie Booth.* **MUS** *Dennis Wilson.*
CAST Basil Fawlty *John Cleese* Sybil Fawlty *Prunella Scales* Polly *Connie Booth* Manuel *Andrew Sachs* Major Gowen *Ballard Berkely* Miss Tibbs *Gilly Flower* Miss Gatsby *Renee Roberts.* Video *BBC.*

Que?

The origins of *Fawlty Towers* are well known: in 1972 the >*Monty Python* team stayed in a hotel in Torquay on a location shoot, which gave them a somewhat jaundiced view of Britain's hotel industry, particularly after the proprietor threw Eric Idle's briefcase into the street for fear that it contained a bomb. The following year John Cleese wrote six scripts for >*Doctor in the House* sequel *Doctor at Large,* setting one of them in just such a seedy hotel, and two years later he wrote the first six-episode series of *Fawlty Towers* together with his then wife Connie Booth.

The series starred Cleese as manic, blustering hotelier Basil Fawlty, Prunella Scales as his long-suffering, over-coiffeured wife Sybil ('sour old bag'), and Connie Booth as pert maid Polly, apparently the only sane person in the hotel. Spanish waiter Manuel (Andrew Sachs) meanwhile darted about incompetently, much bullied by his employer and scorned for his inadequate grasp of English. Manuel's usual response to an order was an uncomprehending 'Que?', whereupon Fawlty would offer by way of apology to his guests, 'You'll have to excuse him – he comes from Barcelona.' (When Spanish TV later bought the series, they avoided offending Barcelona viewers by transforming the waiter into an Italian in the dubbing process.) In the name of comedy, Manuel was infamously used as a battering ram to open a fire exit and dragged around by his ear.

Polly, Basil, Manuel and Sybil from Fawlty Towers *in a rare moment of camaraderie.*

Plots were based on misunderstanding and Basil's tireless efforts to impress those guests he believed were important whilst mercilessly insulting those he considered inferior. When Polly and the kitchen staff went out for the evening, a solo Basil attempted to pretend to his American guests that the hotel was actually fully staffed. A visit by German tourists ('Don't mention the war!') ended with Basil goose-stepping around the dining room making a finger moustache above his upper lip. Imagined romantic intrigues behind the hotel's bedroom doors led Basil into paroxysms of indignation and ill-fated attempts to spy through keyholes and from wardrobes. And when a woman complained that her half-eaten prawn cocktail was inedible, the hotelier responded with 'Well, only half of it is inedible, apparently' and agreed to refund the full price only if she brought up the eaten half during the night. Through all this Basil and Sybil maintained a relationship based entirely on mutual irritation.

Much of the humour of *Fawlty Towers* came from the performances, with John Cleese in particular the master of comic movement. According to series director Bob Spiers, Cleese wrote every detail of his performance into the scripts, with no move or gesture the result of improvisation. Each episode took Cleese and Booth six weeks to write (the industry norm is ten days), and ran to 120 pages of script for one half-hour (the norm being 65).

Prunella Scales' previous comedy credits include *Marriage Lines* with Richard Briers and *Seven of One* with Ronnie Barker. Ex-Python Cleese has since gone on to international acclaim for such feature films as *Clockwise* and *A Fish Called Wanda*.

A US-made show, *Amandas,* starring Bea Arthur (>*The Golden Girls*), tried to duplicate the formula, but failed to achieve either the same comic brilliance or critical success, even when it appropriated some episodes word for word.

The episodes were: A Touch of Class/The Builders/The Wedding Party/The Hotel Inspectors/Gourmet Night/The Germans/Communication Problems/The Psychiatrist/Waldorf Salad/The Kipper and the Corpse/The Anniversary/Basil the Rat.

Filthy Rich and Catflap

UK 1987, 6 x 30m, col BBC1. A Paul Jackson Production for BBC TV.

CR *Ben Elton.* **PR** *Paul Jackson.* **WR** *Ben Elton, Rik Mayall.* **CAST** Filthy Ralph *Nigel Planer* Richard Rich *Rik Mayall* Eddie Catflap *Adrian Edmondson.*

A short-lived reuniting of Nigel Planer, Rik Mayall and Adrian Edmondson from >*The Young Ones,* in the sitcom story – mainly scripted by Ben Elton – of Richie Rich's bid for TV stardom. Unfortunately for Rich, his attempts to enter the stellar showbiz ranks are undone by his own incompetence, the brainless violence of his bodyguard, Catflap, and the dodgy dealings of his dipso agent, Filthy Ralph.

Dismissed as 'The Young Ones: The Next Generation', *Filthy Rich and Catflap* certainly continued with that show's formula of excessive violence, scatology and inexplicable surrealist interludes. Yet, viewed through a generous lens, it was possible to see in *Filthy* a lurking critique by Elton of the traditional sitcom (evidenced by the characters' habit of self-referentialist comment on the show, and Eddie's demolishing of the set in the finale, to reveal the studio behind) and the tawdry nature of showbiz fame.

The only problem was that the jokes weren't terribly good. Funny, but not *that* funny.

THE FLINTSTONES

USA 1960–6, 166 x 30m, col ABC. Hanna-Barbera. UK tx *1961–6 ITV.*

CR *Joseph Barbera, William Hanna.* **PR** *William Hanna, Joseph Barbera.* **DR** *Various, including William Hanna, Joseph Barbera, Charles A Nichols, Ray Patterson.* **WR** *Joseph Barbera, William Hanna, Warren Foster, Mike Maltese, R Allen Saffian, Barry Blitzer, Tony Benedict, Herb Finn, Jack Raymond, Sydney Zelinka, Arthur Phillips, Joanna Lee.* **MUS** *Hoyt S Curtin, William Hanna, Joseph Barbera (theme).* **CAST** *(voices)* Fred Flintstone *Alan Read* Wilma Flintstone/Pebbles *Jean Vander Pyl* Barney Rubble/Dino *Mel Blanc* Betty Rubble *Bea Benaderet (1960–4)/Gerry Johnson (1964–6)* Bamm Bamm *Don Messick.* Video *Video Collection.*

The animated life and times of Stone Age suburban family the Flintstones and their best friends and neighbours the Rubbles, who all lived in the prehistoric city of Bedrock, 250 miles below sea level in Cobblestone County. Fred Flintstone, operator of a dinosaur-powered crane at the Rock Head & Quarry Cave Construction Co. (slogan: 'Own Your Own Cave and Be Secure'), and his wife Wilma had a split-level cave complete with such ingenious Stone Age gadgetry as a Stoneway piano, a bird with a long beak which acted as a phonograph, and an automatic garbage disposal unit in the famished shape of a buzzard-like pigasaurus stashed under the sink. The vacuum cleaner was a baby mastodon with a long trunk. To travel around, the Flintstones hopped into their Cavemobile, propelled by the occupants' feet. At first Fred and Wilma had only Dino, their pet dinosaur, around the cave to play with. Then in February 1963 they were blessed with a baby daughter, born in Bedrock's Rockapedic Hospital (after panicking Fred had initially admitted Dino, instead of Wilma), who they called Pebbles. Not to be outdone, Barney and Betty Rubble adopted a baby boy they found on their doorstep, little Bamm Bamm, an infant possessed of alarming strength. (The kid twosome later had a spin-off show of their own, *Pebbles and Bamm Bamm*; there was also another kiddie knock-on, *The Flintstones Kids.*)

Originally to be called 'The Flagstones' until the name ran into copyright problems, The Flintstones was dreamed up in response to a request from Columbia for a prime-time animated sitcom with 'kidult' appeal. Cartoon masters Joseph Barbera and William Hanna began by taking Jackie Gleason's >*The Honeymooners* as their model, then artist and storyboard man Dan Gordon suggested characters out of the Stone Age dressed in leopard skins, and the concept fell into place.

Like Gleason's Ralph Kramden in *The Honeymooners,* Fred Flintstone was a well-meaning know-all who fancied himself capable of carrying out get-rich-quick schemes and, like Kramden, had a long-suffering wife and neighbours who became embroiled in his antics. Barney, genial but none too bright, in the style of Kramden's neighbour Ed Norton, acted as foil to Fred. *The Flintstones* also drew on the old stockpile of sitcom jokes – Fred had an ogre of a boss, forgot his wedding anniversary, was always trying to sneak away to go bowling, and

Yabba Dabba Doo!

Flintstones, meet the Flintstones
They're a modern Stone Age family
From the town of Bedrock
They're a page right out of history...

had problems with his mother-in-law. More comedy came from the showbiz in-jokes and puns: attorney Perry Masonry, who never lost a case, turned up, as did actor Stony Curtis (voiced by Tony Curtis), while Weirdly and Creepella Gruesome burlesqued the then popular >*The Addams Family* and >*The Munsters*. Most of the show's satirical thrust, however, was aimed at consumerism and the insatiable desire of affluent America for ever more home gadgets.

The Flintstones was not easy to sell. CBS and NBC both turned it down (a prime-time cartoon was too much of an unknown entity), but after weeks of negotiation ABC said yes, Reynolds Tobacco Company bought half the show for their Winston Cigarettes, and Miles Laboratories bought the other half for their One-a-Day vitamins. It premiered on 30 September 1960 and instantly assumed historic status as the first animated TV sitcom, the first animated TV series longer than the standard six or seven minutes, and the first animated series to feature human characters. Reviews were largely hostile (Jack Gould of the *New York Times* dubbed the programme an 'inked disaster'), but the show was given an Emmy nomination, won a Golden Globe, was voted the most original new series by *TV Radio Mirror* and pulled in viewers by the million.

Well, whaddya know, Barn... Along with numerous other classic shows of the sixties, *The Flintstones* was revived in the nineties as a (live action) feature film. The part of Fred went to sitcom star John Goodman from >*Roseanne*.

Frank Stubbs Promotes

UK 1993–4, 13 x 30m, col ITV. Noel Gay Television/ Carlton.

CR *Simon Nye.* **EXEC PR** *Charles Armitage, Robin Banks Stewart.* **PR** *Hilary Bevan Jones.* **DR** *Various, including Tom Cotter, Nick Hurran, Richard Standeven, John Glennister.* **WR** *Simon Nye.* **MUS** *Brian May.* **CAST** Frank Stubbs *Timothy Spall* Archie Nash *Trevor Cooper* Dave Giddings *Nick Reding* Diane Stubbs *Hazel Ellerby* Petra Dillon *Lesley Sharp* Dawn Dillon *Daniella Westbrook.*

The misadventures of a chronically optimistic – but doomed to fail – latterday spiv, who throws over his ticket tout business to promote an array of comically dubious products, from kit cars to the memoirs of an ex-con. The show was adapted by Simon Nye (the creator of >*Men Behaving Badly*) from his novel *Wideboy*, though in the process of becoming videotape it filched conspicuously from the >*Only Fools and Horses* school of light criminal comedy. It starred hamster-faced Timothy Spall from >*Auf Wiedersehen, Pet*, who later progressed to the cricket comedy *Outside Edge*. The 1994 season was transmitted under the shorter title of plain *Frank Stubbs*. Former Queen guitarist Brian May contributed the music.

FRASIER

USA 1993–, 100 x 30m, col NBC. Grub Street/Paramount Pictures. UK tx *1994– C4.*

CR *David Angell, Peter Casey, David Lee.* **EXEC PR** *David Angell, Peter Casey, David Lee, Christopher Lloyd, Linda Morris, Vic Raeuseo.* **DR** *Various, including James Burrows, Kelsey Grammer, Pamela Fryman, William Lucas Walker, David Lee, Jeffrey Melman, Andy Ackerman, Philip Charles MacKenzie.* **WR** *Various, including David Angell, Peter Casey, David Lee, Sy Dukane and Denise Moss, Chuck Ranberg and Anne Flett-Giordano, Don Siegel and Jerry Perzigan, Leslie Eberhard, Christopher Lloyd, Ken Levine and David Isaacs, Linda Morris and Vic Rauseo.* **MUS** *Bruce Miller.* **CAST** Dr Frasier Crane *Kelsey Grammer* Dr Niles Crane *David Hyde Pierce* Martine Crane *John Mahoney* Daphne Moon *Jane Leeves* Roz *Peri Gilpin* Kate Costas *Mercedes Ruehl* Gil Chesterton *Edward Hibbert* Bulldog *Dan Butler.*

Hi, you're on the air with Dr Frasier Crane. If you can feel, I can heal.

A spin-off from >*Cheers* that relocated the elegantly pompous Dr Frasier Crane (Kelsey Grammer) to his home town of Seattle where he moved into a luxury apartment and began a psychiatrist phone-in show on radio KACL–780 AM. Alas, Crane's hoped-for easy and urbane life was ended when anally retentive younger brother (and fellow shrink), Niles, off-loaded their crotchety ex-cop dad Martin on him, complete with dog Eddie. Soon afterwards, daffy Brit Daphne (played by former >*Benny Hill Show* dancer Jane Leeves) moved in as Martin's home help and physiotherapist, to become the object of unrequited lust for the fragile Niles, the latter having a less than successful marriage to the unseen Maris ('I-do-love Maris. Why, the other week I kissed her for absolutely no reason at all!'). Meanwhile, Frasier's self-esteem, never too hot at the best of times, was steadily shaken at work and at play, particularly in his tendency to pursue pathetically doomed affairs.

A steady troupe of *Cheers* stars (Shelley Long, Ted Danson, Bebe Neuwirth) made guest appearances, underlining the show's genealogical connection to the Boston barcom. Yet *Frasier* was more than TV therapy for *Cheers* fans suffering withdrawal. It had sublime scripts, sublimer (ensemble) acting, and a range of comedy techniques that went from verbal wit ('The man is a fascist. He's like Himmler without the whimsy') to quasi-slapstick (Niles' famed dancing manoeuvre to grab a book which revealed Frasier's love life) in a glorious split second. Not to mention matchless dialogue. Niles: 'Well, as some illustrious person said, "Popularity is the hallmark of mediocrity."' Frasier: 'You made that up, didn't you?' Niles: 'Yes, but I stand by it.'

Awards duly followed, including three consecutive Emmys in 1993, 1994 and 1995, for Best Comedy. There were also individual acting Emmys for Grammer and Hyde Pierce. Perhaps the

only caution is that the show lacked the moral depth of the sitcom as true art (eg >*All in the Family*, >*M*A*S*H*, >*The Phil Silvers Show*, *Cheers*); on occasion *Frasier* was only about its own cleverness. A dance on the surface of life.

As no shortage of sage pundits noted, there was an irony in Grammer – who learned the art of comedy by watching Jack Benny – playing a psychiatrist, since he was unable to straighten out his own conspicuously troubled life. His father and sister were murdered (in separate incidents), he was a cocaine addict, a battered husband, a two-time divorcee and served a prison sentence for alcohol-related offences. His public willingness, however, to discuss the intimate corners of his psyche (and those parts of himself that he lent to the character of Frasier) only increased his celebrity in America, making him one of the most stellar stars in the TV firmament. In acknowledgement, Paramount paid Grammer $250,000 per episode.

Classic episodes include: 'My Coffee with Niles'; 'Adventures in Paradise, Parts I and II' (in which Frasier finds himself on holiday alongside ex-wife Lilith); 'Moondance'; 'The Show Where Lilith Comes Back'; 'Frasier Crane's Day Off'; 'Seat of Power'; 'The Show Where Sam Shows Up' (Malone from *Cheers* flies in to talk over his forthcoming marriage, and Frasier finds that he has slept with Sam's bride-to-be; even worse, it turns out she has slept with… Cliff.); and 'The Matchmaker'.

◀◀◀ *Kelsey Grammer (with dog) and the cast of* Frasier, *a hit spin-off from* Cheers. *The show garnered Grammer a cool $250,000 per episode and made him one of the brightest – and richest – stars in US TV heaven.*

FRENCH AND SAUNDERS

UK 1987–96, 33 x 30m, 2 x 40m, col BBC2. BBC TV.

CR *Dawn French and Jennifer Saunders.* **PR** *Jon Plowman.* **DR** *John Birkin, Bob Spiers.* **WR** *Dawn French and Jennifer Saunders.* **CAST** *Dawn French, Jennifer Saunders; plus Simon Brint, Rowland Rivron, Kevin Allen, Patrick Barlow, Sue Perkins, Mel Giedroyc.*

Award-winning sketch show from Dawn French and Jennifer Saunders, originally the female duo of >*The Comic Strip Presents*. Comic actresses rather than comediennes, French and Saunders, along with Victoria Wood, ground-broke women's TV comedy in Britain. Here the formula for the funnies was an invented gallery of recurring characters (the country women who thought any mishap or amputation 'stuff and nonsense', the two sexist slobs who chorused 'I'd give her one'), unnervingly exact observations on contemporary lifestyle (including a 'Modern Mother' skit that eventually spun off >*Absolutely Fabulous*) and spoofs of TV and the movies. As the seasons progressed, the show relied increasingly on these TV/film pastiches of, inter alia, *Batman, La Dolce Vita, Thelma and Louise, Baywatch;* yet, basically, the elaborate spoofs only contained two jokes: the visual immaculateness of the parody, and the moment when French and Saunders stepped out of character to bicker in their time-honoured fashion (French being the bossy one, Saunders the naïf). There was mileage in the screen send-ups, but not quite as much as given.

Musical backing (and comic intervention) came

from Rowland Rivron and Simon Brint as Raw Sex, while songster Kirsty MacColl was a regular guest in the third series. Others to appear over the seasons included Patsy Kensit, Helen Mirren and Lenny Henry (French's husband).

French and Saunders first met at the Central London School of Drama, where they trained to be teachers. As a 'joke' they performed at Peter Richardson's club The Comic Strip (the crucible of British alternative comedy) in Soho, and Richardson encouraged them to polish and perfect their act. After transferring to TV via guest spots in >*The Young Ones* and then as stars of *The Comic Strip Presents*, they featured in the 'flatcom' >*Girls on Top* (1985–6, with Tracey Ullman and Ruby Wax), before treading the studio floor in *French and Saunders*. They have also pursued lustrous solo careers: Saunders most visibly with *Absolutely Fabulous* and French with *Murder Most Horrid* and >*The Vicar of Dibley*.

THE FRESH PRINCE OF BEL AIR

USA 1990–6, Approx 125 x 30m, col NBC. A Stuffed Dog Company and Quincy Jones Entertainment Productions in Association with NBC Productions. UK tx *1991– BBC2.*

CR *Benny Medina, Jeff Pollack, Susan Borowitz, Andy Borowitz.* **EXEC PR** *Various, including Susan Borowitz, Andy Borowitz, Quincy Jones, Kevin Wendle, Winifred Hervey Stallworth, Gary H Miller.* **PR** *Various, including Werner Walian, Samm-Art Williams, Cheryl Gard, Benny Medina, Jeff Pollack, Lisa Rosenthal, Leslie Ray, David Steven Simon.* **DR** *Various, including Debbie Allen, Jeff Melman, Rita Rogers Blye, Ellen Falcon, Shelley Jensen.* **WR** *Various, including Susan Borowitz, Andy Borowitz, Samm-Art Williams, Shannon Gaughan, Cheryl Gard, Rob Edwards, Lisa Rosenthal, John Bowman, Sandy Frank, Leslie Ray, David Steven Simon, David Zuckerman, Maiya Williams.* **MUS** *Quincy Jones.* **CAST** Will Smith *himself* Philip Banks *James Avery* Vivian Banks *Janet Hubert-Whitten/Daphne Reid* Carlton Banks *Alfonso Ribeiro* Hilary Banks *Karyn Parsons* Ashley Banks *Tatyana M Ali* Geoffrey (the Butler) *Joseph Marcell* Jazz *Jeff Townes ('DJ Jazzy Jeff')* Nicky Banks *Ross Bagley.*

>> ***Now this is the story all about how my life got flipped, turned upside down and I'd like to take a minute just sit right there and I'll tell you how I became the prince of a town called Bel Air...*** <<

Funky comedy co-produced by multiple Grammy-winning music business legend Quincy Jones and starring real-life rapper Will Smith. Smith plays Will, a fun-loving black homeboy from a Philadelphia ghetto who is sent west by his mother to live with rich relatives in their mansion at 805 St Claud Road, Bel Air. There Will is in the care of Uncle Philip and Aunt Vivian Banks, plus their insane snooty butler, Geoffrey (British RSC and former *EastEnders* actor

▶▶▶ *Former* Comic Strip *players Dawn French (left) and Jennifer Saunders in the double-act skit show* French and Saunders.

Joseph Marcell). Though Will challenges Philip for forsaking his humble roots, pompous attorney Philip can tell Will a thing or two about black experience when necessary. The Banks' preppy son Carlton – who makes the perfect foil for streetwise Will – and narcissistic daughter are rivals from the start with the newcomer, though youngest daughter Ashley is his friend and confidante. Outside the home, Will attends the exclusive Bel Air Academy, and later the University of Los Angeles, both of which staid institutions he alarms.

A teen comedy of clashing cultures, *The Fresh Prince of Bel Air* regularly slipped in pertinent comments on the situation of blacks in white society. Will Smith, who played the lead role with a comic timing and infectious enthusiasm that was the show's key to success, previously performed as half of the duo Jazzy Jeff and the Fresh Prince with *Bel Air* co-star Jeff Townes (who played Will's friend). The duo won a Grammy award for their 1988 hit 'Parents Just Don't Understand'.

The show was based on an idea by record executive Benny Medina who, as a boy, had been fostered by Beverly Hills musician Jack Elliott, composer of music for such TV series as >*Barney Miller, Charlie's Angels* and *Fish*.

FRIENDS

USA 1994–, 1 x 60m, 78 x 30m, col NBC. Warner Bros. UK tx *1995– C4.*

◀◀◀ *Shiny, happy New Yorkers – the male/female balance that makes up the cast of* Friends.

CR *David Crane and Marta Kauffman.* **EXEC PR** *Kevin S Bright, David Crane, Marta Kauffman.* **DR** *Various, including James Burrows, Kevin S Bright, Michael Lembeck, Peter Bonerz, Thomas Schlamme, Pamela Fryman, Gail Mancuso, Steve Zuckerman.* **WR** *Various, including David Crane, Marta Kauffman, Alexa Junge, Jeffrey Astrof and Mike Sikowitz.* **MUS** *The Rembrandts (theme song).* **CAST** Chandler Bing *Matthew Perry* Ross Geller *David Schwimmer* Rachel Green *Jennifer Aniston* Monica Geller *Courteney Cox* Phoebe Buffay *Lisa Kudrow* Joey Tribbiani *Matt LeBlanc.*

Hit US sitcom, from the creators of >*Dream On*, featuring six shiny happy New Yorkers, who drank large amounts of caffe latte at 'Central Perk', pontificated on relationships, and became entangled in humorous 'everyday' twentysomething situations. Monica Geller was a chef who shared her Greenwich Village apartment with pampered high school buddy Rachel Green (Jennifer 'Big Hair' Aniston, daughter of soap star John, and god-daughter of Telly 'Kojak' Savalas). Across the hall lived computer programmer Chandler Bing and struggling actor Joey Tribbiani. Phoebe Buffay was a New Age guitar-playing masseuse, and Monica's ex-roomy. Ross Geller was Monica's nerdish brother, whose wife had left him for another woman.

Incurably schmaltzy – the episode entitled 'The One With the Ick Factor' could be said to be something of a hostage to fortune – the show nevertheless boasted sharp writing, and sharp one liners, most of these issuing from the dry-witted Chandler. (For example, Chandler on the virtues of breastfeeding: 'The packaging is attractive to adults.') Moreover, as star David Schwimmer observed: '*Friends* works because it's a fantasy family at a time when the family is so dysfunctional for this generation.' Elliot Gould appeared occasionally as Monica and Ross's father, Jack, while Tom 'Magnum' Selleck was Monica's sometime fortysomething boyfriend, Richard Burke. Charlie Sheen, Jean-Claude Van Damme, Isabella Rossellini were among the other celebs giving cameos.

The show was a huge hit, although with an almost entirely white audience (it was 118th on the viewing list of black Americans). One episode was watched by half the households in America, the nation's highest ever audience rating.

THE FROST REPORT

UK 1966–7, 30 x 30m, bw BBC1. BBC TV.

PR *Duncan Wood, James Gilbert.* **WR** *Various, including David Frost, Michael Palin, Terry Jones, Eric Idle, John Cleese.* **CAST** *David Frost, John Cleese, Ronnie Barker, Ronnie Corbett, Nicky Henson, Tom Lehrer, Julie Felix, Nicholas Smith, Sheila Steafel.*

Always beginning with a 'Hello, good evening and welcome…' by frontman David Frost (previously >*That Was the Week That Was*), each week this show debunked a topical institution or subject in a series of skits. Among these was the immortal class sketch, in which upper-class John Cleese looked down on middle-class Ronnie Barker, who in turn looked down on working-class Ronnie Corbett, who in turn looked down on… Not the least of *The Frost Report*'s claims to entry in the annals of hip TV history is that it brought together the anarchic writing talents of Cleese, Graham Chapman, Terry Jones, Michael Palin and Eric Idle – the >*Monty Python* team, bar one – for the first time. A selection of the show's best moments, *Frost Over England*, was awarded the Golden Rose at the 1967 Montreux Festival.

F TROOP

USA 1965–7, 65 x 30m, bw/col ABC. Warner Bros-TV. UK tx *1967 ITV.*

CR *Richard Bluel.* **EXEC PR** *Hy Averback, William T Orr.* **PR** *Richard M Bluel, Hy Averback.* **DR** *Various, including David Alexander, Hollingsworth Morse, Charles R Rondeau, Leslie Goodwins, Seymour Robbie.* **WR** *Various, including Arthur Julian, Howard Merrill and Stan Dreben, Richard Baer, Austin Kalish and Irma Kalish.* **MUS** *Richard LaSalle, William Lava.* **CAST** Captain Parmenter *Ken Berry* Sergeant Morgan O'Rourke *Forrest Tucker* Corporal Randolph Agarn *Larry Storch* Wrangler Jane *Melody Patterson* Bugler Hannibal Dobbs *James Hampton* Trooper Vanderbilt *Joe Brooks* Trooper Hoffenmuller *John Mitchum* Chief Wild Eagle *Frank deKova* Roaring Chicken *Edward Everett.*

Bilkoesque shenanigans out in the Old West. When Private Wilton Parmenter accidentally leads a Civil War charge the wrong way (ie towards the enemy), he becomes a hero and is given command of work-shy F Troop at Fort Courage on the Indian frontier. Here, behind the back of the

Where Indian fights are colourful sights
And nobody likes a lickin'
Where pale-face and redskin
Both turn chicken...

newly promoted Captain Parmenter, crafty Sergeant O'Rourke has a deal with the local Hekawi Indians whereby he sells their wares to tourists. For the sake of appearances, the troopers and braves occasionally rattle sabres and shoot off guns; things only get sticky when the Shugs, with whom there is no treaty, appear to upset the souvenir cart. Wrangler Jane was the colourful, Calamity-ish type out to marry Parmenter. Also prominent in the cast was O'Rourke's comrade in crookery, Corporal Randolph Agarn.

Game On

UK 1995–6, 12 x 30m, col BBC2. Hat Trick.

CR *Andrew Davies and Bernadette Davis.* **EXEC PR** *Denise O'Donaghue.* **PR** *Geoffrey Perkins and Sioned Wiliam.* **DR** *John Stroud.* **WR** *Andrew Davies and Bernadette Davis.* **CAST** Matthew Malone *Ben Chaplin/Neil Stuke* Martin Henson *Matthew Cottle* Mandy Wilkins *Samantha Janus* Clare Monahan *Tracy Keating.*

Three twentysomething friends, products of the nervous nineties, share a Battersea apartment and their problems – which were mostly about sex. The threesome were: agoraphobic Matthew Malone, diffident ginger-haired bank clerk Martin (who was called the 'ginger tosser' by Matthew) and shag-happy Mandy.

Co-created by Andrew Davies (the pen behind *A Very Peculiar Practice,* and serial adapter of classics for TV, such as *Pride and Prejudice*), the show built up a devoted late-night following. Actress Samantha Janus was the dish who also adorned *Demob* and the crime caper *Pie in the Sky.*

George and Mildred

UK 1976–9, 38 x 30m, col ITV. Thames TV. US tx *1984 Syndicated.*

CR *Johnnie Mortimer and Brian Cooke.* **PR** *Peter Frazer-Jones.* **DR** *Peter Frazer-Jones.* **WR** *Johnnie Mortimer and Brian Cooke.* **CAST** George Roper *Brian Murphy* Mildred Roper *Yootha Joyce* Jeffrey Fourmile *Norman Eschley* Ann Fourmile *Sheila Fern* Tristram Fourmile *Nicholas Bond-Owen* Jerry *Roy Kinnear.* Video *V-Col.*

A spin-off from >*Man About the House* in which basement landlords George and Mildred Roper continued their domestic warfare in the new battleground of tweely suburban 26 Peacock Crescent, Hampton Wick. He was lazy and working-class, she was sex-starved (witness those Freudian banana print trousers) and socially aspirant. Their neighbours were middle-class Jeffrey and Ann Fourmile and their bespectacled son Tristram, who was not allowed to play with 'rough boys'. An element of class conflict was expressed through Fourmile's irritation that Roper (Brian Murphy, later *Brookside*) and his motor-cycle sidecar were

lowering the tone of the newly built development, as did the occasional presence of Roper's friend Jerry (Roy Kinnear). Worse, Roper also led Tristram into such ungenteel – but enjoyable – pursuits as gambling. The characters were stereotypical (intentionally so), with George and Mildred merely a TV version of the old hen-pecked music-hall husband and nagging wife. The routines might have been Victorian, but they were immaculately performed. Like the parent show, *George and Mildred* was written by the team of Mortimer and Cooke, who helped in the creation of an American version of *G&M* called *The Ropers* (ABC, 1979–80).

▲▲▲ George and Mildred *was a spin-off from* Man About the House. *Brian Murphy played workshy Roper, Yootha Joyce his sex-starved wife. The show format sold to the USA as* The Ropers.

GEORGE AND THE DRAGON

UK 1966–8, 26 x 30m, bw ITV. Thames TV.

CR *Vince Powell and Harry Driver.* **PR** *Alan Tarrant, Jack Williams.* **DR** *Shaun O'Riordan.* **WR** *Vince Powell and Harry Driver.* **MUS** *Tom Springfield (theme).* **CAST** George Russell *Sid James* Gabrielle Dragon *Peggy Mount* Colonel Maynard *John Le Mesurier.*

Semi-remembered classic from the vaults of black-and-white TV. To the chagrin of retired Colonel Maynard, his country house had a 'bigger [female] staff turnover than Selfridges' thanks to the lascivious attentions of his chauffeur-cum-dogsbody, George. That is, until the frightening, bellow-lunged Gabrielle Dragon was hired as housekeeper – a woman even George could not fancy. Scheming comic warfare between George and the Dragon ensued. Perhaps the classic episode was 'The Not So Tender Trap', when the Dragon, with the connivance of the Colonel and meek gardener Ralph, conned the grotesquely horrified George into believing he had drunkenly agreed to marry her. Written by Vince Powell and Harry Driver (later >*Bless This House*, >*Love Thy Neighbour*) and with an immortal actors' line-up of Sid James, John Le Mesurier and Peggy Mount.

GET SMART

USA 1965–70, 138 x 30m, col NBC/CBS. Talent Artists and Heyday Productions. UK tx *1966–70 BBC1.*

CR *Mel Brooks and Buck Henry.* **EXEC PR** *Arne Sultan, Mel Brooks.* **PR** *Leonard B Stern, Jess Oppenheimer, Jay Sandrich, Burt Nodella, Arnie Rosen, James Komack.* **DR** *Various, including Paul Bogart, Richard Donner.* **WR** *Various, including Mel Brooks, Buck Henry, Leonard B Stern.* **CAST** Maxwell Smart, Agent 86 *Don Adams* Agent 99 *Barbara Feldon* Thaddeus, the Chief *Edward Platt* Agent 13 *Dave Ketchum* Carlson *Stacy Keach* Conrad Siegfried *Bernie Kopell* Starker *King Moody* Hymie, the Robot *Dick Gautier* Agent 44 *Victor French* Larrabee *Robert Karvelas* 99's Mother *Jane Dulo.*

Spoof show from Mel Brooks (later >*When Things Were Rotten,* and such movies as *Blazing Saddles* and *High Anxiety*) and Buck Henry (>*Quark,* >*Captain Nice*), lampooning the rash of spy dramas (*The Avengers, The Man from UNCLE,* the Bond movies) which appeared on the screen in the sixties.

Get Smart featured the cases of Maxwell Smart, the enthusiastic but incompetent Agent 86 for Washington-based international intelligence agency C.O.N.T.R.O.L. Headed by Thaddeus, 'The Chief', with his headquarters in a music hall, C.O.N.T.R.O.L. waged war against the evil agents of K.A.O.S. who, led by mastermind Siegfried and his assistant Starker, planned to take over the world. Max went undercover as a salesman for the Pontiac Greeting Card Company, and his special equipment included a telephone in a shoe and robot, Hymie, who had a marked tendency to interpret orders literally. When told to 'kill the lights', Hymie blasted them with bullets. Also aiding Maxwell in his spook work was a dog named Fang, plus beautiful and brilliant partner Agent 99 (Barbara Feldon, previously a Revlon model and winner of *The $64,000 Question*). In the 1968–9 season love blossomed between the mismatched Agents 86 and 99 – her name was never given – and they married and had twins soon after.

Sorry about that, chief

When NBC cancelled the show in 1969, CBS picked up *Get Smart* for an extra season. One of the most successful parodies in TV history, *Get Smart* won seven Emmys, including three for Don Adams. The show was originally commissioned by ABC, who later jettisoned it because of an un-American scene' in which the Statue of Liberty was blown up.

The show's catchphrases, which still circulate to this day, were: 'Sorry about that, chief'; 'would you believe...'; and 'the old —— trick').

Don Adams as the incompetent spook Maxwell Smart in Get Smart.

GET SOME IN

UK 1975–8, 1 x 60m, 34 x 30m, col ITV. Thames TV.

CR *John Esmonde and Bob Larbey.* **PR** *Michael Mills, Robert Reed.* **DR** *Michael Mills, Robert Reed.* **WR** *John Esmonde and Bob Larbey.* **MUS** *Alan Braden.* **CAST** Ken Richardson *David Janson* Jakey Smith *Robert Lindsay* Matthew Lilley *Gerald Ryder* Bruce Leckie *Brian Pettifer* Corporal Marsh *Tony Selby.*

Military sitcom from Esmonde and Larbey (>*Please Sir*, >*The Good Life*) following the misfortunes of four national service conscripts in the RAF of the austere fifties. The four were: teddy boy Jakey Smith ('that's Smifff, with three fs'), grammar school boy Ken Richardson, uncoordinated Scot Bruce Leckie, and effete vicar's son Matthew Lilley. Sadistic NCO Marsh was their chief tormentor at RAF Skelton training camp, though predictably outwitted by the recruits, particularly 'Poofhouse' Richardson. After basic training the squad was transferred to RAF

My name is Marsh. B.A.S.T.A.R.D. Marsh.

Midham for instruction in nursing (much to the amusement of nemesis Marsh – until he was ordered to accompany them), before postings to Malta and RAF Druidswater.

Tony Selby made the scheming, bullying Marsh into one of British TV's most memorable sitcom creations, and the series also launched the career of Robert Lindsay, soon to become >*Citizen Smith*. (Indeed, the character of Wolfie Smith owes something to *Get Some In*'s Jakey, hence the same surname.) Those who also served in the sitcom included Lori Wells as Marsh's platinum blonde wife Alice, Madge Hindle as Min the Naafi woman, and Jenny Cyst as Bruce's manly girlfriend (later wife), Corporal Wendy Williams.

The Ghost and Mrs Muir

USA 1968–70, 50 x 30m, col NBC/ABC. 20th Century Fox.

EXEC PR *David Gerber.* **PR** *Howard Leeds, Gene Reynolds, Stanley Rubin.* **DR** *Various, including Hollingsworth Morse, Ida Lupino, Gene Reynolds, Lee Phillips, Gary Nelson, Jay Sandrich.* **WR** *Various, including Jean Holloway, Joseph Bonaduce, Arthur Alsberg and Don Nelson.* **MUS** *Dave Grusin.* **CAST** Carolyn Muir *Hope Lange* Captain Greeg (the ghost) *Edward Mulhare* Jonathan Muir *Harlan Carraher* Candy Muir *Kellie Flanagan* Marta (the housekeeper) *Reta Shaw* Claymore Gregg *Charles Nelson Reilly.*

Small-screen remake of the 1947 movie of the same title, starring Gene Tierney and Rex Harrison. When young widow Carolyn Muir moves with her children into a New England seaside cottage, she finds the place possessed by an old crotchety seadog spook, with whom she falls in love. Pleasant enough fantasy-comedy, seldom seen.

Show trivia: Richard Dreyfuss made an early screen appearance in the 1969 segment 'Buried on Page One', playing the editor of the *Schooner Bay Beacon;* the ghost was played by Edward Mulhare, later to reappear in *Knight Rider;* the Muirs' pooch was called Scruffy; and the name of the haunted house was Gull Cottage.

Gidget

USA 1965, 32 x 30m, col ABC. Columbia.

PR *Bob Laver, Harry Ackerman, William Sackheim.* **DR** *Various, including William Asher, E W Swackhamer, Gene Reynolds.* **WR** *Various, including Ruth Brooks Flippen, Austin and Irma Kalish, Barbara Avedon.* **MUS** *Various, including Howard Greenfield and John Keller ('Gidget' theme), Johnny Tillotson (theme vocals), Dave Grusin, Hugh Montenegro.* **CAST** Frances 'Gidget' Lawrence *Sally Field* Russell Lawrence *Don Porter* Anne Cooper *Betty Conner* John Cooper *Peter Deuel* Jeff 'Moondoggie' Matthews *Steven Miles* Larue (Gidget's best friend) *Lynette Winter.*

The fun-lovin' misadventures of short Francine Lawrence (nicknamed 'gidget' from 'girl-midget') at home, high school and among her surfing buddies on Santa Monica beach. Her father, Professor Lawrence, was a widower, so big sister Anne and her husband John (Peter Deuel, later to star in *Alias Smith and Jones*) helped out with the protective parenting.

Terminally sunny show, which launched the career of Sally Field to screen stardom. Derived from the *Gidget* movies of the late fifties/early sixties, the TV show was revived in 1976 as *The New Gidget* (via the pilot, *Gidget's Summer Reunion*), which found the heroine aged twenty-seven, married to her boyfriend Jeff 'Moondoggie' Griffin (Matthews in the original series), owning her own travel business and – irony of ironies – caring for a teenage niece with a knack of finding trouble.

Gilligan's Island

USA 1964–6, 98 x 30m, bw/col CBS. United Artists/CBS Television/Gladysya Productions. UK tx *1965– ITV.*

CR *Sherwood Schwartz.* **PR** *Sherwood Schwartz.* **DR** *Various, including John Rich, Jack Arnold, Ida Lupino, Stanley Z Cherry.* **MUS** *George Wyle and Sherwood Schwartz ('Ballad of Gilligan's Island' theme), The Wellingtons (theme vocals), John Williams.* **CAST** Jonas Grumby *Alan Hale Jr* Gilligan *Bob Denver* Ginger Grant *Tina Louise* Thurston Howell III *Jim Backus* Lovey Howell *Natalie Schaefer* Mary Ann Summers *Dawn Wells* Roy Hinkley (the Professor) *Russell Johnson.*

Farce in which a group of vacationers become marooned on an uninhabited South Pacific island when their sightseeing boat, the SS *Minnow,* founders. Alan Hale Jr (from *Casey Jones*) played the good-natured skipper, Grumby, while Bob Denver (from the grocery store sitcom *Dobie Gillis*) took the role of Gilligan, the hapless first mate whose attempts to return to civilisation started and ended in ineptitude. For laughs it depended entirely on pratfalls (Gilligan's trousers catching fire, Gilligan accidentally dispatching the radio to the deep, that sort of thing). The characters themselves – who were, in addition to Grumby and Gilligan, movie star Ginger, rustic girl Mary Ann, science teacher the Professor, and the idle rich Thurston and Lovey Howells – had no psychological dimension, being mere ciphers for the plot.

Still, the show's Crusoe-esque fantasy scenario was strong enough for it to survive three years aboard the airwaves, and to spin off two animations: *The New Adventures of Gilligan* (1974) and *Gilligan's Planet* (1982–3). And then, nearly ten years after the original series ended, NBC made a slew of nostalgic TV movie sequels, *Rescue from Gilligan's Island* (1978, with Judith Baldwin replacing Tina Louise from the original cast), *Castaways on Gilligan's Island* (1979), even *The Harlem Globetrotters on Gilligan's Island* (1981). For the record, Gilligan's first name, never used in the series but later revealed by Bob Denver, was 'Willy'.

▶▶▶ *Created by Sherwood Schwartz,* Gilligan's Island *followed the farcical misfortunes of a group of latterday Robinson Crusoes.*

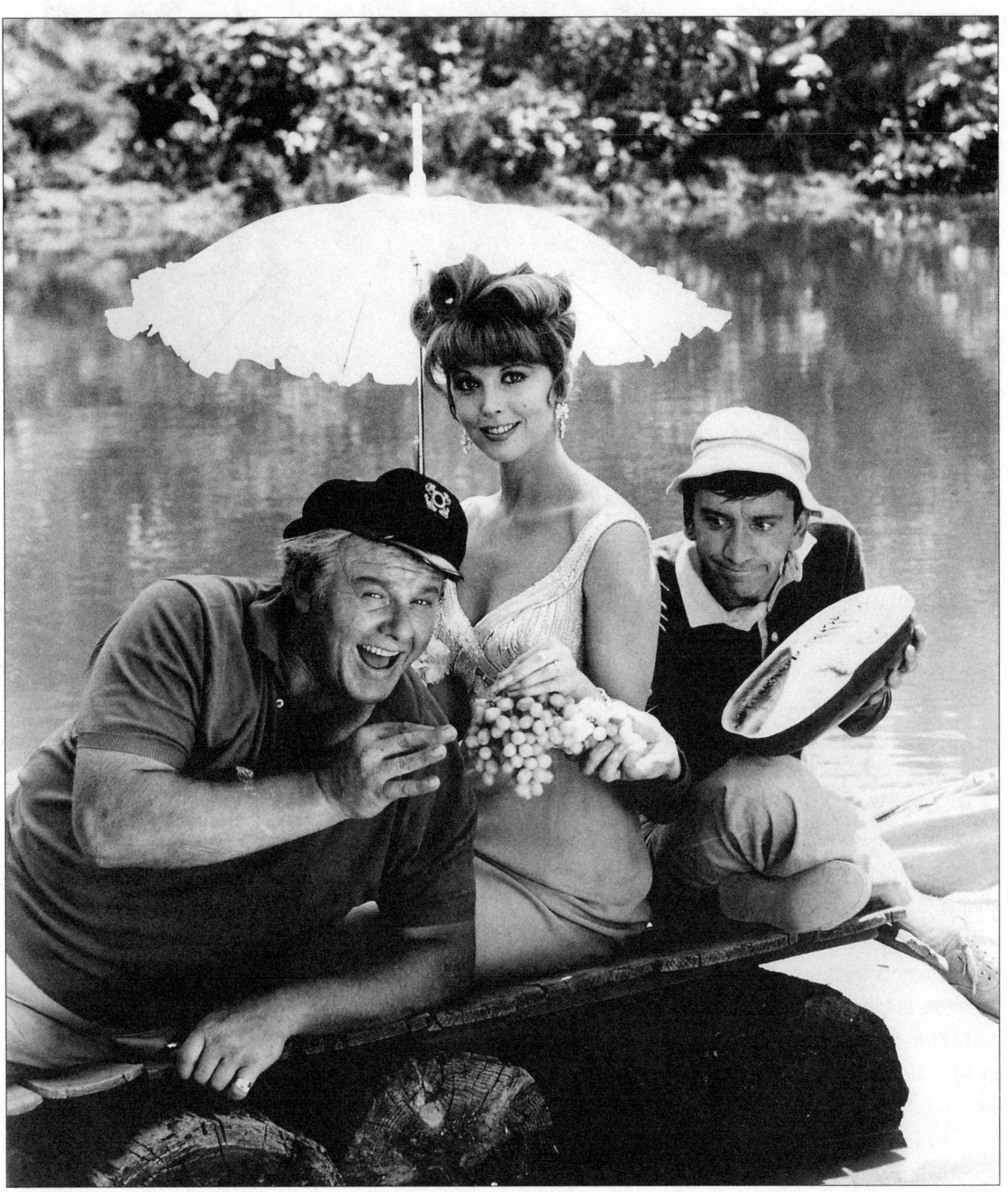

GIRLS ON TOP

UK 1985–6, 13 x 30m, col ITV. Central Independent Television plc.

CR *Dawn French, Jennifer Saunders, Ruby Wax.* **PR** *Paul Jackson, Trevor Walton.* **DR** *Ed Bye.* **WR** *Dawn French, Jennifer Saunders, Ruby Wax.* **MUS** *Chris Difford, Glenn Tilbrook.* **CAST** Amanda *Dawn French* Jennifer *Jennifer Saunders* Shelley *Ruby Wax* Candice *Tracey Ullman* Lady Carlton *Joan Greenwood.*

Female version of >*The Young Ones,* in which four variously out-to-lunch girls share a Chelsea apartment. This was owned by daffy romance writer Lady Carlton (as close a TV parody of Dame Barbara Cartland as the lawyers would allow), who lived downstairs. The tenants were: feminist Amanda, who worked for *Spare Cheeks* magazine; the dull Jennifer (hobby: making things from shells); the mendacious Candice and the loud-mouthed Shelley, an American wannabe actress whose talents had no beginning. At the start of the second season Candice departed for America (as had actress Tracey Ullman). The show was created by >*Comic Strip* veterans Dawn French and Jennifer Saunders (later >*French and Saunders* and all), along with US comedienne Ruby Wax. The script editor was Ben Elton.

Betty White and Bea Arthur in The Golden Girls.

THE GOLDEN GIRLS

USA 1985–93, 180 x 30m, col NBC. Witt-Thomas-Harris in association with Touchstone Television. UK tx *1986–93 C4.*

CR *Susan Harris.* **EXEC PR** *Paul Junger Witt, Tony Thomas, Susan Harris.* **PR** *Various, including Kathy Speer, Terry Grossman, Nina Feinberg, Mitchell Hurwitz, Jim Vallely, Kevin Abbott, John Zifren,*

Jamie Wooten, Marc Cherry. **DR** *Various, including Jay Sandrich, Paul Bogart, Terry Hughes, Lex Passaris, Peter Beyt.* **WR** *Various, including Susan Harris, Kathy Speer, Terry Grossman, Winifred Hervey, Mort Nathan, Barry Fanaro.* **MUS** *Andrew Gold ('Thank You For Being a Friend' theme), George Tipton.* **CAST** Dorothy Zbornak *Bea Arthur* Rose Nylund *Betty White* Blanche Devereaux *Rue McClanahan* Sophia Petrillo *Estelle Getty* Stanley Zbornak *Herb Edelman* Miles Webber *Harold Gould.*

In 1985 >*Soap* creator Susan Harris followed up that success with *The Golden Girls,* a comedy about four middle-aged to elderly women sharing a house together in Miami, sunny Mecca of retirees. Rose (Betty White from >*The Mary Tyler Moore Show*) was a dippy widow who worked as a grief counsellor and frequently remarked on her Norwegian roots – her mother's maiden name was Gerkelnerbigenhoffstettlerfrau. Dorothy (Bea Arthur from >*Maude*) was the acid-tongued teacher whose husband Stan had left her for an air stewardess. Blanche (Rue McClanahan, also from *Maude*), who owned the house, was a man-mad Southern belle, who once took mouth-to-mouth resuscitation classes because she liked kissing. Sophia was Dorothy's tactless octogenarian mother who moved in when her retirement home, Shady Pines, burned to the ground.

Some occasional men drifted through the series. Herb Edelman was seen from time to time as Dorothy's ex-husband Stan, who now seemed to want her back. Rose, for a while, had a boyfriend called Miles who unfortunately turned out to be a mob accountant and had to leave town pronto. And Blanche set her heart on many a passing anything in trousers but never found true love.

The first show to depict women senior citizens positively, *Golden Girls* was directly commissioned by NBC chief Brandon Tartikoff because he had noted the changing demographics of the US population and wanted a show to suit. Though sharply written and brazenly sentimental, it was the humorous, sometimes poignant relationship between the four 'girls' that was the core of its appeal. They may have looked like everyone's favourite aunties or grandmothers, but they traded wicked one-liners over helpings of cheesecake (over a hundred cheesecakes were consumed during the seven-year series) and discussed taboo subjects, from dating midgets to drooping breasts, incontinence, abortion and hot flushes. Their surprisingly broad base of fans included the British Queen Mother, who personally requested their presence at the Royal Variety Performance in 1988.

Golden Girls was a smash hit in sixty countries and highly regarded by the TV industry. It won sixty-five Emmy nominations, ten Emmy Awards, including Best Comedy (twice) and awards for each of its four stars as Best Actress or Best Supporting Actress (making it the only series on television for which all of its leading players have won Emmys), and three Golden Globe Awards. Among the queue of (suitably grey) guest stars on the show were Bob Hope, Don Ameche, Mickey Rooney, Dick Van Dyke and Julio Iglesias.

The show ended its run with a two-parter, 'One Flew Out of the Cuckoo's Nest', in which Bea married Blanche's Uncle Lucas (Leslie Nielsen from

>*Police Squad* and *The Naked Gun* movies) and relocated to Atlanta. A spin-off series, *The Golden Palace* (also by Susan Harris) saw the three remaining Miami matrons enter the hotel trade and buy *The Golden Palace* and its curious staff of three – manager Roland, Oliver, and overworked Chuy, the Mexican chef (played by Cheech Marin, one half of seventies film comedy duo Cheech and Chong).

The success of *The Golden Girls* on British minority Channel 4 led Carlton Television to develop a British version for mainstream ITV. *The Brighton Belles,* 1993, was set on the South Coast and starred Jean Boht, Sheila Hancock, Wendy Craig and Sheila Gish. It became a TV byword for disaster, being withdrawn before the end of its premier season.

Susan Harris went on to create >*Empty Nest,* set in the same Miami neighbourhood as *The Golden Girls,* with the characters from the two shows sometimes overlapping.

Gomer Pyle, USMC

USA 1964–70, 150 x 25m, bw/col CBS. Ashland.

PR *Aaron Ruben, Sheldon Leonard, Ronald Jacobs.* **DR** *Various, including John Rich, Coby Ruskin, Peter Baldwin.* **CAST** Pfc Gomer Pyle *Jim Nabors* Sgt Vincent Carter *Frank Sutton* Pte Gilbert 'Duke' Slattery *Ronnie Schell* Bunny Olsen *Barbara Stuart* Lou-Ann Poovie *Elizabeth MacRae* Pte Frankie Lombardi *Ted Bessell* Pte Lester Hummel *William Christopher* Sgt Charles Hacker *Allan Melvin* Cpl Chuck Boyle *Roy Stuart* Cpl Edward Gray *Forrest Compton.*

After a mere one-season appearance on >*The Andy Griffith Show,* gormless country-boy character Gomer Pyle was sent to join the United States Marine Corps, who stationed him at Camp Henderson, California. There his slapstick antics in Company B caused his immediate superior, leather-necked Sergeant Carter, to believe that Gomer was making a fool out of him – until Carter realized that Gomer was, truly, a wide-eyed naïf, and the two became friends. Not that Gomer's stupidity didn't still cause Sergeant Carter to regularly blow a fuse. Miss Lou-Ann Poovie was Gomer's equally rustic girlfriend. The show was a top ten hit for almost its entire run.

The Goodies

UK 1970–81, 73 x 30m, 2 x c50m, col BBC2/LWT. BBC TV/LWT. US tx *1976 Syndicated.*

CR *Tim Brooke-Taylor, Graeme Garden, Bill Oddie.* **EXEC PR** *Alan Bell (LWT).* **PR** *John Howard Davies, Jim Franklin, Bob Spiers.* **DR** *John Howard Davies, Jim Franklin, Bob Spiers.* **WR** *Bill Oddie, Graeme Garden.* **CAST** Tim *Tim Brooke-Taylor* Graeme *Graeme Garden* Bill *Bill Oddie.*

Originally to be called *Narrow Your Mind,* in reference to Graeme Garden and Tim Brooke-Taylor's earlier show for the BBC, *Broaden Your Mind, The Goodies* was a situation comedy with only the haziest of situations. Garden, Brooke-Taylor and Bill Oddie played three characters – 'Graeme', 'Tim' and 'Bill' – whose brief was to do 'Anything, Anyplace, Anytime'. Without any of the traditional constraints of sitcom, the Goodies were thus free to indulge in an anarchic array of visual slapstick, pop culture parody, and, especially, cartoon-like surrealism. In the BBC Visual Effects Department they found willing collaborators, the Department's trickery allowing the Goodies to tackle many infamous baddies, prime among them giant white kitten Twinkle (a burlesque of *King Kong* which won the show a Silver Rose at the 1972 Montreux Festival).

Graeme Garden, Bill Oddie and Tim Brooke-Taylor in The Goodies.

Aside from the fix-it theme, the only other constants were the Goodies' mode of travel from one caper to another, a tandem-for-three, and their assumed characters: Tim was the upper-class patriot (and coward – *The Goodies* was notably anti-Establishment); Graeme was the mad scientist inventor; and Bill the 'yobbo' conservationist, who used mind-expanding sherbet to achieve 'total awareness'. A musical element often surfaced, even spinning off a string of singles: 'The In-Betweenies', 'Funky Gibbon' and 'Wild Thing'. There was frequent contemporary comparison to >*Monty Python,* but this should not have surprised: both 'teams' came out of the Cambridge Footlights revues of the early sixties and had honed their off-centred comedy on >*At Last the 1948 Show.*

Even over a run of ten years, the novelty of *The Goodies* barely wore off, since there was always something to spoof: punks (which caused the Goodies to wear giant safety pins through their heads); Margaret Thatcher (who had to retire to the Bahamas in *The Goodies,* to be replaced by Tim... until he proved too kind); the kung fu craze, which produced, in the episode 'Ecky Thump', a *Goodies* Up North version in which the lethal weapons were black puddings; and the British Royal Family – always. Not until the move to LWT in 1980 did the show go off the mark, by which time it was apparent that a new generation of comedians, those grouped around >*Not the Nine O'Clock News,* had their finger closer to the funny bone of humour.

Classic episodes include: 'Kitten Kong'; 'Ecky Thump'; 'Goodies Rule – OK?' (Christmas 1975 Special); 'Earthanasia' (1977 Christmas Special).

THE GOOD LIFE

UK 1975–8, 28 x 30m, col BBC1. BBC.

CR *John Esmonde and Bob Larbey.*
PR *John Howard Davies.* **WR** *John Esmonde and Bob Larbey.* **MUS** *Burt Rhodes.* **CAST** Tom Good *Richard Briers* Barbara Good *Felicity Kendal* Margot Leadbetter *Penelope Keith* Jerry Leadbetter *Paul Eddington.*

Much-loved sitcom from the seventies, which centred on the attempt of forty-year-old Tom Good, a draughtsman for the JJM Company, to drop out of the rat race and go self-sufficient. Thus Tom, and his unfeasibly perky wife Barbara, dug up their Surbiton back garden and turned it over to a pig, a goat and numerous hens. Tom's hit-or-miss DIY and agricultural methods were a major source of the show's twee but feel-good humour, as were the shocked reactions of snobbish next-door neighbour Margot Leadbetter, leading light of the local music society. It was Margot's constant fear that the Goods would bring the social tone of 'The Avenue' down irrevocably; however, since sitcoms cannot contain genuinely unpleasant characters, Margot's snootiness was more than tempered by her generous friendship to her odd-couple neighbours in their times of need. Meanwhile, Margot's husband Jerry (who still worked for JJM), looked on the Goods with a bemused affection.

Accorded the accolade of a special Royal Command performance, the show established the cast foursome as some of the best-loved faces on TV. All went on to continued small-screen success: Briers with *Ever Decreasing Circles* (another Esmonde and Larbey series), Keith in >*To The Manor Born* and *Next of Kin,* Felicity Kendal – whose coquettish sex appeal was one of *The Good Life*'s unacknowledged keys to success – in *Solo* and *The Mistress,* and Eddington in the >*Yes, Minister* cycle.

GOODNIGHT SWEETHEART

UK 1993–, 44+ x 30m, col BBC1. Alomo/SelecTV.

CR *Laurence Marks and Maurice Gran.* **PR** *John Bartlett.* **DR** *Terry Kinane, Robin Nash.* **WR** *Various, including Laurence Marks and Maurice Gran, Paul Makin.* **CAST** Gary Sparrow *Nicholas Lyndhurst* Yvonne Sparrow *Michelle Holmes/Emma Amos* Phoebe Bamford *Dervla Kirwan/Elizabeth Carling* Ron Wheatcroft *Victor McGuire* PC Reg Deadman *Christopher Ettridge* Eric *David Ryall.*

Time-travel comedy in which nineties TV repair man Gary Sparrow (Nicholas Lyndhurst, >*Butterflies,* the dim-witted Rodney in >*Only Fools and Horses*) found a secret entrance – Duckett Passage – to the London of the wartime forties.

▲▲▲ The Good Life *for Felicity Kendal (left) and Richard Briers (standing).*

There he fell in love with barmaid Phoebe (Dervla Kirwan from *Ballykissangel*), his resultant absences giving him some explaining to do with his contemporary wife, Yvonne. At one stage, a shopping development threatened to block Sparrow's route to the past – but no sitcom with thirteen million viewers was going to allow a row of shops to stand in its way; accordingly, Sparrow leased the offending unit, and used it to sell Second World War memorabilia. Naturally, Sparrow's time-flitting led to all sorts of anachronistic and culture clash problems – among the most humorously sweet of them, the occasion when he arrived at Phoebe's with a bottle of wine bought from a nineties off-licence, only to discover that the wine was... German. In general, however, Sparrow found the crusading anti-Hitler forties – in which he passed off his modernity by pretending to be a secret agent with an American background – more appealing than contemporary reality.

The show was created by the ubiquitous Lawrence Marks and Maurice Gran *(Shine On Harvey Moon, Birds of a Feather)*, who, just when its formula seemed to be passing its use-by date, introduced the neat plot element of Sparrow's son by his wartime squeeze. As the son was also a time-traveller, this gave Sparrow even more line-spinning to do with his nineties spouse. *Goodnight Sweetheart* was produced by the independent company Alomo, which took its name from its three main movers: Executive producer Allan McKeown, Laurence Marks and Maurice Gran – Al', lo', mo'.

GOOD TIMES

USA 1974–9, Approx 80 x 30m, col CBS. Tandem Productions.

CR *Eric Monte and Michael Evans.* **PR** *Norman Lear.* **DR** *Various, including Jack Shea, Gerren Keith.* **MUS** *Dave Grusin, Alan Bergman, Marilyn Bergman.* **CAST** Florida Evans *Esther Rolle* James Evans *John Amos* James Evans Jr ('JJ') *Jimmie Walker* Michael Evans *Ralph Carter* Thelma Evans Anderson *BernNadette Stanis* Sweet Daddy *Teddy Wilson* Mr Bookman (the janitor) *Johnny Brown* Willona Woods *Ja'net DuBois* Penny Gordon Woods *Janet Jackson.*

Sitcom concerning the sorrows and joys of black American parents Florida and James Evans, as they struggled to bring up their brood of three in a high-rise ghetto ('cockroach towers') on the South Side of Chicago. Much the most problematic of the offspring was James Evans Jr ('JJ'), who had one eye for the ladies and the other for quick get-out-of-the-ghetto schemes, usually of dubious probity. The jive-talking JJ, with his trademark expression of 'Dyn-O-Mite!', became a TV anti-hero of the seventies, but his negative aspects as a role model caused star Esther Rolle to quit the show temporarily. Also to leave, but permanently, was John Amos (for *Roots*), and to make up the cast numbers Janet Jackson was shipped in as battered girl Penny, while the role of next-door neighbour Willona Woods was given more prominence. Originally ingenious – it was America's first black family sitcom – and socially aware, *Good Times* ended as little more than a stage on which for JJ to strut his funky stuff.

The show was a spin-off from >*Maude,* in which Esther Rolle's Florida had featured as a maid, that show itself being a spin-off from >*All in the Family.*

GRACE UNDER FIRE

USA 1993–8, 107+ x 30m, col ABC. Carsey-Werner. UK tx *1995– BBC2.*

CR *Chuck Lorre.* **EXEC PR** *Various, including Kevin Abbott, Brett Butler, Chuck Lorre, Jeff Abugov.* **PR** *Various, including Wayne Lemon, Dava Savel, Miriam Trogdon, Ed Yeager, Danny Zucker.* **DR** *Various, including Michael Lessac, Harry Murray.* **WR** *Various, including Chuck Lorre, Dottie Dartland, Dava Savel, Brett Butler and Wayne Lemon.* **MUS** *Dennis C Brown.* **CAST** Grace Kelly *Brett Butler* Russell Norton *Dave Thomas* Quentin Kelly *Jon*

Boyfriend: 'See you tonight, huh.' Grace: 'Why don't you just wear a big sign that says, "I know what Grace's tongue tastes like"?'

Paul Steuer/Sam Horrigan Patrick Kelly *Cole/Dylan Sprouse* Elizabeth Louise 'Libby' Kelly *Kaitlin Cullum* Dougie *Walter Olkewicz* Nadine Swoboda *Julie White* Wade Swoboda *Casey Sander* Jimmy Kelly (Grace's ex-husband) *Geoffrey Pierson* Rick Bradshaw *Alan Autry.*

Sardonic blue-collar comedy in which recovering alcoholic Grace Kelly divorces her abusive husband and supports her three kids on her lonesome – with a little help from her friends next door, Nadine and Wade, and local druggist Russell. Actress Brett Butler gave perfect delivery as sharp-witted, sharper-tongued Grace (whose jobs included working in an oil refinery), a turn acknowledged by a Best Comedy Actress Award from Viewers for Quality Television. Like >*Murphy Brown,* a show which managed to be simultaneously funny and smart on single momming in the nineties.

GREEN ACRES

USA 1965–71, 170 x 25m, col CBS. Filmways. UK tx *1966–8 BBC1.*

▶▶▶ *From the producer of* The Beverly Hillbillies *came the situation-reversed* Green Acres.

CR *Jay Sommers, Paul Henning.* **EXEC PR** *Paul Henning.* **PR** *Jay Sommers.* **DR** *Various, including Richard L Bare.* **WR** *Various, including Jay Sommers, Dick Chevillat.* **MUS** *Eddie Albert and Eva Gabor ('Green Acres' theme vocal), Vic Mizzy.* **CAST** Oliver Wendell Douglas *Eddie Albert* Lisa Douglas *Eva Gabor* Fred Ziffel *Hank Patterson* Ed Dawson *Tom Lester* Eustace Haney *Pat Buttram.* Video *Columbia House.*

After >*The Beverly Hillbillies,* in which the country folks went to town, producer Paul Henning cannily reversed the comedic formula with *Green Acres.* Here successful Manhattan lawyer

Green acres is the place to be
Farm living is the life for me
Land spreading out
So far and wide
Take Manhattan
Just give me that countryside.

New York
Is where I'd rather stay
I get allergic smelling hay
I just adore a penthouse view
Darling, I love you
But give me Park Avenue...

Oliver Wendell Douglas drags socialite wife Lisa and her finery – to her considerable dismay – to ramshackle 160-acre Haney farm, outside Hooterville, in a bid to get back to nature.

Originating in the radio series *Granby's Green Acres,* the broadbrush humour of the show came from the culture clash of city-meets-country, plus the language difficulties of the Hungarian-accented Lisa (played by Eva Gabor, younger sister of Zsa Zsa), who misunderstood almost everything said to her. There was also a scene-stealing pig, Arnold, owned by neighbour Fred Ziffel, who performed party tricks to order and watched TV.

The show was closely related to another US sitcom, >*Petticoat Junction,* also set in Hooterville and produced by Paul Henning.

A reunion TVM, *Return to Green Acres,* was aired in 1990.

Show trivia: Pat Buttram, who played Mr Haney, modelled his character on Elvis' manager, Colonel Parker; the Douglas' cow was called Eleanor.

HALE AND PACE

UK 1988–, Approx 61 x 25m, 1 x 52m, col ITV. LWT.

PR *Charlie Hanson.* **DR** *Various, including Peter Orton.* **WR** *Various, including Gareth Hale and Norman Pace, Nick Woodey.* **MUS** *Peter Brewis.* **CAST** *Gareth Hale, Norman Pace; with Ainsley Harriott, Annette Badland, Paula Hannis, Maggie Henderson.*

Skit-based show from comedians Gareth Hale and Norman Pace, featuring such invented characters as the patronizing children's TV presenters Billy and Johnny, and the cockney gangsters The Two Rons (a parody of the infamous Kray twins). Clearly oblivious to the concept of good taste – one sketch featured the controversial microwaving of a cat – Hale and Pace were former teachers, who rose through the alternative comedy circuit, making their début on TV in Channel 4's mid-eighties shows *Pushing Up Daisies* and *Coming Next...* before exposure in >*The Young Ones* and >*Saturday Live* persuaded LWT to give them a show of their own. LWT's faith was well placed: the comic twosome won the Golden Rose of Montreal. For the same company, Hale and Pace also spun off the two Rons into a short sitcom series entitled *The Management.*

HANCOCK'S HALF-HOUR

UK 1956–61, 56 x 30m, 1 x 43m, bw BBC. BBC TV.

CR *Ray Galton and Alan Simpson.* **PR** *Duncan Wood.* **DR** *Duncan Wood.* **WR** *Ray Galton and Alan Simpson.*

▶▶▶ *Tony Hancock, 'the lad himself'.*

CAST Anthony Aloysius St John Hancock *Tony Hancock* Sid *Sid James; plus Bill Kerr, Irene Handl, June Whitfield, Warren Mitchell, Patricia Hayes, Patrick Cargill, Kenneth Williams, Hattie Jacques, Frank Thornton, Liz Fraser.* Video *BBC.*

At 23 Railway Cuttings, East Cheam, the bumptious Anthony Aloysius St John Hancock dreamed of rising above his humble origins whilst gloomily observing life's petty frustrations (including, in 'The Missing Page', coming to the end of a thriller only to find that the page has been torn out). Room-mate Sid provided the common-sense foil. Transferring from radio, the show's bitter-sweet scripts (by Ray Galton and Alan Simpson) perfectly suited the deadpan delivery and comic timing of Hancock, the self-proclaimed 'the lad himself', and over ten million viewers tuned in.

Hancock to jury: 'Does Magna Carta mean nothing to you? Did she die in vain?'

The final season was transmitted under the title *Hancock* and, despite the absence of Sid James and Hancock's trademark black Homburg hat, produced the two classic *Hancock* episodes (two, even, of the high-water marks in British TV humour): 'The Blood Donor' ('A pint? That's nearly an armful!') and 'The Radio Ham'. Thereafter, Hancock defected to ITV and unwisely dispensed with the scripts of Galton and Simpson (who went on to create >*Steptoe and Son*). This, plus Hancock's decision to read his lines off autocue rather than memorize them, saw quality drop through the floor. Some accordingly deduced that Hancock was nothing without his scribes (Kenneth Williams, for one, confided to his diary that Hancock was a 'philistine nit... an indifferent performer saved by... Galton and Simpson'), but there was clearly more to it than that. A nineties revival of the original *Half-Hour* scripts with Paul Merton (from *Have I Got News for You* and *The Paul Merton Show*) in the lead was an embarrassing flop.

The son of a hotelier and part-time entertainer, Hancock made his stage début in the RAF with ENSA (Entertainments National Service Association) and touring gang shows. He then moved into pantomimes, cabaret and radio, appearing in

Educating Archie in 1951. The radio series *Hancock's Half-Hour* began in 1954. Famous as much for his real-life alcoholism and self-doubt as for his comic performances, Hancock – the archetypal sad clown – committed suicide on 25 June 1968 in a hotel room in Sydney, Australia, at the age of forty-four. His suicide note read: 'This is quite rational... there was nothing left to do. Things seemed to go wrong too many times.'

▼▼ *'Aaayh!'* Happy Days *for Henry Winkler and Ron Howard.*

HAPPY DAYS

USA 1974–84, 255 x 30m, col ABC. Miller-Milkis/ Paramount TV. UK tx *1975–84 ITV.*

CR *Garry Marshall.* **PR** *Garry Marshall, Edward K Milkis, Thomas L Miller, Jerry Paris.* **DR** *Various, including Jerry Paris, Mel Ferber, Don Weis, Peter Baldwin.* **WR** *Various, including Rob Reiner, Garry Marshall, William S Bickley.* **MUS** *Bill Haley ('Rock Around the Clock' theme), Gimel and Fox ('Happy Days' theme).* **CAST** Richie Cunningham *Ron Howard* Arthur 'the Fonz' Fonzarelli *Henry Winkler* Howard

Cunningham *Tom Bosley* Marion Cunningham *Marion Ross* Joanie Cunningham *Erin Moran* Warren 'Potsie' Weber *Anson Williams* Ralph Malph *Danny Most* Charles 'Chachi' Arcola *Scott Baio* Arnold Takahashi *Pat Morita* Al Delvecchio *Al Molinaro* Lori Beth Allen *Lynda Goodfriend* Jenny Piccolo *Cathy Silvers* Leather Tuscadero *Suzy Quatro* Pinky Tuscadero *Roz Kelly.*

Nostalgia fest, set in smalltown Milwaukee in the fifties, which began as a sketch on *Love, American Style* in 1972 but gained its production impetus from the success of the rock'n'roll movie *American Graffiti*. Initially the show centred on 'hum-drum' teenager Richie Cunningham (Ron Howard from >*The Andy Griffith Show* and the star of *American Graffiti*), and his worldly-wise friend at Jefferson High, Potsie Weber (Anson Williams, born Anson William Heimlich). The guys hung out at a burger joint called Arnold's Drive In, invariably with fellow buddy Ralph Malph. It became apparent by the second season, however, that the real star of the show was none of these characters but a minor creation brought in by show supremo Garry Marshall to lessen the show's tendency towards Middle-American gooeyness: the leather-jacketed biker, Arthur 'the Fonz' Fonzarelli. The streetwise Fonz (played by Henry Winkler, holder of a Masters in drama from Yale) was so cool that he had only to click his fingers and the chicks came running. To incorporate the Fonz into more of the narrative action, the scriptwriters moved him into the apartment over Richie's parents' garage. By 1977 *Happy Days* was the most popular programme on US TV. Kids everywhere imitated the Fonz, his biker look and gestures, particularly his thumbs-up 'Aaayh!' His iconic nature was further confirmed when the Smithsonian Institution in Washington put his leather jacket on display.

As the show gained in years and stature, it dropped the nostalgia and became a character-based sitcom, and Richie's parents Howard and Marion came increasingly to the fore. (Mrs C's line, 'Are you feeling *frisky,* Howard?' became something of a show catchphrase.) The cast changed surprisingly little until the eighties, when Ron Howard, Danny Most and Anson Williams all left the show. By that time their characters were far from teenage; they had all grown up, gone to college, got jobs and, in the case of Richie, got married to Lori Beth. The main addition to the cast was Chachi, Fonzie's cousin, who fell in and out of love with Richie's sister Joanie (actors Baio and Moran – who had previously starred in *Daktari* – were also on/off lovers in real life). At one stage they were given their own series, *Joanie Loves Chachi*. It flopped. But two other spin-offs from *Happy Days* became major successes. In 1975 two blue-collar girls, Laverne DeFazio (played by Penny Marshall, sister of Garry, and previously a fixture in >*The Bob Newhart Show*) and Shirley Feeney, appeared in *Happy Days* for a double date with Richie and the Fonz, and promptly waltzed off to their own >*Laverne and Shirley* series. In 1978 actor Robin Williams, in his first real screen exposure, dropped into Milwaukee as Mork, an extraterrestrial from Ork. The episode was so

successful that he was given his own show, >*Mork and Mindy,* almost overnight.

Happy Days ended its 255-episode, ten-year run in 1984. Since then Ron Howard has forged a career as a major-league Hollywood director *(Backdraft, Cocoon),* and Henry Winkler has become an award-winning producer. Tom Bosley, who played Cunningham senior, later starred in the clerical crime caper, *The Father Dowling Mysteries.*

HARRY AND THE HENDERSONS

USA 1991–3, 72 x 30m, col Syndicated. Amblin Entertainment. UK tx *1991–3 BBC1.*

PR *Lin Oliver.* **MUS** *Leon Redbone ('Your Feet's Too Big' theme).* **CAST** Harry *Kevin Peter Hall/Sawan Scott/Brian Steele* George Henderson *Bruce Davison* Nancy Henderson *Molly Cheek* Ernie Henderson *Zachary Bostrom* Sarah Henderson *Carol-Ann Plante.*

A TV knock-on from the 1987 film *Bigfoot and the Hendersons.* While vacationing in the Pacific North-West, the Henderson family ran over a large hairy creature. This turned out to be a bigfoot or sasquatch, which the Hendersons took home for its convalescence. To protect Harry – for it was he – from the authorities, the Hendersons were obliged to perform farcical acts of cover-up. Lively enough family fodder. Initially Harry was played by Kevin Peter Hall, who had taken the role in the movie. The theme music was Leon Redbone's 'Your Feet's Too Big'.

HARRY ENFIELD'S TELEVISION PROGRAMME

UK 1990–2, 16 x 30m, col BBC2. Hat Trick.

CR *Harry Enfield, Paul Whitehouse, Geoffrey Perkins, Charlie Higson.* **EXEC PR** *Denise O'Donoghue.* **PR** *Geoff Posner, Geoffrey Perkins.* **DR** *Geoffrey Perkins.* **WR** *Harry Enfield, Charlie Higson, Paul Whitehouse, Geoffrey Perkins.* **CAST** Dave Nice/Lee/Stavros/Tim Nice-But-Dim/Wayne Slob/Mr 'You Don't Want to Do That' *Harry Enfield* Alf Git/Lance/Mike Smash *Paul Whitehouse* Waynetta Slob *Kathy Burke.*

After a celebrated stint on >*Saturday Live,* comedian Harry Enfield gained his own BBC2 show, which introduced a collection of new comic-cut caricatures, usually performed in co-operation with Paul Whitehouse (later >*The Fast Show*) or Kathy Burke. Though Enfield's performances were highly controlled, the satire was barely restrained: his spoof DJs Mike Smash and Dave Nice (fave rave: 'You Ain't Seen Nothing Yet' by Bachman-Turner Overdrive) demolished any lingering credibility of an entire generation of DJ presenters at BBC Radio 1. No less comically cruel were some of his other creations: upper-class twit Tim Nice-But-Dim, the Old Gits, wide-boys Lee and Lance, Wayne and Waynetta Slob (the latter giving birth to a daughter called 'Spudulika'), Mr 'You Don't Want to Do That', The Scousers (a lampoon of Liverpool-set soap, *Brookside*), and Mr Cholmondley-Warner and Mr Greyson, whose forties-style documentary presentations were later translated into a series of advertisements for a telephone company. Unwilling to preserve characters beyond a short screen life (the 'poptabulous' DJs Mike and Dave went to TV hell in a 'tip-top, tippety-top' 1994 special, *Smashey and Nicey – The End of an Era*), Enfield was obliged to invent new ones at a prodigious rate. Accordingly, *Harry Enfield and Chums* (BBC1, 1994–), which was effectively *Harry Enfield's Television Programme* under another title and channel, saw the birth of the Self-Righteous Brothers, Kevin the Teenager, Tory Boy, Lovely Wobbly Randy Old Ladies and Considerably Richer Than You. More uneven in quality than the *Television Programme,* it also suffered in comparison with the rapid-fire pace of *The Fast Show* from Enfield's own 'chums', Whitehouse and Charlie Higson (who, like Whitehouse, co-created the *Television Programme;* he also occasionally performed in it).

In addition to skit shows, Enfield has also tried his face at sitcoms in *Gone to the Dogs* (as Little Jim Morley) and >*Men Behaving Badly.* A 1989 spoof documentary on the life of a thespian, *Norbert Smith... A Life* (C4) was awarded an international Emmy.

HI-DE-HI!

UK 1980–9, Approx 70 x 30m, col BBC1. BBC TV.

CR *Jimmy Perry and David Croft.* **PR** *David Croft, John Kilby.* **DR** *David Croft, Jimmy Perry, John Kilby.* **WR** *Jimmy Perry and David Croft.* **MUS** *Jimmy Perry ('Holiday Rock' theme).* **CAST** Jeffrey Fairbrother *Simon Cadell* Ted Bovis *Paul Shane* Gladys Pugh *Ruth Madoc* Spike Dixon *Jeffrey Holland* Mr Partridge *Leslie Dwyer* Fred Quilley *Felix Bowness* Yvonne Stuart-Hargreaves *Diane Holland* Barry Stuart-Hargreaves *Barry Howard* Peggy Ollerenshaw *Su Pollard* Sylvia *Nikki Kelly* Betty Rikki Howard *Mary Penny Irving* Squadron Leader Clive Dempster *David Griffin* The Yellowcoat boys *Terence Creasey, the Webb twins.* Video *BBC.*

Good morning, campers! It's Maplin's Holiday Camp at Crimpton-on-Sea, circa 1959, and the staff and entertainers are assembled for *Hi-De-Hi!,* Jimmy Perry and David Croft's affectionate send-up of that peculiarly British institution, the seaside holiday camp. Episodes follow the farcical misadventures of the entertainment staff of the cut-price camp (a barely veiled Butlins, where Perry had once worked as a Redcoat) as they forcibly jolly along the holidaying proles. Chief Entertainments Officer is the donnishly misplaced Jeffrey Fairbrother (played by Simon Cadell, grandson of famous West End actress Jean Cadell and later Croft's son-in-law), under whom serve the spivvy camp host Ted Bovis, Welsh senior Yellowcoat Gladys Pugh (who tries to speak posh, but usually malaprops) and young comic Spike. Dim-witted and accident-prone maid Peggy, meanwhile, tries to rise above her chalet in life and don a yellow blazer. Also to be seen are the snobby, bickering ballroom dancers Barry and Yvonne, ex-jockey Fred Quilley (now in charge of the camp horses) and drunken child-hating Punch and Judy man Mr Partridge. In the later seasons Fairbrother is replaced as CEO by Squadron Leader Clive Dempster DFC.

A show of camp humour, in more ways than one. By the later seasons, the writers' inventiveness was wearing thin, but audiences seemed not to care, and the show remained popular until the last (its highest position in the BARB ratings was number three, in 1984). Perry and Croft's previous joint exercises in nostalgic lampoonery were >*Dad's Army* and >*It Ain't Half Hot, Mum,* while Croft (with Jeremy Lloyd as partner) had given a comedic doing over to the British department store in >*Are You Being Served?* and to the spy genre in >*'Allo, 'Allo.* Many of the *Hi-De-Hi!* cast came back for *You Rang, M'Lord,* Croft and Perry's spoof on *Upstairs, Downstairs.*

Why do people wear digital watches? Mark Wing-Davey in The Hitchhiker's Guide.

THE HITCHHIKER'S GUIDE TO THE GALAXY

UK 1981, 6 x 35m, col BBC2. BBC TV. US tx *1982 PBS.*

CR *Douglas Adams.* **PR** *Alan J W Bell.* **WR** *Douglas Adams.* **MUS** *Paddy Kingsland.* **CAST** Arthur Dent *Simon Jones* Ford Prefect *David Dixon* Voice of the Book *Peter Jones* Zaphod Beeblebrox *Mark Wing-Davey* Trillian (aka Trisha McMillan) *Sandra Dickinson* Marvin *David Learner* Voice of Marvin *Stephen Moore.* Video *BBC.*

I think you should know I'm feeling very depressed

Seconds before Earth is destroyed by a Vogon Constructor Fleet (to make way for a hyperspace by-pass), Ford Prefect, an alien from planet Betelgeuse and researcher for the best-selling intergalactic reference book *The Hitchhiker's Guide,* rescues typical Englishman Arthur Dent from the impending doom. Arthur, surprised to hear that Ford Prefect is not, in fact, from Guildford, finds himself on a journey through space, where he meets such exotic beings as part-time, two-headed Galactic President Zaphod Beeblebrox and his starship-driving girlfriend Trillian (Sandra Dickinson), Marvin the paranoid Android ('I think you should know I'm feeling very depressed'), the unpoetic Vogons, the useless Golgafrinchians and a pair of pan-dimensional beings who are searching for the Ultimate Question to Life, the Universe and Everything. (They already have the *answer* – it's 42.) As they travel, Prefect and Dent ponder on such questions as: Why are people born? Why do they die? Why do they spend so much of the intervening time wearing digital watches? They finish up at the Restaurant at the End of the Universe, with a prime view over the exploding heavens.

Douglas Adams' brilliant satire on modern times and sci-fi conventions began as a radio play and then became a novel before being serialized for TV under the hand of Alan J W Bell. Notorious for its low sci-fi budgets, the BBC graced the show with superior – for the BBC, at least – special effects, with sophisticated computer animation converting the viewer's screen into the Guide when necessary. The guest stars, who formed something of an in-joke, were headed by Peter Davison (Dickinson's husband and the sixth incarnation of *Dr Who*) and David Prowse, previously Darth Vader in the movie *Star Wars*. Prowse played the bodyguard for plutonium rocker Hotblack Desiado. Adams himself appeared in the second episode, where he disrobed and, *pace* the credits of >*The Fall and Rise of Reginald Perrin,* walked into the sea.

HOGAN'S HEROES

USA 1965–71, 168 x 30m, col CBS. Bing Crosby Productions. UK tx *1967–9 ITV.*

CR *Bernard Fein, Albert S Ruddy.* **EXEC PR** *Edward H Feldman.* **DR** *Various, including Gene Reynolds, Edward H Feldman.* **WR** *Various, including Lawrence Marks.* **CAST** Col Robert 'Papa Bear' Hogan *Bob Crane* Col Wilhelm Klink *Werner Klemperer* Sgt Hans Schultz *John Banner* Cpl Peter Newkirk *Richard Dawson* Cpl Louis LeBeau *Robert Clary* Sgt James Kinchloe *Ivan Dixon* Sgt Andrew Carter *Larry Hovis* Helga *Cynthia Lynn* Sgt Richard Baker *Kenneth Washington.*

John Banner, Bob Crane and Werner Klemperer in POW farce Hogan's Heroes.

Tasteless prison-camp farce set in Germany's Stalag 13 during the Second World War. Ostensibly the establishment was run by pompous Nazi Colonel Klink and dim, strudel-gorging sidekick Sergeant Schultz, but in fact it was under the control of US inmate Colonel Hogan (Bob Crane, from *The Donna Reed Show*). With his Allied pals – chiefly French cook LeBeau, Sergeant James Kinchloe and Cockney Corporal Newkirk – Hogan ran rackets galore and circles around Klink. The POWs also lived in a state of some luxury, and even had a sauna. To justify their continued presence in the camp – since they could leave at any time through a special door in the fence – Hogan's merry men were charged with secret anti-Jerry sabotage and espionage missions by the Allied High Command. Despite a similarity to the stage play *Stalag 17* which was strong enough to invite a lawsuit, the show ran for six raucous seasons. It once again made the news in 1978 when actor Bob Crane was found beaten to death in his condo in Scottsdale, Arizona.

Show trivia: actor Werner Klemperer was the son of the famous Jewish-German conductor Otto Klemperer; Larry Hovis, who played Sergeant Carter, was a regular writer-performer for >*Rowan and Martin's Laugh-In* and had previously served in the military sitcom >*Gomer Pyle, USMC;* Ivan Dixon later directed the cult spy movie *The Spook Who Sat by the Door;* Robert Clary's real name was Robert Widerman, and he had been interned in a Nazi concentration camp as a child.

Schultz: When it comes to war, I do not like to take sides

Home Improvement

USA 1991–8, 178 x 30m, col ABC. Disney/ Touchstone Television/Wind Dancer Group Productions/Buena Vista Television. UK tx *1994– C4.*

CR *Matt Williams, David McFadzean, Carmen Finestra.* **EXEC PR** *Matt Williams, David McFadzean, Carmen Finestra.* **PR** *John Pasquin, Gayle S Maffeo.* **DR** *Various, including John Pasquin, Andy Cadiff, Peter Bonerz.* **WR** *Various, including Matt Williams, David McFadzean, Carmen Finestra, Billy Riback, Elliot Stern.* **CAST** Tim Taylor *Tim Allen* Jill Taylor *Patricia Richardson* Brad Taylor *Zachery Ty Bryan* Randy Taylor *Jonathan Taylor Thomas* Mark Taylor *Taran Smith* Wilson *Earl Hindman* Al Borland *Richard Karn* Lisa *Pamela Denise Anderson* Heidi *Debbe Dunning.*

Smash hit sitcom from Matt Williams (creator of >*Roseanne*) starring Tim Allen as Tim Taylor – chauvinist, gadget-crazy, know-it-all presenter of a DIY cable programme called 'The Tool Show'. At home, however, his wife Jill sensibly kept him away from the appliances, since his every attempt to 'fix' them ended in calls to the fire brigade. Together Tim and Jill tried to bring up their three tow-headed sons, who liked to be bad but always ended up comfortingly good.

Misread by some as an unreconstructed piece of macho posturing, *Home Improvement* in truth effectively and amusingly satirized the unreconstructed male, down to the home truth that it was Jill, not Tim, who held the reins of real power. There were other notable comedic elements to the show: as with any domestic comedy, there was a next-door neighbour, but in the case of Wilson he was permanently hidden from view by a fence and given to guru-like sayings on Tim's perennial problem of trying to understand the female mind; and, as with *Roseanne,* the closing credits showed 'bloopers' committed by the cast. A hit till it quit, *Home Improvement* found the perfect casting in Allen – a former stand-up comic – as Taylor, who tried to be the archetypal MCP but was truly a nice guy underneath. The show received several awards, and even praise from the right-wing Family Guide

Wilson offers some more off-the-fence tips to Tim Taylor in Home Improvement.

for portraying a 'secure family unit... in a TV landscape littered with atypical or dysfunctional families'.

Perhaps the funniest thing about *Home Improvement*, however, was that it gave Pamela Anderson her big screen break playing Lisa, the, er, 'Tool Time Girl'.

The Honeymooners

USA 1955–6, 39 x 30m, bw CBS, 1966–71, 13 x 60m, col CBS, 1984–5, 68 x 30m, col CBS. CBS Entertainment. UK tx *1958 ITV, 1987 BBC2.*

CR *Jackie Gleason, Joe Bigelow, Harry Crane.* **EXEC PR** *Jack Philbin.* **PR** *Jack Hurdle.* **DR** *Various, including Frank Satenstein, Jackie Gleason.* **WR** *Jackie Gleason, Marvin Marx, Walter Stone, Andy Russell, Herbert Finn, Leonard Stern, Sydney Zelinka.* **MUS** *Jackie Gleason (theme), Sammy Spear.* **CAST** Ralph Kramden *Jackie Gleason* Ed Norton *Art Carney* Alice Kramden *Audrey Meadows (1955–6)/Sheila MacRae (1966–71)* Trixie Norton *Joyce Randolph (1955–6)/Jane Kean (1966–71)*

The saga of Ralph and Alice Kramden, the not-so-newlyweds who lived in a grimy, rundown apartment at 328 Chauncey St, Brooklyn. (*The Honeymooners'* set was about the bleakest in TV sitcom history – a kitchen/living-room with a fridge, a table and view out on to the bricks of the neighbouring building.) The show centred on portly Ralph (Jackie Gleason, >*The Life of Riley*), a blustering New York City bus driver always on the look-out for scams for making/saving money. Yet these, whether it was off-loading a warehouseful of useless can-openers on late-night TV, or withholding a rent increase, always ended in disaster. Ever willing to help Ralph in his ambitions was best friend Ed Norton, a cheery but incompetent sewer-cleaner who lived upstairs with spouse Trixie. Continually displeased by the duo's schemes was Ralph's practical wife Alice, whose devastating put-downs and complaints were regularly met by the response, 'One of these days, Alice, one of these days... POW! Right in the kisser.'

Much of *The Honeymooners'* appeal lay in the fact that it was at heart an old-fashioned romance. 'The guy really loved this broad,' creator Gleason maintained. 'They fight, sure. But they always end in a clinch.' And, sure enough, the episode's curtain would fall on harmony and Ralph proclaiming, 'Alice, you're the greatest!' – a moment the scriptwriters dubbed 'kissville'. There was also the comic drama of the indefatigable bus driver always keeping his head in the clouds while the rest of him was sinking fast, and the contribution of gifted physical actor Art Carney (the Hardy to Gleason's Laurel), in whose hands the chalking of a pool cue could become a feat of comic choreography. Unlike its heavily polished and scripted contemporary >*I Love Lucy, The Honeymooners* came complete with adlibs and improvisations, giving it an energy rare in prime-

Alice, you're the greatest!

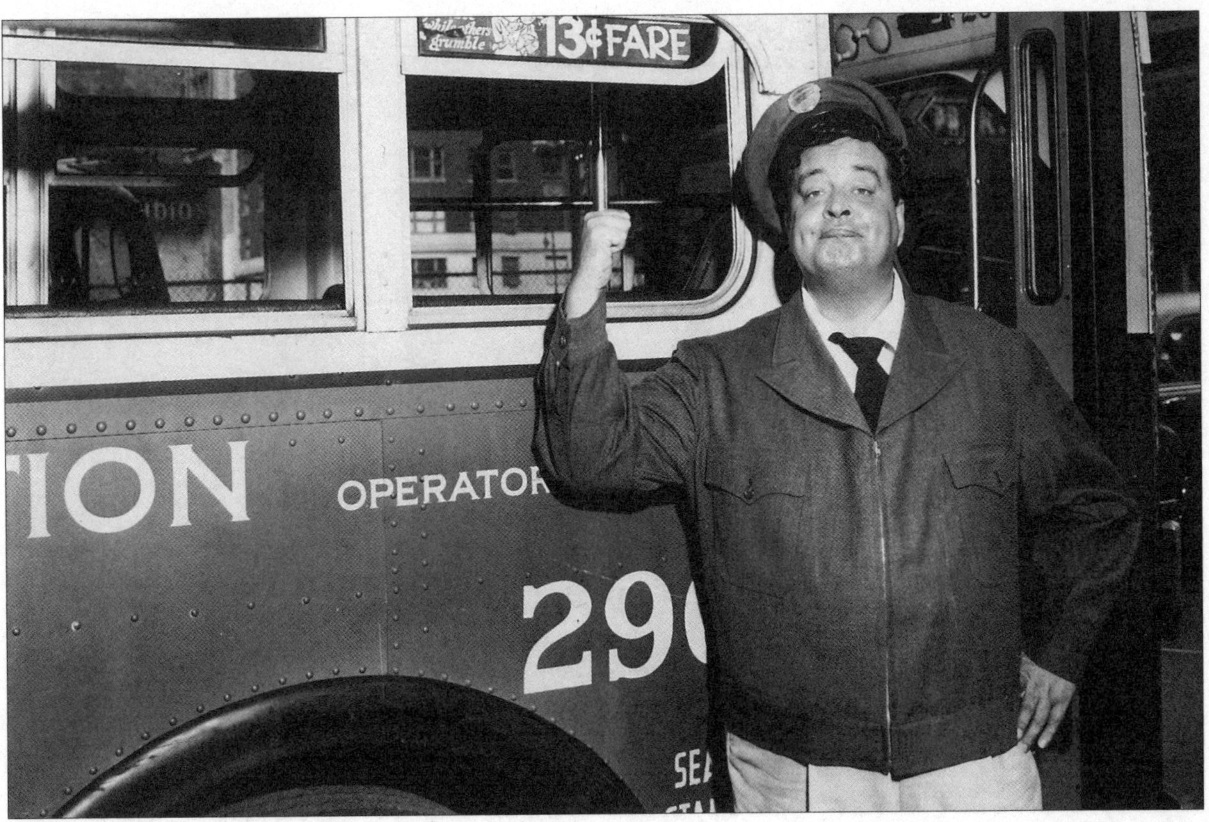

▲▲▲ *Jackie Gleason rode to the heights of the ratings as bus driver Ralph in* The Honeymooners.

time sitcomland, even to this day.

The Honeymooners spent most of its history as a segment within other programmes, running only one season as an independent show. It was first seen as a sketch in *DuMont's Cavalcade of Stars* in 1951, then on CBS as part of *The Jackie Gleason Show. The Honeymooners* finally became a series in its own right in 1955, when the Buick Motor Company sponsored the freestanding sitcom to the tune of over six million dollars – then the largest sponsorship commitment in TV history. (The ultimate compliment to *The Honeymooners* would come later, however, with Hanna-Barbera's shameless, and admitted, cartoon imitation, >*The Flintstones*.) One of the first examples of a live-audience, single-set filmed situation comedy, *The Honeymooners* was filmed twice weekly before a live audience of 1,100 people crowded into New York's Adelphi Theater.

In 1956 *The Honeymooners* – the first TV show to tune into the frustrations of America's urban blue-collar workers – ended after only one season, but in 1966 it was revived in the form of one-hour episodes of Gleason's then-current variety series, with Broadway-style musicals padding out the

▲▲▲ *Astronaut Tony Nelson (Larry Hagman, right) is landed in another supernatural sitcom mishap inevitably involving the cross-legged Jeannie (Barbara Eden) in* I Dream of Jeannie.

episodes by some thirty minutes. A collection of reruns was aired as a 'new' series in 1971, and four 'specials' were shot between 1976 and 1978. In the eighties 'lost episodes' of *The Honeymooners* were broadcast (by Showtime, a pay-cable network owned by Viacom), but these were in fact skits from *DuMont's Cavalcade* and *The Jackie Gleason Show* edited together to make sixty-eight new *Honeymooners* half-hours.

I DREAM OF JEANNIE

USA1965–70, 139 x 25m, col NBC. Columbia. UK tx *1966–70 ITV.*

CR *Sidney Sheldon.* **EXEC PR** *Sidney Sheldon.* **DR** *Various, including Gene Nelson, Alan Rafkin, E W Swackhamer, Hal Cooper, William Asher, Claudio Guzman, Theodore J Flicker, Larry Hagman, Hal Cooper.* **WR** *Various, including Sidney Sheldon, Tom Waldman and Frank Waldman, Arthur Alsberg and Bob Fisher, William Davenport.* **MUS** *Hugh Montenegro.* **CAST** Jeannie *Barbara Eden* Capt Anthony 'Tony' Nelson *Larry Hagman* Capt Roger Healey *Bill Daily* Dr Alfred Bellows *Hayden Rorke.*

When NASA astronaut Tony Nelson (Larry Hagman, later the US *Good Life* sitcom and sudster *Dallas*) crashes on a desert island, he finds a beautiful blonde genie in a bottle. She accompanies him back to Cape Canaveral, where she seeks to magically improve his lot in life. Unfortunately, Jeannie – who is only visible to Nelson and buddy Roger Healey – is both over-zealous and petulantly jealous. Still, with just a blink of her eyes she easily undoes the mayhem she causes each episode. The story ends happily ever after when Jeannie and Tony – who had previously been engaged to general's daughter Melissa – marry in the final season.

A likeable, light supernatural sitcom, *I Dream* was intended by US network NBC to ride the tail of rival ABCs >*Bewitched*. With starette Barbara Eden in skimpy harem attire, it also pandered to an obvious male fantasy (would she really do *anything* for him?), and many turned on.

I Love Lucy

USA 1951–61, 179 x 30m, bw CBS. Desilu Productions. UK tx *1955–65.*

CR *Jess Oppenheimer, Madelyn Pugh, Bob Carroll.* **EXEC PR** *Desi Arnaz.* **PR** *Jess Oppenheimer, Desi Arnaz.* **DR** *Ralph Levy, Marc Daniels, William Asher, James V Kern.* **WR** *Jess Oppenheimer, Madelyn Pugh, Bob Carroll Jr, Bob Schiller, Bob Weiskopf.* **MUS** *Eliot Daniel (theme), Wilbur Hatch and the Desi Arnaz Orchestra.* **CAST** Lucy Ricardo *Lucille Ball* Ricky Ricardo *Desi Arnaz* Ethel Mertz *Vivian Vance* Fred Mertz *William Frawley* Little Ricky Ricardo *Richard Keith* Jerry (the agent) *Jerry Hausner* Mrs MacGillicuddy (Lucy's mother) *Kathryn Card* Caroline Appleby *Doris Singleton.*

The scatter-brained antics of NY housewife and showbiz wannabe Lucy Ricardo snap the patience of her fiery Cuban bandleader husband, whose fractured English degenerates into a stream of Spanish epithets. Meanwhile, nosy apartment neighbours the Mertzes look on.

The prototype sitcom with its polished scripts and performances, its structure of neighbouring inter-relating couples, its theme of frustration, *I Love Lucy* grew from Ball's CBS radio show *My Favorite Husband* (in which she perfected her trademark dottiness and crying fits), with Richard Denning originally slated to play opposite her on TV. Instead, she decided to film a pilot with her real-life spouse, the Cuban musician-actor Desi Arnaz (the two had met on the set of Arnaz's Hollywood feature, *Too Many Girls*), which sold them and the concept to CBS. Almost immediately after it went on the air, *I Love Lucy* became a smash hit, rose to the top of the ratings and stayed there for most of its years on CBS. A kind of *I Love Lucy* mania gripped the USA; the 1953 episode in which the Ricardos' baby boy was born (its transmission, extraordinarily enough, coinciding with Ball's real-life delivery of Desi Arnaz Jr) attracted 44 million viewers. President Dwight Eisenhower's inaugural address the next night could only manage 29 million viewers.

The sheer classiness of the plots, gags, editing (from four cameras, rather than the usual one), and performances lifted the show above all its predecessors and peers, with the partial exception of the raw-energy >*The Honeymooners*. The National Academy of Television Arts and Sciences bestowed five Emmys. Meanwhile, the revolutionary decision to film the *I Love Lucy* shows, rather than broadcast them live, meant that the high-quality prints of each episode could be reshown. As a result, the show sold around the world (including to Britain, where it was one of the first programmes shown on the fledgling ITV network). It has been estimated that *I Love Lucy* has been on the air somewhere in the world throughout the last forty years. Not the least effect of the show's use of film was that it shifted TV production away from New York, where it started, to Hollywood, where the film facilities were.

In the summer of 1958 a collection of reruns entitled *The Top Ten Lucy Shows* revealed the

More scatter-brained domestic mayhem for Lucy and Des in the classic I Love Lucy.

difficulty of selecting an all-time list – it contained thirteen episodes. Among these was the episode where Lucy manoeuvred her way on to Ricky's TV show (he having worked his way up, as the fiction had it, from bandleader at the Tropicana, via ownership of the Ricky Ricardo Babaloo Club), in order to promote a health tonic commercial, and then got drunk sampling the highly alcoholic product. (Lucy's attempts to break into showbiz, and Ricky's attempts to keep her at home as a housewife, were the show's staple plot.) Then there was the time when she tried to bake her own bread, threw in two entire packets of yeast, and ended up pinned to the wall of her kitchen when she opened the oven. And the time Lucy (whose maiden name, for the record, was MacGilicuddy) and neighbour Ethel were looking for mementos of Hollywood to take home to New York and tried to prise loose the block of cement bearing John Wayne's footprint from in front of Grauman's Chinese Theater.

I Love Lucy was made by the independent company owned by Arnaz and Ball, Desilu (named from a meld of their first names), which became one of the most successful in Hollywood. It was bought out in 1967 for $20 million. Some six years before this, however, Arnaz and Ball had divorced, with former speakeasy hostess Ball going on to star in sitcom, *The Lucy Show* (co-produced with new husband Gary Morton). There she played Connecticut widow and mother of two, Lucy Carmichael. Despite a shift down in quality and a confusing change of title to *Here's Lucy,* its longevity alone (it lasted until 1972) established Ball, if proof were needed, as America's TV comedienne *sans pareil.*

I'M DICKENS, HE'S FENSTER

USA 1962–3, 32 x 25m, bw ABC. Heyfay. UK tx *1964 ITV.*

CR *Leonard Stern.* **PR** *Leonard Stern.* **CAST** Harry Dickens *John Astin* Arch Fenster *Marty Ingels* Kate Dickens *Emmaline Henry* Mel Warshaw *Dave Ketchum* Banister *Frank DeVol.*

Intermittently amusing show, something like >*Abbott and Costello* for the sixties, concerning two carpenters-cum-builders whose best-laid plans became pratfalls. At the least, it proved a useful step up the career ladder for John Astin, soon to head >*The Addams Family.* Co-lead Marty Ingels, one of TV's great journeymen, later appeared in Phyllis Dyller's riches-to-rags sitcom, *The Pruitts of Southampton*, and as the recurring character Sol Pomeroy in >*The Dick Van Dyke Show.* In the early eighties he became the voice of Pac Man in Hanna-Barbera's cartoonized video game of that name. He was the second husband of Shirley Jones from >*The Partridge Family.*

IT AIN'T HALF HOT, MUM

UK 1974–81, 56 x 30m, col BBC1. BBC TV.

CR *Jimmy Perry and David Croft.* **PR** *David Croft.* **DR** *John Kilby, Phil Bishop, Bob Spiers.* **WR** *Jimmy Perry and David Croft.* **MUS** *Jimmy Perry and Derek Taverner (theme).* **CAST** RSM B L Williams *Windsor Davies* Bombardier Solomons *George Layton* Bombardier 'Gloria' Beaumont *Melvyn Hayes*

▲▲▲ *The cast of Croft and Perry's 70s military sitcom find* It Ain't Half Hot, Mum.

Gunner 'Lofty' Sugden *Don Estelle* Gunner 'Paderuski' Graham (aka 'La-de-dah') *John Clegg* Gunner Mackintosh *Stuart McGugan* Gunner Parkin *Christopher Mitchell* Colonel Reynolds *Donald Hewlett* Captain Ashwood *Michael Knowles* Rangi Ram *Michael Bates* Gunner 'Nosher' Evans *Mike Kinsey* Gunner 'Nobby' Clarke *Kenneth MacDonald* Char Wallah Muhammed *Dino Shafeek* Punka Wallah *Babar Bhatti*.

Coarse-cut comedy from Croft and Perry (previously the sublime >*Dad's Army*), concerning the misadventures of a Royal Artillery concert party in India during the Second World War. Most of the humour comes from the efforts of blustering Welsh Sergeant-Major Williams to instil in the effete entertainers ('a bunch of poofs') some semblance of military order. On sitcom parade alongside Williams was the assorted platoon of diminutive 'Lofty' Sugden, Bombardier Solomons (George Layton), Scottish Gunner Mackintosh, Gunner Parkin (possessor of a 'fine pair of shoulders' according to Williams, who thought he

Meet the gang, 'coz the boys are here
The boys to entertain you...

was the boy's father), egg-headed pianist 'Lah-de-dah' Gunner Graham, and Gunner Beaumont, who cross-dressed into 'Gloria' in cabarets for the troops. (Beaumont's transvestism was the other wellspring of the show's laughs.) The entertainers' idiotic commissioned officers were Colonel Reynolds and the drippy Captain Ashwood. Also seen were the local wallahs, including a blacked-up Michael Bates *(>Last of the Summer Wine),* whose stereotyped pidgin English as Rangi Ram suggested that the show – which climbed as high as number two in the BARB ratings – might have been better titled, 'It Ain't Half Racist, Mum'.

A spin-off single, 'Whispering Grass', performed by actors Windsor Davies and Don Estelle in their Lofty and Sergeant Major personae, became a number one hit in 1975.

It's a Square World

UK 1960–4, 32 x 30m, bw BBC. BBC TV.

CR *Michael Bentine.* **PR** *G B Lupino, John Street, Joe McGrath.* **WR** *Michael Bentine, John Law.*
CAST *Michael Bentine, Frank Thornton, Clive Dunn, Ronnie Barker, Benny Lee, Dick Emery, Leon Thau, Joe Gibbons, Freddie Earlie, John Bluthal, Louis Mansi, Janette Rowsell, Len Lowe, Anthea Wyndham.*

After leaving the radio *Goon Show* for a solo career in TV, Michael Bentine first tried his hand at kiddie-time animation (the classic *The Bumblies* of 1954), before testing the adult airwaves in *After Hours.* Then came *It's a Square World,* which essentially combined Goonery with the animation techniques of *The Bumblies* to create a visual TV surrealism that prefigured the more famous exploits of *>Monty Python.* The series was built around Bentine in the guise of a lecturer/commentator, whose illustrative models had a habit of coming to 'life'. Perhaps the most famous – and controversial – of the resultant gags saw a Chinese junk sailing up the Thames to attack the House of Commons. (The sequence was banned temporarily by the BBC for fear that it was too political at general election time.)

Those assisting Bentine in the live-action sequences included Clive Dunn (later *>Dad's Army*), Frank Thornton (later *>Are You Being Served?*), Dick Emery (*>The Army Game*), Louis Mansi (later *>'Allo, 'Allo*), and, in his first lead TV role, Ronnie Barker (later *>Porridge*). Bentine followed *Square World* with *It's All Square* for ITV (1966–7), the children's show *Michael Bentine's Potty Time* and the 1977 BBC1 special, *Michael Bentine's Square World.*

It's Garry Shandling's Show

USA 1986–90, Approx 60 x 30m, col SHO/Fox. Showtime. UK tx *1987–91 BBC2.*

CR *Garry Shandling, Alan Zweibel.* **EXEC PR** *Bernie Brillstein, Brad Gery, Garry Shandling.* **PR** *Alan Zweibel.* **DR** *Various, including Alan Rafkin, Paul*

Miller, Stan Lathan, Thomas Schlamme. **WR** *Various, including Garry Shandling, Alan Zweibel, Jeff Franklin.* **MUS** *Joey Carbone (theme).* **CAST** Garry Shandling *himself* Mrs Ruth Shandling *Barbara Cason* Nancy Bancroft *Molly Cheek* Leonard Smith *Paul Wilson* Pete Schumaker *Michael Tucci* Jackie Schumaker *Bernadette Birkett* Grant Schumaker *Scott Nemes* Phoebe Bass *Jessica Harper.*

Post-modern sitcom from toothsome comic Garry Shandling, in which he played a fictitious version of himself, an angst-ridden goofball plagued by odd characters and his own neuroses. Although set exclusively in Shandling's condo, the plots went far, far away; in one episode Shandling hosted the 1988 elections; in another, the condo was turned into a private theme park, 'Shandlingland'. The epitome of post-modernist TV, the show consciously referenced the classics of the past, with its opening monologue *pace* >*The Jack Benny Show,* the direct addresses to the audience ('breaking the fourth wall') borrowed from *The Burns and Allen Show,* and the single set echoing both >*I Love Lucy* and >*The Honeymooners.* Elaborately concerned to stress the artificiality of TV, the show was full of self-referentialism, even opening the credits with the gag line, 'This is the theme to Garry's show'. Yet, the show ensured mainstream watchability by cannily foregrounding the staples of sitcoms everywhere – funny family and friends – and followed a conventional sub-plot in Garry's relationship with girlfriend Phoebe. At the end of the show's run, the two even married to live happily ever after. The non-fictitious Shandling, meanwhile, moved to the blackly humorous side of life in >*The Larry Sanders Show for HBO.*

The Jack Benny Show

USA 1950–65, Approx 170 x 30m, bw/col CBA/ NBC. UK tx *1956– BBC.*

EXEC PR *Ralph Levy.* **PR** *Various, including Irving Fein, Fred DeCordova, Ralph Levy, Hilliard Marks.* **R** *Various, including Ralph Levy, Fred DeCordova.* **WR** *Various, including Neil Morrow, John Tackaberry, Ed Beloin, Sam Perrin, George Balzer.* **MUS** *Leo Robin and Ralph Rainger ('Love in Bloom' theme).* **CAST** Jack Benny *himself* Mary Livingston *herself* Rochester *Eddie Anderson* Don Wilson *himself* Prof LeBlanc/Si (Mexican foil) *Mel Blanc* Fred (Jack's director) *Fred DeCordova* Dennis Day *himself* Mr Kitzel (Jewish foil) *Arte Auerbach* Sam (Jack's writer) *Herbert Vigran.*

One of the first comedians to see the possibilities of TV, Jack Benny (aka Benjamin Kubelsky) transferred his long-running radio show to the new medium virtually unchanged. This centred on his fictionalized persona as a pompous ageing actor (who always claimed to be 'thirty-nine') and the world's outstanding miser, regularly and comically brought low by the foils who were his workmates. (Added for the screen, by Benny, were an affected camp walk and equally affected hand to the cheek.) As such the programme's elements of extended

Robber to Jack Benny: 'Your money or your life!'
[silence]
Robber: 'Quit stalling. I said your money or your life.'
Jack Benny: '...I'm thinking it over.'

sketches, invented characters and 'family' of regulars marked a departure from the variety model of early TV humour, making *The Jack Benny Show,* along with >*I Love Lucy,* the prototype sitcom. And, like the humour of *I Love Lucy,* Jack Benny's lacked malice, instead resting on his perfect comic timing, understatement and invented, self-deprecating persona.

The show's regulars, all veterans from the radio version, were Don Wilson as Benny's announcer and friend, secretary Mary Livingston (Benny's real-life wife, born Sadie Marks), Eddie Anderson, who played Benny's black manservant Rochester, and Mel Blanc (the voice of Bugs Bunny and later that of Barney in >*The Flintstones*), who voiced Benny's antique Maxwell car and played his hapless violin teacher, Professor LeBlanc. (Despite Benny's acted ineptitude on the violin, he had been a child prodigy with the instrument.) Among the guests were Lucille Ball herself, Carol Burnett, Ginger Rogers and John Wayne (in one of his very few TV appearances). Ronald Colman made semi-regular appearances as Benny's neighbour. The show – sometimes known as *The Jack Benny Program* – was as loved on TV as it had been on radio, and it lasted from 1950 through to 1965. By then Benny was aged seventy-one and, although he much reduced his schedule, he continued to produce TV specials until his death in 1974.

JEEVES AND WOOSTER

UK 1990–3, 23 x 52m, col ITV. US tx *1991–3 PBS. Picture Partnership Productions/Carnival Films.*

PR *Brian Eastman.* **DR** *Robert Young, Simon Langton, Ferdinand Fairfax.* **WR** *Clive Exton.* **MUS** *Anne Dudley.* **CAST** Bertie Wooster *Hugh Laurie* Jeeves *Stephen Fry* Aunt Agatha *Mary Wimbush/Elizabeth Spriggs* Aunt Dahlia *Brenda Bruce/Vivian Pickles.*

Top-hole TV version of P G Wodehouse's stories of dimwit socialite Bertie Wooster and his capable valet Jeeves, starring Hugh Laurie and Stephen Fry in lively plots that contained the perfect formulaic blend of hair-brained money-making schemes, mad pashes and formidable dowager aunts. Designer Eileen Diss was responsible for the sumptuous sets. The later episodes were set in New York, after Bertie's escape from his imminent marriage to Honoria Glossop.

The Jeeves and Wooster stories had been adapted for TV before in the BBC's *P G Wodehouse's World of Wooster* (BBC1, 1965–7), with Ian Carmichael as Wooster and Dennis Price as the gentleman's gentleman. However, it was Fry and Laurie, seemingly born to play the parts, who established the definitive version.

Fry and Laurie first performed together in the 1981 Cambridge Footlights (with Emma Thompson), and their award-winning show 'The Cellar Tapes' was transmitted by the BBC in 1982. After stints, individually and together, on *Alfresco,* >*The Young Ones,* >*Saturday Live,* >*Blackadder, This Is David Lander* and *Happy Families,* the two opened their own BBC show, *A Little Bit of Fry and Laurie,* in 1989, a year later changing channel for *Jeeves and Wooster.*

What ho!

JULIA

USA 1968–71, 86 x 30m, col NBC. 20th Century Fox. UK tx *1969–71 ITV.*

PR *Hal Kanter.* **DR** *Various, including Hal Kanter.*
CAST Julia Baker *Diahann Carroll* Corey Baker *Marc Coppage* Dr Morton Chegley *Lloyd Nolas* Marie Waggerdorn *Betty Beaird* Earl J Waggerdorn *Michael Link* Hannah Yarby *Lurene Tuttle.*

The first TV series since *Beulah* (ABC, 1950) to star a black woman and, unlike *Beulah*'s maid-heroine, one which starred a black woman in a 'prestige' role. *Julia* was a half-hour comedy about a beautiful young nurse raising her six-year-old son single-handedly after her air force pilot husband was killed in Vietnam. Moving to Los Angeles, Julia Baker found a job at the medical office of Astrospace Industries. Julia's work, home life and social activities all provided grist for the show's humour mill. The show was totally integrated – to the nervousness of NBC executives, who then decided it had no chance of survival and scheduled it in a 'coffin spot' opposite CBS's *The Red Skelton Show;* indeed, NBC only aired *Julia* for the kudos of making a show with a black principal. Against network expectation, the show became popular with white audiences as well as black and became a fully-fledged hit.

In the world of the show, Julia lived with son Corey in a modern, mixed-race apartment building, where his best friend was white Earl J Waggerdorn. Other characters in Julia's home life were Earl's dad Leonard, landlord Sol Cooper and mother's helper Carol Deering. At work, the middle-class heroine had equally harmonious relations with her white employer, feisty, kind-hearted Doctor Morton Chegley, his wife Melba, fellow nurse Hannah Yarby and plant employee Eddie Edwards. Romantic partners were, however, strictly black. Paul Cameron was Julia's occasional boyfriend for the first two seasons and was replaced by Steve Bruce, a widower with a four-year-old daughter Kim, during the show's final year.

It soon became apparent, though, that this rather cute, romanticized version of black/white relations was running behind real time. This was 1968, an era of ghetto riots and a new black militancy, and Julia's trouble-free, colourless integration into the white community bore little relation to the reality of black experience in the USA. The show came under fire from black nationalists and the liberal white press for being false and distorted, and partly because of this political pressure star Diahann Carroll decided to quit after the third season.

Diahann Carroll (born Carol Diann Johnson), a singer with motion-picture experience, later secured an Oscar nomination for her role in *Claudine* (1974), giving a romantic-comedy performance of a depth not suggested by her pretty plastic turn in *Julia*. In the 1980s she returned to undemanding glamour as Dominique Devereaux, Blake Carrington's half-sister in *Dynasty.*

KATE AND ALLIE

USA 1984–8, Approx 111 x 30m, col CBS. Reeves Entertainment. UK tx *1982–9 C4.*

▲▲▲ *A distaff Odd Couple,* Kate and Allie *(Susan Saint James and Jane Curtin).*

CR *Sherry Kobin.* ***EXEC PR*** *Mort Lachman, Merrill Grant, Bill Persky, Saul Turtletaub, Bernie Orenstein.* ***PR*** *Bob Randell, Anne Flett, Chuck Ranberg.* ***DR*** *Various, including Bill Persky, Linda Day.* ***WR*** *Various, including Bob Randell, Sherry Kobin.* ***CAST*** Kate McCardle *Susan Saint James* Allie Lowell *Jane Curtin* Emma McCardle *Ari Meyers* Chip Lowell *Frederick Koehler* Jennie Lowell *Alison Smith* Ted Bartelo *Gregory Salata* Charles Lowell *Paul Hecht* Bob Barskey *Sam Freed* Lou Carello *Peter Onarati.*

Female version of >*The Odd Couple*. Kate and Allie were two New York divorcees obliged by shaky finances to share an apartment. Their kids came too. Although Kate, a hi-energy Swinging Sixties liberal, and Allie, a quiet conservative, had little in common, they bonded like glue, even setting up a catering business together. Towards the end of the show's run Allie remarried, but continued to live with Kate since her television sportscaster husband, Bob Barskey, worked during the week in Washington DC.

Wryly amusing sitcom, with perfectly cast leads in Susan Saint James (previously the co-star, with Rock Hudson, of *McMillan and Wife*) and Jane Curtin (formerly the mom of the 'Conehead' family on >*Saturday Night Live*). Curtin collected two Emmys for her portrayal of Allie. Among the later entries on her CV was *Third Rock from the Sun*.

KEEPING UP APPEARANCES

UK 1990–95, 40 x 30m, 4 x c60m, col BBC1. BBC TV. US tx *1992– PBS.*

CR *Roy Clarke.* **PR** *Harold Snoad.* **DR** *Harold Snoad.* **WR** *Roy Clarke.* **MUS** *Nick Ingman (theme).*
CAST Hyacinth Bucket *Patricia Routledge* Richard Bucket *Clive Swift* Daisy *Judy Cornwall* Rose *Shirley Stelfox Mary Millar* Onslow *Geoffrey Hughes* Elizabeth *Josephine Tewson* Emmett Hawksworth *David Griffin* Vicar *Gerald Sim/Jeremy Gittins* Daddy *George Webb.*

Situation comedy from Roy Clarke featuring Mrs Hyacinth Bucket – 'It's pronounced bouquet!'– a matronly class climber obsessed with her social standing. To elevate this she went to extreme lengths, dressed for elevenses and polished the leaves of her trees. The laugh, of course, was that Bucket, despite her airs and graces, had no accurate notion of 'U' behaviour and was permanently undone by her own gaffes. Worse, her council-house relatives turned up regularly to embarrass her. They were slutty sisters Daisy and Rose, brother-in-law Onslow (Daisy's husband, the vest-wearing driver of an S-reg Cortina), and senile Daddy, who believed that the war was still on. (Another sister, unseen, lived in a 'big house on the hill'.) And though Hyacinth sought to impress her neighbours and believed they admired her, they tended to flee as she hoved into view. Her singing was held to be a particular peril. Through all this, Hyacinth's meek husband Richard endured a life of exasperated resignation.

It's pronounced bouquet!

The aural joke of bucket/bouquet was not new, it dated back to the days of British black-and-white cinema, but Clarke's (>*Last of the Summer Wine*, >*Open All Hours*) observations of social mores and class nuances were turned to exquisitely painful degree. Meanwhile, Patricia Routledge (born Katherine Patricia Routledge) positively bloomed as the suburban matron from hell. She was named Top Television Comedy Actress in 1991. Two years later she was awarded an OBE for services to acting. After *Keeping Up Appearances* she appeared in the star vehicle *Hetty Wainthrop Investigates,* a comedy caper about an OAP detective.

Some *Keeping Up Appearances* trivia: Hyacinth and Richard's unseen son Sheridan, who only ever phoned home when he needed money, was studying to be a quantity surveyor; actor Clive Swift was once married to authoress Margaret Drabble, while actress Josephine Tewson (who played horrified neighbour Elizabeth) was the sometime wife of Leonard Rossiter; Geoffrey Hughes used to play Eddie Yates in northern soap *Coronation Street;* the Buckets lived in Blossom Avenue; Richard's job before retirement was Deputy Manager of Finance and General Services.

THE KENNY EVERETT VIDEO SHOW

UK 1978–80, 24 x 30m, col ITV. Thames TV.

PR *David Mallett.* **DR** *John Birt.* **WR** *Ray Cameron, Barry Cryer, Kenny Everett.* **CAST** *Kenny Everett, Cleo Rocas.*

A shock-jock before the term was invented, radio DJ Maurice James Cole – aka Kenny Everett – first took his patented madcap humour to TV in the children's show, *Nice Time,* in 1968. Here his unlikely co-hosts were Jonathan Routh from *Candid Camera* and a then unknown Warwick University academic by the name of Germaine Greer. For Greer, Everett and the show's director, John Birt, *Nice Time* proved to be a crucial rung on the TV career ladder (Routh was already on the way out of TV to become an amateur painter, and find his recreational fun tossing wooden dwarfs in Jamaica), and in 1970 LWT awarded Everett his own show, *The Kenny Everett Explosion.* But it was the follow-up series, *The Kenny Everett Video Show* for Thames, in which Everett really found his *métier.* His enthusiasm for the medium, especially the nascent video gadgetry, was positively infectious. Presenting from a studio bare apart from a wall of TV monitors, Everett led the audience at home on a thirty-minute weekly tour of gleefully adolescent erotics, courtesy of Arlene Phillips' dance troup Hot Gossip, and equally gleeful and adolescent comic sketches, featuring such Everett creations as Sid Snot, Marcel Wave, punk Gizzard

The zany Kenny Everett.

Puke, and a Dolly Parton-like celeb of unfeasible décolletage (known off-air as 'Cupid Stunt'). Everett's chief on-screen collaborator was Cleo Rocas, who played the buxom Miss Whiplash. It was, of course, 'all done in the best possible taste'. Not.

With the show's end, Everett then fronted the short-lived *The Kenny Everett Video Cassette* (Thames TV, 1981), before presenting *The Kenny Everett Television Show* (1982–8) for the BBC. If this lacked the verve and originality (and Hot Gossip) of the *Video Show*, it nevertheless produced Everett's greatest video gag, a Bee Gees sketch in which Everett played all three toothsome, tandoori-tanned brothers at the same time. Interviewed (by Everett), the 'Bees Gees' answered all questions with lines from their songs. Asked, 'How do you sell so many records?', they chorused, 'Because we're living in a world of fools…' It was one of the truly hysterically funny moments of eighties British comedy.

A prominent supporter of the Conservative Party (Everett once did a Tory Conference sketch in which he suggested 'we should bomb Russia' and 'kick away' the walking stick of then Labour leader Michael Foot), Everett died of an AIDS-related condition in 1995.

KING OF THE HILL

USA 1997–, 30+ x 30m, col Fox. 20th Century Fox Television/Film Roman Productions/3 Arts Entertainments. UK tx *1997– C4.*

CR *Mike Judge, Greg Daniels.* **EXEC PR** *Howard Klein, Phil Roman, Michael Rotenberg, Greg Daniels, Mike Judge.* **PR** *Joseph A Boucher, Richard Raynis.* **DR** *Various, including Jeff Myers, Monte Young, Chuck Sheetz, Cyndi Tang, Tricia Garcia, Wesley*

▶▶▶ King of the Hill, *another looney 'toon success for Mike Judge.*

Archer, Shain Cashman, Klay Hall, Adam Kuhlman, Gary McCarver, John Rice. **WR** *Various, including Mike Judge, Greg Daniels, Johnny Hardwick, Jim Dauterive.* **MUS** *Brian David Blush and Roger Meade Clyne (theme).* **CAST** *(voices)* Hank Hill/Boomhauer/Dooley *Mike Judge* Peggy Hill *Kathy Najimy* Bobby Hill *Pamela Segall* Luanne Platter/Joseph Gribble *Britanny Murphy* Dale Gribble *Johnny Hardwick* Bill Dauterive *Stephen Root.*

Hank Hill resides in the 'burb of Arlen, Texas, with his wife Peggy, awkward twelve-year-old son Bobby, and live-in niece Luanne. The assistant manager of the Strickland Propane company, Hank likes to drink beer with his redneck buddies, ride his pick-up truck, and keep his tools in the right place. The voice of reason – as he sees it – in a world gone awry, he tries to keep life simple.

The problem is, Hank is besieged by his own idiosyncrasies (he's anally retentive to the degree that he measures the grass after cutting), those of his family, and those of the world. And his friends – military barber Bill Dauterive, conspiracy theorist Dale Gribble, and gibberish-spouting Boomhauer – are plain crazy.

An Everydad, Hank Hill was the lead character in *King of the Hill,* an animated ironic browse through the American suburban South. Co-fathered by Mike Judge of >*Beavis and Butt-head* and Greg Daniels from >*The Simpsons, King of the Hill* combined obvious elements of both those shows (the familyness of *The Simpsons,* the distinctive graphic simplicity of *B&B*) in a way that viewers liked; the show was the first major post-*Simpsons* cartoon hit.

Looked at another way, however, what *King of the Hill* left out from its precursors was equally important to its success, viz. the *Simpsons*' busy cultural referencing and *B&B*'s nihilism. Written with casual, ironic genius, *King of the Hill* poked fun at its targets, but not too hard, while its slack pace allowed time for characterization. (The dim-witted, monotone Hill clan had some pleasingly amusing quirks: Bobby, in between trying to please his father – but never quite succeeding – by participating in Little League, could watch TV for hours without moving a muscle; while Peggy, scribe of the column 'Peggy Hill's Musins' for the local paper, had such large feet she had to drive a hundred miles to 'Lubbock's Very Big Shoes' for her footwear.) The theme running through the show, if you cared to look, was the right of Americans to be left alone.

KNOWING ME, KNOWING YOU... WITH ALAN PARTRIDGE

UK 1994–5, 6 x 30m, 1 x 50m, col BBC2. Talkback. **EXEC PR** *Peter Fincham.* **PR** *Armando Iannucci.* **DR** *Dominic Brigstocke.* **WR** *Steve Coogan, Henry Normal, Patrick Marber.* **CAST** *Steve Coogan, with Rebecca Front, Doon Mackichan, David Schneider.*

Spoof chat show hosted by the smarmy, logorrhoeic and hugely incompetent 'Alan Partridge'. A-ha.

A transfer from radio to TV (via >*The Day Today*) of comedian Steve Coogan's presenter persona, initially a Pringle-clad sportscaster but then

elevated to talkshow supremo. In the new medium, Partridge proved to be an even more squirmingly accurate send-up of the self-importance of broadcasting and those who front it. A 1995 Xmas special was broadcast under the title of 'Knowing Me, Knowing Yule with Alan Partridge'; naturally, the joys of Christmas were lost on Partridge, who resorted to telling Norwich bellringers to 'shut up', shamelessly dropping plugs for the car brand he

A-ha! Steve Coogan (standing) as spoof talkshow supremo Alan Partridge in Knowing Me, Knowing You.

advertised (Rover Vitesse), and erroneously and insensitively comparing a disabled golf caddy to other disabled people 'like Einstein and Daniel Day-Lewis'.

The most telegenic of the wave of absurdist nineties humourists who grew around Radio 4's 'On the Hour', Coogan first came to TV providing voices for >*Spitting Image* (Neil Kinnock, Mick Jagger) and Allied Carpets advertisements. In 1993 he developed the characters of lager-drinking Mancunian Paul ('bag o'shite') Calf and his shag-happy sister Pauline Calf for *Saturday Zoo,* these developing through *Paul Calf's Video Diary* into the immortal 1994 *Three Fights, Two Weddings and a Funeral* (aka *Pauline Calf's Wedding Video*), which was awarded a BAFTA. The character of Paul Calf reappeared in the 1995 series *Coogan's Run,* which also memorably featured Coogan's nerdy software salesman Gareth Cheeseman, an invention who did little for the sales of the Ford Probe. In the same year Partridge himself reappeared in 'The [General] Election Night Armistice' episode of *The Saturday Night Armistice* show, coming back to the small screen for a fully-fledged series, *I'm Alan Partridge,* in 1997. This refined the abusive, self-hating Partridge to a yet funnier degree. A-ha.

KYTV

UK 1990–3, 18 x 30m, col BBC2. BBC TV.

PR *Jamie Rix.* **DR** *John Kilby, John Stroud.* **WR** *Angus Deayton, Geoffrey Perkins.* **MUS** *Philip Pope.*
CAST Mike Channel *Angus Deayton* Mike Flex *Geoffrey Perkins* Anna Daptor *Helen Atkinson Wood* Martin Brown *Michael Fenton-Stevens* Continuity Announcer *Philip Pope.*

Sitcom parodying satellite TV. Set in station KYTV, named for fictitious Sir Kenneth Yellowhammer ('When it comes to quality, we stop at nothing'), it remorselessly spoofed every aspect of satellite programming, in particular the technical deficiencies and cultural crudity that dogged the extraterrestrial networks in the early eighties. The target was difficult to miss, but sometimes the *KYTV* team skewered it with panache. A spoof fly-on-the-wall documentary about a suburban family, in which the said clan descended into alcoholism, crime and working in a petrol station, and suffered the paedophile attentions of the KYTV interviewer, was a particular highlight. Other episodic highlights included a poor British version of the glitzy *Baywatch,* entitled 'Herne Bay Watch', and 'The Making of David Chizzlenut' – 'a chance to look behind the scenes of a classic drama production'. The show came from the same team who had written and presented Radio 4's lampoon of local commercial radio, *Radio Active,* prime among them the rising Angus Deayton *(Have I Got News for You,* >*One Foot in the Grave).* The title of *KYTV* was intended to suggest a brand of lubricant jelly commonly used as a sex aid.

The Larry Sanders Show

USA 1992–8, 88+ x 30m, col HBO. HBO/Brillstein-Grey Productions. UK tx *1995– BBC2.*

EXEC PR *Brad Grey, Garry Shandling, Peter Tolan, Paul Simms.* **PR** *John Ziffren, Paul Simms.* **DR** *Various, including Todd Holland, Garry Shandling, Dennis Erdman, Paul Flaherty, Thomas Schlamme, Michael Lehman, John Riggi, Ken Kwapis.* **WR** *Various, including Garry Shandling, Peter Tolan,*

Maya Forbes, Steve Levitan, Jon Vitti. **CAST** Larry Sanders *Garry Shandling* Artie (Arthur) *Rip Torn* Hank Kingsley *Jeffrey Tambor* Paula *Janeane Garafalo* Jeannie Sanders *Megan Gallagher* Phil *Wally Ward* Jerry *Jerry Piven* Beverly *Penny Johnson* Darlene *Linda Doucett.*

Spoof TV chat show. Modelled on David Letterman and Jerry Langford (the character played by Jerry Lewis in the movie *King of Comedy*), 'host' Sanders oozed schmooze on screen and vitriol off, and paranoid ego all the while. A wincingly brilliant lampoon of its subject, with masterful performances by Garry Shandling (grown inestimably in comic maturity since >*It's Garry Shandling's Show*) in the title role, nuclear-powered Rip Torn as producer Artie, and Jeffrey Tambor as Sanders' second banana, the obsequious Hank 'Hey Now' Kingsley (a character not a million miles from Johnny Carson's sidekick, Ed McMahon).

Viciousness, expletives and arty overlapping conversations all ensured the programme low ratings. However, those who liked it liked it, and happened to be the glitterati of the US screen trade. Robin Williams, Sharon Stone, Roseanne, Billy Crystal, David Duchovny, Jay Leno and the Letterman himself all appeared. In a proof positive that life and art are just the same, actress Linda Doucett (who played Hank's comely assistant Darlene) was removed from the show when she ceased to be Shandling's girlfriend (to be replaced by Scott Thompson from the Canadian sitcom *Kids in the Hall*). Moreover, Shandling then hit his manager (and best friend) Brad Grey for a $100 million lawsuit, because Grey had not given Shandling a cut of the profits from his other clients...

The Larry Sanders Show came to an end in 1998, with a running theme of the network trying to replace star Sanders, but not before humiliating him by making him hug his guests. Don't flip!

Among the classic *Sanders* are: 'Broadcast Nudes' (in which Hugh Heffner and Hank want Darlene to pose for *Playboy*, but 'very tasteful, no bush'); 'Hank's Wedding'; Hank's Sex Tapes'; and 'Hank's Night in the Sun'.

>> ***Producer Artie to host Larry Sanders: 'You're a talkshow animal... You're like one of those goddam creatures out of Greek mythology. Half man, half desk.'*** <<

LAST OF THE SUMMER WINE

UK 1973–, 171 x 30m, 4 x 60m, col BBC1. BBC TV.

CR *Roy Clarke.* **PR** *James Gilbert, Bernard Thompson, Sydney Lotterby, Alan J W Bell.* **DR** *Various, including Bernard Thompson, Sydney Lotterby, Alan J W Bell.* **WR** *Roy Clarke.* **CAST** William 'Compo' Simmonite *Bill Owen* Norman 'Cleggy' Clegg *Peter Sallis* Cyril Blamire *Michael Bates* Foggy Dewhurst *Brian Wilde* Seymour Utterthwaite *Michael Aldridge* Sid *John Comer* Ivy *Jane Freeman* Nora Batty *Kathy Staff* Wally Batty *Joe Gladwin* Wesley Pegden *Gordon Wharmby* Edie Pegden *Thora Hird* Eli *Danny O'Dea* Smiler *Stephen Lewis* Auntie Wainwright *Jean Alexander.* Video *BBC.*

Long, long-running sitcom (indeed, the world's longest-running sitcom) about three reprobate Yorkshire pensioners, developed from a 1973 *Comedy Playhouse* piece entitled 'Of Funerals and Fish' by Roy Clarke (later >*Open All Hours, Rosie,* >*Keeping Up Appearances*). Filmed on location in Holmfirth, the show was novel in that it asked you to laugh with OAPs, rather than at them (in this predating >*The Golden Girls* by a decade). The original terrible threesome were unkempt Compo (Bill Owen, ex-lyricist for Ken Dodd), widower Norman 'Cleggy' Clegg and ex-Signals sergeant Blamire, with their adventures turning into misadventures either through Compo's delinquent behaviour or Blamire's misplaced self-confidence. Over the passing seasons Blamire (Michael Bates, also >*It Ain't Half Hot, Mum,* d. 1976) was replaced by another ex-army man, Foggy Dewhurst, then by retired teacher Seymour Utterthwaite, before Dewhurst returned. It was notable that, whatever the particular configuration of the three characters, their (essentially overgrown schoolboy) antics were always met with stony-faced disapproval by the village's womenfolk, especially Nora Batty (Compo's landlady and improbable object of desire, her wrinkly-stockinged legs like 'a pair of Chinese lanterns') and café proprietor Ivy; underneath the geriatric novelty of *Last of the Summer Wine* lurked the old stalwart of British TV comedy: the battle of the sexes. That and a sense of gentle, peculiarly English whimsy, with an almost exclamation mark-free humour built out of fond observation, character and meandering conversation...

In 1988–90, a prequel, *First of the Summer Wine,* was aired on BBC1 (12 x 30m) featuring Compo, Cleggy, Utterthwaite and Dewhurst in their pre-war Dales youth.

Clegg: 'We might all have been better off if the Wright brothers 'ad never got off the ground with an aeroplane.'

Blamire: 'There's always the atomic bomb.'

Clegg: 'I know. But if they'd had to drop it from a bicycle it might 'ave made them think a bit...'

LAVERNE AND SHIRLEY

USA 1976–83, 178 x 25m, col ABC. Miller-Milkis/ Henderson/Paramount TV. UK tx *1977–83 ITV.*

CR *Garry K Marshall.* **EXEC PR** *Garry K Marshall, Thomas L Miller, Edward K Milkis.* **DR** *Various, including James Burrows, Jay Sandrich, Howard Storm, Joel Zwick.* **WR** *Various, including Michael McKean, David L Lander.* **MUS** *Norman Grimble and Charles Fox ('Making Our Dreams Come True' theme).* **CAST** Laverne DeFazio *Penny Marshall* Shirley Feeney *Cindy Williams* Andrew 'Squiggy' Squigman *David L Lander* Lenny Kosnoski *Michael McKean* Carmine Ragusa *Eddie Mekka* Frank DeFazio *Phil Foster* Edna Babbish *Betty Garrett*

A smash hit for America's ABC network and, like >*Mork and Mindy,* a spin-off from >*Happy Days.* In its original format the slapstick show concerned two feisty fifties girls, Laverne DeFazio and Shirley Feeney, who worked as bottle cappers at Milwaukee's Shotz Brewery and roomed together at 730 Hampton Street. After their dismissal from

Laverne and Shirley *was one of two hit spin-offs from* Happy Days: *the other was* Mork and Mindy.

the brewery in the 1980 season, the duo moved to California, where they hoped to break into the movies but instead ended up behind the counter of the Bardwell Department Store. They were accompanied in their move west by comic greaser neighbour-friends, Lenny (Michael McKean from >*Saturday Night Live*) and Squiggy (David L Lander, aka David Landau), who took up the unlikely occupation of talent scouting for the movies. When a contract dispute forced actress Cindy Williams (born Cynthia Williams) to leave the show, her character married an army medic and moved overseas, so ending a long-running comedic worry about Shirley retaining her virginity in an increasingly permissive age. The more raucous Laverne (favourite drink: milk and Pepsi mixed), was left alone as a single gal wage-slaving for the Ajax Aerospace Company and hoping to find romance.

One of the few blue-collar sitcoms (and one of the very few to centre on women), *Laverne and*

Shirley was created by Garry K Marshall, who cast his sister Penny (previously >*The Bob Newhart Show*) in the role of Laverne. Penny Marshall – the sometime spouse of Rob Reiner from >*All in the Family* – later became a big-shot Hollywood director, helming such features as *Awakenings, Big, Jumping Jack Flash* and A *League of their Own*.

Two cartoon versions of *Laverne and Shirley* were made by Hanna-Barbera, *Laverne and Shirley in the Army* (1981–2) and *Laverne and Shirley with the Fonz* (1982–3).

LEAVE IT TO BEAVER

USA 1957–63, 234 x 30m, bw CBS/ABC. Gomalco Productions/Universal TV.

CR *Bob Mosher, Joe Connelly.* **PR** *Harry Ackerman, Joe Connelly, Bob Mosher.* **DR** *Various, including Norman Tokar, Hugh Beaumont.* **WR** *Various, including Joe Connelly, Bob Mosher, Dick Conway, Roland MacLane.* **MUS** *Dave Khan (theme), Melvin Lenard.* **CAST** June Cleaver *Barbara Billingsley* Ward Cleaver *Hugh Beaumont* Theodore 'Beaver' Cleaver *Jerry Mathers* Wally Cleaver *Tony Dow* Eddie Haskell *Ken Osmond* Miss Canfield *Diane Brewster* Miss Landers *Sue Randall* Larry Mondello *Rusty Stevens* Whitey Whitney *Stanley Fafara* Clarence 'Lumpy' Rutherford *Frank Bank* Mr Fred Rutherford *Richard Deacon* Gilbert Bates *Stephen Talbot.*

Long-running family sitcom – the first to deal with life from a kid's point of view – set within the middle-class Cleaver household of 485 Maple Drive (later 211 Pine Street), Mayfield, U S of A. Kindly Ward and June Cleaver (a Mom always ready with neat hair and milk and cookies) were the perfect parents for offspring Theodore 'Beaver' Cleaver – aged seven when the series began – and his older

▼▼▼ *For faminy life from the kids' point of view,* Leave It To Beaver.

brother Wally, aged twelve. Larry, Whitey and Gilbert were Beaver's pals, and Wally's buddies were Clarence 'Lumpy' Rutherford (whose father Fred was Ward's boss) and the unctuous Eddie Haskell – sycophant to adults, bully to rugrats, and probably the first really nasty kid on TV. Miss Canfield and Miss Landers were Beaver's schoolteachers.

Beaver was a typically rumbustious youth, more interested in pet frogs than in girls, while Wally was beginning to discover that there were other things in life than pets'n'toys, and the show's storylines dwelt on the good-natured tiffs between the siblings and their necessary chidings from their ever-loving elders. Over the six years that the show ran, the stories gradually moved away from the little boy premise until, in the final season, Beaver was about to enter his teens and Wally was ready for college. Yet, throughout, Beaver and Wally and their assorted buddies were reassuringly, believably real, unlike the saccharine goody two-shoes who infested most family sitcoms in the late fifties (a time when the genre was in full spate, a reflection of the baby boom, with Danny Thomas, >*Father Knows Best, The Donna Reed Show, The Real McCoys* and *Dennis the Menace* all on air).

Leave It To Beaver premiered on CBS in October 1957 and moved to ABC a year later. In the 1957 pilot, Ward Cleaver was played by Casey Adams, Wally by Paul Sullivan, and 'Frankie', an Eddie Haskell-like brat, by Harry Shearer, later a regular on >*Saturday Night Live.* Creators Mosher and Connelly had written together since 1942 on over 1,500 >*Amos'n'Andy* radio and TV scripts. They went on to create >*The Munsters,* but left some of their best dialogue back in suburban Mayfield.

»

June Cleaver: 'Ward, Wally's best friend is Eddie Haskell and yours is Fred Rutherford. What's wrong with this family?'

Ward: 'Can I help it if both Wally and I are humanitarians?'

June: 'Oh, you have a girl, Eddie?'

Eddie Haskell: 'Oh, yes. She goes away to boarding school. My father says that's a pretty good sign her family has money. My father says you shouldn't waste time with people who don't count.'

June: 'Well, it's nice of you to come over anyway, Eddie.'

«

Twenty years after *Leave It To Beaver* ended its original run, the Cleaver family, played by virtually all the original cast, were reunited in a TV movie, *Still the Beaver* (1983). Beaver was now thirty-three, grossly overweight, out of work and undergoing a divorce, and was having trouble communicating with his two young sons. Wally was a successful attorney but had troubles at home, while Eddie Haskell was a crooked contractor. Dad was no longer around (actor Hugh Beaumont had died) and wife June made regular trips to his grave to ask advice. Viewers apparently wanted more, and so a series, *Still the Beaver,* ran on the Disney Channel, 1985–6, followed by *The New Leave It To Beaver* in 1986 on WTBS. The original *Leave It To Beaver* remains one of the most popular reruns in America.

Beaver trivia: Ken Osmond, who acted Eddie Haskell, later joined the LAPD and was awarded a medal for valour; June's maiden name was Bronson; Hugh Beaumont was an active Methodist lay preacher; the schools Wally and Beaver attended were Mayfield High School and Grant Avenue Grammar School; the place where they played ball was Metzger's Field; actress Barbara Billingsley always wore a string of pearls around her neck, because she was self-conscious about a deep wrinkle that looked like a scar.

THE LENNY HENRY SHOW

UK 1984–8, 36 x 30m, col BBC1. BBC TV/Crucial Films.

CR *Lenny Henry, Stan Hey, Andrew Nickolds.* **PR** *Geoff Posner, Geoff Atkinson.* **DR** *Various, including Juliet May.* **WR** *Lenny Henry, Andrew Nickolds, Stan Hey.* **CAST** *Lenny Henry, with Vas Blackwood, Gina McKee, Ellen Thomas, Pip Torrens, Naim Khan, Nimmy March, Michael Mears, Malcolm Rennie.*

Showcase for talents of black British comedian Lenny Henry. Over the seasons it changed humorous hue, as Henry flirted with formats (stand-up, sketches, sitcom), although a constant was his talent for developing broad comic caricatures, such as PC Ganga, drag queen Deeva, Jamaican pensioner Deakus, Reverend Nat West and, especially, testosteroned crooner Theosophilus P Wildebeest. (In an immortal gag, Wildebeest once asked a female member of the audience, 'Do you have any African in you? Do you want some?') For the 1987–8 season, the show was entirely given over to a twelve-episode sitcom built around Henry's egotistical DJ, Delbert Wilkins, who ran a pirate radio station in London – the Brixton Broadcasting Corporation. He was assisted in this by his more responsible chum, Winston (Vas Blackwood). 'Crucial'.

A former winner of talent programme *New Faces,* Henry (born Lenworth Henry, 1958) got his screen break on the Saturday morning kiddie classic *Tiswas,* then joined the cast of the all-black, South London-set sitcom *The Fosters* in 1976. Skit show *Three of a Kind,* with Tracey Ullman and David Copperfield, followed in 1981, then an ill-advised sojourn on *OTT,* Central's much-panned adult version of *Tiswas.* Three years later Henry switched to the BBC with his own *Show,* by which time exposure to the alternative comedy scene (not least because Henry had married >*Comic Strip* actress Dawn French) had moved Henry towards a more radical humour, less dependent on the clubland-type gags he started out with. More recently (1994–), Henry led the restaurant sitcom *Chef!,* in which he played temperamental meistercook Gareth Blackstock.

THE LIFE OF RILEY

USA 1949–50, 20 x 30m, bw DuMont, 1953–8, 90 x 30m, bw NBC. UK tx *1959–60 ITV.*

PR *Andy Potter, Irving Brecher, Tom McNight.* **CAST** Chester A Riley *Jackie Gleason/William Bendix (1953–8)* Peg Riley *Rosemary DeCamp/Marjorie Reynolds (1953–8)* Junior *Lanny Rees/Wesley Morgan (1953–8)* Babs *Gloria Winters/Lugene Sanders (1953–8)* Jim Gillis *Sid Tomack/Tom D'Andrea* Honeybee Gillis *Gloria Blondell (1953–8)* Digby 'Digger' O'Dell *John Brown.*

Misadventures of Chester A Riley, a none-too-bright aircraft riveter who lived at 113 Blue View Terrace, Los Angeles, where he opined from his armchair on the world's problems and interfered in family life – with chaotic results. Long-suffering wife Peg and children Junior and Babs were left to sort out the comic mess. Also seen were Riley's gravedigger friend Digby O'Dell ('Guess I'd better be shovelling off') and sardonic friend Jim Gillis.

The Life of Riley was the prototypical sitcom of the Bumbling Pop sort, and starred Jackie Gleason in its début 1949 season. Although Gleason's interpretation of the radio favourite secured the show an Emmy, it did not catch on with Joe Audience and the show was cancelled. (Gleason went on to >*The Honeymooners.*) When it was revived three years later, Riley was played by William Bendix – the actor who had played Riley on radio. In this form it enjoyed a five-year run. Riley's catchphrase was: 'What a revoltin' development this is!'

A 1948 pilot episode had featured yet another actor as Riley, Herb Vigran, later a stalwart on >*The Jack Benny Show.*

LIFE WITH FATHER

USA 1953–5, 26 x 25m, bw CBS. McCadden. UK tx *1963 ITV.*

PR *Ben Feiner, Fletcher Markle.* **CAST** Clarence Day Sr *Leon Ames* Vinnie Day (wife) *Lurene Tuttle* Clarence Day Jr *Ralph Reed/Steven Terrell* Whitney Day *Ronald Keith/B G Norman/Freddy Ridgeway* Harlan Day *Harvey Grant* John Day *Freddie Leiston/Malcolm Cassell* Margaret *Dorothy Bernard.*

Domestic sitcom based on the popular book, play and film by Clarence Day. Set in 1880s New York, it chronicled the misadventures of the upper-middle-class Day family, as ruled over by their stubbornly Victorian pater.

Likeable early evening fare, with convincing period atmosphere, and notable for being the first live colour show made in Hollywood for US network TV. The part of Day senior was taken by veteran character actor Leon Ames (born Leon Waycoff), shortly to star in another sitcom, >*Mister Ed.* Ames was the winner, in 1981, of a lifetime achievement award from the Screen Actors Guild. Meanwhile, further down the cast list, actress Marion Ross, later Mrs Cunningham in >*Happy Days,* was to be found as the maid, Nora.

THE LIKELY LADS

UK 1965–9, 26 x 30m, bw/col BBC2/BBC1. BBC TV.

CR *Ian La Frenais and Dick Clement.* **PR** *Dick Clement.* **WR** *Ian La Frenais and Dick Clement.* **MUS** *Ronnie Hazlehurst.* **CAST** Terry Collier *James Bolam* Bob Ferris *Rodney Bewes* Audrey (Terry's sister) *Sheila Fern.*

A sitcom which arose out of a sketch Dick Clement wrote with friend Ian La Frenais for the exam part of his BBC directors course. Set in the North-East of England, it concerned two young electrical workers, Terry Collier (ex-trainee chartered accountant James Bolam, *When the Boat Comes In, Only When I Laugh*) and Bob Ferris (Rodney Bewes, *Dear Mother, Love Albert*), who

Rodney Bewes (left) and James Bolam as The Likely Lads *brewing up trouble and bitter laughs over a pint of beer.*

were markedly different in character and attitudes, particularly towards the class system. Terry was brash, aggressive, only interested in girls, and resigned to his proletarian station in life. Bob was Terry's alter ego, diffident, cautious, scared of authority (particularly if it had a posh accent), and almost pitiful in his belief that he could escape the class trap if he only worked hard enough. (It was not difficult to see the show as a critique of the supposed social mobility of the Swinging Sixties.) Despite their over-a-pint philosophizing, each would view the other's approach with leaden dismay. Not least because their escapades, usually originated by Terry, always ended in tears.

In 1973 Terry and Bob were brought back for a revival, *Whatever Happened to the Likely Lads?* (BBC1, 1973–4, 47 x 30m). Unusually for a sequel, this was as well written and acted as the original and, if anything, even sharper on the foibles of the class system. Here the ill-fated pair were four years older, with Terry having spent the intervening time in the army and a failed marriage. Bob, meanwhile, had risen up the career ladder to a white-collar job and become engaged to the boss's pushy daughter, the frightening Thelma (Brigit Forsyth). Bob had also bought a house of his own and taken to holidays on the Costa Brava and meals in restaurants. Terry's attack on such bourgeois delusions was remorseless. There was also a touching vein of social commentary on the bewildering changes to the industrial North-East during the seventies.

With the end of the TV run (by which time Bob and Thelma had married), the misadventures of Bob and Terry continued in a 1975 radio version, then a 1976 feature film, *The Likely Lads*.

A Little Bit of Wisdom

UK 1974–6, 7 x 25m, col (1976 season) ITV. ATV.

PR *Les Chatfield.* **WR** *Lew Schwarz, John Kane, Jon Watkins, Ronnie Taylor.* **CAST** Norman Wisdom *himself* Albert Clark *Robert Keegan* Linda Clark *Frances White* Alec Potter *Neil McCarthy.*

A hot star after the success of the 1953 movie *Trouble in Store,* the 'gump'-suited, peaked-capped Norman Wisdom became a regular fixture on the small screen in such variety-oriented shows as *It's Norman* (1953), and *The Norman Wisdom Show* (BBC, 1956). Wisdom also tried his hand at the sitcom in *Norman* (ITV, 1970), *Nobody is Norman Wisdom* (ITV, 1973) and the last season of *A Little Bit of Wisdom* (the first two seasons presented non-linked playlets). In this seven-week stint, Wisdom was given a permanent job as a clerk in a builder's office, where he caused slapstick mayhem in between his blushes at the boss's daughter. It persuaded 7.8 million viewers to tune in. Thereafter, Wisdom largely disappeared from the British screen, although he continued to be a superstar in the Stalinist country of Albania, where he was dictator Enver Hoxha's favourite artiste.

The Liver Birds

UK 1969–78, 79 x 30m, bw/col BBC1. BBC TV.

CR *Carla Lane, Myra Taylor, Lew Schwarz.* **PR** *Sydney Lotterby, Douglas Argent, Roger Race.* **DR** *Ray Butt, Bernard Thompson, Douglas Argent.* **WR** *Carla Lane, Myra Taylor, Lew Schwarz.* **MUS** *The Scaffold (theme), Ronnie Hazlehurst.* **CAST** Beryl Hennessey *Polly James* Dawn *Pauline Collins* Sandra Hutchinson *Nerys Hughes* Mrs Hutchinson *Mollie Sugden* Carol Boswell *Elizabeth Estensen* Mrs Boswell *Eileen Kennally/Carmel McSharry* Lucien Boswell *Michael Angelis* Paul *John Nettles* Robert *Jonathan Lynn* Derek Paynton *Tom Chadbon.*

Classic flatshare sitcom, usually attributed to Carla Lane alone, but in fact created with fellow housewife Myra Taylor and veteran screen scribe Lew Schwarz. It began as a 1969 *Comedy Playhouse* one-off, before going into a series of three episodes later the same year. In these episodes the two 'Birds' sharing the poky bedsit in

Huskisson Road, Liverpool, were Pauline Collins' prim Dawn and Polly James' raucous Beryl, but James and Collins never rapported and in January 1971 when the show went into full production, Nerys Hughes arrived to play the diffident, socially aspirant Sandra – the perfect foil. The Birds then set forth on a season of 'likely girl', fella-chasing misadventures around Merseyside, the perfect beat for their chirpy antics. By the third season, however, Lane had gone solo as writer (though the BBC brought in, bizarrely enough, >*Monty Python*'s Eric Idle to act as her script editor), and she began to introduce the undertone of lonesome tragicomedy which would prove her TV trademark. Accordingly, the Birds, though they continued to room together, began to have separate lives: Sandra began a steady relationship with Paul (a pre-*Bergerac* John Nettles) and in 1974, on the same day as Princess Anne's wedding, Beryl married Robert (played by

Beryl (left) and Sandra were the flat-sharing Liver Birds.

Jonathan Lynn, previously >*Doctor in the House*, later the co-writer of >*Yes, Minister*) and left the series. Her successor was Carol Boswell, who wore multi-coloured jumpsuits and red hair, and had a morose brother called Lucien, whose hobby of rabbit-keeping led to the catchphrase, 'It's me rabbits...' (The show's other catchphrase was the durable, 'You dancing?'/'You asking?' from the Scaffold's theme lyric.) Carol's Catholic, gin-swilling Ma, meanwhile, became the prototype for *Bread*'s Nellie Boswell, down to the shared surname. The series ended with Sandra finding a suitable match in vet Derek. It was 1978 and the days of the freewheeling *Liver Birds* were over.

A 1996 revival (produced by Philip Kampff) only proved the point. Here Nerys Hughes and Polly James played their original characters as older, but not necessarily wiser. Shorn of their youth and original social context, they were tragic, certainly, but not at all comic.

THE LOVERS

UK 1970–1, 14 x 30m, col ITV. Granada.

CR *Jack Rosenthal.* **PR** *Jack Rosenthal, Les Chatfield.* **DR** *Michael Apted.* **WR** *Jack Rosenthal, Geoffrey Lancashire.* **MUS** *Derek Hilton (theme).* **CAST** Geoffrey ('Bubbles Bon Bon') *Richard Beckinsale* Beryl *Paula Wilcox* Mum (Beryl's) *Joan Scott* Roland *Robin Nedwell.*

Jack Rosenthal sitcom in which Paula Wilcox sought to preserve her virginity on the sitting-room sofa against the desperate advances of Richard Beckinsale (later >*Rising Damp*, >*Porridge*), who was trying to lose his. To this end, Beckinsale's gauche Geoffrey, a Manchester bank clerk, agreed to a trial marriage, even a real engagement. All to no avail. (The trial marriage plot looked hopeful, until the scheming Beryl brought along a chaperone.) The series reached number three in the BARB ratings in 1971.

Dated, but funny. A big-screen version, with Wilcox still resisting 'Percy Filth', was released by British Lion in 1972. Wilcox virtually reprised her frigid role in >*Man About the House*.

LOVE THY NEIGHBOUR

UK 1972–6, 40 x 25m, col ITV. Thames TV.

CR *Harry Driver and Vince Powell.* **PR** *Ronnie Baxter, Stuart Allen, Anthony Parker.* **DR** *Stuart Allen, Ronnie Baxter.* **WR** *Various, including Harry Driver and Vince Powell, Johnnie Mortimer, Sid Colin, Lawrie Wyman and George Evans.* **CAST** Eddie Booth *Jack Smethurst* Joan Booth *Kate Williams* Barbie Reynolds *Nina Baden-Semper* Bill Reynolds *Rudolph Walker* Arthur *Tommy Godfrey* Jacko Jackson *Keith Marsh* Nobby Garside *Paul Luty.* Video *BRAVE/SMO.*

One of the first British comedies to deal exclusively with the subject of race relations, placing bigoted white trade unionist Eddie Booth and wife next door to black couple, Bill and Barbie Reynolds. Eddie, whose aim in life was to preserve 'our white heritage', called his neighbour 'Sambo' and 'nig-nog'; in turn, Bill called him 'snowflake' and 'honky'. Much of the bickering took place at the workers' social club, where Eddie was supported by cronies Jacko, Arthur and Nobby. To add another element of conflict, Eddie was a socialist and Bill a Tory. Meanwhile, as is so often the case in sitcomland, the two wives got on like a house on fire.

Co-creator Vince Powell claimed that the intention behind the show's trade in racist epithets 'was to take the sting out of them, and make them less hurtful'. Whatever, it was never very funny, but its novel subject matter kept it high in the ratings, frequently in top position, for five years. If politically unsophisticated, it at least got two black characters into a prime-time British comedy and almost certainly paved the way for Britain's first all-black comedy series, *The Fosters* (1976–7, LWT, starring Norman Beaton, Lenny Henry and Carmen Munroe).

In 1973 a feature film version of *Love Thy Neighbour (by EMI and Hammer)* was released on a suspecting public in the UK, while in the USA an attempt to repeat the show's success, also called *Love Thy Neighbour* (starring Ron Masak and Harrison Page, and set in San Fernando), lasted a bare season on ABC.

Writers Vince Powell and Harry Driver began their careers as a comedy double act, but turned to scriptwriting when Driver contracted polio. Their shows include >*George and the Dragon,* >*Never Mind the Quality, Feel the Width, For the Love of Ada, Spring and Autumn, Nearest and Dearest.* They jointly contributed to *Harry Worth* and >*Bless This House,* while Driver alone was a regular storyliner for sudster *Coronation Street.*

MAN ABOUT THE HOUSE

UK 1973–6, 39 x 25m, col ITV. Thames TV.

CR *Johnnie Mortimer and Brian Cooke.* **PR** *Peter Frazer-Jones.* **WR** *Johnnie Mortimer and Brian Cooke.* **CAST** Chrissy Plummer *Paula Wilcox* Jo *Sally Thomsett* Robin Tripp *Richard O'Sullivan* George Roper *Brian Murphy* Mildred Roper *Yootha Joyce.*

Popular Johnnie Mortimer and Brian Cooke sitcom about two chicks (prissy Chrissy, dumb-blonde Jo) who inadvertently ended up sharing their Earls Court flat with a guy (student chef Robin). Since, in the seventies, mixed-sex households were considered risqué, there resulted lots of 'whoops-I-didn't-know-you-were-in-the-bath' gags and hiding from visiting old-fashioned mums.

The trio's basement-living, mean-minded landlord and his sex-starved wife were eventually spun off to their own show, >*George and Mildred,* while Robin (played by Richard O'Sullivan from the >*Doctor in the House* cycle) went on to culinary disasters in >*Robin's Nest.* Actress Paula Wilcox, who in playing Chrissy virtually reprised her Beryl character from >*The Lovers,* moved on to another mildly risqué seventies sitcom, *Miss Jones and Son* (1977–8, 12 x 30m col, created by Richard Waring), in which she played a single mother.

A feature film version of *Man About the House* was released by Hammer/EMI in 1974, and the format sold to America as *Three's Company.* Broadcast on ABC, 1977–84, it starred John Ritter, Joyce DeWitt, Suzanne Somers, Audra Lindley and Norman Fell. Ray Charles and Julia Rinker sang the theme song.

The Many Loves of Dobie Gillis (aka Dobie Gillis)

USA 1959–63, 147 x 30m, bw CBS. CBS/20th Century Fox.

CR *Max Shulman.* **EXEC PR** *Martin Manulis.* **DR** *Various, including Rod Amateau, Stanley Z Cherry, Guy Scarpitta.* **WR** *Various, including Max Shulman, Joel Kane, Bud Nye, Arnold Horwitt.* **MUS** *Lionel Newman.* **CAST** Dobie Gillis *Dwayne Hickman* Maynard G Krebs *Bob Denver* Herbert T Gillis *Frank Faylen* Winifred 'Winnie' Gillis *Florida Friebus* Thalia Menninger *Tuesday Weld* Zelda Gilroy *Sheila James* Milton Armitage *Warren Beatty* Davey Gillis *Darryl Hickman* Chatsworth Osborne Jr *Steve Franken* Clarice Armitage/Mrs Chatsworth Osborne Sr *Doris Packer* Jerome Krens *Michael J Pollard.*

Dobie Gillis was the quintessential American fifties teenager, with an eye for money, beautiful cars and girls. Unfortunately, his romantic aspirations were somewhat hampered by his background – he was the grocer's son. One bane of his life was plain but brainy Zelda, who wanted to snare him; another was handsome Milton Armitage (Warren Beatty in one of his earliest screen roles), who rivalled him for the attentions of the girl he dreamed of, snobbish Thalia Menninger. Meanwhile, Dobie and goatee-bearded beatnik buddy Maynard ('work!?!') tried to ease through life with a minimum of effort, all the while pondering their futures. In an attempt to 'find themselves', Dobie and Maynard (who was played by Bob Denver, later >*Gilligan's Island*) enlisted in the army in the 1961 season but, not finding this to their liking, left for the easier pastures of St Peter Prior Junior College, where they remained until the last episode in 1963. The characters were developed from the stories of humourist Max Shulman.

In May 1977, CBS aired a pilot for an intended revival show, *Whatever Happened to Dobie Gillis?* This found the fortysomething Dobie Gillis married to... Zelda. He was also a partner in the family grocery shop. Maynard, still a beatnik, came back to visit. The new series never happened, but there was another reunion, *Bring Me the Head of Dobie Gillis*, in 1988.

Married... With Children

USA 1987–97, 259 x 30m, col Fox. Columbia Pictures TV/ELP Communications/Leavitt Productions. UK tx *1990– ITV/Sky1.*

CR *Michael G Moye, Ron Leavitt.* **EXEC PR** *Michael G Moye, Ron Leavitt, Katherine Green, Richard Gurman, Kim Weiskopf.* **PR** *John Maxwell Anderson, Sandy Sprung, Marcy Vosburgh, Kevin Curran, Barbara Blachot Cramer, Stacie Lipp.* **DR** *Various, including Linda Day, Tony Singletary, Amanda Bearse, Gerry Cohen, Sam W Orender.* **WR** *Various, including Michael G Moye and Ron Leavitt, Sandy Sprung and Marcy Vosburgh, Jerry Perzigian, Ralph R Farquhar.* **CAST** Al Bundy *Ed O'Neill* Peggy Bundy *Katey Sagal* Kelly Bundy *Christina Applegate* Bud Bundy *David Faustino* Steve Rhoades *David Garrison* Marcy Rhoades D'Arcy *Amanda Bearse* Jefferson D'Arcy *Ted McGinley* Buck the Dog *Buck.*

Like >*Roseanne* and >*The Simpsons,* a domestic comedy which kicked against TV's idealized portrait of the US suburban family – only more so. Centring on the bickering, white-trash Bundy household of Chicago, the show featured Al, a former high school football star turned salesman for Gary's Shoe Accessory, and his couch potato wife, Peg. Their quarrels were invariably about sexual dissatisfaction, particularly her too frequent amorous advances. This left Al – who much preferred reading about it to doing it – to peruse his favourite reading matter, *Playboy* and *Big 'Uns,* and Peg to go off shopping at the mall. Their children were equally unwholesome; daughter Kelly spent her evenings leaving heel prints on the headlining of assorted boyfriends' cars, while girlfriendless son Bud enjoyed the company of a blow-up doll. The Bundys were also notably keen on violence, with Al once telling a court that a burglar 'broke into my house, so I broke into his face'. Steve and Marcy were their neighbours.

Political correctness small. Comic popularity big. *Married... with Children* was one of America's longest-running sitcoms.

MARTY

UK 1968–9, 12 x 30m, bw BBC2. BBC TV.

PR *Dennis Main Wilson, Roger Race, Michael Mills.* **WR** *Marty Feldman, Barry Took, John Cleese, Graham Chapman, Terry Jones, Michael Palin, Philip Jenkinson, Donald Webster.* **CAST** *Marty Feldman, Tim Brooke-Taylor, John Junkin, Mary Miller.*

For so long the backroom scribbler and third banana, bug-eyed Marty Feldman finally got a show of his own, with this late-evening BBC2 shot. There was plenty of offbeat visual gagging – most of the future >*Monty Python* team were contributing scripts – and studio tomfoolery; unfortunately, the cautious Corporation decided to temper this with such Middle-England guests as *The Black and White Minstrel Show.* Of course, with something for everyone, the show could hardly fail. And didn't: it was quickly repeated on BBC1, where it reached number four in the ratings. *The Marty Feldman Comedy Machine* (ATV, 1971–2, with Spike Milligan) and *Marty Back Together Again* (BBC1, 1974) followed for TV, before Feldman decamped to Hollywood and the Mel Brooks movies, *Young Frankenstein* and *Silent Movie,* that would bring him international renown.

Feldman, who was the brother of actress Fenella Fielding, died in Mexico City in 1982.

THE MARY TYLER MOORE SHOW

USA 1970–7, 120 x 25m, col CBS. MTM Enterprises Inc. Production. UK tx *1972–5 BBC1.*

CR *James L Brooks, Allan Burns.* **PR** *James L Brooks, Allan Burns, David Davis, Stan Daniels, Ed Weinberger.* **DR** *Jay Sandrich, Marjorie Mullen, James Burrows, Harry Mastrogeorge, Mel Ferber, Doug Rogers.* **WR** *Various, including James L Brooks, Allan Burns, Treva Silverman, Ed Weinberger, Stan Daniels, David Lloyd, Bob Ellison.* **MUS** *Sonny Curtis ('Love Is All Around' theme lyrics,*

◄◄◄ *The cast of the Emmy-laden* The Mary Tyler Moore Show.

vocals), Pat Williams. **CAST** Mary Richards *Mary Tyler Moore* Lou Grant *Ed Asner* Ted Baxter *Ted Knight* Murray Slaughter *Gavin McCleod* Rhoda Morgenstern *Valerie Harper* Phyllis Lindstrom *Cloris Leachman* Georgette Frankin *Georgia Engel* Sue Anne Nivens *Betty White.*

After success in >*The Dick Van Dyke Show* Mary Tyler Moore spent several years in an ill-fated attempt to emulate Ginger Rogers, before starring in this show about Mary Richards, a career-girl-about-Minneapolis-town, who worked in the newsroom of TV station WJM-TV. The character represented a breakthrough in TV comedy history since she was, along with Marlo Thomas' Anne Marie in *That Girl* (1966–71), the first small-screen woman who was single by choice. Moreover, her sheer urbanity was a conscious attempt to win back younger city-dwellers to the CBS network after a decade of rural farce.

At WJM-TV Richards' boss was irascible but gold-hearted Lou Grant ('Oh! Mr Grant!' Richards was to exclaim on many an occasion); Murray Slaughter was the sarcastic head newscaster, and Ted Baxter the obtuse anchorman. Sue Anne Nivens (Betty White, >*The Golden Girls*) was the hostess of the station's *Happy Homemaker* show. While many of the laughs in this polished and realistic series – the dialogue in *TMTMS* was probably more natural than in any comedy to that date – came from the workplace situation, it also (like *The Dick Van Dyke Show*) focused on the main character's home life. Those featured on the domestic set included Richards' best friend, window dresser Rhoda Morgenstern, and busybody apartment neighbour Phyllis Lindstrom.

The show was created by James L Brooks (later >*Taxi*, >*The Simpsons*) and Allan Burns, and

Oh! Mr Grant

developed for television by Moore and her husband, Grant Tinker, via their company Mary Tyler Moore Productions. Subsequently, MTM became one of the main independent production companies in Hollywood, issuing such hits as *Hill Street Blues* and *Remington Steele*.

For many fans and critics alike, *The Mary Tyler Moore Show* represents the moment that the sitcom achieved the status of art. Over the show's seven-year run, it won a record twenty-seven Emmys, including Outstanding Comedy Emmys in 1975, 1976 and 1977. Among the Emmy awards was a 1976 Outstanding Writing in a Comedy Series Emmy for the last, highly emotional episode, 'The Final Show'. In this WJM-TV was taken over by a new owner who sacked all the staff – except Ted.

There was a bonanza of spin-off shows. They were: >*Rhoda, Lou Grant, The Betty White Show, The Love Boat* and *Phyllis*.

THE MARY WHITEHOUSE EXPERIENCE

UK 1990–2, 13 x 30m, col. Spitting Image Productions/BBC TV.

CR *Rob Newman, David Baddiel.* **PR** *Marcus Mortimer.* **WR** *Rob Newman, David Baddiel, Steve Punt, Hugh Dennis.* **CAST** *Rob Newman, David Baddiel, Steve Punt, Hugh Dennis.*

Transfer to TV of the alternative(ish) radio comedy show of the same name, unusual for its alternating (at a frenetic three-minute-culture pace) between stand-up and sketches. Irreverent and controversial – its name was an ironic reference to British TV's moral watchdog, Mary Whitehouse of the Viewers and Listeners Association – the *Experience* comprised writing-performing teams of Steve Punt and bishop's son Hugh Dennis (both previously >*Carrott's Lib*), and David Baddiel and Rob Newman. At a time when nearly all the other British rock'n'roll nineties comedians were appearing on Channel 4, the *Experience* proved a blush-saver for the BBC, so long the home of cutting-edge TV humour.

The 'fab four of TV comedy', as the BBC billed them, returned to TV in various permutations and projects, including *Newman and Baddiel in Pieces, Stab in the Dark* and *The Imaginatively Titled Third Punt and Dennis Show,* but only Baddiel's 1994 *Fantasy Football League* really scored. A laddish late-night mix of soccer trivia and humour, epitomized by the 'Phoenix from the Flames' recreations of great football moments, this was hosted by Baddiel with Frank Skinner from *Blue Heaven* and *Packet of Three,* his flatmate in real life.

M*A*S*H

USA 1972–83, 1 x 15m, 250 x 30m, col CBS. 20th Century Fox. UK tx *1973–84.*

CR *Larry Gelbart.* **EXEC PR** *Larry Gelbart, Gene Reynolds.* **PR** *Various, including Don Reo, Burt Metcalfe, Gene Reynolds.* **DR** *Various, including Larry Gelbart, Charles S Dubin, Don Weis, Gene Reynolds, Jackie Cooper, Burt Metcalfe, Alan Alda, Harry Morgan, Joan Darling, Hy Averback.* **WR** *Various, including Larry Gelbart, Alan Alda,*

Glen Charles, Les Charles, Jim Fritzell, Everett Greenbaum, Den Wilcox, Thad Mumford. **MUS** *Johnny Mandel ('Suicide is Painless' theme music), Mark Altman (theme lyrics).* **CAST** Capt Benjamin Franklin 'Hawkeye' Pierce *Alan Alda* Capt 'Trapper John' McIntyre *Wayne Rogers* Maj Margaret 'Hotlips' Houlihan *Loretta Swit* Cpl Maxwell Klinger *Jamie Farr* Lt Col Henry Blake *McLean Stevenson* Maj Frank Burns *Larry Linville* Capt B J Hunnicutt *Mike Farrell* Cpl Walter 'Radar' O'Reilly *Gary Burghoff* Maj Charles Emerson Winchester III *David Ogden Stiers* Col Sherman Potter *Harry Morgan* Father Francis Mulcahy *George Morgan/William Christopher.*

Through early morning fog I see
visions of the things to be
the pains that are withheld for me
I realise and I can see...
... that suicide is painless
It brings on many changes
and I can take or leave it if I please.

Developed from Robert Altman's 1970 hit movie about the misadventures of a weary MASH (Mobile Army Surgical Hospital) during the Korean War, this show was the unlikeliest hit comedy of the seventies. Not only did it satirize war at a time when the US was losing the Vietnam conflict, it also foregrounded such taboo TV subjects as interracial marriage, adultery and homosexuality. On its side it had witty, skilful writers and a likeable collection of oddball characters, notably sensitive-but-cynical surgeon Hawkeye Pierce, Trapper John, head nurse Major 'Hotlips' Houlihan (who, though censorious about other people's morals, was having an affair with Frank Burns, the most incompetent surgeon in the unit), telepathic clerk Radar, and transvestite theatre assistant Klinger (played by Jamie Farr, the only one of the cast to have served in Korea). Commanding officer Henry Blake ignored all antics as long as his doctors performed in the operating theatre. Though humorous, the show did not avoid the explicit physical and emotional detail of war. In a key episode, 'Sometimes You Hear the Bullet', a friend of Hawkeye's died on the operating table, much to the network's nervousness. The series had high production values, was shot on film, had a top-grade set (left over from Altman's movie) and, rare for prime-time TV, allowed the cast adequate rehearsal time. There was also a constant, but unselfconscious, sense of inventiveness, most notable in 'The Interview', a black-and-white episode which viewed events as if through a TV documentary lens.

In 1976 the show's original writer, Larry Gelbart, left, partly because he was worn out battling with studio executives over the controversial storylines. ('War is hell,' commented Gelbart. 'So is TV.') Thereupon Alan Alda took over as the show's creative consultant, and as one of its principal writers and directors. His Hawkeye character became more and more central to the events at the 4077th, causing actor Wayne Rogers to quit for his own spin-off show, *Trapper John, M D.* At the end of the third season McLean Stevenson also

▶▶▶ *There is never likely to be a more unlikely hit comedy than* MASH.

departed the unit, his Colonel Blake character – shatteringly for the audience – being shot down on his return to the USA (the 'Abyssinia, Henry' episode). Their places were taken by Mike Farrell (as BJ, Hawkeye's chief conspirator in skewering military pretensions) and ex-*Dragnet* and ex-*Naked City* star Harry Morgan (as Colonel Potter, a man with a fine creative line in slang, viz. 'busload of bushwah'). At the beginning of the 1977–8 season David Ogden Stiers joined up as aristocratic Bostonian Charles Emerson Winchester, to replace Larry Linville's Burns as the 4077th's arch-pain-in-the-butt. (Burns, as the storyline had it, had gone AWOL because Hoolihan had thrown him over for Lt. Col. Penobscott.)

Under Alda's tutelage, the show came to rely for its humour on the irreverent wisecracking banter between the characters, with fewer banana-skin pratfalls. It also developed a strong vein of sentimentality, with Hawkeye becoming a 'saint in surgical garb'. In 1983, having earned fourteen Emmys, *M*A*S*H* bowed out with a two-and-half-hour special, 'Good-bye, Farewell and Amen' – to that date the most watched TV programme in history. With the signing of the armistice, the medics bid their final adieus, with Hawkeye and BJ delivering their first and only salute to Colonel Potter. As Alda claimed rightly, 'We came to tell jokes, and stayed to touch the edges of art.'

Ironically, the one man on record as not liking the TV *M*A*S*H* was a certain Richard Hornberger. Under the pseudonym Richard Hooker he wrote the original *M*A*S*H* novel. He was a conservative Republican, and would not watch the TV version because of its liberal sensibilities.

A sequel, *AfterMASH* (1983–4), presented Potter, Klinger and Father Francis Mulcahy adjusting to civilian life at General Pershing's Veteran's Administration Hospital in River Bend, Missouri.

... 'cause suicide is painless
it brings on many changes
and I can take or leave it if I please...
... and you can do the same
thing if you choose.

MAUDE

USA 1972–8, 140 x 30m, col CBS. Tandem Productions. UK tx *1976 ITV.*

PR *Norman Lear.* **DR** *Various, including Hal Cooper, Tony Csiki.* **CAST** Maude Findlay *Bea Arthur* Walter Findlay *Bill Macy* Carol *Adrienne Barbeau* Philip *Brian Morrison/Kraig Metzinger* Dr Arthur Harmon *Conrad Bain* Vivian Cavender Harmon *Rue McClanahan* Florida Evans *Esther Rolle* Henry Evans *John Amos* Mrs Nell Naugatuck *Herminone Baddeley* Victoria Butterfield *Marlene Warfield.*

Controversial spin-off from >*All in the Family,* centring on Archie Bunker's upper-middle-class cousin-in-law, Maude Findlay, from the suburb of Tuckahoe, NY. There she lived with fourth husband Walter, the alcoholic owner of Findlay's Friendly Appliances, divorced daughter Carol, and nine-year-old-son Philip.

Whereas Bunker caused critical heat for his blue-collar bigotry, Maude did the same by being too pro-Women's Lib. In one episode she had an abortion, in another she was treated for manic depression, in another she called Walter 'a son of a bitch'. In the process actress Bea Arthur was elevated to stardom, winning a 1977 Emmy for Outstanding Lead Actress in a Comedy. (A decade later she was again on Emmy-winning form, this time in >*The Golden Girls,* where she was joined by fellow *Maude* actress Rue McClanahan.) Maude Findlay, meanwhile, became one of the classic characters of the US small screen. The show reached as high as number four in the Nielsens. Only a smattering of episodes were screened in the UK.

A spin-off, >*Good Times,* followed the life of Maude's black maid, Florida Evans.

McHALE'S NAVY

USA 1962–6, 138 x 25m, bw ABC. ABC/Sto-Rev/MCA/Universal.

PR *Edward J Montagne, Si Rose.*
DR *Various, including Sidney Lanfield.*
CAST Lt Cmdr Quinton McHale *Ernest Borgnine* Capt Wallace B Binghampton *Joe Flynn* Ensign Charles 'Chuck' Parker *Tim Conway* Harrison 'Tinker' Bell *Billy Sands* Happy Haines *Gavin MacLeod* Lt Elroy Carpenter *Bob Hastings* Fuji Kobiaji *Yoshio Yoda* Quartermaster George 'Christy' Christopher *Gary Vinson* Seaman Lester Gruber *Carl Ballantine* Seaman Virgil Edwards *Edson Stroll.*

US navy lark featuring the hustlers who crewed PT 73 (a motor torpedo boat) in the Pacific during the Second World War. Ernest Borgnine took a break from playing psychopathic heavies in Hollywood to reveal a surprisingly sure comic touch

James Cromwell gives Hermione Baddeley a hug in Maude.

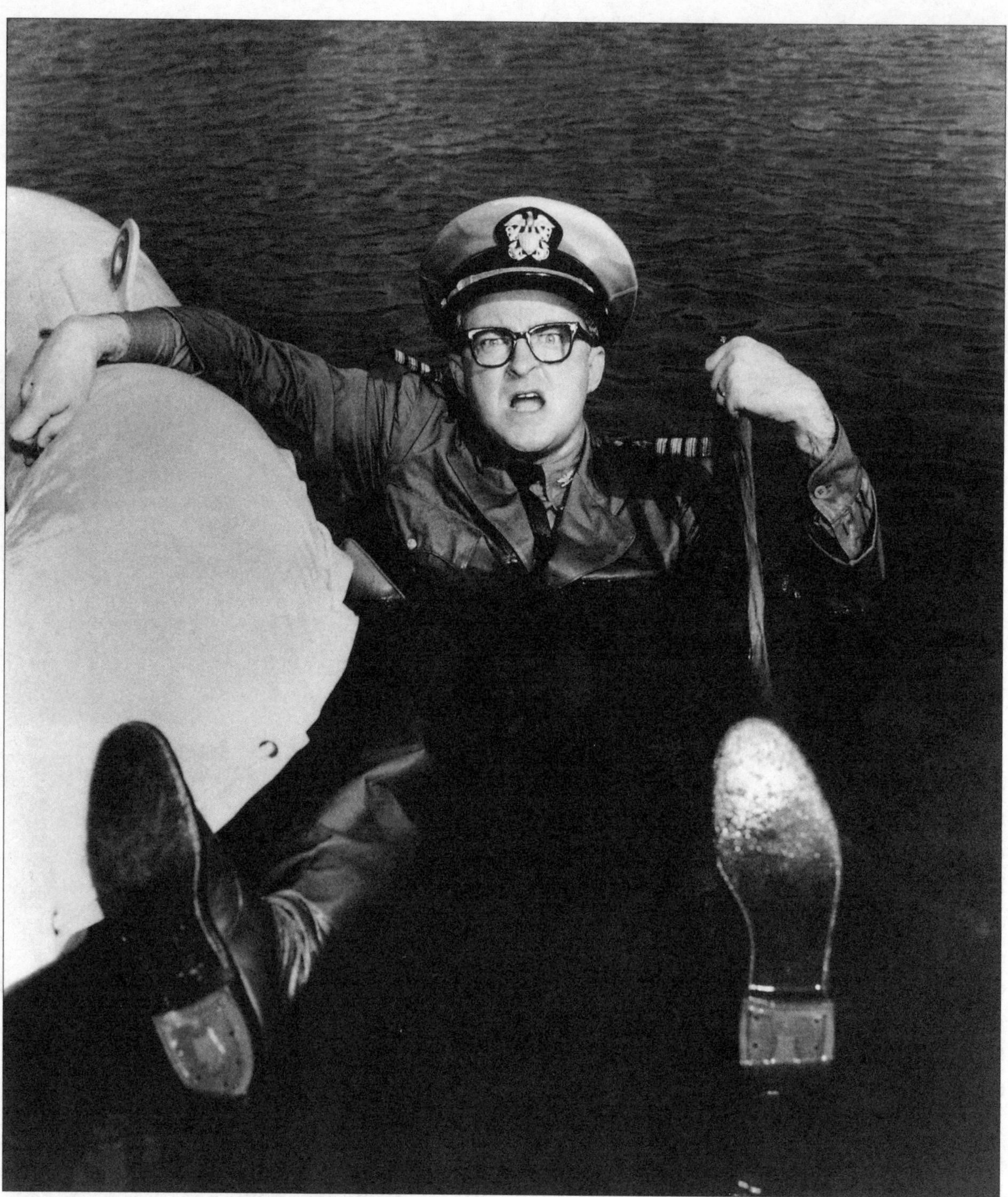

as the sly McHale. For the last season, McHale and men were transferred to the Mediterranean, where their entertaining antics continued to plague their hapless CO, Wallace B Binghampton ('Old Lead Bottom'). Based on the TV play *Seven Against the Sea,* in which Borgnine had also starred, *McHale's Navy* was one of the more successful of the military sitcoms which marched across the American small screen in the early sixties. There were two spin-off feature films from the show, *McHale's Navy* and *McHale's Navy Join the Airforce.*

MEN BEHAVING BADLY

UK 1991–, 25+ x 30m, col ITV/BBC1 (from 1994). Thames TV/Hartswood Films Ltd.

CR *Simon Nye.* **PR** *Beryl Vertue.* **DR** *Martin Dennis.* **WR** *Simon Nye.* **MUS** *Alan Lisk.* **CAST** Gary *Martin Clunes* Dermot *Harry Enfield* Tony *Neil Morrissey* Dorothy *Caroline Quentin* Deborah *Leslie Ash* George *Ian Lindsay* Anthea *Valeri Minifie* Les *Dave Atkins.*

Politically incorrect – but woefully funny – sitcom about a pair of adolescent-minded males, who share a squalid flat and a consuming interest in girls. In the first two seasons the men behaving badly were Gary (jug-eared Martin Clunes, whose first TV part was in *Dr Who* and who also starred in *No Place Like Home*) and Dermot (the ubiquitous Harry Enfield, >*Harry Enfield's Television Show*), but then Dermot moved out, leaving Gary to find a new lodger. The successful applicant was Tony (Neil Morrissey, formerly Sammy the Shammy in *Noel's House Party,* and *Boon*), who impressed Gary with his claim to be 'in the music business'. A comic misunderstanding whereby Gary worried that his new flatmate was a 'pillow-biter' (homosexual) was soon ironed out, and the twosome settled down to a soul-mateyness, which survived the disclosure that Tony actually ran a secondhand record stall (later abandoned for a career as a busker). For Tony himself, a principal attraction of the flat was the upstairs neighbour, blonde, Twiggy-like Deborah (Leslie Ash, *Quadrophenia, C.A.T.S. Eyes*), whom he lusted after relentlessly.

Meanwhile, Gary maintained a romantic relationship of sorts with long-suffering State Registered Nurse Dorothy (Caroline Quentin, ex-wife of Paul Merton, *Jonathan Creek, Kiss Me Kate*). By the fourth season, despairing of Gary's adolescent behaviour and lack of commitment, Dorothy's eye began to wander. Her casual mention of a friend called Tim caused Gary to explode jealously: 'Maybe you'd like to jiggle around on Tim's todger while I bring you a series of tasty snacks?' In fact, Dorothy was having an affair with Jamie, to whom she became engaged – until Jamie called it off – much to Gary's gloating. Gary and Dorothy then recommenced their relationship, although more rockiness ensued in 'Playing Away', when Gary returned home unexpectedly and found Dorothy *in flagrante* – with Tony. This indiscretion was overcome when Dorothy lied to Gary and told him that Tony was a useless lover. Gary promised not to rub Tony's face in it – and then proceeded to rub Tony's face in it.

◀◀◀ *More watery mishaps in McHale's Navy.*

Created and written by Simon Nye (also >*Frank Stubbs Promotes, Is it Legal?, True Love, How Do You Want Me?*), and based on his novel of the same name, *MBB* dextrously balanced the cathartic and the cynical. It allowed male viewers to indulge in vicarious 'laddism', whilst allowing female viewers to ridicule the bad but lovable Tony and Gary. Meanwhile, it was also a genuine sitcom in that the humour came from the characters and their context. 'I don't do mad, plot-driven farragoes,' Nye remarked. 'You have to allow your characters time to talk.' A garland of prizes was bestowed on *MBB,* including the Comedy Awards' Best ITV Comedy, and the first National Television Award for Situation Comedy.

The behind-the-scenes mover and shaker of *MBB* was the venerable Beryl Vertue (whose daughter was Harry Enfield's main squeeze when *MBB* began). Originally an artists' agent, Vertue moved into production with Eric Sykes' comedy *The Plank* and the movie version of *Till Death Us Do Part.* As deputy chairman of the Robert Stigwood Group, Vertue pioneered the selling to foreign companies of the basic formats of British comedies, among them >*Till Death Us Do Part* (which became >*All in the Family* in the USA), >*Steptoe and Son* (*Sanford and Son* in the USA), and *Upstairs, Downstairs (Beacon Hill).* When, inexplicably, ITV decided not to film a second series of *MBB,* Vertue sold the show to the BBC. The inevitable US 're-version' starred stand-up comic Rob Schneider and Ron Eldred (Shep in *ER*) and came from Carsey-Werner. It screened on NBC from 1996, and also featured Justine Bateman and Ken Marino.

MISTER ED

USA 1960–6, 143 x 25m, bw Syndicated/CBS. Filmways. UK tx *1962–5.*

CR *Arthur Lubin.* **PR** *Various, including Al Simon, Arthur Lubin, George Burns.* **DR** *Various, including Arthur Lubin.* **WR** *Various, including Bob O'Brian, William Burns, Lou Derman, Ben Starr.* **CAST** Wilbur Post *Alan Young* Carol Post *Connie Hines* Roger Addison *Larry Keating* Kay Addison *Edna Skinner* Colonel Gordon Kirkwood *Leon Ames* Winnie Kirkwood *Florence MacMichael* Mr Ed *(voice) Allan 'Rocky' Lane.*

On moving to the country, architect Wilbur Post finds that he has also bought a palomino horse, Mr Ed… who can talk. American fantasy sitcom that inaugurated a host of similarly premised shows, among them >*My Favorite Martian,* >*Bewitched,* >*I Dream of Jeannie.* It was derived from the *Francis the Talking Mule* movie series by their director Arthur Lubin, but in a fashion that was studio bound and too feebly nonsensical to swallow. Equine scatology, in fact. Despite this, *Mister Ed* was awarded the 1963 Golden Globe for Best TV Show. The voice of Mr Ed was supplied by the great B-western hard man Allan 'Rocky' Lane (1901–73), while English actor Alan Young (born Angus Young) played his human foil. Leon Ames from >*Life With Father* played neighbour Colonel Gordon Kirkwood.

Show trivia: *Mister Ed* began life as a syndicated series, before being picked up by a network. Watching TV was one of the talking horse's favourite hobbies – although he refused to watch Westerns because his relatives always got killed.

THE MONKEES

USA 1966–8, 58 x 30m, col NBC. Screen Gems/Raybert/NBC. UK tx *1966–8 BBC1.*

CR *Bert Schneider, Bob Rafelson.* **EXEC PR** *Ward Sylvester.* **PR** *Bert Schneider, Bob Rafelson.* **DR** *Various, including Bob Rafelson, James Frawley, Bruce Kessler, Mickey Dolenz, Peter H Thorkelson (Peter Tork), Russ Mayberry, Alexander Singer.* **WR** *Various, including Bob Rafelson, Lee Sanford, Stanley Z Cherry, Neil Burstyn, Mickey Dolenz, Joel Kane, Jon C Anderson.* **MUS** *Tommy Boyce and Bobby Hart (main theme), Peter Tork and Joseph Richards ('For Pete's Sake' end credits).* **CAST** Davy Jones *himself* Mike Nesmith *himself* Peter Tork *himself* Mickey Dolenz *himself* Mr Babbitt (landlord) *Henry Corden* Mrs Purdy (neighbour) *Jesslyn Fax.*

▼▼ *Hey, hey, we're* The Monkees, *and people say we monkey around. Jones, Dolenz, Tork and Nesmith put on a show.*

Hey, hey, we're the Monkees
And people say we monkey around...

So opened the theme tune of the weekly life-on-the-road misadventures of the Monkees, an artificially created American mop-top pop-group based on the Beatles of *A Hard Day's Night* and *Help!* vintage. More than four hundred applicants were screened by producers Bert Schneider and Bob Rafelson before they chose as the 'pre-fab four' English actor Davy Jones (previously Ena Sharples' grandson in soap *Coronation Street*), folk singer Peter Tork, former *Circus Boy* actor Mickey Braddock (now called Mickey Dolenz), and Michael Nesmith, whose mother had invented the liquid paper used in typing corrections.

Each episode featured picaresque madcap antics (emphasized by such innovative shooting techniques as slow motion and distorted lenses), plus a couple of musical numbers. To these the Monkees only contributed the vocals, since Peter Tork was the only one, despite TV appearances, who could play a chord.

Better than a manufactured product had a right to be, *The Monkees* won the 1966 Emmy for Outstanding Comedy. Several of the band's songs even reached number one in the charts ('Last Train to Clarksville', 'Daydream Believer', 'I'm a Believer'), though having lyricists such as Neil Diamond, Neil Sedaka, Carole King and Harry Nilsson helped. A 1968 Monkees film, *Head*, directed by Rafelson and co-written by him with Jack Nicholson (the two would team up again for *Five Easy Pieces*), proved too off-the-wall for the teenyboppers who were the main Monkee maniacs, and died a death by box office. By then, anyway, the band had split up, except for a TV special released in 1969 entitled *33⅓ Revolutions Per Monkee*.

Until 1997, that is. Then, without a trace of doubt in their minds, the Monkees (now in their fifties) took the first train to nostalgiaville and announced a new album, together with a TV special, *Hey, Hey, we're the Monkees*.

'Oooh, I'm a believer, I'm a believer, I'm a believer, yes I am.'

An update of *The Monkees,* called *The New Monkees,* with an entirely new cast and set of characters, was syndicated in 1987, but isn't worth describing.

MONTY PYTHON'S FLYING CIRCUS

UK 1969–74, 45 x 30m, col BBC2. BBC TV. US tx *1974–6 PBS.*

CR *Barry Took, John Cleese, Terry Gilliam, Eric Idle, Graham Chapman, Terry Jones, Michael Palin.* **PR** *John Howard Davies, Ian MacNaughton.* **DR** *Ian MacNaughton.* **WR** *John Cleese, Michael Palin, Graham Chapman, Terry Jones, Eric Idle, Terry Gilliam.* **MUS** *John Philip Sousa ('Liberty Bell March' theme).* **CAST** *John Cleese, Terry Jones, Graham Chapman, Eric Idle, Terry Gilliam, Michael Palin; plus Carol Cleveland.*

And now for something completely different...

Landmark BBC comedy series – originally to be called *Owl Stretching Time,* then *Vaseline Review,* then *Cynthia Fellatio's Flying Circus* – of free-form sketches and blackout. With the exception of American illustrator Terry Gilliam, the *Python* team shared an Oxbridge background and had honed their talents on such mid-sixties TV shows as *Do Not Adjust Your Set, >At Last the 1948 Show, The Complete and Utter History of Britain* and *>The Frost Report,* before coming together in *Python* at the instigation of BBC comedy veteran Barry Took. Although *Python* found its humour in almost anything, its favourite targets were quintessentially British: pompous, small-minded bureaucrats (John Cleese's Minister of Silly Walks), upper-class twits, lower-class wearers of knotted handkerchiefs ('Gumbies'), and accountants. But there was no political point to *Python* comedy (unlike the satirical thrust of many of its peers); it was entirely relativist ridicule.

The show also delighted in undermining the conventions of TV. Jokes failed to have punch lines, episodes were concluded with false endings, while characters, notably the blimpish Colonel and the Spanish Inquisition Cardinals Ximanez, Fang and Biggles, flitted from skit to skit. Often the only link was a surreal Gilliam cartoon (the descending giant foot, the dropping sixteen-ton weight) or Cleese's 'And now for something completely different...' Yet, for all its inspired brilliance, the anarchic series was as often miss as hit; for every quotable Dead Parrot, Cheese Shop, Spam, Crunchy Frog, and Argument Clinic sketch there were two of instant forgettableness. Indeed, the first season was so poorly received that in the Midlands area of Britain it was replaced by a farming programme. BBC bosses, meanwhile, were accusing the *Python* team of 'wallowing in sadism'. Still, by 1971, the show was enough of a cult hit to spin off a movie version, *And Now For Something Completely Different* (1972: essentially a rehash of show sketches). In 1972 the show was awarded a BAFTA.

▲▲▲ *John Cleese as the Minister of Silly Walks in* Monty Python's Flying Circus.

Praline (John Cleese): Hello, I wish to register a complaint... Hello? Miss?

Shopkeeper: (Michael Palin): What do you mean, miss?

Praline: Oh, I'm sorry, I have a cold. I wish to make a complaint.

Shopkeeper: Sorry, we're closing for lunch.

Praline: Never mind that, my lad, I wish to make a complaint about this parrot what I purchased not half an hour ago from this very boutique.

Shopkeeper: Oh yes, the Norwegian Blue. What's wrong with it?

Praline: I'll tell you what's wrong with it. It's dead, that's what's wrong with it.

Shopkeeper: No, it's resting, look!

Praline: Looky my lad, I know a dead parrot when I see one, and I'm looking at one right now.

Shopkeeper: No, no sir, it's not dead. It's resting.

Praline: Resting?

Shopkeeper: Yeah, remarkable bird the Norwegian Blue, beautiful plummage, innit?

Praline: The plummage don't enter into it – it's stone dead.

Shopkeeper: No, no – it's just resting.

Praline: All right then, if it's just resting I'll wake it up. **[shouts into cage]** ***Hello Polly! I've got a nice cuttlefish for you when you wake up, Polly Parrot!***

Shopkeeper: **[jogging the cage]** ***There, it moved.***

Praline: No he didn't. That was you pushing the cage.

Shopkeeper: I did not.

Praline: Yes, you did. **[takes parrot out of cage, shouts]** ***Hello Polly, Polly!*** **[bangs it against counter]** ***Polly Parrot, wake up. Polly!*** **[throws parrot into air and lets it fall to floor]** ***Now that's what I call a dead parrot.***

Shopkeeper: No, no, it's stunned...

After a five-year run and with Cleese in particular tiring of the 'anything goes' structurelessness, the group pulled down the *Python* big top to pursue brilliant individual careers (including >*Fawlty Towers*, >*Rutland Weekend Television*, >*Ripping Yarns*). To the relief of *Python* fans everywhere, however, *Python* continued to exist as a cinema being, continuing the collective craziness in a cycle of *Python* films: *Monty Python and the Holy Grail* (1974), *Monty Python's Life of Brian* (1979), and *Monty Python's Meaning of Life* (1983).

Of course, when the show *was* good, it was surreally sublime, as in the famous Dead Parrot sketch (see left).

MOONLIGHTING

USA 1985–9, 1 x 120m, 66 x 60m, col ABC. Picturemaker Productions. UK tx *1986–9 BBC2.*

CR *Glenn Gordon Caron.* **EXEC PR** *Glenn Gordon Caron.* **PR** *Jay Daniel.* **DR** *Various, including Alan Arkush, Peter Werner, Will Mackenzie, Christian I Nyby, Paul Krasny, Robert Butler, Sam Weisman.* **WR** *Various, including Glenn Gordon Caron.* **MUS** *Lee Holdridge and Al Jarreau (theme).* **CAST** Maddie Hayes *Cybill Shepherd* David Addison *Bruce Willis* Agnes Dipesto *Allyce Beasley* Herbert Viola *Curtis Armstrong* Virginia Hayes *Eve Maria Saint* Sam Crawford *Mark Harmon.*

Stylish romantic comedy, inspired by the 1940 film *His Girl Friday,* which rescued the stalled career of Cybill Shepherd and projected Bruce Willis to stardom.

Shepherd played former model Maddie Hayes who, after being swindled by embezzlers, decides to turn the Los Angeles detective agency, which she has among her assets, from a tax dodge to a profit maker. As her partner in the Blue Moon agency she takes in Willis's lascivious and wisecracking David Addison. Their subsequent lust-hate relationship was the essence of the show, with the investigations almost incidental. Sexual chemistry sparked on screen; he wolf-whistled after her, sang the lyrics from sixties girl-watchin' songs, but Maddie resisted – until season two, when the producers succumbed to the obvious temptation: a heavily hyped bed scene between Maddie and David, which raised the ratings to heavenly heights. The other leading cast members were Allyce Beasley as daffy receptionist Miss Dipesto and Curtis Armstrong as clerk Herbert Viola, the object of her unrequited sighs.

There was considerable cross-over between the stars and their on-screen characters (although, if Shepherd's off-screen statements are to be believed, this did not stretch to the sexual chemistry). Cybill Shepherd was an ex-model herself, indeed 1968's Model of the Year, and came to *Moonlighting* as the one-time star of feature film *The Last Picture Show* (1971) and NBC's Texan rancher series *The Yellow Rose* (1983–4). Willis had previously landed only one screen role, a bit part as a crook in *Miami Vice,* and turned up among three thousand hopefuls to read for the part of David Addison with a punk haircut, khaki army trousers and three earrings. He was the last to read and got the part.

Created by Glenn Gordon Caron, the show was the epitome of post-modern TV, with its quirky but effective rummages through the cutting-room floors of the past. One episode, 'Atomic Shakespeare', was written entirely in iambic pentameters; another, dealing with an unsolved murder from the forties, was filmed in *noir* style; and nearly every instalment incorporated some tricky self-referential statement to camera.

Although almost fanatically popular, the show was cancelled in 1989. It had been beset throughout by three-way conflicts between Shepherd, Willis and Caron, and increasingly production had run over time and budget. Moreover, the storyline, in which Maddie had become pregnant (by either astronaut Sam Crawford or Addison), miscarried, and married a near stranger, had taken the scriptwriters up a dark alley from which they were having difficulty getting out. The plug was accordingly pulled. This proved no hardship to Willis, who moved into the major league with films like *Die Hard* and *Pulp Fiction,* and has become phenomenally popular. Shepherd's career, however, again went into abeyance, until she found the plot again in >*Cybill.*

THE MORECAMBE AND WISE SHOW

UK 1961–83, Approx 60 x 30m, 100 x 60m, bw/col. ATV/BBC TV/Thames TV. US tx *1980– Syndicated.*

PR *Various, including Colin Clews (ATV), John Ammonds (BBC).* **WR** *Various, including Sid Green and Dick Hills (ATV), Eddie Braben (BBC/Thames).* **CAST** *Eric Morecambe, Ernie Wise.*

you can't see the join. . .

Not so much a comic double act as a British institution.

Eric Morecambe (born John Eric Bartholomew) and Ernie Wise (Ernest Wiseman) began their partnership in 1941. It was then interrupted by Morecambe's wartime service as a miner, but resumed in 1947 as part of *Lord George Sanger's Variety Service,* the duo making their way to the new medium of TV in 1951 as part of the BBC's *The Youth Parade.* A show of their own followed, the dismal *Running Wild* (BBC) of 1954, before extensive touring perfected their timing and rapport. When they were offered another chance of their own series, by ATV in 1961, they did not waste it. Playing their stage personae of Eric the mischievous pipe-smoking sceptic and Ernie the pompous, short-fat-hairy-legged foil (with 'twenty-three A-levels, all of them in maths'), they mugged and sight-gagged happily, in between introducing musical artistes, the Beatles included.

In 1968 the duo were poached by the BBC, where they produced their greatest work; the catchphrase 'you can't see the join' (about Ernie's wig), Eric's pretence of being strangled behind the stage curtain, Ern's plays 'wot I wrote', Eric's skewed specs – all date from this time. So too does the classic 'Breakfast Sketch', in which the pair prepared the morning meal to the music of 'The Stripper'. Most of the scriptwriting was done by Eddie Braben, who often gave the gags a touch of sure-fingered absurdity: a mock TV advertisement for a cold remedy ended with an unseen questioner saying to the flu-ridden Morecambe, 'Fed up?' and then suggesting, 'Why not try' – at which point a gun-shot was heard.

It was also for the BBC that Morecambe (the name was taken from Bartholomew's home town) and Wise produced their legendary Christmas specials, which entrapped stellar celebrities in affectionate antics. Peter Cushing was never paid, newscaster Angela Rippon stepped out from behind her desk to high-kick her way through 'Let's Face the Music and Dance' and 'You're Adorable', while Shirley Bassey tried to sing 'Smoke Gets in Your Eyes' as Eric and Ern pulled her foot from a hole in the stage, then replaced her dainty footwear with an army boot. The 1976 guests were John Thaw and Dennis Waterman from thick-ear actioner *The Sweeney* (Morecambe and Wise guested on a comedic 1978 episode of that show in return), and ex-Prime Minister Harold Wilson. The special in 1977 was watched by 27 million people, by which time Morecambe and Wise had become as much a part of the British yuletide as plum pudding and the Queen's Speech.

In 1979 the duo moved to Thames TV (the first skit showed them being dumped from a BBC van outside Thames TV's HQ), but their sojourn there was plagued from the outset by Morecambe's poor health. He died in 1984 of a heart attack. An era in British comedy had ended. The work of Morecambe and Wise, however, continues to live on in repeats and videos, not to mention the living homage that is Vic Reeves (>*Vic Reeves' Big Night Out*).

'Bring me sunshine...'

MORK AND MINDY

USA 1978–82, 92 x 30m, 1 x 60m, col ABC. Miller-Milkis Productions/Henderson Production Co Inc/Paramount TV. UK tx *1979–83 ITV.*

CR *Garry K Marshall, Tony Marshall, Dale McRaven, Joe Gauberg.* **EXEC PR** *Garry K Marshall, Tony Marshall.* **PR** *Bruce Johnson, Dale McRaven.* **DR** *Various, including Bob Claver, Howard Storm.* **WR** *Various, including Dale McRaven, Ed Scharlach, Bruce Johnson, Robin Williams, April Kelly, Tom Tenowich, Deborah Raznicka.* **CAST** Mork *Robin Williams* Mindy McConnell *Pam Dawber* Frederick McConnell *Conrad Janis* Cora Hudson *Elizabeth Kerr* Orson *Ralph James* Exidor *Robert Donner* Mearth *Jonathan Winters* Nelson Flavor *Jim Stahl* Franklin Delano Bickley *Tom Poston* Remo DaVinci *Jay Thomas* Jean DaVinci *Gina Hecht.*

Shazbat! A spin-off from a 1978 episode of >*Happy Days* in which Mork from Ork (Robin Williams) landed on earth and tried to kidnap Richie Cunningham. Audience reaction to the episode was

▼▼ *ET Mork finds a strange Earth life form in* Mork and Mindy.

Pam Dawber: 'He* [Robin Williams] *is the show, I'm lucky I got my name in the title.

so favourable that it was decided to give the alien a show of his own.

For his second coming to Earth, Mork landed at Boulder, Colorado, in a giant egg and with a mission to study earthlings and report his findings back to His Immenseness, Orkan leader Orson ('Cosmic breath'). In Boulder, Mork was befriended by Mindy McConnell, daughter of music store owner Fred. To the latter's oft-stated disapproval, Mork moved into Mindy's apartment. Initially, their relationship was, in fact, platonic, but eventually they married, and honeymooned on Ork – where Mork discovered he was pregnant and laid an egg. From this emerged their son, Mearth, played by middle-aged, 225-pound US comedian Jonathan Winters. On Ork beings grew younger, not older.

Mork and Mindy was a pleasant twist to a sci-fi perennial, for the invading Mork was no bug-eyed monster but a zany and endearing child-man, an innocent abroad in the universe (although Gore Vidal's play *Visit to a Small Planet* and the 1963 TV show >*My Favorite Martian* prefigured it). Mork's habits were strange – he slept upside down in a cupboard, drank through his finger, wore his suit backwards – but he was likeable.

The role of Mork, initially offered to Dom DeLuise, was perfectly suited to the wacky, stream-of-consciousness style of Williams, a former stand-up comic at Los Angeles' Comedy Store. Understanding this, the producers allowed Williams to do his own stuff, marking scripts: 'Mork can go off here'. The show made Williams a star, and he followed it with a string of major films, including *Good Morning Vietnam* (1987), *The Fisher King* (1989) and *Toys* (1992).

Williams' comic skills aside, the series had an almost fatal tumble in quality in season two, when the producers jettisoned the show's zappy sci-fi sitcom format in favour of would-be-clever surrealism. Two principal cast members were sacked, Conrad Janis (also an accomplished jazz player, who had cut records with Coleman Hawkins) and Elizabeth Kerr (who played Mindy's with-it Grandma). The audience ratings plummeted, and the producers restored the old format – plus Janis and Kerr – for season three. Among the other regular characters seen were Exidor, a UFO prophet who thought Mork was crazy, and neighbour Mr Bickley. Jim Stahl played Mindy's yuppie cousin, Nelson. Lead guest actors were headed by Raquel Welch as beautiful captain Nirvana, who captured Mork in 'Mork vs the Necrotons'.

If *Mork and Mindy* was something different on TV, it also used some classic sci-fi techniques, such as juxtaposing the alien with the human as a means of commentary on the latter. In case the audience missed the point, Mork's end-of-episode reports to Orson were explicit comments on the state of humanity. Unfortunately, these tended to be cute (people should be nice to each other, etc) rather than meaningful.

Na nu, na nu

▶▶▶ *Rowan Atkinson as the walking disaster that was* Mr Bean.

MR BEAN

UK 1990–6, 14 x 30m, col ITV. Tiger Aspect/Central TV/Thames TV. US tx *1992–6 HBO.*

CR *Richard Curtis.* **PR** *John Howard Davies, Sue Vertue.* **DR** *John Howard Davies, John Birkin, Paul Weiland.* **WR** *Rowan Atkinson, Richard Curtis, Robin Driscoll, Ben Elton.* **MUS** *Howard Goodall.* **CAST** Mr Bean *Rowan Atkinson* Irma Gobb *Matilda Ziegler* various roles *Robin Driscoll.*

Near-silent comedies starring rubber-faced Rowan Atkinson (>*Blackadder,* >*Not the Nine O'Clock News*) as the clueless Mr Bean. The misadventures had their side-splitting moments (Mr Bean's attempt to obtain a picture on his TV with an indoor aerial comes to mind), if only because of Atkinson's impeccable timing, but were often just plain dumb antics, telegraphed in advance and derivative of Charlie Chaplin and Monsieur Hulot. There were many specials, with 'Merry Christmas Mr Bean' showing to 18.5 million in December 1992, making it the most watched programme, apart from soaps, in the British yuletide week. A spin-off movie, *Mr Bean: The Ultimate Disaster Movie* (directed by Mel Smith) was released in 1997.

The episodes were: Mr Bean/The Return of Mr Bean/The Curse of Mr Bean/Mr Bean Goes to Town/The Trouble with Mr Bean/Mr Bean Rides Again/Merry Christmas, Mr Bean/Mr Bean in Room 426/Do-It-Yourself Mr Bean/Mind the Baby, Mr Bean/Back to School, Mr Bean/Torvill and Bean/Tee Off, Mr Bean/Goodnight Mr Bean/The Library/Mr Bean's Red Nose Day/The Bus Stop/Blind Date/Hair by Mr Bean of London.

The Mrs Merton Show

UK 1994–7, 18 x 30m, col BBC2. BBC TV.

PR *Peter Kessler, Mark Gorton.* **DR** *Pati Marr.* **CAST** Mrs Merton *Caroline Aherne.*

With the death of the British chat show in the nineties, there were only spoofs left, such as >*Knowing Me, Knowing You… with Alan Partridge* – and this programme, featuring studio pensioner Mrs Merton (played by thirtysomething comedienne Caroline Aherne, *The Dead Good Show,* >*The Fast Show*). It was full of winking innuendo and vicious swipes, in front of an elderly, extremely partisan Mancunian audience.

Brilliant, in fact. Mrs Merton's archly styled questions (to Debbie McGee: 'So tell me. What attracted you to millionaire Paul Daniels?') were simply devastating. A BAFTA Award followed, though eventually the idea burst its own bubble, as cautious A- and B-list celebrities began to refuse the Mancunian granny's invitation to have her verbal knitting needles jabbed into them. And *Mrs Merton*'s heavily manufactured irony suited the iconoclastic mid-nineties, but not all times. The show's band featured Peter Hook from rock music combo New Order, who was Aherne's sometime husband (she was occasionally credited as Caroline Hook).

Mrs Merton was famed for her piercing look, but there was a prosaic reason for it: Aherne suffered partial blindness in one eye.

◀◀◀ *Yvonne DeCarlo and Fred Gwynne in* The Munsters, *a spoof horror show.*

The Munsters

USA 1964–6, 70 x 25m, bw CBS. MCA/Universal. UK tx *1965–7 BBC1.*

CR *Joe Connelly, Bob Mosher.* **PR** *Joe Connelly, Bob Mosher.* **DR** *Jack Marquette, Harry Larrecq, Lawrence Dobkin, Ezra Stone, Charles Rondeau, Donald Richardson, Gene Reynolds, Joseph Pevney, Earl Bellamy, Norman Abbott.* **WR** *Bob Mosher, Joe Connelly, James Allardice, Dick Conway, Richard Baer, Dennis Whitcomb.* **MUS** *Jack Marshall.* **CAST** Herman Munster *Fred Gwynne* Lily Munster (née Dracula) *Yvonne DeCarlo* Grandpa Munster *Al Lewis* Edward Wolfgang ('Eddie') Munster *Butch Patrick* Marilyn Munster *Beverly Owen (1964)/Pat Priest (1964–6).* Video *CIC.*

Spoof horror show created by Bob Mosher and Joe Connelly (also >*Amos'n'Andy,* >*Leave It To Beaver*). Contemporary with, and seen by some as cruder than, >*The Addams Family,* with which it has similarities. The Munsters live at 43 Mockingbird Lane, a peaceful elm-shaded average suburban street in America. But the Munsters are a little different from ordinary folks. Their three-storey Victorian house has not seen a paintbrush since it was built. Shutters hang askew, weeds grow abundantly, vultures nest in the trees, and there's a dungeon in the basement. In the garage stands the fabulous (if archaic) Munster Koach and a drag speedster, the Dragula. The Munsters hail from Transylvania and head of the household is Herman Munster (played by Fred Gwynne, formerly of >*Car 54, Where Are You?*), modelled on Frankenstein's monster, seven feet three inches tall, with a flat head, lantern jaw, jagged scar on his forehead, and bolts through his neck. A devoted family man, Herman works hard at the Gateman, Goodbury & Grave Funeral Home to provide for his family, wife Lily, Grandpa, son Eddie and niece Marilyn. Lily (played by film star Yvonne DeCarlo, born Peggy Yvonne Middleton) is aged 137, with long black hair with a white streak and a penchant for Chanel No. 13. Hauntingly beautiful, she is almost as pretty as the day she died. Grandpa Munster (played by Al Lewis, also from *Car 54*), aged somewhere between sixty-two and 479, is a practical joker who sleeps in a coffin in the cellar. He is idolized by ten-year-old Eddie, a happy youngster with Wolfboy fangs and pointed ears. Eddie thinks Grandpa's tricks are 'neat'. Innocent of the effect they have on others, the Munsters – who believe themselves to be the typical American clan – think it is other people who are odd. And no one is more unfortunate than 'poor Marilyn', their ugly live-in niece, who just happens to be a blue-eyed blonde.

Most of the jokes in *The Munsters* came from the ghoulish ones' culture clash with suburban America, and were straightforward inversions of the norm. Niece Marilyn was, in fact, a ravishing Monroe lookalike. Lily's response to a handsome male was, 'He looks like Cary Grant, poor man.' Standard family advice was, 'Remember, every cloud has a dark lining.' The gag was overworked until it wore out its welcome, but there was an explicit message of decent liberal tolerance behind the humour and the affectionate characterization of the happy monster family. (The creators of *The Munsters* themselves came from recent immigrant families to America).

After many fruitless weeks searching Los Angeles and the Midwest for a suitable Victorian-Gothic structure, the Munster house was built in its entirety on the studio lot and aged with chemicals and lighting. The main stars spent hours in make-up. Aside from his flat head and neck-bolts, Fred Gwynne (d. 1993), even though the series was filmed in black-and-white, was required to have his face painted green, a process which took over an hour and a half, every day of shooting. *The Munsters* ran for seventy episodes, followed by numerous repeats on both sides of the Atlantic. Memorable episodes include: 'Herman the Great', in which Herman tries to earn extra cash by wrestling; and 'Lo-cal Munster', in which Lily forces Herman to diet for his army reunion. A movie, *Munster Go Home,* featuring the TV cast, was released in 1966. Gwynne, DeCarlo and Lewis again reprised their roles for a 1981 TVM, *The Munsters' Revenge,* an eminently forgettable disaster. So too was the 1989–91 series, *The Munsters Today,* an attempt to revamp the formula with the entirely new cast of John A Shuck, Lee Meriweather, Jason Marsden, Hilary van Dyke and Howard Morton.

THE MUPPET SHOW

UK 1976–80, 130 x 30m, cól ITV. ATV/Henson Associates. US tx *1976–81 Syndicated.*

CR *Jim Henson, Frank Oz.* **EXEC PR** *David Lazer.* **PR** *Jack Burns, Jim Henson.* **WR** *Jim Henson, Jack Burns, Marc London, Jerry Juhl.* **CAST** Kermit the Frog/Waldorf/Rowlf/Doctor Teeth/Captain Link Hearthrob/The Swedish Chef *Jim Henson* Miss

Piggy Lee/Sam the Eagle/Fozzie Bear/Animal *Frank Oz* Gonzo (the stunt animal)/Dr Bunsen Honeydew/ Zoot/Beauregard *Dave Groelz* Statler/Scooter/ Sweethums/Janice *Richard Hunt* Rizzo the Rat *Steve Whitmire* Pops/Sgt Floyd Pepper/Robin the Frog/Lew Zealand/Dr Julius Strangepork *Jerry Nelson.*

Fixtures on US TV, including *Sesame Street,* for over a decade, Jim Henson's bizarre creatures – half marionette, half glove puppet (hence their name) – only received a show of their own courtesy of British impresario Lew Grade, who bankrolled *The Muppet Show* in the UK.

The premise of each episode was that the Muppets were obliged to put on a variety performance at the Muppet Theatre, with Kermit the Frog as MC. Naturally, there was more drama behind the stage than on it; frustrating Kermit's efforts were would-be-comedian bears, regular balcony hecklers in the irascible shape of Statler and Waldorf, a right-wing Eagle, and argumentative Miss Piggy (who was also in lurve with him). Caught in the frantic efforts was the week's human guest star, there to be ritually mock humiliated. (Those who so suffered included Julie Andrews, Carol Burnett, Peter Sellers, Christopher Reeve and James Coburn.) There were also occasional running Muppet skits, such as Veterinarians Hospital, Pigs in Space and Muppet News Flash. Providing the music were Rowlf, the shaggy piano player, and Dr Teeth and the Electric Mayhem, with Animal on the drums and hippie Floyd on guitar.

A world-wide success, the show led to feature film spin-offs: *The Muppet Movie* (1979), *The Great Muppet Caper* (1981), *The Muppets Take Manhattan* (1984), *Muppet Christmas Carol* (1991).

Although Jim Henson himself died in 1990, the Muppets came back to the small screen in 1996 in *Muppets Tonight!,* an update of the old format that saw the featured creatures doing their putting-on-a-show routine for K-MUP TV. A troupe of new characters was added, of whom the dreadlocked Clifford ('your homey made of foamey'), Johnny Fiama, the poor man's Sinatra, and a line of dancing cheeses shone out. A *Muppet Treasure Island* appeared in the same year.

MURPHY BROWN

USA 1988–98, 247 x 30m, col CBS. Shulovsky-English Productions/Warner Bros TV. UK tx *1992– Sky 1.*

CR *Diane English.* **EXEC PR** *Various, including Diane English, Joel Shulovsky, Steven Peterman.* **PR** *Various, including Ned E Davis, Bill Diamond, Rob Bragin.* **DR** *Various, including Barnet Kellman, Lee Shailat, Peter Bonerz, Bill Bixby, Lee Zlotoff, Peter Baldwin, Burt Brinckerhoff.* **WR** *Various, including Diane English, Russ Woody, Denise Moss and Sy Dukane.* **MUS** *Steve Dorff.* **CAST** Murphy Brown *Candice Bergen* Corky Sherwood *Faith Ford* Jim Dial *Charles Kimbrough* Frank Fontana *Joe Regalbuto* Miles Silverberg *Grant Shaud* Eldin Bernecky *Robert Pastorelli* Phil *Pat Corley* Kay Carter-Shepley *Lily Tomlin* Haley Joel Osment *Avery Brown* Peter Hunt *Scott Bakula* Audrey Cohen *Jane Leeves* Stan Lansing *Garry Marshall* Carl (the cameraman) *Ritch Brinkley.*

Dan Quayle's least favourite show – the single-mom sitcom Murphy Brown.

Sitcom starring Candice Bergen (daughter of Oscar-winning ventriloquist Edgar Bergen, and formerly best known for the anti-western movie *Soldier Blue*) as star TV news reporter Murphy Brown of Washington DC's magazine programme *FYI*. A graduate of the Betty Ford clinic, Brown had notorious difficulty in retaining secretaries – who were simply marked with a number in the credits – and sustaining relationships, while her town house was in a permanent state of repainting. Crafted and honed in the >*Mary Tyler Moore Show* manner (with which it has obvious similarities), the series was influential enough for former US Vice President Dan Quayle to cite the unmarried pregnant Brown as symbolizing the collapse of American family values that caused the LA riots. The TV industry, meanwhile, considered Bergen's show good enough to bestow a clutch of Emmys on it.

When Brown gave birth to her son ('I have breasts for the first time and the only man in my life doesn't know what to do with them'), she went through nannies at home at the same rate as she went through secretaries at work, until she hit on the solution – to give the job to Eldin, the house painter. Which was fine with him, as long as he was referred to as 'Big Guy' and not 'Nanny'.

MY FAVORITE MARTIAN

USA 1963–6, 107 x 30m, bw/col CBS. A Jack Chertok Production.

CR *John L Greene.* **PR** *Jack Chertok.* **DR** *Various, including Alan Rafkin, Sheldon Leonard, Sidney Miller.* **MUS** *George Greeley.* **CAST** Uncle Martin *Ray Walston* Tim O'Hara *Bill Bixby* Lorelei Brown *Pamela Britton* Angela Brown *Ann Marshall* Detective Bill Brennan *Alan Hewitt* The Police Chief *Roy Engle* Harry Burns *J Pat O'Malley.*

The progenitor of the long line of alien-in-the-home sitcoms. On his way to the office, Los Angeles *Sun* journalist Tim O'Hara (Bill Bixby in his breakthrough role) sees a spaceship crash, and befriends its occupant – a professor of anthropology from Mars who is on a research trip. Taken to O'Hara's apartment as 'Uncle Martin', the human-looking alien (he had retractable antennae) causes sticky situations galore for his host, thanks to mischievous use of his powers of levitation, telepathy and invisibility.

The show rode the wave of its own novelty into the top ten of the Nielsens, eventually spinning off a

A perplexed Bill Bixby in My Favorite Martian.

sixteen-episode animated version, *My Favorite Martians* (Filmation, 1973–5).

Ray Walston, the actor who played 'Uncle Martin', was previously best known for his role as Luther Bliss in the film version of *South Pacific*.

My Mother the Car

USA 1965–6, 22 x 30m, col NBC. United Artists/Cottage Industries/MGM. UK tx *1965 ITV.*

PR *Rod Amateau.* **WR** *Various, including Lila Garrett, Bernie Kahn.* **CAST** Dave Crabtree *Jerry Van Dyke* Mother (Gladys), the Car (voice) *Ann Sothern* Barbara Crabtree *Maggie Pierce* Randy Crabtree *Randy Whipple* Cindy Crabtree *Cynthia Eilbacher* Captain Bernard Mancini *Avery Schreiber.*

Jerry Van Dyke (brother of Dick) starred as Dave Crabtree, a lawyer who buys a 1928 Porter car, only to find that it is the machinating metal reincarnation of his domineering mother. To his embarrassment, she is also taste-challenged and insists on leopard-print seat covers.

It was intended as off-beat, but viewed simply as off-beam. A candidate for the worst sitcom ever, it was pulled after a single season. The original premise had been even more tasteless: the car was to be the spirit of Crabtree's deceased wife. After due consideration, however, that idea was rejected as too necrophiliac. The villain of the piece was Captain Mancini, who constantly sought to part Dave from his valuable vintage car. Producer Rod Amateau pursued his interest in the comedic possibilities of cars with *The Dukes of Hazzard.*

My Three Sons

USA 1959–65, 369 x 25m, bw/col ABC/CBS. Don Fedderson Production. UK tx *1961– ITV.*

CR *Peter Tewksbury.* **PR** *Don Fedderson.* **DR** *Various, including Fred DeCordova, Gene Reynolds.* **MUS** *Frank De Vol.* **CAST** Steve Douglas *Fred MacMurray* Mike Douglas *Tim Considine* Robbie Douglas *Don Grady* Chip Douglas *Stanley Livingston* Michael Francis 'Bub' O'Casey *William Frawley* Uncle Charley O'Casey *William Demarest* Kate Miller Douglas *Tina Cole* Barbara Harper Douglas *Beverly Garland* Ernie Thompson Douglas *Barry Livingston.*

Hugely successful sitcom vehicle for film star Fred MacMurray, in which he played Steve Douglas, a widower trying to raise three sons – Mike, Robbie and Chip – through the usual rites of boyish, middle-American passage (camping trips, Little League, dating). And, as if Steve did not have enough problems, beautiful women were always chasing him and trying to move in on the boys. There was help, though, at 837 Mill Street, from father-in-law 'Bub', then (when actor William Frawley died) from crusty ex-sailor Uncle Charlie, who moved in as housekeeper. The inevitable lovable dog was called Tramp.

By the end of the run, the show's premise had changed considerably: Steve had adopted orphaned Ernie and remarried (Barbara Harper being the lucky woman), and Mike, the eldest son, had married, moved away from home and had children of his own (three sons, of course). Steve's work – which he barely had time for – as a consulting aviation engineer had meanwhile taken him from the Midwest to North Hollywood.

It was like *Disney*-time, only more so – but well enough done to win the 1962 Golden Globe for Best TV Programme.

MY TWO DADS

USA 1988–90, Approx 61 x 30m, col NBC. Michael Jacobs Productions/Tri Star. UK tx *1990–1 C4.*

PR *Michael Jacobs, Danielle Alexander.* **DR** *Various, including Andrew D Weyman, Andrew Cardiff, John Tracy, John L Lobue, Florence Stanley, Peter Baldwin.* **MUS** *Greg Evigan.* **CAST** Michael Taylor *Paul Reiser* Joey Harris *Greg Evigan* Nicole Bradford *Staci Keanan* Judge Wilbur *Florence Stanley* Ed Klawicki *Dick Butkus.*

One of many post-nuclear family sitcoms to come off the TV conveyor belt in the late eighties. When Marcy Bradford died, her twelve-year-old daughter Nicole was inherited by two single men, since it could not be determined which one was her biological father. And in order to provide proper co-parenting, the judge ordered the two to flat-share. The resultant compromises and disputes between starch-shirted financial adviser Michael Taylor and Bohemian artist Joey Harris, as they worried over Nicole's growing up, provided consistent chuckles. The theme was written and performed by star Greg Evigan.

NEVER MIND THE QUALITY, FEEL THE WIDTH

UK 1967–71, 39 x 30m, col ITV. ABC TV/Thames TV.

CR *Vince Powell and Harry Driver.* **PR** *Ronnie Baxter, Stuart Allen.* **DR** *Various, including Ronnie Baxter.* **WR** *Vince Powell and Harry Driver.* **CAST** Patrick Michael Kevin Aloysius Brendan Kelly *Joe Lynch* Emmanuel 'Manny' Cohen *John Bluthal* Father Ryan *Eamon Kelly* Rabbi Levy *Cyril Shaps.*

Situation comedy from Vince Powell and Harry Driver (>*George and the Dragon*, >*Love Thy Neighbour*) about two tailors, Jewish jacket-maker Manny Cohen and Irish trouser-maker Patrick Kelly,

▲▲▲ *Tailored for laughs, John Bluthal and Joe Lynch in* Never Mind the Quality, Feel the Width.

▲▲▲ *Rik Mayall as Thatcherite MP Alan B'Stard in* The New Statesman.

who had a small business in London's East End. The lowbrow humour exploited their stereotyped differences in religion and ethnicity, with Rabbi Levy and Father Ryan officiating.

The show was derived from a presentation for *Armchair Theatre* (with Frank Finlay as Kelly). It was originally made by ABC, but when that company lost its franchise, Thames took over the production.

THE NEW STATESMAN

UK 1987–92, 27 x 25m, 1 x 78 m, col ITV. Alomo/ Yorkshire TV. US tx *1990– PBS.*

CR *Laurence Marks and Maurice Gran.* **EXEC PR** *Michael Pilsworth, John Bartlett.* **PR** *David Reynolds, Tony Charles, Andrew Benson, Bernard McKenna.* **DR** *Graeme Harper, Geoffrey Sax.* **WR** *Laurence Marks and Maurice Gran.* **MUS** *Mussorgsky ('Pictures from an Exhibition' theme), Alan Hawkshaw.* **CAST** Alan Beresford B'Stard *Rik Mayall*

Sarah B'Stard *Marsha Fitzalan* Piers Fletcher-Dervish *Michael Troughton* Crippen *Nick Stringer* Roland Gidleigh-Park *Charles Gray* Sidney Bliss *Peter Sallis* Sir Greville *Terence Alexander* Count Otto von Munchweiller *Benedick Blythe* Krimhilde Kleist *Briggitte Kahn* Norman Bormann *R R Cooper.*

Knock-about political satire starring Rik Mayall as Alan Beresford B'Stard, a connivingly amoral far-right Tory MP (Haltemprice constituency) who jackbooted over all in the pursuit of money, power and sex. Michael Troughton played his wimpish assistant Piers Fletcher-Dervish and Marsha Fitzalan his aristo bisexual wife, Sarah. The fourth season saw B'Stard, after a spell in a Russian gulag (courtesy of a vengeful Sarah), returning home to find himself unemployed – having been unavoidably detained during the General Election – the Leaderene gone from office, Sarah in the arms of Teutonic lover Count Otto von Munchweiller, and Britain in the grip of recession. B'Stard thus transferred his avaricious attentions to Europe, becoming the MEP for a lucrative corner of Saxony, while conniving the hapless Fletcher-Dervish into the useful job (for B'Stard, that was) of European Commissioner for Internal Relations.

As a parody of the Essex wing of Thatcherism it was faultless. Among the awards garnered was an International Emmy. From the reliable firm of Laurence Marks and Maurice Gran *(Birds of a Feather, >Goodnight Sweetheart).*

NIGHT COURT

USA 1984–92, Approx 93 x 30m, col NBC. Warner Bros/Starry Night Productions.

PR *Various, including Reinhold Weege.* **DR** *Various, including James Burrows, John Larroquette, Thomas Klein, Lee Bernhard, Reinhold Weege.*
CAST Judge Harold T Stone *Harry Anderson* Court Clerk Lana Wagner *Karen Austin* Selma Hacke *Selma Diamond* Asst DA Dan Fielding *John Larroquette* Liz Williams *Paula Kelly* Bailiff Nostradamus 'Bull' Shannon *Richard Moll* Christine Sullivan *Markie Post* Art *Mike Finneran* Billie Young *Ellen Foley* Phil/Will *William Utay* Roz Russell *Marsha Warfield.*

Judge Harold T Stone presides over 'Night Court', a Manhattan courtroom that has an endless passage of loony nocturnal defendants. Which is fine, since bejeaned, flippant Judge Stone and his motley crew of clerks and DAs are pretty odd, too.

A long-running hit comedy for NBC, the show introduced many new TV faces, such as Richard Moll as the thick-headed court officer Nostradamus 'Bull' Shannon, John Larroquette as the sex-starved prosecutor Dan Fielding, and Markie Post as the sexy public defender Christine Sullivan; the familiar faces were headed by John Astin (>*The Addams Family*) as Buddy Ryan, a mental patient who was in fact Judge Harry's father. Mel Tormé appeared occasionally as a guest star.

NIGHTINGALES

UK 1990–2, 13 x 30m, col C4. Alomo.

CR *Paul Makin.* **PR** *Esta Charkham, Laurie Greenwood, Rosie Bunting.* **DR** *Tony Dow.* **WR** *Paul Makin.* **MUS** *Clever Music.* **CAST** Carter *Robert Lindsay* Bell *David Threlfall* Sarge *James Ellis.*

Surreal two-set (office rest room, lavatory) sitcom about a trio of security guards – Carter, Bell and Sarge – who whiled away the job's inactive midnight hours with flights of fantasy, power plays, pranks and squabbles. Storylines included Bell having to attend a psychiatrist because he raped a horse (he, in fact, harboured a hidden fantasy to sleep with Carter); a competition for Security Guard of the Year (prizes: an egg cup and a house brick); Carter and Bell forgetting Sarge's birthday – luckily Eric the Werewolf remembered; and the arrival of a distressed and heavily pregnant Mary on Christmas Eve. She was allowed to stay after signing a contract agreeing that she was not an allegory, whereupon she gave birth to a goldfish and a succession of white goods. Meanwhile, a fourth watchman, Mr Smith, had been dead for three years, but the others had kept his body hidden on the premises so that they could claim his salary.

Blackly weird, a kind of TV *Waiting for Godot, Nightingales* was dreamed up by Paul Makin, and based on a post-drama school stint as a security guard at Birmingham's National Exhibition Centre. Brilliantly realizing the idea and scripts (by Makin) were three of Britain's best actors: James Ellis (from *Z Cars*), David Threlfall

◀◀◀ *David Threlfall, James Ellis and Robert Lindsay in the security guard sitcom* Nightingales.

There's nobody here but us chickens!

(*Paradise Postponed, Diana: Her True Story* – as Prince Charles) and Robert Lindsay (>*Get Some In*, >*Citizen Smith, GBH*).

No – Honestly

UK 1974–5, 13 x 30m, col ITV. London Weekend TV. US tx *1975 PBS.*

CR *Terence Brady and Charlotte Bingham.* **PR** *Humphrey Barclay.* **DR** *Bill Turner, David Askey.* **WR** *Terence Brady and Charlotte Bingham.* **MUS** *Lyndsey De Paul (theme).* **CAST** Charles 'CD' Danby *John Alderton* Clara Danby *Pauline Collins* Lord Burrell *James Berwick* Lady Burrell *Fanny Rowe.*

Starred husband-and-wife team of John Alderton (from >*Please Sir!, My Wife Next Door*) and Pauline Collins (>*Liver Birds*) in a sickly sweet 'domcom' where they played the newly wedded Danbys. He was a calm thespian, she was the deeply dippy, book-writing (tales of 'Ollie the Otter') daughter of a peer. Episodes were wrapped around with *Burns and Allen Show*-esque addresses to camera. The same idea, with the cast changed to Donal Donelly and Liza Goddard, became *Yes – Honestly* (1976–7, ITV).

No – Honestly's theme song, as warbled by Lyndsey De Paul, reached the top ten in 1974.

Alderton and Collins later teamed again for the late eighties countrified drama *Forever Green.*

No Problem!

UK 1983–5, 22 x 30m, col C4. London Weekend TV C4.

CR *Mustapha Matura, Farukh Dhondy.* **PR** *Charlie Hanson, Mickey Dolenz.* **WR** *Mustapha Matura, Farukh Dhondy.* **CAST** Sensimilia *Judith Jacob* Bellamy *Victor Romero Evans* Beast *Malcolm Frederick* Toshiba *Chris Tummings* Terri *Shope Shodeinde* Angel *Janet Kay* Susannah *Sarah Lam.*

Home-alone comedy show featuring the Powell kids of Willesden, London, whose parents had returned to Jamaica for an extended holiday.

The show was the first original sitcom made for British minority network, Channel 4, and was almost absurdly true to its liberal brief, being written by two black writers, Farukh Dhondy and Mustapha Matura, for the Black Theatre Co-Operative. Raucous. But funny. The producers included Mickey Dolenz, formerly of >*The Monkees.*

Not in Front of the Children

UK 1967–70, 35 x 30m, col BBC1. BBC TV.

CR *Richard Waring.* **PR** *Graeme Muir.* **WR** *Richard Waring.* **CAST** Jennifer Corner *Wendy Craig* Henry Corner *Paul Daneman/Ronald Hines* Trudi *Roberta Tovey/Verna Greenlaw* Robin *Hugo Keith-Johnson* Amanda *Jill Riddick.*

Domestic comedy by Richard Waring, starring Wendy Craig as the matriarch-referee of the disputatious Corner family. It derived from a 1967

Comedy Playhouse presentation called 'House in a Tree', and blueprinted the scatty middle-class housewife persona that Craig would take to Waring's *And Mother Makes Three/Five* (Thames 1971–6, as Sally Harrison) and then to Carla Lane's >*Butterflies.*

A radio version of *Not in Front* was broadcast between 1969 and 1970.

NOT ONLY... BUT ALSO...

UK 1965–6/1970–3, 14 x 45m, 7 x 30m, 2 x 50m, bw/col BBC2. BBC TV.

CR *Peter Cook and Dudley Moore.* **PR** *Joe McGrath, Dick Clement, John Street, James Gilbert.* **WR** *Peter Cook, Dudley Moore, John Law, Robert Fuest.* **CAST** *Peter Cook, Dudley Moore.*

Revue-style show with *Beyond the Fringers* Peter Cook and Dudley Moore. Originally scheduled as a one-off, it achieved instant success – and thus a full series, its absurdist skits neatly capturing the psychedelic unreality of the Swinging Sixties. There was a Gerry Anderson puppet pastiche entitled 'Superthunderstingcar', the Leaping Nuns of St Beryl, the 'Good vs Evil' cricket match, the one-legged man auditioning for a Tarzan film, and Cook's immortal interpretation of Bo Diddley's R'n'B music (*'Momma's got a brand new bag, we're gonna groove it'* – 'Now this, presumably, is a reference to the fact that mother, having bought the bag, decided to make some indentations on it...'). In each week's opening credits, the show's logo was depicted in the unlikeliest of situations, most memorably being carved by cavemen on a hillside above a chalk horse; the closing song 'Goodbye-ee', meanwhile, made the top twenty in 1965. (Moore, the son of a railwayman, was a musical prodigy; he had won an organ scholarship to Oxford, and later led a jazz combo at Cook's Establishment Club.) But the undoubted highlight of *Not Only... But Also* episodes was Cook and Moore's 'Dagenham' routine, in which two brain-dead, cloth-capped proletarians, Pete and Dud, met for a chat, beginning with something mundane and ending up with something sublimely fantastic. A visit to the zoo prompted a discussion on the immensely long tongue of the humming-bird, which would enable it to kiss at obscenely long distances: 'That means you could stand on the Chiswick flyover and kiss someone on the Staines by-pass.' As for women, 'She got off at the stop before me but I knew what she was after...'

> **»** ***'Tap, tap, tap at the bloody window pane. I looked out – you know who it was? Bloody Greta Garbo...'*** **«**

Guests included Spike Milligan, Peter Sellers, Barry Humphries and John Lennon, the latter once appearing as the commissionaire of a gents' lavatory.

A TV treasure for all time.

NOT THE NINE O'CLOCK NEWS

UK 1979–82, 28 x 30m, col BBC1. BBC TV. US tx *1981 Syndicated.*

CR *John Lloyd.* **PR** *John Lloyd, Sean Hardie.* **WR** *Various, including Mel Smith, Rowan Atkinson,*

▶▶▶ *Nice video, shame about the song. Rowan Atkinson and Pamela Stephenson in* Not the Nine O'Clock News.

Griff Rhys Jones, John Lloyd, Arnold Brown, Andy Hamilton, Colin Bostock-Smith, Nigel Planer, Peter Richardson, Philip Pope, Guy Jenkin, Richard Curtis, Howard Goodall, Laurie Rowley, Andrew Marshall, Terry Kyan. **CAST** *Rowan Atkinson, Pamela Stephenson, Mel Smith, Griff Rhys Jones, Chris Langham (first season only).*

Satirical skit show from the twilight of the seventies, one of the first to break with the oldster comedy (of the >*Two Ronnies* type) which then dominated the BBC's airwaves. Conducted at a clip of 75 seconds each, the sketches were energetically iconoclastic and wonderfully offensive; everyone from Margaret Thatcher to Angela Rippon to Abba was done over, with a gag about a squashed hedgehog causing apoplexy amongst the responsible classes (ie anyone over twenty-five). The show scored a direct hit on pop's New Romanticism in 'Nice Video, Shame About the Song', and on >*Monty Python* – once the Young Turks of comedy themselves – in a sketch about a humble carpenter who thought he was the new messiah, John Cleese. Other highlights included a spoof studio discussion on football hooliganism ('Cut off their goolies,' agreed the social worker), an interview with Gerald the Gorilla ('Wild? I was absolutely livid'), while the words of the 'Trucking Song' passed into legend. The alternative voice-overs of news footage – from which

... American Express, that'll do nicely, sir, and would you like to feel my tits?

the show took its title – had their moments, too, particularly Pamela Stephenson's bullseye impression of newscaster Angela Rippon's exaggerated pronunciation of African leader 'Mugabe'. Although Rowan Atkinson, Griff Rhys Jones, Pamela Stephenson and Mel Smith are fixed in the memory as the presenters, Rhys Jones only joined in season two, to replace Chris Langham (who became a >*Muppet Show* writer).

The most obviously punk-influenced comedy show to be broadcast on GB TV, the series launched the careers not only of its performers (who returned in such classics as >*Blackadder*, >*Alas Smith and Jones*, although Stephenson, the wife of ex-*Hazell* star Nicholas Ball, then of Billy Connolly, eventually quit showbiz to work in LA as a psychiatrist), but also of the writers. Richard Curtis went on to pen >*Blackadder*, *The Vicar of Dibley* and *Four Weddings and a Funeral;* Andy Hamilton and Guy Jenkin begat >*Drop the Dead Donkey*, and Andrew Renwick >*One Foot in the Grave*.

In 1980 the show won a Silver Rose at the Montreux Festival, and three years later the format was sold to the USA as *Not Necessarily the News* (1983, HBO).

Cut off their goolies

NURSES

USA 1991–4, 67 x 30m, col ABC. Witt-Thomas-Harris. UK tx *1992–4 C4.*

CR *Susan Harris.* **DR** *Various, including Terry Hughes, Andy Cardiff, Peter D Beyt, Bob Berlinger.*
CAST Sandy Miller *Stephanie Hodge* Annie Roland *Arnetia Walker* Greg Vincent *Jeff Altman* Julie Milbury *Mary Jo Keenen* Gina Cuevas *Ada Maris* Dr Hank Kaplan *Kip Gilman* Paco Ortiz *Carlos Lacamara* Jack Trenton *David Rasche* Casey MacAfee *Loni Anderson* Luke Fitzgerald *Markus Flanagan* Dr Riskin *Florence Stanley.*

Medical mirth at Miami's Community Medical Center. The show was loosely spun off from creator Susan Harris' >*Empty Nest*, which featured the Center's Dr Harry Weston; here the featured characters were a group of overworked, underpaid – and mismatched – RNs. Nice gal Annie, a single mom, was in charge. Greg was a Vietnam vet, with more than a few cracked slates. Julie was phobic about... germs. Mexican Gina was culturally bemused. Sandy was the caustic-tongued divorcee. Dr Hank was the one good doctor. It wasn't funny enough to make you spill your bedtime drink, but there were some nice one-liners injected into the scripts. Quipped Sandy to a Ku Klux Klan member admitted (in 'Kind, Kompassionate and Karing') for treatment: 'We keep all our sheets here numbered... just in case you were thinking of wearing one home.' John Ratzenberger from >*Cheers* guested as hospital administrator Mr Haffner. Also donating cameos were Richard Mulligan, Estelle Getty and Adam 'Batman' West.

THE ODD COUPLE

USA 1970–5, 100 x 25m, col ABC. Paramount TV. UK tx *1971–5 ITV.*

PR *Garry K Marshall, Jerry Belson, Harvey Miller, Sheldon Keller.* **DR** *Various, including Garry K Marshall, Jerry Paris, Jay Sandrich, Charles R Rondeau.* **WR** *Various, including Garry K Marshall, Jerry Belson, Peggy Elliot and Ed Sharlach, Dick Bensfield and Peggy Grant, Albert E Lewis.* **MUS** *Neal Hefti, Kenyon Hopkins.* **CAST** Felix Unger *Tony Randall* Oscar Madison *Jack Klugman* Off Murray Greshner *Al Molinaro* Speed *Garry Walberg* Vinnie *Larry Gelman* Cecily Pigeon *Monica Evans* Gwendolyn Pigeon *Carol Shelly* Gloria Unger *Janis Hansen* Blanche Madison *Brett Somers* Myrna Turner *Penny Marshall.*

A compulsively tidy photographer, Felix Unger, shares an apartment with a slobbish sportswriter for the *New York Herald,* Oscar Madison.

Sitcomized extrusion of Neil Simon's hit Broadway play. Wryly, sometimes brilliantly, written, with a successful, bickering chemistry between its principals – but bound to suffer, ever so slightly, in comparison with the 1968 movie version, with its wondrous casting of Jack Lemmon and Walter Matthau.

In what would become a habit, producer Garry K Marshall (>*Happy Days,* >*Laverne and Shirley*) cast his sister Penny in his show, here to play Oscar's secretary, Myrna Turner. Also seen were Oscar and Felix's daffy English upstairs neighbours, the Pigeon sisters, Felix's poker-playing buddies, Speed, Vinnie and Murray the cop (Al Molinaro, >*Happy Days*), and Felix and Oscar's ex-spouses – the men were both divorced – Gloria and Blanche. (Blanche was played by actor Jack Klugman's real-life wife, Brett Somers.) By the final season Felix moved out to remarry Gloria, leaving Oscar to return alone to the apartment – which to his joy he could now make as untidy as he wanted. Klugman won a 1974 Golden Globe for his portrayal of Oscar.

In 1982 the sitcom version was revived as *The New Odd Couple,* with two black stars Ron Glass and Desmond Wilson in the Felix and Oscar roles. It screened on ABC until 1983.

Nearly twenty years after the original TV show ended its run, Felix and Oscar (played again by Randall and Klugman) were reunited in the 1993 TV movie, *Odd Couple: Together Again,* when Felix was temporarily thrown out of his house by his wife, who wanted to plan for daughter Edna's wedding in peace. He moved back in with Oscar, who was still living in the same old apartment.

OH BROTHER!

UK 1968–70, 19 x 30m, col BBC1. BBC TV.

CR *David Climie and Austin Steele.* **PR** *Duncan Wood, Johnny Downes.* **WR** *David Climie and Austin Steele.* **CAST** Brother Dominic *Derek Nimmo* Father Anselm *Felix Aylmer* Master of the Novices *Colin Gordon.*

Starred Derek Nimmo as the bumbling Brother Dominic of Mountacres Priory. The character, who was promoted up the clerical career ladder for a sequel, *Oh Father!* (1971, 7 x 30m, BBC1, where he became curate to Father Harris), was essentially a resurrection of Nimmo's bashful, plummy-voiced Noote from >*All Gas and Gaiters*. And, thus, mildly watchable.

ONE FOOT IN THE GRAVE

UK 1990–7, 29 x 30m, 5 x 50–95m, col BBC1. BBC TV.

CR *David Renwick.* **PR** *Susan Belbin.* **DR** *Susan Belbin.* **WR** *David Renwick.* **MUS** *Eric Idle (theme).* **CAST** Victor Meldrew *Richard Wilson* Margaret Meldrew *Annette Crosbie* Patrick *Angus Deayton* Pippa *Janine Duvitski* Nick Swainey *Owen Brennan* Ronnie *Gordon Peters* Mildred *Jean Challis/Barbara Ashcroft* Ronnie *Gordon Peters.* Video *BBC.*

David Renwick's acidly amusing 'trials of retirement' sitcom following the misadventures of splenetic Victor Meldrew (played by former mortuary assistant Richard Wilson, *Only When I Laugh*) as he sought to understand the illogical behaviour of household appliances and everyone else. Particular bugbears were 'crap' in the front garden and the failure of mail order firms to supply the correct goods. Meanwhile, his Scottish wife Margaret (Annette Crosbie) found even her considerable patience tried by his diatribes and accidents. In 1992 the Meldrews moved to a modern estate in suburban Bournemouth, where neighbours Patrick (Angus Deayton, >*KYTV, Have I Got News for You*) and his bus-driving wife Pippa, and Nick Swainey, found themselves unfortunate enough to experience close encounters with the

I don't believe it . . .

grumbling curmudgeon, a man whose view of yuletide was that 'All the miseries of the world seem a hundred times worse at Christmas'.

Unusually reluctant to stay with the traditional confines of the sitcom, *One Foot in the Grave* broached pathos, even surrealism, yet remained constantly credible owing to Renwick's highly controlled writing. The show proved the most popular BBC sitcom of the early nineties, and sold to America, where it was remade as *Cosby*, with Bill Cosby from >*The Cosby Show*.

Trivia: Meldrew's job before retirement was security guard for Mycroft, Watts & Associates; the Meldrews' first address was 37 Wyngate Drive; the second address was 19 Riverbank. Their telephone numbers were 770301 and 4291.

ON THE BUSES

UK 1970–5, 70 x 25m, col ITV. London Weekend TV.

CR *Ronald Wolfe and Ronald Chesney.* **PR** *Stuart Allen, Bryan Izzard.* **DR** *Various, including Stuart Allen.* **WR** *Various, including Ronald Wolfe and Ronald Chesney, Bob Grant and Stephen Lewis, George Layton and Jonathan Lynn.* **CAST** Stan Butler *Reg Varney* Jack *Bob Grant* Inspector Blake ('Blakey') *Stephen Lewis* Mum *Cicely Courtneidge/Doris Hare* Olive *Anna Karen* Arthur *Michael Robbins* Jessie (conductress) *Yootha Joyce* Video *Video Collection/LWT.*

Like Chesney and Wolfe's earlier series, >*The Rag Trade,* this was a workplace sitcom of cheerfully lowbrow humour. The setting was The Luxton Bus Company, ruled over by the black-hearted Inspector Blakey, tormentor of ferrety driver Stan (ex-music hall performer Reg Varney, >*The Rag Trade, Beggar Thy Neighbour, Down the Gate*) and his lothario conductor, Jack. Stan lived with his mum, his plain sister Olive (former stripper Anna Karen, later Peg Mitchell's sister in soap *EastEnders*) and idle brother-in-law Arthur (Michael Robbins). Stories centred on Stan and Jack's labour-management battles with the dim-witted Blakey (catchphrases: 'I 'ate you Butler', 'I'll get you Butler') and the attempts by the lads to woo the conductresses. A bus depot in Wood Green, London, provided the exteriors. For many its gorblimey laffs were just the ticket, and it rode to the top of the BARB ratings in 1970, 1971 and 1972.

Three movies based on the show were released in the cinema: *On the Buses* (the highest-earning British film of 1971), *Mutiny on the Buses,* and *Holiday on the Buses.* None of them was worth the fare. The show's format was sold to America as *Lotsa Luck.*

ONLY FOOLS AND HORSES

UK 1981–96, 33 x 30m, 13 x 50m, 3 x 60m, col BBC1. BBC TV.

CR *John Sullivan.* **PR** *Ray Butt, Gareth Gwenlan.* **DR** *Various, including Ray Butt, Gareth Gwenlan, Tony Dow, Martin Shardlow, Susan Blebin, Mandie Fletcher.* **WR** *John Sullivan.* **CAST** Derek 'Del Boy' Trotter *David Jason* Rodney Trotter *Nicholas Lyndhurst* Grandad Trotter *Lennard Pearce* Uncle Albert *Buster Merryfield* Cassandra Parry/Trotter *Gwyneth Strong* Raquel *Tessa Peake-Jones* Boycie *John Challis* Marlene *Sue Holderness* Mike Fisher *Kenneth MacDonald* Trigger *Roger Lloyd-Pack* Denzil *Paul Barber* Mickey Pearce *Patrick Murray* Roy Slater *Jim Broadbent.*

◀◀◀ *Reg Varney (right) headed the cast of* On the Buses.

▲▲▲ *Nicholas Lyndhurst, David Jason and Lennard Pearce in* Only Fools and Horses.

Uproariously funny John Sullivan sitcom that took its title from the Cockney saying, 'Only fools and horses work' (also an episode title in Sullivan's earlier hit, >*Citizen Smith*). It followed the wide-boy antics of South London's Del Boy Trotter (immortally performed by David Jason, >*Open All Hours*), who sold 'dodgy gear' from his clapped-out yellow Robin Reliant – the legend 'Trotter's Independent Trading Company' emblazoned on the side – and had delusions of imminent wealth. The Brut-splashed, gold-swathed Del Boy was helped in the family firm by naïve younger brother, 'plonker' Rodney (Nicholas

You plonker

Lyndhurst, >*Butterflies*), the proud possessor of two GCSEs. They lived in a council flat (no. 368) in high-rise Mandela House, Peckham, with Grandad, and then (after the death of actor Lennard Pearce) old sea-dog Uncle Albert. Also seen was a coterie of credibly bizarre friends, most of whom, like Del (favourite drink: Drambuie and grapefruit juice) were habitués of the Nag's Head: brain-fused road sweeper Trigger (Roger Lloyd Pack, *The Vicar of Dibley,* father of Emily Lloyd); gangster-like businessman Boycie and his good-time gal wife, Marlene ('all the boys like Marlene'); and nerve-shattered lorry driver Denzil. Although Sullivan had originally intended the sitcom to be about 'three men of different generations, all without a woman in their lives', by the early nineties Rodney had married the middle-class Cassandra and Del Boy had fallen in love with former stripogram/actress Raquel (Tessa Peake-Jones, *So Haunt Me, Up the Garden Path*), who later bore him a son, Damian ('The Son of Del' episode).

The 1991 season saw the last full series of *Only Fools and Horses,* although it continued to exist in Christmas specials (which, like >*Morecambe and Wise* of yore, became the turkey and cranberry sauce of British yuletide TV) until a 'final' three-parter in 1996, in which Del and Rodney walked off into the sunset after finding a watch worth £6 million in their garage. A record 24.35 million viewers tuned in.

OPEN ALL HOURS

UK 1976–85, 25 x 30m, col BBC2/1. BBC TV. US tx *1982 TEC.*

CR *Roy Clarke.* **PR** *Sydney Lotterby.* **DR** *Sydney Lotterby.* **WR** *Roy Clarke.* **MUS** *Max Harris.*
CAST Arkwright *Ronnie Barker* Granville *David Jason* Nurse Gladys Emmanuel *Lynda Baron* Mrs Featherstone *Stephanie Cole* Mavis *Maggie Ollerenshaw.*

Roy Clarke (>*Last of the Summer Wine,* >*Keeping Up Appearances*) situation comedy set in a Yorkshire corner shop, which opened as a 1974 *Comedy Playhouse* and received its first run on BBC2, where it picked up only modest custom. A repeat on BBC1 in 1979, however, took it to the very pinnacle of the ratings.

Ronnie Barker *(Hark at Barker,* >*The Two Ronnies)* starred as the stammering, scrooge-like shopkeeper Arkwright who, in between counting his money, bullied his daydreaming assistant, nephew Gr-Gr-ranville, and lusted after big-bosomed, Morris Minor-driving Nurse Gladys Emmanuel. To counter the rising tide of supermarkets, Arkwright opened his shop first thing in the morning till last thing at night, and conned his customers into buying goods they did not want. Among the regulars in the shop were Mrs Featherstone (Stephanie Cole, later *Waiting for God*) and Mavis.

Gr-Gr-ranville

Seaside postcard-type laughs, always crucially dependent on Barker's performance as Arkwright. But then, Clarke had tailor-made the part for Barker (it was originally tried out in Barker's *Seven of One* show), and he was never s-s-s-s-short of superb.

The format sold to America as *Open All Night* (1981–2), with George Dzundza as Gordon Feester, the owner of a Californian '364' store.

PARKER LEWIS CAN'T LOSE

USA 1990–3, Approx 60 x 30m, col FOX. Clyde Phillips Productions/Columbia Pictures TV. UK tx *1992– BSkyB.*

CR *Clyde Phillips and Lon Diamond.* **EXEC PR** *Clyde Phillips.* **PR** *Lon Diamond, Russell Marcus, Robert Lloyd Lewis.* **DR** *Various, including Max Tash, Bryan Spicer, Andy Tennant, Rob Bowman, Thom Eberhardt.* **WR** *Various, including Lon Diamond and Clyde Phillips.* **MUS** *Dennis McCarthy.* **CAST** Parker Lloyd Lewis *Corin Nemec* Mikey Randall *Billy Jayne* Jerry Steiner *Troy W Slaten* Principal Ms Grace Musso *Melanie Chartoff* Mr Martin Lewis *Timothy Stack* Mrs Lewis *Anne Bloom/Mary Ellen Trainor* Annie Sloan *Jennifer Guthrie* Francis Lawrence 'Larry' Kubiac *Abraham Benrubi.*

Initially slated as a carbon copy of *Ferris Bueller* (the movie and the TV show) this US sitcom chronicling the machinations and misadventures of ice-cool, rule-defying Santa Domingo High School student Parker Lewis actually had a style all its own. Made with a single camera, full of unusual angles and special video effects, it erred towards a cartoon-like bizarreness which ensured youth appeal. Adults liked it, too.

Unfortunately for Lewis (motto: 'Not a problem') his quest for ultimate cool during puberty was frequently frustrated by his little sister Shelly. Not to mention principal Grace Musso. Mikey and Jerry were Parker's best buds, Annie Sloan his girlfriend. From 1993 the show went out as plain *Parker Lewis.*

THE PARTRIDGE FAMILY

USA 1970–4, 96 x 25m, col ABC. Columbia Pictures Corporation. UK tx *1971–4 BBC1.*

CR *Bernard Slade.* **EXEC PR** *Bob Claver.* **PR** *Paul Junger Witt, Michael Warren, Mel Swope, Bob Claver, William S Bickley.* **DR** *Various, including Bob Claver, E W Swackhamer, Lou Antonio, Russ Mayberry, Claudio Guzman, Earl Bellamy, Herb Wallerstein, Jerry London, Ralph Senensky, Lee Philips, Richard Kinon.* **MUS** *Wes Farrell and Diane Hilderbrand ('When We're Singing' theme and lyrics), Danny Janssen ('Come On Get Happy' lyrics), Hugh Montenegro.* **CAST** Shirley Partridge *Shirley Jones* Keith Partridge *David Cassidy* Laurie Partridge *Susan Dey* Danny Partridge *Danny Bonaduce* Christopher Partridge *Jeremey Gelwaks/Brian Forster* Tracy Partridge *Suzanne Crough* Reuben Kinkaid (manager) *Dave Madden* Rickey Stevens *Ricky Segall.*

▶▶ *Come on get happy!* The Partridge Family *go on the road again. The musical sitcom launched David Cassidy (right) to teenybop stardom.*

The Partridge Family

In which a widowed suburban mom, Shirley Partridge, joins her kids' band as a singer – and, hey presto, they become a big sensation. Embarking in a painted school bus, the Partridge family duly tour the US of A making music and having squeaky clean sitcom fun.

Though Shirley Jones was ostensibly the star, her real-life stepson David Cassidy – who played the eldest Partridge boy, Keith – quickly emerged as the real draw, and for a brief rocket-glare moment became the biggest teen idol on Earth.

For the record, *The Partridge Family* line-up was: Shirley Partridge, sixteen-year-old Keith, fifteen-year-old Laurie, ten-year-old Danny, seven-year-old Chris and five-year-old Tracy. The dog was Simone. In the 1973–4 season, next-door neighbour Ricky (aged a cute four) joined the band. Among the *Family*'s spin-off chart hits were the sixties covers, 'Breaking Up is Hard to Do', and 'Walking in the Rain'.

The guest actor list included Jodie Foster (as Julie Lawrence), Farah Fawcett, Cheryl Ladd, and Richard Pryor and Lou Gossett Jr, who both appeared in the immortal 'Soul Club' episode where Shirley organized a block party to save their characters' Detroit nightclub. (Keith Partridge, of course, wrote a song for the occasion, 'It's a Sort of Afro thing', and Black Panthers danced in the street to it...)

A 1974 animated spin-off, *Partridge Family: 2200 AD* (directed by Joy Batchelor and John Halas), posited the phenomenon of widow Partridge (her forename changed to Connie and voiced by Sherry Alberoni) leading the clan on a rock'n'roll tour of the planets.

PETTICOAT JUNCTION

USA 1963–9, 148 x 25m, col. Filmways. UK tx *1964– ITV.*

CR *Paul Henning.* **PR** *Paul Henning, Charles Stewart, Al Simon, Dick Wesson.* **MUS** *Paul Henning and Curt Massey (theme).* **CAST** Kate Bradley *Bea Benaderet* Billie Jo *Jeannine Riley /Gunilla Hutton* Bobbie Jo *Pat Woddell/Lori Saunders* Betty Jo *Linda Kaye Henning* Homer Bedloe *Charles Lane* Uncle Joe *Edgar Buchanan* Charley Pratt *Smiley Burnett* Floyd Smoot *Rufe Davis* Dr Janet Craig *June Lockhart* Fred Ziffel *Hank Patterson* Sam Drucker *Frank Cady.*

Countrified farce about the proprietress of the Shady Rest Hotel, at the end of the Hooterville line. She was Kate Bradley, and she was supported in her endeavours to keep the hotel running and the steam-age line open (bad-guy rail executive Homer Bedloe of CF & W wanted to close it down) by her three buxom, beautiful daughters, Billie Jo, Bobby Jo and Betty Jo. Zany Uncle Joe was the manager.

The show was created for actress Bea Benaderet, formerly elderly cousin Pearl Bodine in >*The Beverly Hillbillies,* by Paul Henning, with a faith which was well justified. Benaderet (and the rest of the cast) rose above its studio-bound production, and the show ran for 148 episodes. Benaderet herself died in the sixth season, which led to a loss of quality in the last episodes. Henning's own daughter, Linda Kaye Henning, played Betty Jo. The show was closely related to another Henning production, >*Green Acres.*

THE PHIL SILVERS SHOW

USA 1955–9, 143 (inc pilot) x 30m, 1 x 60m, bw CBS. CBS. UK tx *1957–61 BBC1.*

CR *Nat Hiken.* **PR** *Nat Hiken, Al De Caprio, Edward J Montagne.* **DR** *Nat Hiken, Al De Caprio.* **WR** *Various, including Nat Hiken, Arnold Auerbach, Terry Ryan, Barry Blitzer, Aaron Rubin, Vincent Bogert, Harvey Orkin, Tony Webster, Coleman Jacoby, Arnie Rosen, Billy Friedberg, Leonard Stern, Phil Sharp, Neil Simon.* **MUS** *John Strauss.* **CAST** M/Sgt Ernie Bilko *Phil Silvers* Cpl Rocco Barbella *Harvey Lembeck* Pte Sam Fender *Herbie Faye* Col John Hall *Paul Ford* Pte Duane Doberman *Maurice Gosfield* Sgt Rupert Ritzik *Joe E Ross* Cpl Henshaw *Allan Melvin* Pte Dino Paparelli *Billy Sands* Pte Zimmerman *Mickey Freeman* Nell Hall *Hope Sansberry* Sgt Grover *Jimmy Little* Sgt Joan Hogan *Elizabeth Fraser.* Video *Fox/Columbia House.*

Master Sergeant Ernie Bilko, based at mythical Fort Baxter, Kansas, was the biggest and most charming rogue in the US Army. With little to do in the world of the Midwest, Bilko was incurably occupied in get-rich-quick schemes, spending most of his time gambling (in the episode 'The Twitch', he even managed to run a book on an officer's lectures on Beethoven), conjuring up scams, and out-manoeuvring his unfortunate and all too trusting commanding officer, the hapless Colonel Hall, who was reduced to calling his post 'the Little Las Vegas'. The Bilko-Hall relationship was central to the genius of the show, a modern reworking of the dumb master/clever servant relationship found as far back as ancient Greek theatre. Highly resourceful, Bilko could talk his way out of any situation. His example was followed by most of his subordinates whom he involved as willing aides and accomplices (although he was not above fleecing them in times of desperation). A favourite target for his con tricks was the ill-fated Rupert Ritzik. Seargeant Joan Hogan, who worked in the base's office, was Bilko's mild romantic interest during the first three seasons, but was later phased out. Bilko also endlessly flattered the Colonel's wife ('Hello Miss – the Colonel didn't tell me his daughter was visiting – why it's *Mrs* Hall...'), with the result that she was one of his staunchest defenders. Bilko's wooing technique was known as the 'Bilko Blitz', an unbeatable combination of a 'man in

▶▶▶ *Phil Silvers as the irrepressible Bilko.*

uniform, moonlight and music'. Of course, underneath the Machiavellian clown exterior, Bilko had a heart of gold; in the classic spoof on Elvis joining the army, 'Rock'n'Roll Rookie', Bilko eventually refused to exploit his new musical recruit, 'Elvin Pelvin', after overhearing him sing 'Bilko is the Best' to the tune of 'Love Me Tender'. Down on the guest list, the show provided early screen appearances for Alan Alda (as Carlisle Thompson in 'Bilko, the Art Lover'), Fred Gwynne and Dick Van Dyke. A musical special, 'Keep in Step', was released in 1959, the same season that saw Bilko and entourage move from Kansas to Camp Fremont, California ('a lousy idea,' admitted producer Edward J Montagne, 'but by then we had told all the jokes'). In a moral conclusion to the long-running satire on army life, the final episode, 'Weekend Colonel', saw Bilko behind bars. Colonel Hall had won the war.

The original title was *You'll Never Get Rich,* which remained as the subtitle when the series became *The Phil Silvers Show* two months after its premiere. Although there was fine support from the cast – headed by Paul Ford's Hall and Maurice Gosfield's Doberman ('the slob of the century') – it was Silvers' show in name and fact, his oxygen-consuming performance frequently leaving everyone else to gasp 'But Sarge...!' It was perhaps the greatest sitcom act of all time, and won Silvers three Emmys.

Silvers was born Philip Silver in New York, the son of Jewish immigrants. He made his show business début at the age of eleven, and featured in numerous films over the next decade, signing to MGM in 1940. But it was as Bilko that he found fame, and the character overshadowed everything

But Sarge. . .!

he did thereafter. A *New Phil Silvers Show,* in which he played maintenance superintendent Harry Grafton, lasted only the 1963–4 season on CBS. *Just Polly and Me, The Slowest Gun in the West* and *Summer in New York* fared even worse. After several years of illness and clinical depression, Silvers died in 1985.

The Bilko character, meanwhile, turned up in cartoon form in Hanna-Barbera's *Boss Cat* (which even had Gosfield voicing his 'toon representation, blue Benny the Ball). In 1996 a movie version of *Bilko* was released (directed by Jonathan Lynn) with Steve Martin as the eponymous conman, but it never quite came off, and viewed like endless foreplay.

PLEASE SIR!

UK 1968–9, 40 x 25m, col ITV. London Weekend TV.

CR *John Esmonde and Bob Larbey.* **PR** *Mark Stuart, Phil Casson.* **DR** *Mark Stuart.* **WR** *John Esmonde and Bob Larbey.* **CAST** Bernard Hedges *John Alderton* Price *Richard Davies* Doris Ewell *Joan Sanderson* Norman Potter *Deryck Guyler* Mr Cromwell (the Headmaster) *Noel Howlett* Mr 'Smithy' Smith *Eric Chitty* Eric Duffy *Peter Cleall* Frankie Abbot *David Barry* Maureen Bullock *Liz Gebhardt* Peter Craven *Malcolm McFee* Dennis Dunstable *Peter Denyer* Sharon Eversleigh *Penny Spencer* Penny Wheeler/Hedges *Jill Kerman.*

Actor John Alderton, in his first starring role since playing Dr Moon in soap *Emergency – Ward 10,* was sensitive teacher Bernard 'Privet' Hedges, the form master of unruly 5C at inner-city Fenn Street School. The class – played by actors clearly much older than fifth-formers – caused Bernard considerable heartache, but many of the show's best moments came in the staff room with the interchanges between cynical Welsh teacher Price and the straight-laced deputy head, Doris Ewell. Norman Potter was the uniformed, Hitlerian school porter. Towards the end of the run, Hedges acquired a wife in Penny Wheeler. The show was inspired by the 1967 movie *To Sir with Love,* starring Sidney Poitier, Judy Geeson and Lulu.

After Alderton left *Please Sir!* (to eventually appear in *My Wife Next Door,* and >*No – Honestly*), the series continued for several seasons as *The Fenn Street Gang,* concentrating on 5C's antics after leaving their alma mater. This was likewise created and (mainly) written by John Esmonde and Bob Larbey, who then went on to pen >*Get Some In,* the self-sufficiency sitcom >*The Good Life, Ever Decreasing Circles,* with Larbey alone creating *A Fine Romance* and *As Time Goes By*.

The format of *Please Sir!* was sold to the USA as >*Welcome Back, Kotter,* where it launched the career of John Travolta.

▶▶▶ *John Alderton was the trouble-struck teacher of 5C in* Please Sir!

POLICE SQUAD!

USA 1982, 6 x 30m, col ABC. Paramount TV. UK tx *1982.*

CR *Jim Abrahams, David Zucker, Jerry Zucker.* **PR** *Bob Weiss.* **DR** *Jerry Zucker, Reza S Badiyi, Paul Krasny, Joe Dante, George Stanford Brown, Jim Abrahams.* **WR** *Various, including Jim Abrahams, David Zucker, Jerry Zucker, Tino Insana, Robert Wuhl, Nancy Steen, Pat Proft, Neil Thompson.*

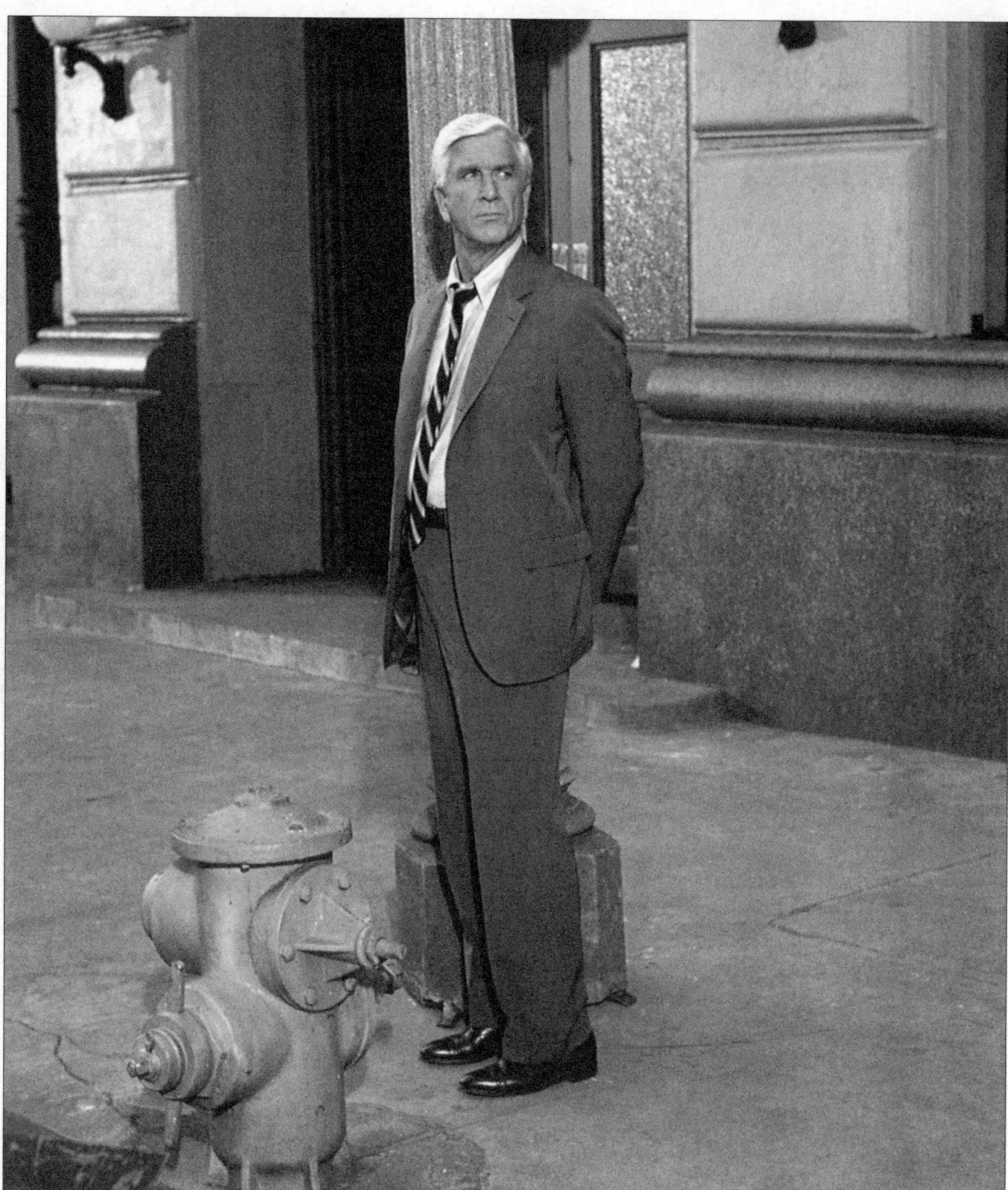

***MUS** Ira Newborn.* **CAST** Detective Frank Drebin *Leslie Nielsen* Captain Ed Hocken *Alan North* Norberg *Peter Lupus* Abraham Lincoln *Rex Hamilton* Johnny the Snitch *William Duell* Al *John Wardell* Ted Olson *Ed Williams.* Video *Paramount.*

This short-lived spoof police show came from the creators of *Airplane!* and featured that film's star, Leslie Nielsen (also *The New Breed, >The Golden Girls*), as fearless, deadpan Inspector Frank Drebin of Police Squad. The comedy came from a deluge of sight gags (giant policeman Al was only ever seen from the neck down), non sequiturs and literalisms; when Drebin requested a colleague to 'Cover Me!', the officer did so – with a coat. In his fight to keep the streets clean, Drebin had the help of forensic scientist Ted Olson (who had an unhealthy interest in young children) and stoolie shoeshine Johnny, who could give more information on any given subject than the *Encyclopedia Americana*. Although it fared abysmally on TV (ABC executives reportedly believed it required too much concentration from the average viewer), it became the basis for the successful movies *The Naked Gun* ('From the Files of Police Squad!'), *Naked Gun 2½* and *Naked Gun 33⅓*.

The six episodes were: A Substantial Gift (The Broken Promise)/Ring of Fear (A Dangerous Assignment)/The Butler Did It (A Bird in the Hand)/ Revenge and Remorse (The Guilty Alibi)/Rendezvous at Big Gulch (Terror in the Neighbourhood)/ Testimony of Evil (Dead Men Don't Laugh).

◀◀◀ *I said cover me, Al... Leslie Nielsen deadpans it up as fearless Lieutenant Frank Drebin in* Police Squad!

PORRIDGE

UK 1974–7, 18 x 30m, 2 x c60m, col BBC1. BBC TV.

***CR** Dick Clement and Ian La Frenais.* ***PR** Sydney Lotterby.* ***DR** Sydney Lotterby.* ***WR** Dick Clement and Ian La Frenais.* **CAST** Fletcher *Ronnie Barker* Godber *Richard Beckinsale* Chief Officer Mackay *Fulton MacKay* Warden Barrowclough *Brian Wilde* Mr Venables, the Governor *Michael Barrington* Lukewarm *Christopher Biggins* Blanco *David Jason* Warren *Tony Osiba* 'Orrible Ives *Ken Jones* Harry Grout *Peter Vaughan* Heslop *Brian Glover* Harris *Ronald Lacey* Ingrid *Patricia Brake.* Video *BBC*

» ***Norman Stanley Fletcher... you are an habitual criminal who accepts arrest as an occupational hazard and presumably accepts imprisonment in the same casual manner...*** **«**

So intoned the judge over the opening credits of Dick Clement and Ian La Frenais' (*>The Likely Lads >Auf Wiedersehen, Pet*) sitcom about an ageing Muswell Hill lag sentenced to a five-year term at HM Prison Slade in darkest Cumbria. There the genial, crafty, quick-quipping Fletcher (Ronnie Barker, *Hark at Barker, >Open All Hours*) shared a cell with naïve Birmingham offender Godber (Richard Beckinsale, *>The Lovers, >Rising Damp*), and generally ran comic rings around the warders – notably strutting Scotsman Chief Officer Mackay and kindly (but dim) Warden Barrowclough – while earning the awestruck admiration of his fellow cons. These included Bunny Warren (Sam Kelly, *>'Allo,*

'Allo), brain-dead murderer Blanco (David Jason, >*Only Fools and Horses*), gay cook Lukewarm, and 'Black Jock' McClaren. Harry Grout (the frightening Peter Vaughan, >*Citizen Smith*) was the Mr Big who still ran his racket from the prison wing. Mr Venables was the do-gooder governor. By the end of the run Rawley, the judge who had sentenced Fletcher, had also joined the inmates of Slade (imprisoned on corruption charges), and Fletcher himself had tired of prison life and was determined never to reappear behind bars again.

Porridge was stacked with shining performances, brilliant characterization and droll humour. It was derived from a play, 'Prisoner and Escort', seen on Barker's 1973 anthology for BBC2, *Seven of One*. A sequel, *Going Straight* (1978, 6 x 30m), followed Fletcher's fortunes on release and his resumed life with his family. His son, Raymond, was played by Nicholas Lyndhurst (>*Butterflies, Only Fools and Horses*). A cinema version of *Porridge,* with the TV cast, was released by Black Lion/Witzend in 1979.

Classic episodes include: 'A Day Out'; 'Men without Women' (in which Fletcher, with the connivance of wife and daughter, hatches a compassionate leave plan for a weekend at home); and 'Final Stretch'.

QUARK

USA 1978, 1 x 60m, 7 x 30m, col NBC. NBC/ Columbia.

CR *Buck Henry.* **PR** *Buck Henry, David Gerber, Mace Neufeld, Bruce Johnson.* **DR** *Peter H Hunt, Hy Averback.* **WR** *Buck Henry, Steve Zacharias.* **MUS** *Perry Botkin Jr.* **CAST** Adam Quark *Richard Benjamin* Gene/Jean *Tim Thomerson* Ficus Panderato *Richard Kelton* Betty I *Tricia Barnstable* Betty II *Cyb Barnstable* Andy the Robot *Bobby Porter* Otto Palindrome *Conrad Janis* The Head *Alan Caillou.*

It is 2222 AD, and Commander Adam Quark is head of an interplanetary garbage crew whose mission on behalf of the united Galaxy Sanitation Patrol is to clean up the Milky Way. In order to receive his assignments he returns his patrol ship to giant space station Perma One, operation headquarters, where disembodied Secretary General The Head rules the universe from a TV screen. Orders also come from Superintendent Otto Palindrome (Conrad Janis, >*Mork and Mindy*), Perm One's woolly brained chief architect with four arms.

Under Quark himself served First Officer Gene/Jean, a transmute with male and female chromosomes who was sometimes tough and sometimes delicate, Science Officer Ficus, a humanoid vegetable, Andy the Robot, and Ergo the ship's mascot (a temperamental blob of protoplasm with one eye). Glamorous ex-cheerleaders Betty I and Betty II (a clone), who were so similar that no one could tell them apart, were the co-pilots.

Whilst ridding the galaxy of litter, this motley crew met with adventure and such colourful galactic inhabitants as the evil High Gorgon, Zoltar the Magnificent and Zorgon the Malevolent. But the series was first and foremost a spoof on space adventure epics such as *2001: A Space Odyssey, Flash Gordon* and, especially, *Star Wars.*

Quark first appeared as a pilot in 1977 and débuted as a TV series in 1978 with a one-hour special. Its slick blend of in-jokes, innuendo and slapstick gained a devoted cult following but not a mass audience. Termination followed. The mastermind of the show was Buck Henry, who had earlier hit the jackpot with his sixties spy spoof, >*Get Smart*.

RAB C NESBITT

UK 1990–3, 18 x 30m, col BBC2. BBC TV.

PR *Colin Gilbert.* **DR** *Colin Gilbert.* **WR** *Ian Pattison.* **CAST** Rab C Nesbitt *Gregor Fisher* Mary Nesbitt *Elaine C Smith* Jamesie Cotter *Tony Roper* Gash Nesbitt *Andrew Fairlie* Burney Nesbitt *Eric Cullen.*

The string-vested Glasgow street philosopher made his début in *Naked Video* sketches, before spinning off into a series (via 1989 one-off *Rab C Nesbitt's Seasonal Greet*) which took the British sitcom for a header into the sewer.

Operating on a perpetually full tank of alcohol, Nesbitt (a touching injured-warrior performance by Gregor Fisher) ranted in foul-mouthed Scottish about life and the Establishment in between raucous squabbles with wife Mary and revolting spawn, 'Wee Burney' (Eric Cullen, d. 1996) and Gash. At least they were united in killing the rats which infested their apartment (the weapon of choice being a frying pan). Also seen was Nesbitt's lugubrious drinking partner, Jamesie.

Painfully, perceptively funny.

Gregor Fisher, who played Nesbitt, later starred in *The Tales of Para Handy*, a 1994 revival of Neil Munro's stories about a Scottish cargo boat skipper, which had first sailed the airwaves as the 1959 show, *Para Handy – Master Mariner*.

THE RAG TRADE

UK 1961–3, 35 x 30m, bw BBC. BBC TV.

CR *Ronald Wolfe and Ronald Chesney.* **PR** *Dennis Main Wilson.* **WR** *Ronald Wolfe and Ronald Chesney.* **CAST** Paddy *Miriam Karlin* Mr Fenner *Peter Jones* Reg *Reg Varney* Carole *Sheila Hancock* Little Lil *Esma Cannon* Judy *Barbara Windsor* Sandra *Sheena Marshe* Janet *Amanda Reiss* Betty *Patricia Denys* Myrtle *Claire Davenport* Olive *Stella Tanner* Gloria *Carmel Cryan.*

Everybody Out!

London's East End workshop of Fenner Fashions was the setting for Wolfe and Chesney's situation comedy of workplace strife, much loved but clearly indebted to the cinema hit *I'm Alright Jack*.

Militant machine shop steward Paddy (Miriam Karlin, later *So Haunt Me*) led the work-shy women workers, with her ever-ready cry of 'Everybody out!' becoming something of a national catchphrase. Their complaints against unscrupulous boss Mr Fenner (Peter Jones) were usually well founded, however, since he was always on the look-out for ways and means of making them work more for less. A not inaccurate picture of shopfloor life in the early sixties, it was assisted by a cast of heavenly configuration, featuring – in addition to Karlin – Reg Varney (later >*On the Buses*), Sheila Hancock, Peter Jones and Barbara Windsor (>*Carry On Laughing*). The format sold to the USA as *The Rag Business,* set in the LA dress-making industry, but failed to make it beyond a 1978 pilot for ABC.

For a crude revival of *The Rag Trade* by LWT (1977–8, 26 x 30m, col), a decade after the original closed down, only Karlin and Jones resumed their old roles. New faces seen included Christopher Beeny, Anna Karen (>*On the Buses*) and Gillian Taylforth *(EastEnders).*

RED DWARF

UK 1988–, 42 x 30m, col BBC2. BBC TV/A Paul Jackson Production/Grant Naylor Productions.

CR *Rob Grant and Doug Naylor.* **PR** *Ed Bye, Rob Grant, Doug Naylor, Hilary Bevan Jones.* **DR** *Ed Bye, Juliet May, Grant Naylor.* **WR** *Various, including Rob Grant, Doug Naylor, Paul Alexander, James Hendries.* **MUS** *Howard Goodall (theme).* **CAST** Dave Lister *Craig Charles* Arnold Rimmer *Chris Barrie* Cat *Danny John-Jules* Kryten *David Ross/Robert Llewellyn* Holly *Norman Lovett/Hattie Hayridge* Kochanski *Claire Grogan/Chloe Annett.* Video *BBC.*

Space-age sitcom. This tale of inter-galactic curry-eating slob Dave Lister (Craig Charles, *Captain Butler*), the last human alive, originated as a sketch for BBC Radio 4's *Son of Cliché,* but owed much to such sci-fi screen vehicles as *Dark Star,* >*Quark* and >*Hitchhiker's Guide to the Galaxy.* As incarnated for TV, Dave was a twenty-third-century Liverpudlian with a penchant for derivatives of the expletive 'smeg', and the sole survivor of a radiation leak aboard the mining vessel of the title. Brought out of a three-million-year-long 'stasis' by ship's computer Holly, Lister was given company in the form of a hologram of his ex-boss, the pompous Arnold Rimmer (Chris Barrie, >*Spitting Image,* >*The Brittas Empire*). Also aboard was Cat, a narcissistic, Little Richard-type dude who had evolved in the ship's hold from Lister's pet feline, and was a humanoid except for fangs and six nipples. (Alas for hip Cat, he had an alter ego – the far-from-cool Duane Dibley.)

Much of the humour of the show, especially in the first two seasons, came out of the characters and their inter-relationships, but was also schoolboyish ('No way are these my boxer shorts – these bend') and bizarre (the Talking Toaster). Indeed it could be described as >*The Young Ones* in space. But the comedy was generous and skilful, and it was also more serious than initially appeared. Rimmer was a semi-parody of a Thatcherite – Lister was the proletarian end of the class struggle aboard *Red Dwarf* – and two shows from season four, 'Dimension Jump' and 'Meltdown', were held back by the BBC at the time of the Gulf War because of their anti-war content. A weakness was the writers' tendency to borrow plots from other sci-fi works wholesale; the time-reverse idea in the episode

▲▲▲ *Going not so boldly into space, the crew of* Red Dwarf.

'Backwards' is suspiciously similar to that in Philip K Dick's sci-fi classic *Counterclock World*.

On its first voyages along the airwaves *Red Dwarf* bumped along the bottom of the ratings (although it scored high in Audience Appreciation). The third season, which opened with 'Backwards' – a classic for all its apparent plagiarism – saw changes in format, and the introduction of more recognizably sci-fi situations. The personnel also changed as stand-up comic Hattie Hayridge replaced Norman Lovett as Holly, while the subservient android Kryten (who was programmed to be polite, and thus could only manage 'sme' as an insult) became a regular crew fixture. The production values were also upped, and the series won the World Television Award for its special effects. In 1994 *Red Dwarf* was awarded an International Emmy. By this time Lister had mislaid *Red Dwarf,* and the boys were rocketing around the universe in the *Starbug*. After a break of three years (largely caused by co-creator Rob Grant jumping ship and the trial – and subsequent acquittal – of actor Craig Charles on a rape charge), the show was revived from TV stasis to become BBC2's longest-running sitcom. In the interval addicted fans had made it the Corporation's most popular video buy. Actress Chloe Annett (previously teen soap *Byker Grove*) replaced former Altered Images singer Claire Grogan as the recurring character Kochanski, Lister's unrequited (and holographic) love interest. Two attempts were made to launch *Red Dwarf* on US airwaves – the first, in 1992, featuring Jane Leeves from >*Frasier* – but both proved abortive.

The episodes to date have been: Season 1: The End/Future Echoes/Balance of Power/Waiting for God/Confidence and Paranoia/ME; Season 2: Kryten (guest Tony Slattery)/Better Than Life/Thanks for the Memory/Stasis Leak/Queeg/Parallel Universe/; Season 3: Backwards/Marooned/Polymorph/Body Swap/Timeslides (guest Koo Stark)/The Last Day; Season 4: Camille/DNA/Justice/White Hole/ Dimension Jump/Meltdown; Season 5: Holoship/ The Inquisitor/Terrorform/Quarantine/Demons and Angels/Back to Reality; Season 6: Psirens/Legion/ Gunmen of the Apocalypse/Emohawk-Polymorph 3/ Rimmerworld/Out of Time; Season 7: Tikka to Ride/ Stoke Me a Clipper/Ouroborus/Duck Soup/Blue/ Beyond a Joke/Epideme/Nanarchy.

»***It's cold outside, there's no kind of atmosphere,***
I'm all alone, more or less.
Let me fly far away from here,
Fun, fun, fun in the sun, sun, sun.

I want to live shipwrecked and comatosed
Drinking fresh mango juice,
Goldfish shoals nibbling at my toes
Fun, fun, fun in the sun, sun, sun,
Fun, fun, fun in the sun, sun, sun... «

REN AND STIMPY

USA 1991–, 38+ x 25m, col Nickelodeon. Carbunkle/SpumCo/Nickelodeon. UK tx *1994– BBC2.*

CR *John Kricfalusi (aka John K).* **EXEC PR** *Vanessa Coffey.* **PR** *John Kricfalusi, Bob Camp, Jim Smith, Jim Ballentine, Frank Sapperstein.* **DR** *Various, including John Kricfalusi, Bob Camp, Vincent Waller, Greg Vanzo.* **WR** *Various, including John Kricfalusi, Bob Camp, Vincent Waller, Jim Smith, Will McRobb, Bill Wray, Jim Gomez, Elinor Brake, Richard Purcel.* **CAST** *(voices)* Ren Hoek *John Kricfalusi/Bob Camp* Stimpson J 'Stimpy' Cat *Billy West.*

Happy Happy Joy Joy... Launched on US kiddie cable channel Nickelodeon in 1991 as part of its promotion of creator-based animations, *Ren and Stimpy* featured an irritable, nuclear-fried chihuahua and a stupid fat cat of those names. And an avalanche of lateral jokes, surreal graphics, grossed-out violence and bodily functions. In one memorable, but not untypical episode ('Big House Blues') the pair escaped from a dog pound after Stimpy sicked up a fur ball on Ren so that he was mistaken for a poodle and taken home by a kindly girl. The stories went far into outlandishness ('The Rubber Nipples Salesman'), deep into sacrosanct American culture ('Out West' featured red-necked Western folk singing 'The Lord Loves a Hanging') and tended to bite the hand that fed them by viciously satirising tiny time TV – especially the advertisements on which Nickelodeon depended for its revenue.

Educationalists issued dire warnings, but what

the heck. It made great television – for adults. Understanding that Ren and Stimpy was a sly joke mostly lost on its supposed pre-teen audience, many networks and stations gave it a respectable evening, even night-time, airing.

It was too good to last. Eventually, Nickelodeon dispensed with creator Kricfalusi's services (either because of his inability to meet deadlines, or because the product, particularly the homo-erotic relationship between Ren and Stimpy, was becoming too controversial), and lesser men and women took the cartoon's helm.

RHODA

USA 1974–8, 110 x 25m, col CBS. MTM. UK tx *1974–80 BBC2.*

CR *James L Brooks, Allan Burns.* **EXEC PR** *James L Brooks, Allan Burns.* **PR** *Lorenzo Music, David Davis, Charlotte Brown.* **DR** *Various, including James Burrows, Charlotte Brown, Bob Claver, Howard Storm, Alan Rafkin, Joan Darling.* **WR** *Various,*

▼▼ *Valerie Harper (left) won an Emmy for her starring turn as Rhoda.*

including Charlotte Brown, David Davis. **MUS** *Billy Goldenburg.* **CAST** Rhoda Morgenstern Gerard *Valerie Harper* Brenda Morgenstern *Julie Kavner* Ida Morgenstern *Nancy Walker* Martin Morgenstern *Harold J Gould* Joe Gerard *David Groh* Gary Levy *Ron Silver* Carlton, the doorman (voice only) *Lorenzo Music* Myrna Morgenstein *Barbara Sharma* Jack Doyle *Ken McMillan* Ramon Diaz Jr *Rafael Campos* Johnny Venture *Michael Delano* Donny Gerard (Joe's son) *Todd Turquand.*

The character of Rhoda first appeared as the overweight, over-anxious neighbour in >*The Mary Tyler Moore Show* before being slimmed down, made more obviously Jewish, and given a show of her own. She was also relocated to New York, where she initially lived with her parents, Ida and Martin, before moving in with her dowdy sister Brenda (played by Julie Kavner, later the voice of Marge in >*The Simpsons*). She also got a job as a window dresser and fell in love with Joe, owner of the New York Wrecking Company. They married (in the highest-rated TV special of the 1974 season) but separated soon after – largely because the scriptwriters decided that the abrasive but vulnerable Rhoda worked comically best as a single girl, although she later took up with Vegas lounge singer Johnny Venture in an on/off relationship. Also seen was Rhoda's friend Myrna Morgenstein, and towards the end of the run Rhoda joined Jack Doyle and Ramon Diaz in the shaky Doyle Costume Company. Unseen but heard was Carlton, the mad doorman at Rhoda's apartment block. In Britain *Rhoda* was first aired in BBC2's 'Tankee Treble' slot in autumn 1974, and was so popular that it was screened weekly from February 1975.

Valerie Harper won the 1976 Outstanding Lead Comedy Actress Emmy for her portrayal of Rhoda.

RIPPING YARNS

UK 1977–9, 9 x 30m, col BBC2. BBC TV.

CR *Michael Palin and Terry Jones.* **PR** *Alan J W Bell.* **DR** *Terry Hughes, Alan J W Bell, Jim Franklin.* **WR** *Michael Palin and Terry Jones.* **CAST** *Michael Palin.*

Irreverent parodies of Boy's Own literature from those cheeky ex >*Monty Python*s Michael Palin and Terry Jones.

A 1976 one-off, Tompkinson's Schooldays (BBC2) inaugurated the series, which presented such delightful dottiness as stiff-upper-lipped British heroes crossing the Andes by frog (Captain Snetterton) and escaping from the ever-so-secure Stalag Luft 112B. No matter the scenario, the period detail was spot on. Palin played the lead character in each Yarn, and those providing cameos were John Cleese and Eric Idle. It was awarded a BAFTA for light entertainment.

The episodes were: Tompkinson's Schooldays/ The Testing of Eric Olthwaite/Escape from Stalag Luft 112B/Murder at Moorstones Manor/Across the Andes by Frog/The Curse of the Claw/Whinfrey's Last Case/Golden Gordon/Roger of the Raj.

▶▶ *Captain Snetterton (Michael Palin) puts on a stiff upper lip in* Ripping Yarns.

BRITIS
FROGS
MOIST

RISING DAMP

UK 1974–8, 28 x 30m, col ITV. Yorkshire TV.

CR *Eric Chappell.* **PR** *Vernon Lawrence, Ronnie Baxter, Len Lurcuck, Ian MacNaughton.* **DR** *Vernon Lawrence, Ronnie Baxter, Len Lurcuck, Ian MacNaughton.* **WR** *Eric Chappell.* **CAST** Rupert Rigsby *Leonard Rossiter* Philip Smith *Don Warrington* Alan Moore *Richard Beckinsale* Miss Ruth Jones *Frances de la Tour* Spooner *Derek Newark* Brenda *Gay Rose.*

Originally a stage show called *Banana Box,* Eric Chappell's masterly series about the sneering, jeering landlord Rigsby ('My-y-y God...') and his seedy Northern boarding house was one of ITV's few quality comedy hits in the seventies. Almost as obnoxious a character as the elder Steptoe or Alf Garnett, the arms-folded, eyes-rolling Rigsby (dressed always in a sleeveless cardigan) lusted ceaselessly after his one female boarder, spinster university administrator Ruth, and endlessly battled with his two male boarders, effete medical student Alan and, scion of an African chieftain, Philip. Rigsby's snide manner was splendidly evidenced in the first episode when the fashionably hirsute Alan defended himself saying 'Jesus had long hair.' 'Yes,' replied Rigsby with perfect timing, 'but I bet he never had a hairdryer.' Always rebuffed in his advances to Ruth, Rigsby took out his frustrations on his cat Vienna (who could sometimes be heard screeching in fright off stage), and by interfering in the attempts of Alan to bring girls back to the flat. The series was compelling not only because of its writing and acting (especially Rossiter's virtuoso performance as Rigsby), but because it struck a chord with anybody who had ever lived in rented digs.The show topped the BARB ratings in both 1977 and 1978.

Of the TV cast only Richard Beckinsale (previously >*The Lovers,* >*Porridge,* and who died during the fourth season of *Rising Damp*) did not appear in the original play, and both Rossiter and Frances de la Tour had distinguished stage careers. An insurance clerk until he was twenty-seven, Rossiter had achieved notable success in the theatre for his renditions of Arturo Ui and Richard III. On television he had put in a long spell in *Z Cars* in the sixties. After *Rising Damp,* the lugubrious, Liverpudlian actor appeared in the 1980 film version of the series, and the TV sitcom >*The Fall and Rise of Reginald Perrin.* He died during a production of Joe Orton's *Loot* in 1984.

◀◀◀ *'My-y-y God'. Leonard Rossiter as the parsimonious landlord Rigsby in* Rising Damp.

ROBIN'S NEST

UK 1977–81, 36 x 30m, col ITV. Thames TV. US tx *1983 Syndicated.*

CR *Johnnie Mortimer and Brian Cooke.* **PR** *Peter Frazer-Jones.* **WR** *Various, including Johnnie Mortimer and Brian Cooke, George Layton, Adele Rose, Dave Freeman, Ken Hoare, Bernard McKenna, Willis Hall, Jon Watkins, Richard Waring and Gail Renard.* **MUS** *Richard O'Sullivan (theme).* **CAST** Robin Tripp *Richard O'Sullivan* Vicky Nicholls *Tessa Wyatt* James Nichols *Tony Britton* Marion

Nichols *Honor Blackman/Barbara Murray* Albert Riddle *David Kelly* Gertrude *Peggy Aitchison.*

Spin-off from >*Man About the House* in which Robin Tripp qualifies as a chef, moves into a Notting Hill pad with air hostess girlfriend Vicky Nicholls (Tessa Wyatt, ex-wife of Radio 1 DJ Tony Blackburn) and opens the bistro of the title. Comically hindering in this endeavour are one-armed Irish washer-upper Albert Riddle and Vicky's divorced, interfering father, James, who (despite not approving of his daughter's live-in arrangement) co-owns the restaurant, and likes to try his hand at waiting, when not using the place as an upmarket pick-up joint. Honor Blackman (previously *The Avengers*) played the occasional character of James's wife and Vicky's mother. The show was later remade in America as *Three's a Crowd* (ABC 1984–5).

A predictable, thus easily digestible, Mortimer and Cooke sitcom which topped the ratings in 1978.

ROSEANNE

USA 1988–97, 221 x 30m, col ABC. Carsey-Werner Productions. UK tx *1989–97 C4.*

CR *Matt Williams.* **EXEC PR** *Various, including Marcy Carsey, Tom Werner, Roseanne Barr, Tom Arnold.* **DR** *Various, including Ellen Falcon, Gail Mancuso, Andrew D Weyman, Jeff Margolis, John Whitesell, John Pasquin.* **WR** *Various, including Matt Williams, David McFadzean, Bill Pentland, Tom Arnold.* **CAST** Roseanne Conner *Roseanne Barr (aka Roseanne Arnold, Roseanne)* Dan Conner *John Goodman* Darlene Conner/Healy *Sara Gilbert* Becky Conner/Healy *Lecy Goranson/Sara Chalke* David Jacob 'DJ' Conner *Michael Fishman* Jackie Harris *Laurie Metcalf* David Healy *Johnny Galecki* Mark Healy *Glenn Quinn* Fred *Michael O'Keefe* Crystal Anderson *Natalie West* Arnie Thomas *Tom Arnold* Booker *George Clooney* Ed Conner *Ned Beatty* Beverly Harris *Estelle Parsons* 'Nana-Mary' Harris *Shelley Winters* Nancy Bartlett *Sandra Bernhard.*

A blue-collar comedy, set in the Illinois town of Lanford, about a caustic and corpulent mother, Roseanne Conner. Making up the rest of her family were equally large husband Dan and assorted children: boy-mad Becky, small son DJ and cynical Darlene. Jackie was Roseanne's single sister (until she got mixed up with Fred, and had baby Andy), and much disliked by Dan. Though Roseanne put down her kids mercilessly (when one complained of being bored, she advised, 'Go play in the traffic'), the viewer was never left in any doubt that she loved the brats. She also worked outside the home in a variety of dead-end jobs, including on the production line at a plastics factory, bussing tables at Lobo's Lounge, and later co-running the Lunch Box diner. After Dan gave up his dry-wall business for a motorbike shop, the family enjoyed a middle-class income, until the early nineties recession forced Dan out of business. When times got hard, Roseanne was obliged to use son DJ to con the electricity man. Aside from the problems of cash shortage, the comedy focused on the 'usual' problems of family life, including generational conflict. Stories of this type included Dan's father Ed marrying Roseanne's

Go play in the traffic

friend Crystal, Becky's elopement with Mark, and Darlene's drug use at art college.

The series was based (through the comic magnifying glass of Matt Williams, later >*Home Improvement*) on a character created by Roseanne Barr, a Jewish waitress turned stand-up comic from Salt Lake City who came to prominence after an appearance on *The Tonight Show*. Not long after the instant success of *Roseanne,* Barr divorced husband Bill Pentland; in 1991 she married reformed cocaine addict Tom Arnold, whom she brought into the series as co-executive producer and as the character Arnie, neighbour of the Conners. Arnold subsequently starred in *The Jackie Thomas Show,* a ratings disaster for the ABC network, and was divorced by Roseanne. Aside from the regular cast, those appearing in *Roseanne* (which grossed over $91 million per year at its peak in revenues) have included Shelley Winters as Roseanne's grandmother Mary, Estelle Parsons as Roseanne's mother Bev, Sandra Bernhard as neighbour Nancy and Mariel Hemingway as a lesbian stripper (who gave Roseanne a much publicized 'sapphic kiss' in the episode 'Don't Ask, Don't Tell'). With a famously fast turnover of writers – a scriptwriter's life expectancy on Roseanne was much like that of a subaltern in the trenches of the Western Front – the show deteriorated somewhat in its latter seasons, as Roseanne remodelled her character (and herself, thanks to the surgeon's knife) into something distinctly glamorous, rather than proletarian-looking. A vein of sentimentality also became evident, with Roseanne having a baby, and the show bowing out with a storyline in which the Conners won the state lottery.

Roseanne trivia: The Conners' address was 714 Delaware Street, Lanford; in the end credits of the episode 'The Dark Ages', Laurie Metcalf can be seen polishing a trophy – her 1992 Emmy, the first acting Emmy to be bestowed on *Roseanne;* in the following year, Roseanne herself won the Emmy for Outstanding Lead Actress in a Comedy.

ROWAN AND MARTIN'S LAUGH-IN

USA 1967–73, 150 x 50m, col NBC. Romart Inc. UK tx *1968–71 BBC2.*

PR *George Slatter, Paul W Keyes, Ed Friendly, Carolyn Raskin.* **CAST** *Various, including Dan Rowan, Dick Martin, Ruth Buzzi, Garry Owens, Goldie Hawn, Judy Carne, Lily Tomlin, Arte Johnson, Larry Hovis, Pigmeat Markham, Alan Sues, Jud Strunk, Dave Madden, Jeremy Lloyd, Dick Whittington, Johnny Brown, Henry Gibson, Ann Elder, Charlie Brill, Jo Anne Worley, Mitzi McCall, Teresa Graves, Byron Gilliam, Richard Dawson, Moosie Drier, Patti Deutsch, Sarah Kennedy, Todd Bass, Donna Jean Young.*

Running wild variety show. Hosted by nightclub comedians Dan Rowan and Dick Martin, each *Laugh-In* formed a madcap sixty minutes satirizing the contempory scene in skits, songs and slapstick. Using almost all new talent – including the then

Here come de judge

unknowns Goldie Hawn and Lily Tomlin – it fast built up a repertoire of stock characters and catchphrases which were used over and over until the mere mention of them was funny (the 'shtick technique'; the British >*Fast Show* would do the same thing in the nineties). Among the most famous of them were: 'Sock it to me' (at which Judy Carne got drenched); 'Here come de judge'; 'You bet your bippy'; Lily Tomlin's sardonic, nasal-voiced telephone girl; Arte Johnson's German soldier peering over the potted plant to say 'Verrry interrrestink'; Goldie Hawn's giggling blonde; Ruth Buzzi's umbrella-wielding old lady. Regular skit-slots included the talent show send-up 'The Flying Fickle Finger of Fate', 'Hollywood News' with Ruth Buzzi, the Cocktail Party and the joke wall at the end of each episode.

Eventually *Rowan and Martin's Laugh-In* (sometime just plain *Laugh-In*) was undone by its own success; its now famous performers moved off to do other things. Only Garry Owens and Ruth Buzzi, in addition to Rowan and Martin, were in the show for the duration. But for three years it ruled the American airwaves, its enthusiasm and daring seeming to catch the liberated mood of the late sixties. Even President Nixon dropped in. A cynical 1977 revival, however, was almost universally divellicated... 'Look that up in your Funk and Wagnall's.'

◀◀◀ *John Wayne gets in on the comic act in* Rowan and Martin's Laugh-In. *Also on the show's guest list was the well-known comedian, Richard Millhouse Nixon.*

RUTLAND WEEKEND TELEVISION

UK 1975–6, 12 x 30m, col BBC2. BBC.

PR *Ian Keill.* **WR** *Eric Idle.* **MUS** *Neil Innes.* **CAST** *Eric Idle, Neil Innes, David Battley, Henry Woolf, Gwen Taylor.*

Eric Idle's follow-up to >*Monty Python's Flying Circus* cast him as the programme controller of fictional Rutland Weekend Television, based in England's smallest county. From there issued forth sub-*Python* parodies of TV – and one solid gold masterpiece in the 1978 one-off sequel, *The Rutles* (65m col, BBC2, aka *All You Need is Cash*).

This presented a (spoof) documentary history of the 'pre-Fab Four': Dirk, Nasty, Stig and Barry – the Rutles, from their beginning in Egg Lane, Liverpool, in 1959, when Ron Nasty and Dirk McQuickly first bumped into each other, and Ron invited Dirk to help him stand up. They were then joined by Stig O'Hara, a guitarist of no fixed hairstyle, and finally Barrington Womble on drums. *The Rutles* then followed the story of the band through their early days at the Cavern to their worldwide success and their recording sessions at Shabby Road. Interviews with (real) rock faces such as Mick Jagger and Ron Wood were intercut with footage of the band performing such Rutles classics as 'W C Fields Forever', 'Goose-Step Mama' and 'Cheese and

Onions'. A band of whom it could safely be said that they were legends in their own lunchtime. And then, of course, there was the mystery of Stig. Was he still alive? Well, if you sing the title song of 'Sgt Potter's Only Darts Club Band' backwards it sounds like 'Stig has been dead for ages honestly'...

An unsurpassable send-up of the Beatles and the slew of serious programmes made about them. Eric Idle and Gary Weis directed Lorne Michael's production for Above Average Productions. The main cast was: Dirk McQuickly/Narrator/S J Krammerjhad *Eric Idle* Barry Wom *John Halsey* Stig O'Hara *Ricky Fataar* Ron Nasty *Neil Innes* Eric Manchester *Michael Palin* The Interviewer *George Harrison* (!) John Belushi *Ron Decline* Brian Thigh *Dan Ackroyd* Mrs Emily Pules *Gilda Radner* Bill Murray the K *Bill Murray*. The music was by Neil Innes.

A treasure for all time.

SATURDAY NIGHT LIVE

USA 1975–, 1000 x 90m, col NBC. NBC Studios/ Broadway Video.

CR *Lorne Michaels, Dick Ebersol.* **EXEC PR** *Lorne Michaels.* **PR** *Various, including Lorne Michaels, Jean Doumanian.* **DR** *Various, including Dave Wilson, Paul Miller.* **WR** *Various, including Michael O'Donaghue.* **CAST** *Various, including Chevy Chase, John Belushi, Dan Ackroyd, Gilda Radner, Jane Curtin, Bill Murray, Albert Brooks, Jim Henson's Muppets, Don Novello, Tom Davis, Joe Piscopo, Eddie Murphy, Christine Ebersole, Jim Belushi, Billy Crystal, Harry Shearer, Nora Dunn, Dennis Miller, Christopher Guest, Pamela Stephenson, Jon Lovitz, Damon Wayans, Robert Downey, Jr, Victoria Jackson, Phil Hartman, Jan Hooks, Kevin Nealon, Dana Carvey, Mike Myers, Chris Farley, Ellen Cleghorne, Rob Schneider, Tim Meadows, Molly Shannon, Tracy Morgan, Cheri Oteri, Julia Louis-Dreyfus, Laurie Metcalf.*

S*NL* began as an experiment by the NBC network to create a showcase for young comedians whose material was unsuitable for prime-time broadcasting, but who might attract a young (and relatively affluent) audience. The ninety-minute programme was broadcast live from New York and hosted by George Carlin, who was allowed to wear a T-shirt by NBC, but only if he wore a jacket over the top. The show's mix of improvisation, skits and rock music took a while to catch on, but when it did it became essential baby-boom viewing, its preoccupations – sex, drugs and rock'n'roll – being also those of its audience. A small rep company of performers ('The Not Ready for Prime Time Players') did the in-front-of-camera antics, Chevy Chase being the luminary of the first season with his slapstick routines and catchline of 'Good evening. I'm Chevy Chase and you're not!'. He also made a memorable bumbling President Ford (whose mishaps included stapling his ear to his desk), and his popular satirical newscasts. Around Chase coalesced what would become known as the 'original cast'; it included Jane Curtin, John Belushi and Dan Ackroyd, with the latter two developing the 'Blues Brothers' routine they would take into the movies. Jim Henson's Muppets (see >*The Muppet Show*) were a regular fixture, as were the Coneheads, a group of egg-headed aliens who got by in the USA by pretending to be from France. Almost everyone buzzed around in bee costumes.

In 1976 Chase left to pursue an independent career, and three years later Belushi and Ackroyd followed him. By now burnout was clearly affecting *SNL,* and in 1980 Lorne Michaels, the show's creator and producer, also quit.

An entirely new *SNL* cast was brought in for the 1980–1 season, to heavily critical reviews. Of the new cast only Eddie Murphy shone out, and in 1981 a new production team took over. Ratings steadily improved, despite a high turnover of cast members. Those joining the intake of 1984 included Billy Crystal, whose obsequious interviewer Fernando ('You look mahvelous') became a standard fixture. By the late eighties, with Lorne Michaels again on the production tiller, and a stable cast in Jon Lovitz, Nora Dunn, Dennis Miller, Dana Carvey, Jan Hooks, Victoria Jackson and Mike Myers, the show reached another peak, exemplified by the spinning-off to movie mega-success of Myers and Carvey's 'Wayne's World' skit. By 1998 *SNL* had won fourteen Emmys.

A British copy was broadcast as *>Saturday Live/Friday Night Live.*

SATURDAY LIVE/FRIDAY NIGHT LIVE

UK 1985–8, Approx 32 x 60m, col C4.Thames TV.

CR *Geoff Posner, Geoff Perkins.* **PRESENTERS** *Ben Elton, plus Michael Barrymore, Tracey Ullman, Lenny Henry.*

Revue-style series for upcoming comedians, based on the American model *>Saturday Night Live.* After a problematic start involving misguided scheduling (it was put on too early in the evening for its sometimes dubious items) and rotating presenters (including Michael Barrymore), the show was shifted to a 10.00pm time-slot and Ben Elton, 'the smug git in the shiny suit', was hired in as permanent host. In between right-on, anti-Thatcher rants, he introduced the unknown likes of Julian Clary (as the Joan Collins Fan Club, with Fanny the Wonder Dog), Josie Lawrence, Jack Docherty, Jo Brand ('The Sea Monster'), Craig Charles, Stephen Fry and Hugh Laurie. The showcase, however, was stolen by Harry Enfield, whose Greek kebab-shop owner Stavros ('Hello, matey peeps', 'Up the Arse[nal]!') was only eclipsed by his Turbo-Nutter driving plasterer, Loadsamoney ('Look at my wad!'). Created for Enfield by Paul Whitehouse and Charlie Higson (later *>The Fast Show*), Loadsamoney was probably the most telling caricature of Essex Man in the 1980s. When, ironically enough, Loadsamoney became appropriated by the selfsame Essex Man as a hero, Enfield introduced the Northern 'Buggarallmoney' as a counterbalance, before killing off the character entirely. To mark its change of transmission day, the programme was retitled *Friday Night Live,* although the format of live turns remained the same.

Look at my wad!

SEINFELD

USA 1990–8, 150 x 30m, col NBC. Castle Rock Entertainment West-Shapiro. UK tx *1993–8, BBC2.*

CR *Jerry Seinfeld, Larry David.* **EXEC PR** *Jerry Seinfeld, George Shapiro, Howard West, Alec Berg, Jeff Schaffer.* **DR** *Various, including Tom Cherones, David Steinberg, Jason Alexander, Joshua White.* **WR** *Various, including Jerry Seinfeld, David Steinberg.* **CAST** Jerry *Jerry Seinfeld* Elaine Benes *Julia Louis-Dreyfus* George Costanza *Jason Alexander* Cosmo Kramer *Michael Richards.*

Jerry: 'Look at this woman feeding her baby greasy disgusting coffee-shop corned-beef hash. Isn't that child abuse?'

George: 'I'd like to have a kid... of course, I'd have to get a date first.'

The American sitcom sensation of the nineties. Though reminiscent of >*Rhoda* (the NY apartment set, open house to a group of quirky loser friends) and >*Dick Van Dyke* (the comedian-lead playing himself), *Seinfeld* consciously redrew the boundaries of the sitcom. The show featured nerdy, white-sneakered stand-up comic Jerry Seinfeld pontificating on the absurd minutiae of life with fellow 'schlubs' – former girlfriend Elaine, luckless George (Jason Alexander, >*Duckman*) and shock-haired neighbour Kramer. There were no plots, no canned laughter, no moral pieties. 'No Hugs, No Lessons' was the producers' mantra. That this tricky act of dramatizing everyday life – obsessively observed – could last thirty minutes, let alone entertain 76 million Americans per episode, was due to precision-tuned scripts and a flurry of set-piece jokes that cunningly linked into a whole.

Zen and the art of sitcom maintenance.

The off-beatness of *Seinfeld* was much imitated, but never bettered. A final episode on 14 May 1998 drew 30 million viewers.

Seinfeld trivia: Jerry Seinfeld's first stand-up comedy performance was at Manhattan's Catch a Rising Star Club in 1976; his TV début was in >*Benson*, playing a gag writer whose gags weren't funny; in an attempt to persuade Seinfeld to continue the show beyond the ninth season, NBC reputedly offered him $5 million per episode; an in-flight screening of *Seinfeld* once had to be switched off because the passengers were laughing so much that they were making the plane rock out of control.

Classic *Seinfeld* episodes include: The Contest (in which the gang see who can go for the longest without self-gratification)/Soup Nazi/The Rye/The Note (in which Kramer thinks he's spotted Joe DiMaggio in Dinky Donuts)/The Puffy Shirt/The Library (in which Jerry is busted by the library for keeping 'Tropic of Cancer' out since 1971)/The Bubble Boy/The Virgin (Jerry dates a virgin, played by >*Frasier*'s Jane Leeves, and all looks good, until Elaine tells her about how men behave after sex)/ The Chicken Roaster/Fusilli Jerry and The Marine Biologist/The Fix-Up/The Outing (in which Jerry and George are mistakenly believed to be a gay item; Jerry's father homophobically blames his mother, saying, 'It's those shorts you made him wear when he was four!'... 'We're not gay,' protests George, adding, 'Not that there's anything wrong with that.')/ The Fix Up/The Note.

Much ado about nothing, NBC's sitcom sensation Seinfeld.

A SHOW CALLED FRED

UK 1956, 6 x 30m, bw ITV. Associated Rediffusion.

DR *Dick Lester.* **WR** *Various, including Spike Milligan, John Antrobus, Dave Freeman.* **CAST** *Peter Sellers, Spike Milligan, Kenneth Connor, Valentine Dyall, Patti Lewis, Max Geldray.*

Derived from radio's *The Goon Show,* via Peter Sellers' *Idiot Weekly, Price 2d,* to present an enjoyable half-hour of studio zaniness. Sample: a theatre audience watches the stage curtain open – to reveal an audience looking at them. Sellers and Spike Milligan led the team, which carried on the foolery in *Son of Fred* (1956). The director of both shows was Dick Lester, later to helm the Beatles' films.

THE SIMPSONS

USA 1989–, 200+ x 30m, col Fox. Gracie Films/20th Century Fox Television. UK tx *1990– Sky1.*

CR *Matt Groening.* **EXEC PR** *Various, including James L Brooks, Matt Groening, Sam Simon, Al Jean, Mike Reiss, Josh Weinstein.* **PR** *Various, including George Meyer, Richard Sakai, David Silverman, Jon Vitti, John Swartzelder, Frank Mula, David Sacks, Bill Oakley, Josh Weinstein.* **DR** *Various, including Rich Moore, David Silverman, Jim Reardon, Wes Archer, Mark Kirkland, Susie Dieter.* **WR** *Various, including John Swartzelder, Adam I Lapidus, Conan O'Brien, Greg Daniels, Jay Kogen, Al Jean and Mike Reiss, Jon Vitti.* **MUS** *Danny Elfman.* **CAST** *(voices)* Homer Simpson/Krusty the Clown *Dan Castellaneta* Marge Simpson *Julie Kavner* Bartholomew J 'Bart' Simpson *Nancy Cartwright* Lisa Simpson *Yeardley Smith* Mrs Karbappel *Marcia Wallace* Mr Monty Burns/Principal Skinner/Ned Flanders/Waylon Smithers/Otto the Bus Driver *Harry Shearer* Moe/Chief Wiggum/Dr Nick Riviera *Hank Azaria.* Video *Fox.*

Ay carumba! Animated events in the life of a dysfunctional blue-collar American family that became the first cartoon since >*The Flintstones* to become a prime-time hit.

The immediate Simpsons clan (who had just four digits per hand, yellow skin, and hailed from Springfield) were: pop Homer, aka 'Bonehead', who worked as the safety inspector at the local nuclear power plant; his wife Marge (voiced by Julie Kavner from >*Rhoda*), possessor of an enormous blue beehive; ten-year-old Bart (an anagram of brat), a spiky-haired underachiever; his sister Lisa, the resident, baritone sax-playing intellectual; and Maggie the baby, who crawled everywhere with a dummy in her mouth.

The Simpsons were dreamed up by 'Life in Hell' cartoonist Matt Groening (who swore the characters were not autobiographical, even though his parents and two sisters had the same names as the Simpsons), and débuted as inserts in >*The Tracey Ullman Show* and developed into a series of its own by Fox – through the agency of comedy deity James

'Why you little…' Homer and Bart display family (dis) harmony in The Simpsons.

L Brooks – to become one of the phenomena of all TV time. (Tracey Ullman later sued to the tune of £1.5 million for a share of the profits, claiming 'I breast-fed those little devils.' She lost.) Celebrities queued for guest voice spots; Maggie's first word was uttered by Liz Taylor, and others who loaned their vocal chords included Danny De Vito, Ringo Starr, The Ramones, Kirk Douglas, Meryl Streep, Leonard Nimoy, Kelsey Grammer, Joe Frazier, Buzz Aldrin, Dustin Hoffman, Bob Hope and Tom Jones. David Duchovny and Gillian Anderson voiced their *X-Files* characters in the 'Springfield Files' episode, when Homer, having drunk ten pints of Duff at Moe's Tavern, saw an 'alien'.

In the beginning the show centred on Bart and his pranks and fired off witty, though irrelevent gags, but then subtly shifted its focal point to food-mad Homer – a man who once sold his soul to the devil for a single donut. (He also ate spoiled meat from Apu's Kwik-E-Mart because it was cheap. Twice.) The show simultaneously deepened characterization, not just of the Simpsons, but of the other inhabitants of Springfield, such as Mr Burns, the104-year-old owner of the nuclear plant, his yes-man gay assistant Smithers, and neighbour Ned Flanders; the genius was in the detail. The show also began to lampoon everything in sight: politics, the movies (references to *Citizen Kane* were legion), the TV domestic sitcom – even the all-American nuclear family itself. The moral Establishment showed its irritation in President George Bush's slogan, 'We need a nation closer to the Waltons than the Simpsons'. Bart replied: 'We're just like the Waltons – we're praying for the Depression to end, too'. (To put the comedic knife in even more, *The Simpsons* later had a storyline in which ex-President Bush moved into the Simpsons' street, and Bart wrecked his memoirs.) Yet, as Fox's research showed, people liked the imperfect Simpsons because they were 'a family like us'. *The Simpsons* had realistic get-by-as-best-as-you-can values, epitomised by Homer's loving advice to son Bart: 'Never say anything unless you're sure everyone else feels exactly the same way.' Homer's other words of wisdom include: 'Son, when participating in sporting events, it's not whether you win or lose, it's how drunk you get.'

When, in the mid-nineties, the show suffered a dip in interest, Groening penned a storyline – inspired by *Dallas* – that set the TV nations talking. This was the summer 1995 shooting of Mr Burns. The answer to the whodunnit 'Who Shot Mr Burns?' was revealed in the opening episode of the new season; it was an accident caused by the Simpsons' baby, Maggie. Mr Burns, like JR, survived. The show has been awarded ten Emmys.

In Britain, the Simpsons were first seen on satellite TV after the BBC, having bought *The Tracey Ullman Show,* decided that the little yellow people from Springfield were not funny – and cut them out. It was several years before they were finally broadcast by the BBC.

Doh!

Simpsons trivia: in the episode 'The Front' the scene inside the writers' room features caricatures of *The Simpsons'* own writers; Bart's hit single, 'Do the Bartman', was anonymously penned by Michael Jackson; Bart's voice belongs to Nancy Cartwright – a 38-year-old-woman! – but 'Don't have a cow'; in 1990 *The Simpsons* became the top-rated show in America, ousting the previously untoppable >*Cosby Show;* the T-shirt with Bart's slogan 'Underachiever and Proud of It' was banned in American schools; each *Simpsons* episode cost $200,000 to make.

SLEDGE HAMMER!

USA 1986–8, 41 x 30m, col ABC. A New World International Production. UK tx *1987–9 ITV.*

CR *Alan Spencer.* **EXEC PR** *Alan Spencer, Robert Lovenheime.* **DR** *Various, including Bill Bixby, Thomas Schlamme, Jackie Cooper, Martha Coolidge, Reza Badiyi, Seymour Robbie, Charles Braverman, Charles Dubin, David Wechter.* **WR** *Various, including Mark Curtis and Rod Ash, Chris Ruppenthal, Al Jean and Mike Reiss, Mort Rich and Brian Pollack, Alan Spencer, Jim Fisher and Jim Staal.* **CAST** Det Sledge Hammer *David Rasche* Off Dori Doreau *Anne-Marie Martin* Capt Trunk *Harrison Page.*

Enthusiastic parody of the tough-guy crime genre, featuring square-jawed, brain-free cop Sledge Hammer ('Trust me, I know what I'm doing'). His cases were usually solved by his blonde female sidekick, Detective Doreau, the macho man himself being too busy caressing his .44 Magnum – or 'Gun', as he cooingly called it – and shooting off same at any 'lowlife' he took a right-wing prejudice to. Captain Trunk was his headache-plagued boss.

Inconsequential, but fun. As creator Alan Spencer put it, 'Ultimately what the show is about... is half an hour.' The dreadful punning episode titles – 'Hammer Gets Nailed', 'Brother, Can You Spare a Crime', 'Over My Dead Bodyguard' – gave a fair clue as to the level of humour inside. Among the guests was Heather Lupton ('Here's to You, Mrs Hammer'), who was star David Rasche's wife in real life.

The Smothers Brothers Comedy Hour

USA 1967–9, 1970, 1975, Approx 100 x 60m, col CBS/ABC/NBC.

PR *Saul Ilson, Ernest Chambers, Chris Bearde, Allan Blye.* **MUS** *Various, including Nelson Riddle and his Orchestra.* **CAST** *Various, including Tom Smothers, Dick Smothers, Pat Paulsen, Leigh French, Mason Williams, Bob Einstein, Jennifer Warnes, John Hartford.*

In an attempt to dethrone oater show *Bonanza* from the top of the Nielsens, CBS turned to Tom and Dick Smothers, a duo who mixed folk music and comedy and who the network determined had under-thirties appeal. Although the Smothers Brothers had failed in a sitcom (about an apprentice angel) two years previously, their new show was enormously successful. Indeed, it was too successful.

Dick played the bass and the straight man to guitarist Tom, a stuttering dunce who opined inanely but genially on anything that took his fancy. For the most part, though, the show poked fun at such sacred American institutions as government, church and the establishment. And that was the rub. CBS constantly pressured the Smothers Brothers to tone down their anti-war bent – it was the time of Vietnam – and politically tuned humour. Skits were censored by CBS, one of them ironically enough dealing with film censorship. Also left on the cutting-room floor was Harry Belafonte singing before a montage of the riots at the 1968 Democratic Convention, Pete Seeger singing a protest song ('Waist Deep in the Big Muddy') and an interview with Benjamin Spock.

To no one's great surprise, CBS yanked the show – reputedly at the behest of Nixon and the Republicans – in 1969, even though its ratings were still high. The replacement show was *Hee Haw*. The Brothers came back on ABC the following year, and were revived by NBC in 1975, but to no great watching shakes – the moment had passed. But for two years at the end of the sixties, *The Smothers Brothers* chimed with the changing times more than just about anything on American TV, with the possible exception of NBC's >*Rowan and Martin's Laugh-In*. A 1988 revival, also entitled *The Smothers Brothers Comedy Hour,* lasted but a bare year.

SOAP

USA 1977–82, 93 x 30m, col ABC. Witt-Thomas-Harris Productions. UK tx *1978–82 ITV.*

CR *Susan Harris.* **EXEC PR** *Tony Thomas, Paul Junger Witt.* **PR** *Susan Harris.* **DR** *Various, including Jay Sandrich, J J Lobue.* **WR** *Various, including Susan Harris.* **CAST** Jessica Tate *Katherine Helmond* Chester Tate *Robert Mandan* Corrine Tate *Diana Canova* Eunice Tate *Jennifer Salt* Billy Tate *Jimmy Baio* Benson *Robert Guillaume* The Major *Arthur Peterson* Mary Dallas Campbell *Cathryn Damon* Burt Campbell *Richard Mulligan* Jodie Campbell *Billy Crystal* Danny Campbell *Ted Wass* Father Timothy Flotsky *Sal Viscuso* Dutch *Donnelly Rhodes* Det Donahue *John Byner* Carlos 'El Puerco' Valdez *Gregory Sierra.*

Outrageous prime-time satire of American daytime soaps, which provoked storms of protest while still in production after magazine reports accurately listed its themes as adultery, transvestism, impotency, premarital sex and homosexuality. Religious groups organized campaigns to ban the programme and sponsors were urged to boycott it (which some did). The furore only subsided after ABC promised to tone down future episodes.

Soap, however, was pure irreverent spoof, whose subjects were sent up, not promoted. Revelling in the show's intentionally incomprehensible storylines, each episode started with a cast snapshot and plot summary that ended 'Confused? You will be!' Featured were two sisters and their families, residents of Dunns River, Connecticut, Jessica Tate and Mary Campbell. The delightfully dim Jessica was married to super-rich stockbroker Chester, a chronic philanderer. Their children were sexy Corinne, quiet Eunice and Billy, a fourteen-year-old wisecracking brat. The Tate household was completed by Jessica's father, 'The Major', who wore a uniform and believed that he was still living in the war, and sardonic black butler Benson, who habitually insulted his employers and refused to cook anything he didn't like (an act so successful that Robert Guillaume left for his own spin-off show, >*Benson*).

Across town lived Jessica's sister, Mary Campbell, together with her blue-collar second husband Burt. Burt had some difficulty in relating to gay ventriloquist stepson Jodie (Billy Crystal) and racketeer stepson Danny, the latter having a shotgun marriage to a Mafia boss's daughter. This might have all seemed unusual stuff to the viewer, but the inhabitants of *Soap* were blasé about it. A typical *Soap* joke had Mary Campbell catching her gay son trying on her dress and rebuking him, 'I've told you a hundred times that dress fastens at the back.'

As with the soaps the show aped, ever more far-fetched fare was to come. First there was the murder of Burt's lothario tennis-pro son Peter (Robert Urich, later *Spenser for Hire*), for which Jessica was convicted. Chester, however, turned out to be the real culprit and was sent to prison, but escaped with Dutch. Chester then lost his memory, and wandered out west, leaving Dutch to elope with Eunice, and Jessica to fall in love with Detective Donahue, the man she had hired to find Chester. Meanwhile, Burt was cloned by aliens, and Corinne

Tate's baby turned out to be the spawn of the Devil (literally), which required a quick exorcism. Jessica then had another steamy entanglement, this time with a South American revolutionary, 'El Puerco'.

Having redrawn the boundaries of the situation comedy, creator Susan Harris went on to move them again with >*Golden Girls,* a sitcom about ageing women.

Harris' husband, Paul Junger Witt, was executive producer on *Soap.*

▼▼▼ *Confused? You were if you watched* Soap.

Some Mothers Do 'Ave 'Em

UK 1973–8, 19 x 30m, 3 x 50m, col BBC1. BBC TV.

CR *Raymond Allen, Michael Crawford.* **PR** *Michael Mills.* **WR** *Raymond Allen.* **CAST** Frank Spencer *Michael Crawford* Betty Spencer *Michele Dotrice* Mr Lewis *Glynn Edwards.*

Misadventures of an accident-prone genial simpleton in beret and mac. Throughout every DIY disaster, anti-social malaprop, loss of

employment, his patient wife, Betty, supported. Their daughter, born in the 1973 season, was Jessica (Emma Ware).

A throw-back to the slapstick style of the silent films era, with a camp nerves-twitching, 'harrassed' characterization by Michael Crawford. It proved the laugh of the land. For the 1978 episode in which Frank and Betty had to move from their council house because it was unfit for habitation (and Frank fell into a barrel of tar), 20 million tuned in, taking the show to the top of the BARB ratings. Crawford performed all his own stunts (his previous service in the swashbuckler series *Sir Francis Drake* presumably standing him in good stead) – and they were truly, breathholdingly brilliant.

Ooh Betty. . .

SOUTH PARK

USA 1996–, 24+ x 30m, col Comedy Central. Comedy Central. UK tx *1998– Sky1.*

CR *Trey Parker and Matt Stone.* **PR** *Anne Garefino.* **WR** *Trey Parker and Matt Stone, Dan Sterling, Philip Stark.* **MUS** *Adam Berry, Matt Stone.* **CAST** *(voices)* Stan/Eric *Trey Parker* Kenny/Kyle *Matt Stone* Chef *Isaac Hayes.*

The following programme contains coarse language, and, due to its content, it should not be viewed by anyone. . .

Animated adventures of four foul-mouthed brats – Waspy Stan, confused Jew Kyle, fat boy Eric Cartman, the permanently hooded Kenny – who lived in the snow-swept Colorado town of South Park. Something like Peanuts on acid, its storylines featured anal probes inserted by extraterrestrials, turds that talked, farting – in other words, normal kiddie things. In every episode Kenny got killed, usually by being eaten alive by rats. But he always came back next week. The four traded insults – 'Dildo' 'I saw your mother on the cover of crack whore magazine' – and earned huge piles of money for their backers, the low-rated cable company, Comedy Central. Celebrities queued to play guests spots, with George Clooney settling to play gay dog Sparky (he only got to woof).

Aside from the four eight-year-old boys, other regular characters included goody-two-shoes Wendy Testaburger (with whom Stan was in lurve, but he was so shy he puked at the mere sight of her), class teacher Mr Garrison (who wore a puppet, Mr Hat, on his hand), Stan's militia-man uncle, and soulman school caterer and coach Chef (voiced by Isaac Hayes), who was inclined to tell his diminutive charges to 'hold the football like yo' wuz holding yo' woman'.

South Park originated as an animated Christmas card, commissioned by Fox TV executive Brian Graden from twentysomething animators Matt Stone and Trey Parker in 1995. The resultant 'Spirit of Christmas', which featured the South Park boys and a Christmas showdown between Jesus and Father Christmas (plus a storm of expletives, eg 'Dudes, don't say "pig-fucker" in front of Jesus'), became an underground hit, and Comedy Central called

»hold the football like yo' wuz holding yo' woman.«

soon after. Although the drawings were rude and crude, they formed an effective counterpoint to scripts which could be witty, even exhilaratingly dangerous about the darker recesses of childhood.

'Omigod, they killed Kenny!'

SPIN CITY

USA 1996–, 12 x 30m, col NBC. UBU/Lotery Hill/ Dreamworks. UK tx *1997–, C4.*

CR *Gary David Goldberg.* **EXEC PR** *Gary David Goldberg, Michael J Fox.* **PR** *Walter Barnett, Linda Nieber, Jeff Lowell.* **DR** *Various, including Lee Shallat Chemel, Thomas Schlamme.* **WR** *Various, including Gary David Goldberg and Bill Lawrence, Kirk J Ruddell and Bill Lawrence, Michelle Nader, Amy Cohen, Richard Childs, Michael Craven.* **MUS** *Shelly Parker.* **CAST** Michael Flaherty *Michael J Fox* Mayor Randall Winston *Barry Bostwick* Ashley Schaeffer *Carla Gugino* Stuart Bondek *Alan Ruck* Paul Lassiter *Richard Kind* Nikki Faber *Connie Britton* James Hobert *Alexander Gaberman* Janelle *Victoria Dillard* Stacey Paterno *Jennifer Esposito* Helen Winston *Deborah Rush* Carter Heywood *Michael Brahman.*

His movie career having apparently stalled, the tiny, boyish Michael J Fox returned to the medium that made him in this hit sitcom from Gary David Goldberg – the producer who had originally discovered Fox for >*Family Ties.* Here Fox played Michael Flaherty, deputy mayor of New York, a man whose job had less to do with governing than extricating his inept boss from gaffes and japes (like saving the last dance at the ball for his mistress). Likeable and brisk, it gave Fox the perfect opportunity to show off his immaculate skills of delivery, especially in his romantic one-to-ones with co-star Carla Gugino. The political satire, though, was passé, and it stretched credulity to the breaking point to have a WASP mayor of New York in the nineties. There was one good political joke: an ironic cameo from former Clinton aide George Stephanopolous – the diminutive spin doctor whose metaphorical clothes Fox had borrowed for the show.

SPITTING IMAGE

UK 1984–96, 122 x 30m, 2 x 60m, col ITV. Central TV/Spitting Image Productions.

CR *Peter Fluck and Roger Law (from an idea by Martin Lambie-Nairn).* **PR** *Jon Blair, John Lloyd, Geoffrey Perkins, David Tyler, Bill Dare, Giles Pilbrow.* **DR** *Various, including Bob Cousins, Peter Harris, Sean Hardie, Richard Bradley, John Stroud.* **WR** *Various, including Ian Hislop, Rob Grant, Doug Naylor, Steve Punt, Hugh Dennis, Moray Hunter.* **CAST** *(voices) Various, including Steve Nallon, Chris Barrie, Steve Coogan, Harry Enfield, Jan Ravens, Pamela Stephenson, Rory Bremner, Enn Reitel, Jon Glover, Jessica Martin, John Sessions.*

The latex puppets of the carefully pronounced Fluck and Law débuted in 1984, immediately winning *Spitting Image* a reputation for cruelly accurate satire. Yet, at best, the topical scripts (from among others, Ian Hislop, later *Have I Got News for You,* and future >*Red Dwarf* creators Rob Grant and Doug Naylor) were variable; the show's true turn-on was its utter and complete disrespect. It mercilessly parodied the British Royal Family (previously virtual comedic untouchables), portraying the Queen Mother as an alcohol-guzzling, horse-racing fanatic, Prince Charles (voiced by Chris Barrie) as a huge-eared hippie, whilst fun-loving Fergie and Andrew were so removed from their children that they kept asking them 'What's your name?' Equally fair latex game was provided by politicians of all rank and party: Norman Tebbit was portrayed as a skinhead, John Major was grey and had an obsession with eating peas, Kenneth Baker was a slug, Peter Mandelson a snake.

Towards the end of the show's run, as it tended to broaden its remit to include popsters, media-folk, movie stars (Arnie Schwarzenegger: 'Ja, my villy ist tiny') and jive-talking pontiffs, it lost direction and shambled around like a toothless dog. But a handful of classic skits, songs and images from the eighties remain. A fascistic Margaret Thatcher singing 'Tomorrow Belongs to Us', in the 1987 Election Special. Philip Pope's anti-apartheid ditty, 'I've Never Met a Nice South African' ('cos we're a bunch of murdering bastards/who hate black people'). The search for President Reagan's brain. The reworking of the Police song 'Every Breath You Take' into 'Every Bomb You Make'. The *Sun* journalist pigs. Liberal leader David Steel living in David Owen's pocket (which produced the popular misconception that the former was physically smaller than the latter; a testament to the show's influence). And, of course, 'The Chicken Song', which spoofed the Costa del Brit hit, 'Agadoo' by Black Lace...'Though you hate this song, you'll be humming it for weeks.'

An American version for NBC never caught on, despite two pilots.

STEPTOE AND SON

UK 1964–73, 55 x 30m, 2 x c45m, bw/col BBC1. BBC TV.

CR *Ray Galton and Alan Simpson.* **PR** *Duncan Wood, David Croft, John Howard Davies, Graeme Muir, Douglas Argent.* **DR** *Various, including Douglas Argent.* **WR** *Ray Galton and Alan Simpson.* **MUS** *Ron Grainger, Dennis Wilson.* **CAST** Albert Steptoe *Wilfred Brambell* Harold Steptoe *Harry H Corbett.* Video *BBC.*

Created by >*Hancock's Half-Hour* scriptwriters Ray Galton and Alan Simpson, this situation comedy about a malicious rag-and-bone man and his frustrated son premiered as a 1962 one-off play, *The Offer,* in the BBC's fertile *Comedy Playhouse* slot. From the outset, the show broke most of the rules of TV comedy, ebbing with pathos (even tragedy), rather than laughs. The central characters were the tattered-mitten-wearing father, Albert ('you dirty old man'), and his 38-year-old son, Harold ('you great lummox'). It was Harold's dream to

▲▲▲ *Harry H Corbett and Wilfred Brambell in the blackly comic* Steptoe and Son.

better himself, and to this end he read such tomes as G B Shaw's *Everybody's Political What's What* and listened to classical music on the gramophone in the cluttered sitting-room. He even sought to introduce his father to the joys of Fellini in 'Sunday for Seven Days'. Yet every time he tried to escape the yard his petty jealous father blackmailed him ('arold… I think I'm 'aving an 'art attack, 'arold!') into staying. The ties of blood were simply too strong to escape. And, beneath the bickering and hate, there was love and mutual need: 'He's not a

PLEASE
OFF TAXI DUTY

bad boy,' Albert tells the old burglar who hides out with them in 'Desperate Hours', with real pride on his face. (This classic episode featured Leonard *'Rising Damp'* Rossiter as the old burglar's partner, and the burglars' relationship mirrored that of Steptoe and son.) If the humour was dark, it struck a chord at a time when many believed the nation trapped in decline, and it topped the ratings in 1964, helped by the faultless acting of Dublin-born Brambell and Harry H Corbett (one of Britain's few true method actors). In the General Election of that year, Labour leader Harold Wilson persuaded BBC Director-General Hugh C Greene to postpone transmission of *Steptoe and Son* until after the polls closed, a move Wilson thought won him thirteen extra seats and victory. Greene was later knighted.

The episodes from the fifth season (1970) onwards were transmitted under the title *The Return of Steptoe and Son,* the fourth season having ended in 1965. A radio version ran from 1966 and lasted for fifty-two episodes.

The series spawned two feature films, *Steptoe and Son* (1972) and *Steptoe and Son Ride Again* (1973), and was remade in America as *Sanford and Son* (with the black cast of Red Foxx and Desmond Wilson, 1972–7, NBC).

Among the classic *Steptoe and Son* episodes are: Desperate Hours/The Piano/The Holiday/Oh, What a Beautiful Mourning/Loathe Story (in which Harold's girlfriend is played by Joanna Lumley)/And So to Bed (in an attempt to go upmarket, Harold buys a water bed)/Porn Yesterday.

◀◀◀ Taxi *was a rare example of an American blue-collar comedy.*

SYKES

UK 1960–5, 1971–9, Approx 78 x 30m, bw/col BBC/BBC1. BBC TV.

CR *Eric Sykes.* **PR** *Various, including Dennis Main Wilson, Sydney Lotterby, Philip Barker, Roger Race.* **WR** *Eric Sykes, Johnny Speight.* **CAST** Eric *Eric Sykes* Hattie *Hattie Jacques.*

Much-loved British sitcom in which the ever-seeking-to-better-himself Sykes and his twin sister Hattie (Hattie Jacques, wife of John Le Mesurier from >*Dad's Army*) shared a house at 24 Sebastapol Terrace, Suburbia. Initially, the weekly plots were prompted by the arrival of new gadgets or goods, the episodes being transmitted as 'Sykes and a –', but later seasons settled down into more standard domestic crises. Often to be found on the periphery of the plot was Mr Brown, the belittling neighbour, and Corky (Deryck Guyler from >*Please Sir!*), the pompous policeman.

The episode 'Sykes and a Plank' was expanded into a classic Monsieur Hulot-like silent comedy film, released by Associated London Films in 1964 as *The Plank.*

TAXI

USA 1978–83, 113 x 30m, col ABC. John Charles Walters Productions. UK tx *1980–5, BBC2.*

CR *James L Brooks, Stan Daniels, David Davis, Ed Weinberger.* **EXEC PR** *James L Brooks, Stan Daniels, David Davis, Ed Weinberger.* **PR** *Glen Charles, Les Charles.* **DR** *Various, including James Burrows,*

Noam Pitlik, Danny De Vito, Harvey Miller, Richard Sakai, David Lloyd, Michael Zinberg. **WR** *Various, including James L Brooks, Stan Daniels, David Davis, Ed Weinberger, Glen Charles, Les Charles, Earl Pomerantz, Barry Kemp, Holly Holmberg Brooks, Ken Estin, Sam Simon, Dari Daniels, Michael Leeson.* **MUS** *Bob James ('Angela' theme).* **CAST** Alex Rieger *Judd Hirsch* Louie DePalma *Danny De Vito* Elaine Nardo *Marilu Henner* Bobby Wheeler *Jeff Conaway* Jim Caldwell Igatowski *Christopher Lloyd* Tony Banta *Tony Danza* Latka Gravas *Andy Kaufman* Simka Dahblitz Gravas *Carol Kane* Zena Sherman *Rhea Perlman* John Burns *Randall Carver* Jeff Bennett *J Alan Thomas.*

The aspirations and frustrations of the staff of New York's Sunshine Cab Company was the focal point of this comedy, which was created by ex-MTM staffers, James L Brooks, Stan Daniels, David Davis and Ed Weinberger. Having spent some years on MTM's shows about single, middle-class women (>*The Mary Tyler Moore Show, Phyllis,* >*Rhoda*), the group wanted to do a blue-collar comedy about 'guys'. The principal character of the show was Alex (Judd Hirsch, *Delvecchio*), a philosophical cabbie, and the only sensible person in the garage. Louie DePalma (Danny De Vito) was the malevolent, dwarfish dispatcher, who sat in the cage giving orders. Latka (Andy Kaufman) was the mechanic, and possessor of only the most fractured English. Reverend Jim (Christopher Lloyd), a mind-warped ex-hippie, Bobby, a bit actor, Elaine (Marilu Henner, later >*Evening Shade*), an art gallery assistant, Tony, a boxer, and John, a student, were all part-time drivers who used the garage as a way station on the road to better things (or so they hoped). In the 1980–1 season Latka married a daffy woman from his homeland by the name of Simka. Although the show finished its first two seasons in the top twenty, it slid down the ratings thereafter. ABC unceremoniously cancelled the show, despite critical acclaim for its scripts and ensemble acting (among other Emmys, it won three straight Emmys for Outstanding Comedy Series, plus acting Emmys for Hirsch and De Vito, and a directing and a writing Emmy). In 1981 the NBC network picked up the series for a year, but were unable to revive its ratings fortunes. Popular taste was changing, and the show's sympathy for its misfit characters just did not fit Reaganite times. Guest actors included Rhea Perlman (who married De Vito on set, during a lunchbreak) and Ted Danson, who did a turn as an egotistical hairdresser in 'The Unkindest Cut'. Both went on to star in >*Cheers,* the next work of *Taxi* producers Les and Glen Charles. As did another *Taxi* guest, George Wendt, who appeared in the segment 'Latka the Playboy'.

TERRY AND JUNE

UK 1979–87, 65 x 30m, col BBC1. BBC TV.

CR *John Kane.* **PR** *Peter Whitmore, John B Hobbs, Robin Nash.* **DR** *Various, including David Taylor, Peter Whitmore.* **WR** *Various, including John Kane, Colin Bostock-Smith, Jon Watkins, Dave and Greg Freeman.* **CAST** Terry *Terry Scott* June *June Whitfield* Sir Dennis Hodge *Reginald Marsh* Miss Fennel (secretary) *Joanna Henderson* Beattie *Rosemary Frankau.*

Suburban sitcom about marital ups and downs set in Purley, Surrey, with Terry Scott and June Whitfield playing Terry and June Medford. The series was a virtual TV synonym for blandness; the crises from which *Terry and June* made dramas included visits from Terry's boss, looking after a neighbour's dog, and Terry's misunderstanding about his wife's 'infidelity'. Throughout all these innocent misadventures tubby Terry (played to overgrown schoolboy perfection by Scott) blustered and June smiled knowingly. Although not described as such, the show was a sequel to *Happy Ever After* (1974–8), in which Scott and Whitfield played the Fletchers, trying to get along together after their children had flown the nest.

June Whitfield, archetypal sitcom woman, originally came to prominence as Eth, the fiancée of Ron Glum in radio's *Take It From Here*. She first worked with Terry Scott in 1969 in *Scott On*, and among her other small-screen appearances are *Beggar Thy Neighbour, Idiot Weekly, The Best Things In Life, The Fossett Saga*, the nurse in the *>Hancock's Half-Hour* 'Blood Donor' sketch and, more recently, *>Absolutely Fabulous*. Terry Scott's other television credits include *Hugh and I* and *Son of the Bride*.

Terry and June was later spoofed by camp comic Julian Clary (*>Saturday Live, Sticky Moments with Julian Clary*) in *Terry and Julian* (1992, 6 x 30m, C4) which posited Clary as a homeless Channel 4 celebrity who moves in with a South London lad for innuendo, decorating and flat-sharing bliss. And robbing the Bank of England. June Whitfield even did it the honour of a guest appearance. The writers were Clary, Paul Merton and John Henderson.

THAT WAS THE WEEK THAT WAS

UK 1962–3, 36 x 50m, 2 x c60m, bw BBC. BBC TV.

CR *Ned Sherrin.* ***PR*** *Ned Sherrin.* ***DR*** *Ned Sherrin.* ***WR*** *Various, including John Cleese, David Frost, Malcolm Bradbury, Bernard Levin, Lance Percival, Millicent Martin, William Rushton, Anthony Jay, Gerald Kaufman, Roy Hudd, Eleanor Bron, Al Mancini, David Kernan, Kenneth Cope, John Wells, Timothy Birdsall, Peter Tinniswood, Peter Lewis, Charles Lawson, Dennis Potter, Jack Rosenthal, Robert Gillespie, David Nathan, Christopher Booker, Willis Hall, Keith Waterhouse, Brian Glanville.* ***CAST*** *David Frost, William Rushton, Kenneth Cope, Lance Percival, Al Mancini, David Kernan, Bernard Levin, Timothy Birdsall, John Wells, Eleanor Bron, Roy Hudd, Roy Kinnear, John Bird.*

Or *TW3* as it came to be abbreviated. The show grew out of the boom in British political satire in the early sixties (the founding of Peter Cook's Establishment Club, *Private Eye* magazine), a movement rocket-fuelled by the Profumo scandal. *TW3* took the new satire to TV, with a team of presenters – led by David Frost – who gleefully but skilfully filleted and ridiculed the week's political nonsense and pomposities in sketches, reports and songs (these trilled by Millicent Martin). It courted controversy, and found it, with Tory MPs requesting the Postmaster-General to censor the show. He declined. Highlights included 'A Consumer's Guide to Religion', David Frost's listing of the remnants of Britain's Empire ('and not forgetting Sweet Rockall'), and his coolly savage attack on the

probity of Home Secretary Henry Brooke, 'the most hated man in Britain' (ended, as per his other verbal lashings, with trademark sign-off, 'Seriously, though, he's doing a grand job'). John Cleese, Dennis Potter, Anthony Jay (later >*Yes, Minister*), Jack Rosenthal, David Nobbs (>*The Fall and Rise of Reginald Perrin*) and Keith Waterhouse were among the writers. The ratings were tall, the influence broad, but an American version, also with

▲▲▲ *David Frost (right) and the cast of* That Was the Week That Was.

Frost, plus Buck Henry, Henry Morgan and all (1964–5, NBC), never took off. Meanwhile, back in Britain, the BBC pulled *TW3* before the election year of 1964, fearing that the show might influence the electorate.

Seriously, though, they were doing a grand job.

TILL DEATH US DO PART

UK 1966–74, 53 x 30m, 1 x 45m, bw/col BBC1. BBC TV.

CR *Johnny Speight.* **PR** *Dennis Main Wilson, David Croft.* **DR** *Douglas Argent, Colin Strong.* **WR** *Johnny Speight.* **MUS** *Dennis Wilson.* **CAST** Alf Garnett *Warren Mitchell* Else *Dandy Nichols* Rita *Una Stubbs* Mike *Anthony (Tony) Booth; plus John Junkin, Roy Kinnear, Joan Sims, Pat Coombes.*

▼▼ *Dandy Nichols takes a well-earned rest in* Till Death Us Do Part.

The monstrous caricature of an East End working-class Tory that was Alf Garnett (played by former Radio Luxemburg DJ Warren Mitchell), West Ham supporter and hater of 'yer coons', first appeared in a 1965 BBC *Comedy Playhouse*. There the family was known as the Ramseys, and Gretchen Franklin (later *EastEnders*) played the 'silly moo', otherwise known as wife Else. In translation to a regular series, the cast stabilized as Mitchell, Dandy Nichols (aka Daisy Nichols) as Else, Una Stubbs as daughter Rita, and Anthony Booth (father of Cherie, the wife of PM Tony Blair) as son-in-law Mike, the 'randy scouse git'. To Alf's

eternal ire, Mike had longish hair (occasioning the epithet 'Shirley Temple') and was a Trotskyist, a reader of *Keep Left* newspaper. Week after week, docker Alf treated his family to rants on whatever happened to catch his fancy, delivering the diatribes from the armchair below the flying ducks and pictures of 'yer Majesty' and Winnie Churchill in the sitting-room of their house in Wapping High Street. Particular targets were blacks, the permissive society, women, Edward Heath (for taking Britain into the Common Market and for going to a grammar school, not a 'proper' Tory training ground like Eton). The series attracted numerous complaints – not least from moral guardian Mary Whitehouse, who once counted seventy-eight 'blaadys' in one episode – and from those who failed to see that Garnett was an ironic portrait, not a role model. His creator was Johnny Speight, a former East Ender himself, and an ex-member of the Communist Party. Mitchell's performance was a *tour de force,* perfect in every word and physical gesture, but the rest of the superlative cast was indispensable as comic foils and counterpoints.

In 1981 ATV tried a revival show *Till Death...* (set in Eastbourne), which was followed in 1985 by a BBC sequel to *Till Death Us Do Part,* called *In Sickness and In Health* (1985–92, 46 x 30m, BBC1). In both of these only Mitchell appeared regularly (although Nichols was cast as Else, the actress was in failing health) and both were

Up the 'ammers

Silly moo!

mediocre compared with the original. Also the fact that a right-wing Conservative government was in power made Alf's outrages difficult to pull off with plausibility, while his particular prejudices seemed dated. A more telling parody of working-class Conservatism in the eighties was Harry Enfield's *>Saturday Live* character, Loadsamoney.

The format of *Till Death* sold to America as *>All in the Family,* another sitcom colossus, and the show also became popular in Germany, where the Garnetts were known as the Tetzlaffs.

There were two feature films, *Till Death Us Do Part* (1969) and *The Alf Garnett Saga* (1972), both made by Associated London Films/Black Lion.

To the Manor Born

UK 1979–81, 21 x 30m, col BBC1. BBC TV. US tx *1982 Syndicated.*

CR *Peter Spence.* **PR** *Gareth Gwenlan.* **WR** *Peter Spence, Christopher Bond.* **MUS** *Ronnie Hazlehurst.* **CAST** Audrey Forbes-Hamilton *Penelope Keith* Richard DeVere *Peter Bowles* Mrs Plouvicka (DeVere's mother) *Daphne Heard* Marjory Frobisher *Angela Thorne* Brabinger (the butler) *John Rudling.*

Popular British sitcom (it topped the ratings for three consecutive seasons) built around the British comedic perennial: class. Penelope Keith (*>The Good Life*) starred as snobbish Audrey

Forbes-Hamilton, whose widowed penury obliged her to sell her 400-year-old country pile, Grantleigh Manor, to *nouveauriche* grocer Richard DeVere (Peter Bowles, the *Irish RM, Only When I Laugh*). Moving into the gatehouse, she then endured a love/hate relationship with the gaffing DeVere, until love triumphed and she moved back into Grantleigh as Mrs DV. Throughout, Audrey's friend Marjory was an absolute brick. The setting was the fictional Somerset village of Cricket St Thomas.

Originally intended for radio, but diverted to the small screen by the BBC, the show finally aired on its intended medium in 1997, with Keith Barron (from holiday romp *Duty Free*) as DeVere.

The Tracey Ullman Show

USA 1987–90, 52 x 30m, col Fox. 20th Century Fox/Gracie Films. UK tx *1988, BBC2.*

CR *James L Brooks.* **EXEC PR** *James L Brooks, Heide Perlman, Ken Estin, Jerry Belson, Sam Simon.* **CAST** *Tracey Ullman, Dan Castellaneta, Joe Malone, Julie Kavner, Sam McMurray, Anna Levine.*

Originally a chorus dancer for Les Dawson (a job from which she was sacked after forgetting to attire herself in underwear for one performance), Tracey Ullman first came to notice in *Three of a Kind* (1981–3, BBC1, with Lenny Henry and David Copperfield). Stints on *A Kick Up the 80s* and >*Girls on Top* followed, before she headed to Hollywood and her own skit/playlet series, *The Tracey Ullman Show.* Created by James L Brooks, this allowed Ullman's talent for characterization and mimicry to bloom; yuppie Sarah Downey, Tina the postal worker, anthropologist Ceci (who lived in darkest Africa with her monkeys), South African golfer Kiki Howard-Smith and nervous spinster Kay all became US TV favourites. The show was awarded a 1990 Emmy, but in retrospect her supporting cast (which included Julie Kavner and Dan Castellaneta) seems under-used and the material patchy. History is likely to suggest that the main contribution of *The Tracey Ullman Show* to the general comic well-being of humanity was as the launch pad for >*The Simpsons,* shown in animated segments between the live-action skits.

The Two Ronnies

UK 1971–86, 68 x 30m, 4 x 60m, col BBC1/2. BBC TV.

EXEC PR *James Gilbert, Michael Hurll.* **PR** *Various, including Peter Whitmore, Paul Jackson, Marcus Plantin.* **DR** *Various, including Marcus Plantin.* **WR** *Various, including Gerald Wiley (aka Ronnie Barker), John Cleese, Spike Milligan, David Nobbs, Terry Jones, Michael Palin, John Sullivan.* **CAST** *Ronnie Barker, Ronnie Corbett.*

Here Ronnie Barker and Ronnie Corbett (who had first worked together on >*The Frost Report*), were in a sketch and gag show of unchanging format: mock news items, some skits, a transvestite musical number, a song from a guest MOR chanteuse, Corbett in a sit-down monologue, and the tag sign-off line, 'It's goodnight from me –

and it's goodnight from him.' Perhaps the favourites were the Barker routines where he masticated the English language into glorious innuendoes and malapropisms whilst retaining the straight-faced persona of a bank manager or similar. The spoof serials – Spike Milligan's *The Phantom Raspberry Blower of Old London Town,* and the Charley Farley and Piggy Malone private investigations – also hit the humour spot. Milligan, John Cleese, John Sullivan, David Nobbs, Michael Palin and Terry Jones were all to be found toiling in the show's writing room.

Up Pompeii!

UK 1969–70, 14 x 35m (inc pilot), col BBC1. BBC TV.

CR *Talbot Rothwell.* **PR** *Michael Mills, David Croft, Sydney Lotterby, Paul Lewis.* **WR** *Talbot Rothwell, Sid Collin.* **MUS** *Alan Braden.* **CAST** Lurcio *Frankie Howerd* Senna *Jeanne Mockford* Plautus *William Rushton* Ammonia *Elizabeth Larner* Nausius *Kerry Gardner* Ludicrus *Max Adrian/Wallis Eaton/Mark Dignam* Erotica *Georgina Moon.* Video *BBC.*

Ancient Roman costume romp, loosely derived from the plays of Plautus (via *A Funny Thing Happened on the Way to the Forum*), featuring Frankie Howerd as Lurcio, the slave to the household of philandering senator Ludicrus Sextus. The double entendres in this TV orgy of bad taste, with household slave Lurcio playing middle-aged Cupid to everyone from Sextus' nymphomaniacal daughter Erotica to his effete, lovelorn son

The Prologue...

Nausius, were considered daring at the time. Legend has it that the puns even caused the veteran ex-music-hall star to 'blink a bit'. In between matchmaking, cynical Lurcio commentated on the bawdiness around him in asides to camera ('breaking the fourth wall') and tried to deliver his 'The Prologue'. Among the other characters seen was the mad soothsayer, Senna, always prophesying the town's doom.

As the seventies progressed, the show became tagged as sexist, although its nudge-nudge, seaside postcard-like humour actually poked fun at sex, rather than treating women as sex objects. A feature film version was produced by EMI in 1971. With the close of the show in 1972, Howerd moved on to *Whoops Bagdad!* (1973, 6 x 30m, BBC1), in which he played Arabian servant Ali Oopla – which was merely a change of setting for the same jokes. Howerd's Lurcio returned briefly in a 1975 Easter Monday special, *Further Up Pompeii!.*

In the early nineties, Howerd (and thus *Up Pompeii!*) was rediscovered by a new generation of TV watchers, and the 'weary camel' (as Howerd described himself) achieved a revered status in youth circles. In response London Weekend Television commissioned a 1991 pilot (unsuccessful) for a new version of the show entitled *Up Pompeii, Missus.* Following Howerd's

▶▶▶ *'Titter ye not...' Frankie Howerd stars as Lurcio in* Up Pompeii!

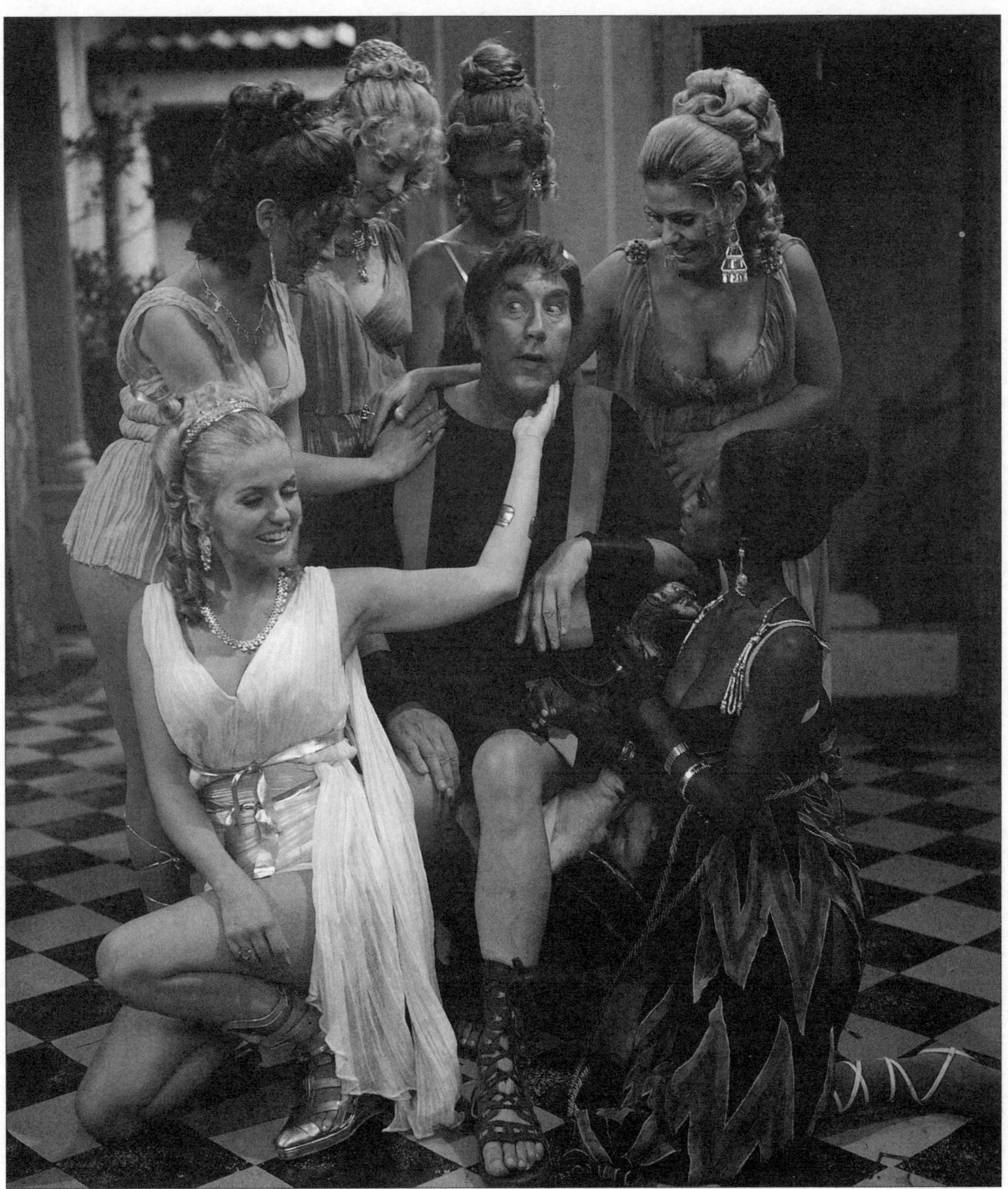

death in 1992, the British satellite station UK Gold aired the BBC series *Then Churchill Said to Me,* in which Howerd played one of the minions (Private Percy Potts, the batman to Lt Col Robin Witherton, as played by Nicholas Courtney) in Churchill's wartime bunker. Originally made in the early eighties, the series had been shelved during the Falklands conflict, and never previously screened.

The catchphrases of *Up Pompeii!* were: 'Titter ye not, missus' and 'Nay, nay, thrice nay'.

VIC REEVES' BIG NIGHT OUT

UK 1990–2, 28 x 30m, 1 x 60m, col C4. Channel X.

EXEC PR *Alan Marks, Robert Jones.* **PR** *Peter Orton.* **DR** *Peter Orton.* **WR** *Vic Reeves and Bob Mortimer.* **CAST** *Vic Reeves, Bob Mortimer.*

'You wouldn't let it lie!' Another moment of inanity in Vic Reeves' Big Night Out.

What's on the end of the stick, Vic?

An almost uncategorizable – although Northern Dadaist variety show might do – entertainment featuring velvet-suited Vic Reeves (born Jim Moir) and ex-solicitor sidekick Bob Mortimer. Developed from a stage show, *Big Night*'s novel creations (Les, Wavy Davy, Graham Lister, the Slitherer – the latter being Paul Whitehouse in his TV début) and cultural parody (Novelty Island, the Wheel of Justice) earned it a devoted late-night audience, with its catchphrases 'What's on the end of the stick, Vic?' and 'You wouldn't let it lie' becoming playground favourites. The nonsense continued, in somewhat watered-down fashion, in the more mainstream *The Smell of Reeves and Mortimer* and the game show spoof *Shooting Stars*.

WAYNE'S WORLD

UK 1992, 8 x 10m, col BBC2. NBC. US tx *1988–94 (as segment of* Saturday Night Live*), NBC.*

CR *Mike Myers.* **CAST** Wayne Campbell *Mike Myers* Garth Angar *Dana Carvey.*

The excellent! adventures of two Heavy Metal teens, smart-arse Wayne (British comedian Mike Myers) and gimpy Garth, as they present a local cable programme from a mid-American basement, with guest star interviews, 'slut court', and omnipresent air guitar-playing. And indulgences in pubescent fantasy, like an in-bed with a fetishistically dressed Madonna. Schwing!

Mirth quotient? Maximum. For nerds. Originally screened as vignettes in >*Saturday Night Live, Wayne's World* spun off a 1992 $100 million-grossing movie (directed by Penelope Spheeris), with its idiosyncratic humour briefly entering the Zeitgeist. Echos of *Wayne's World* continued down the TV nineties in such shows as >*Beavis and Butt-head* and the British DIY TV series, *The Adam and Joe Show,* presented from a Brixton bedsit.

WELCOME BACK, KOTTER

USA 1975–9, 95 x 30m, col ABC. The Komack Co/Wolper Productions. UK tx *1981, ITV.*

CR *Gabe Kaplan and Peter Myerson.* **PR** *David Wolper, James Komack.* **MUS** *John B Sebastian ('Welcome Back' theme).* **CAST** Gabe Kotter *Gabriel Kaplan* Julie Kotter *Marcia Strassman* Vinnie Barbarino *John Travolta* Arnold Horshak *Ron Palillo* Freddie 'Boom Boom' Washington *Lawrence Hilton-Jacobs* Juan Luis Pedro Phillipo de Huevos Epstein *Robert Hegyes* Mr Michael Woodman *John Sylvester White* Beau De Labarre *Stephen Shortridge* Verna Jean *Vernee Watson-Johnson* Judy Borden *Helaine Lembeck* Todd Ludlow *Dennis Bowen.*

Americanized >*Please Sir!* in which Jewish teacher Gabe Kotter (played by co-creator Gabe Kaplan) at Brooklyn's James Buchanan High School has comic problems keeping his class misfits – known as the 'Sweat-hogs' – under control.

The part of star 'Sweat-hog' Vinnie Barbarino

rocket-launched the career of John Travolta, who began leading in such movies as *Saturday Night Fever* while still playing in *Welcome Back*. By the 1978 season most of the 'Sweat-hogs' had taken part-time jobs, and the camera followed their life in work as well as inside school. Much of the show's realism was based on Kaplan's personal experience; he had once been a student in an inner-city remedial class himself.

Up your nose with a rubber hose

WHO DARES WINS

UK 1984–8, 24 x 30m, col C4.

PR *Andy Hamilton.* **DR** *Sandy Johnson, John Stroud.* **WR** *Rory McGrath, Philip Pope, Jimmy Mulville, Tony Robinson.* **CAST** *Tony Robinson, Julia Hills, Rory McGrath, Philip Pope, Jimmy Mulville.*

Sketch show. It recalled >*Not the Nine O'Clock News* in its brashness (signalled both by the comic use of the SAS motto as its title and performer Tony Robinson's stark-naked appearances), but was less tied to politics than its alternative comedy contemporaries. A sequence of skits featuring two zoo pandas, variously plotting their escape (under the alias of a Belgian dentist) and abusing 'Tojos' (Japanese tourists), were solid comedic platinum. All the cast went on to other things, and from the show evolved the influential TV independent company Hat Trick.

WHOOPS! APOCALYPSE

UK 1982, 6 x 30m, col ITV. London Weekend TV.

CR *Andrew Marshall and David Renwick.* **PR** *Humphrey Barclay.* **DR** *John Reardon.* **WR** *Andrew Marshall and David Renwick.* **CAST** President Johnny Cyclops *Barry Morse* Premier Dubienkin *Richard Griffiths* Kevin Pork *Peter Jones* The Deacon (US Security Advisor) *John Barron* Commissar Solzhenitsyn *Alexei Sayle* Foreign Secretary *Geoffrey Palmer* Lacrobat *John Cleese* Jay Garrick *Ed Bishop.*

Black comedy about the globe plunging into World War III, thanks to the machinations and miscalculations of US President Johnny Cyclops (a lobotimized ex-actor from Omaha), Premier Dubienkin of the USSR, and British Prime Minister Kevin Pork. The incident which precipitated the crisis was the attempt to restore Shah Mashiq Rassim to the throne of Iran by use of the Quark bomb – except that, unfortunately, Israel got blown up instead…

Similar in its dark, mad appeal to *Dr Strangelove* and considered by many at the time to be too possible for comfort.

THE WONDER YEARS

USA 1988–93, 115 x 30m, col ABC. New World International. UK tx *1989–95, C4.*

CR *Neal Marlens and Carol Black.* **EXEC PR** *Bob Brush.* **PR** *Neal Marlens and Carol Black, Michael Dinner.* **DR** *Various, including Neal Marlens and*

Carol Black, Michael Dinner, Peter Baldwin, Steven Miner, Arlene Sanford, Peter Horton, Daniel Stern. **WR** *Various, including Carol Black and Neal Marlens, David M Stern, Matthew Carlson.* **MUS** *Joe Cocker ('With a Little Help from My Friends' theme).* **CAST** Kevin Arnold *Fred Savage/Daniel Stern (adult voice)* Wayne Arnold *Jason Hervey* Jack Arnold (Dad) *Dan Lauria* Norma Arnold (Mom) *Alley Mills* Karen Arnold *Olivia D'Abo* Paul Pfeiffer *Josh Saviano* Winnie Cooper *Danica McKellar* Coach Cutlip *Robert Picardo.*

Sitcom about growing up in suburban America between 1968 and 1973, as seen through the eyes of teen Kevin Arnold (an effortlessly brilliant Fred Savage) as he goes through the years at the Robert F Kennedy Junior High School. Narrating the series was the voice of his adult self (Daniel Stern). Use of news clips and music from the Age of Flower Power gave the show a strong nostalgia value, but in general it avoided gratuitous wallowing in golden memories of yesteryear, in favour of domestic drollery (even poignancy) as it followed Arnold's relations with his siblings, parents and friends, particularly best buddy Paul and girlfriend Winnie. Robert Picardo (*China Beach,* later *Star Trek: Voyager*) played the school's Coach Cutlip, while the directors' list included, as well as Stern, Peter Horton, better known as Professor Gary Shepherd in the contemporaneous *thirtysomething.*

Growing up happens in a heartbeat. One day you're in diapers: the next day you're gone.

WRKP IN CINCINNATI

USA 1978–82, 48 x 30m, col CBS. MTM Enterprises. UK tx *1981–2, ITV.*

CR *Hugh Wilson.* **PR** *Various, including Hugh Wilson, Max Tash, Rod Daniel, Blake Hunter.* **DR** *Various, including Jay Sandrich, Frank Bonner, Will MacKenzie, Asaad Kelada, Michael Zinberg.* **WR** *Various, including Hugh Wilson, Blake Hunter.* **MUS** *Tom Wells.* **CAST** Arthur Carlson ('Big Guy') *Gordon Jump* Andy Travis *Gary Sandy* Johnny Caravella ('Dr Johnny Fever') *Howard Hesseman* Gordon Sims ('Venus Flytrap') *Tim Reid* Les Nessman *Richard Sanders* Herb Tarlek *Frank Bonner* Jennifer Marlowe *Loni Anderson* Mama Carlson *Sylvia Sydney/Carol Bruce* Bailey Quarters *Jan Smithers.*

Sitcom set in a small and ailing Cincinnati radio station, that followed the lives of the station's staff, principally modernizing programme director Andy Travis, incompetent station manager Arthur Carlson, nerdy reporter Les Nessman, jive-talking jock Dr Johnny Fever, laid-back black DJ Venus Flytrap, and sexy blonde secretary Jennifer Marlowe.

Picture >*The Mary Tyler Moore Show* in the setting of a small-time rock radio station and you have it. Plus a touch of 'jiggle TV' in the buxom shape of actress Loni Anderson. The show – which came from Moore's MTM company – was amusing enough to last four years, having caught a fair slice of the under-thirties audience (its intended target), but a 1991 syndicated version with three of the original characters – Nessman, Tarlek and Carlson – flopped.

YES, MINISTER

UK 1980–2, 1 x 45m, 21 x 30m, col BBC1. BBC TV. US tx *1982, The Entertainment Channel.*

CR *Anthony Jay and Jonathan Lynn.* **PR** *Stuart Allen, Sydney Lotterby, Peter Whitmore.* **WR** *Anthony Jay and Jonathan Lynn.* **CAST** Rt Hon James Hacker *Paul Eddington* Sir Humphrey Appleby *Nigel Hawthorne* Bernard Wooley *Derek Fowlds.* Video *BBC.*

Satirical sitcom featuring the Right Honourable James Hacker (Paul Eddington, >*The Good Life,* d. 1995), the newly appointed government Minister for Administrative Affairs, whose idealistic schemes were undone by his double-talking, all-powerful civil servant, Sir Humphrey Appleby (Nigel Hawthorne), the Mephistopheles of Whitehall.

The erudite, finely detailed scripts from Jonathan Lynn (>*Liver Birds,* >*Doctor in the House*) and Anthony Jay (who had seen deep into the wormy can of British politics during a spell on *Tonight*), with their elaborate exchanges of dialogue, attracted praise from public and TV industry alike, winning three BAFTA Awards for Best Comedy and selling to over forty countries. Even politicians liked it, despite being pictured as supine idiots in the control of the bureaucracy; indeed, such was the admiration of the then Prime Minister Margaret Thatcher that she enacted a scene with Eddington in *Yes, Minister* character at the National Viewers and Listeners Association Awards in 1984. Presumably this close encounter gave Lynn and Jay ideas, for by 1986 Jim Hacker had been elevated to the premiership in *Yes, Prime Minister* (1986–8, 16 x 30m). Accompanying him to Number 10 was Sir Humphrey, now promoted to Cabinet Secretary; also returning was the put-upon Private Secretary Bernard Wooley (Derek Fowlds, late of *The Basil Brush Show*). The new show lost one of the central comic principles of *Minister,* which was Hacker's inbuilt fear of damaging his prospects for advancement. Nevertheless, it provided a half-hour of hilarity way above the norm of the British sitcom in the eighties. Not the least recognition of this was that Eddington and Hawthorne both received CBEs in the 1987 Honours List, while Anthony Jay was knighted in the same year.

THE YOUNG ONES

UK 1982–4, 12 x 35m, col BBC2. BBC TV.

PR *Paul Jackson.* **DR** *Paul Jackson, Geoff Posner.* **WR** *Ben Elton, Rik Mayall, Lise Mayer.* **MUS** *Peter Brewis.* **CAST** Rick *Rik Mayall* Neil *Nigel Planer* Vyvyan *Ade Edmondson* Mike *Christopher Ryan* Jerzy Balowski *Alexei Sayle.* Video *BBC.*

Along with Channel 4's >*The Comic Strip Presents,* this was one of the first TV appearances of 'alternative comedy' in Britain. The movement began in 1980 when Peter Richardson opened 'London's newest anarchic cabaret' above Raymond's Revue Bar in Soho. The nucleus of the new club were three partnerships, who had previously performed at the Comedy Store: the Outer Limits (Peter Richardson and Nigel Planer), 20th Century Coyote (Rik Mayall and Adrian Edmondson), and Dawn French and Jennifer Saunders. The club was neither from Oxbridge nor

Rick, Mike, Neil and Vyvyan were The Young Ones.

the Northern working-men's institute circuit, and shared little other than an iconoclastic humour. Word spread, however, and TV networks came calling; Channel 4 commissioned the first >*The Comic Strip Presents* for screening in 1982, while the BBC bought *The Young Ones*.

Although it took its title from a Cliff Richard song, *The Young Ones* was far from Christian sweetness. Its characters, all essentially based on routines worked out at the Comedy Store and the Comic Strip, were four students in a shared house: Spotty Rick who, although a Cliff Richard admirer, was a violent vegetarian; Vyvyan, the headbanging punk with studs in his forehead and spikes in his hair, and a pet hamster called 'Special Patrol Group'; Neil, a lentil-eating hippie with lank hair down to his waist; and Mike, a Bogartian wide-boy with delusions of the paranoid conspiratorial variety. This unattractive bunch regularly indulged in cartoon-style violence, kicking each other, the house, and where possible the dominant ideology. Porkpie-hatted Jerzy Balowski (who, along with the rest of his family, was played by Alexei Sayle) was the landlord.

Out of this anarchy and squalidness came a humour that was infantile, slapstick, but also surreal: the food moved, new lands – even different eras – appeared outside the front door, and rock bands dropped in to play in the front room. Highly successful, the show spawned three best-selling books and two hit records by Planer as Neil (whom the actor described as 'an unpleasant, self-pitying bastard'). It also launched high-profile careers for its stars. Mayall, Edmondson and Planer went on to star in >*Filthy Rich and Catflap,* while Mayall and Edmondson also starred together in >*Bottom,* with Mayall alone going on to >*The New Statesman.* Planer tried light comedy in *King and Castle,* then invented the advice-giving thespian *Nicholas Craig – The Naked Actor,* narrated *The Magic Roundabout,* and starred as French teacher Laurence Didcott in *Bonjour la Classe.*

... which was nice

PICTURE ACKNOWLEDGMENTS

The publisher would like to thank the following for supplying images for this book: BFI Films: Stills, Posters and Designs, the Kobal Collection, the Pictorial Press and Scope Features. Every effort has been made to acknowledge all copyright holders. However, should any photographs not be correctly attributed, the publisher will undertake any appropriate changes in future editions of the book. The images listed below are protected by copyright.

14 BBC
16 ABC Filmways / Pictorial Press
21 CBS Tandem Productions / Yorkin Lear
23 BBC / BFI
26 CBS / Kobal Collection
32 ABC / Pictorial Press
34 MTV / Pictorial Press
36 ABC / Kobal Collection
37 ABC / Kobal Collection
38 CBS / BFI
40 ABC / Pictorial Press
42 BBC
44 Thames TV / Scope Features
47 BBC
48 ABC / Kobal Collection
51 NBC / Pictorial Press
54 NBC / Kobal Collection
56 BBC
59 NBC / Pictorial Press
62 BBC / BFI
67 CBS / Pictorial Press
71 HBO / BFI
73 Channel 4 / Hattrick Production / BFI
75 Channel 4 / Disney Publishing UK
80 BBC
82 Thames TV / Pictorial Press
84 Channel 4 / Hattrick Productions
85 BBC
90 Channel 4 / Paramount
93 BBC / BFI
94 NBC / Warner Bros / Channel 4 / BFI
98 Thames TV / Pictorial Press
100 NBC / CBS / Pictorial Press
103 CBS / Kobal Collection
104 CBS / Kobal Collection
107 BBC / BFI
109 BBC / BFI
111 CBS / BFI
113 NBC / Kobal Collection
114 ABC / Kobal Collection
118 BBC / BFI
119 BBC / BFI
121 Disney / Touchstone / Channel 4 / BFI
123 CBS / Kobal Collection
124 NBC / Kobal Collection
126 CBS / Kobal Collection
128 BBC
133 CBS / Kobal Collection
135 Thames TV / Scope Features
136 Roman Production / 3 Arts Entertainments / Channel 4 / BFI
138 BBC
142 Paramount / Kobal Collection
143 Gomalco Productions / Universal TV / Kobal Collection
147 BBC
149 BBC
154 CBS / Pictorial Press
157 CBS / 20th Century Fox / BFI / Pictorial Press
159 CBS / Tandem Productions / Kobal Collection
160 ABC / Sto-Rev / MCA / Universal / BFI
163 NBC / Screen Gems / BFI
165 BBC
169 ABC / Miller-Milkis Production / Henderson Production Company / Paramount
171 ITV / Scope Features
172 CBS / MCA / Universal / Pictorial Press
176 CBS / Pictorial Press
179 ITV / BFI
180 ITV / BFI
182 Channel 4 / BFI
185 BBC / BFI
189 LWT / Scope Features
190 BBC / BFI
193 ABC / Columbia Picture / Kobal Collection
195 CBS UK / Pictorial Press
197 ITV / Scope Features
198 Paramount / BFI
203 BBC
205 CBS / MTM UK / Kobal Collection
207 BBC / BFI
208 Yorkshire TV / BFI
212 Romart Inc UK / Kobal Collection
217 NBC / Castle Rock Entertainment / Pictorial Press
219 Gracie Films / 20th Century Fox / Pictorial Press
223 Witt Thomas Harris Production
227 BBC / Pictorial Press
228 Pictorial Press
232 BBC / BFI
233 BBC BFI
237 BBC / Pictorial Press
238 Channel 4 / BFI
243 BBC / BFI

INDEX

A J Wentworth, BA 18
Abbott, Bud 12
Abbott and Costello Show, The 12
Abbott, Kevin 104, 110
Abbott, Norman 173
Abrahams, Jim 197
Absolutely 12–13
Absolutely Fabulous 13–15
Abuger, Jeff 110
Ackerman, Andy 53
Ackerman, Harry 30, 39, 101, 143
Ackroyd, Dan 214
Adam, Paul 22
Adams, Don 99, *100*
Adams, Douglas 118
Addams, Charles 15
Addams Family, The 15–16
Adventures of Ozzie and Harriet, The 17
Adventures of Pete and Pete, The 17
Adventures of Tugboat Annie, The 18
Aherne, Caroline 81, 173
Alas Smith and Jones 18–19
Albert, Eddie 111
Alda, Alan 155, 156
Alderton, John 183, 196, *197*
Alexander, Danielle 179
Alexander, David 47, 96
Alexander, Jason 74, 216
Alexander, Paul 202
Alexei Sayle's Stuff 19
Alf 19–20
Alice 20
All in the Family 21–2
All Gas and Gaiters 21
Allen, Dave 64
Allen, Debbie 79, 92
Allen, Jack 27
Allen, Keith 57
Allen, Ray 20
Allen, Raymond 223
Allen, Stuart 21, 46, 150, 179, 188, 242
Allen, Tim 120, *121*
Allerdice, James 173
Allison, Judy D 44
'Allo, 'Allo 22–4
Alsberg, Arthur 101, 124
Altman, Jeff 186
Amateau, Rod 152, 178
Ames, Leon 146
Ammonds, John 167
Amos, Emma 108
Amos, John 110
Amos 'n' Andy 24–5
Anderson, Clive 18
Anderson, Eddie 130
Anderson, Harry 181
Anderson, John Maxwell 68, 152
Anderson, Jon C 163
Andrews, Harry 18
Andrews, John 34
Andy Griffith Show, The 25–6
Angell, David 89
Angus, Robert 17
Aniston, Jennifer 95
Antonio, Lou 192
Antrobus, John 27, 218
Applegate, Christina 152
Apps, Edwin 21
Apted, Michael 150
Archer, Wes 218
Are You Being Served 26–7
Argent, Douglas 84, 148, 226, 233
Arkush, Alan 166
Armitage, Charles 88
Armstrong, Curtis 166
Army Game, The 27–8
Arnaz, Desi 125
Arnold, Danny 31, 39
Arnold, Jack 47, 102
Arnold, Roseanne *see* Barr, Roseanne
Arnold, Tom 210
Arthur, Bea 104, *104*, 158
Ash, Leslie 161
Ash, Rod 220
Asher, William 39, 101, 124, 125
Askey, David 66, 69, 183
Asner, Ed 154
Asquith, Robin 46
Astin, John 15, 127
Astrof, Jeffrey 95
At Last the 1948 Show 28–9
Atkinson, Geoff 145
Atkinson, Rowan 41, *42*, 171, *171*, 184, *185*
Auer, Chris 58
Auerbach, Arnold 195
Auf Wiedersehen, Pet 29–30
Austin, Karen 181
Avedon, Barbara 39, 101
Averback, Hy 96, 155, 200
Avery, James 92
Aylmer, Felix 187

Bachelor Father 30–1
Backus, Alice 30
Baddiel, David 155
Baden-Semper, Nina 150
Badiyi, Reza 197, 220
Baer, Parley 17
Baer, Richard 96, 173
Baerwald, Joshua 51
Bagdad Café 31
Bain, Conrad 68
Baker, Roy Ward 77
Bal, Jeanne 30
Baldwin, Peter 36, 106, 114, 175, 179
Ball, Lucille 125, *126*
Ballentine, Jim 204
Balsam, Martin 21
Balzer, George 130
Bamford, Roger 29
Banks, Morwenna 12
Banner, John 119, *119*
Bannister, Trevor 27
Baranski, Christine 61
Barbeau, Adrienne 158
Barbera, Joseph 87
Barclay, Humphrey 66, 69, 183, 240
Bare, Richard L 111
Barker, Philip 229
Barker, Ronnie 96, 129, 191, 199, 235
Barnett, Walter 225
Barney Miller 31–3, *32*
Baron, Lynda 191
Barr, Roseanne 210
Barrie, Barbara 33
Barrie, Chris 49, 52, 202, 225
Barron, Fred 51
Barron, John 78
Barrymore, Michael 215
Bartell, Paul 57
Bartlett, John 108, 180
Barton, Charles 24, 79
Bass, Alfie 27
Bateman, Justine 79
Bates, Michael 140
Battley, David 213
Bavier, Frances 25
Baxter, Ronnie 150, 179, 209
Baxter-Birney, Meredith 79
Beadle, Gary 57
Bearde, Chris 221
Beasley, Allyce 166
Beaton, Norman 66
Beaumont, Hugh 143
Beavis and Butt-head 34–5
Beckett, Keith 35
Beckinsale, Richard 150, 199, 209

Belbin, Susan 188
Belion, Ed 130
Bell, Alan 106
Bell, Alan J. W. 118, 140, 206
Bellamy, Earl 25, 30, 173, 192
Belson, Jerry 187
Beluce, Meeno 37
Belushi, John 214
Belyeu, Faye Oshima 51
Benaderet, Bea 87, 194
Benben, Brian 71
Bendix, William 145
Benedict, Tony 87
Benjamin, H. Jon 70
Bennett, Harold 27
Bennett, Richard 60
Bennett, Ruth 79
Benny Hill Show, The 35–6
Benny, Jack 130–1
Bensfield, Dick 187
Benson 36–7
Benson, Andrew 180
Benson, Robby 75, 76
Bentine, Michael 129
Berg, Alec 216
Bergen, Candice 175
Berger, Gregg 74
Bergman, Alan 79
Berkley, Ballard 84
Berlinger, Robert 61, 186
Bernhard, Lee 181
Bernhardi, Lee 31
Berry, Adam 224
Berry, Ken 96
Berry, Mike 27
Berwick, James 183
Besser, Joe 12
Best of the West 37–8
Beverly Hillbillies 38–9, *38*
Bewes, Rodney 146, *147*
Bewitched 39–41, *40*
Beyt, Peter 104, 186
Bialik, Mayim 45
Bickley, William S 114, 192
Bigelow, Joe 122
Billingsley, Barbara 143
Bingham, Charlotte 183
Birch, Peter 29
Birkin, John 91, 171
Birt, John 135
Bishop, Debby 52
Bishop, Phil 127
Bixby, Bill 44, 175, 177, 220
Black Adder, The 41–3, *42*
Black, Carol 75, 240
Blackwood, Vas 145
Blair, Jon 225
Blanc, Mel 87
Blebin, Susan 189
Bless This House 43–4
Blitzer, Barry 87, 195
Bloodworth-Thomason, Linda 65
Blossom 44–5
Bluel, Richard 96
Bluthal, John 179, *179*
Blye, Allan 221
Blye, Rita Rogers 92
Bob Newhart Show, The 45–6
Bochco, Stephen 70
Boden, Richard 41
Bogart, Paul 21, 31, 99, 104
Bogert, Vincent 195
Bolam, James 146, *147*
Bonaduce, Danny 192
Bonaduce, Joseph 101
Bonerz, Paul 19
Bonerz, Peter 45, 95, 120, 175
Bonet, Lisa 58
Booth, Connie 84, *85*
Booth, Tony 233
Boothroyd, Basil 18
Borgnine, Ernest 159
Borowitz, Andy 92
Borowitz, Susan 92
Bosley, Tom 114
Bostock-Smith, Colin 18, 185, 230
Bostrum, Arthur 24
Bostwick, Barry 225
Bottle Boys, The 46
Bottom 46–7, *47*
Bouchard, Loren 70
Bough, Arthur 26
Bowles, Peter 234
Bowman, John 92
Bowman, Rob 192
Boyd, Jimmy 30
Braben, Eddie 167
Bradbury, Malcolm 231
Bradley, Richard 225
Brady Bunch, The 47–9, *48*
Brady, Terrence 183
Bragin, Rob 175
Braine, Tim 70
Brake, Elinor 204
Brambell, Wilfred 226, *227*
Braun, Zev 31
Braverman, Charles 220
Brecher, Irving 145
Bremner, Rory 225
Bresslaw, Bernard 27
Brewer, Jameson 15
Bridges, Todd 68
Briers, Richard 108, *109*
Bright, Kevin S. 71, 95
Brigstocke, Dominic 137
Brillstein, Bernie 19, 129
Brinckerhoff, Burt 175
Brint, Simon 91
Brisebois, Danielle 21
Brittas Empire, The 49–50
Britton, Pamela 177
Britton, Tony 209
Brody, Ronnie 64
Brooke, Hillary 12
Brooke-Taylor, Tim 28, 106, *107*, 153
Brookes, Mel 99
Brooks, James L. 60, 153, 205, 218, 229, 230, 235
Brown, Arnold 185
Brown, Charlotte 205
Brown, Georg Stanford 197
Brown, Ian 72
Brown, Kristofer 34
Bruckman, Clyde 12
Brush, Bob 240
Bryan, Zachery Ty 120
Bullock, Harvey 20
Bullock, J. M. J. 20
Bunting, Rosie 182
Burke, Delta 65
Burke, Kathy 116
Burns, Allan 153, 205
Burns, George 162
Burns, Jack 174
Burns, William 162
Burrows, James 37, 51, 53, 89, 95, 141, 153, 181, 205, 229
Burstyn, Neil 163
Busby, Zane 44
Butkus, Dick 179
Butler, Brett 110
Butler, Robert 67, 166
Butt, Ray 26, 56, 148, 189
Butterflies 50
Buzzi, Ruth 20, 211
Bye, Ed 46, 104, 202

Cabot, Sebastian 79
Cadell, Simon 117
Cadiff, Andy 120
Calhoun, Monica 31
Callay, Peter 76
Cameron, Ray 135
Camp, Bob 204
Campbell, Duncan 52
Canova, Diana 222
Canterbury, Bill 74
Car 54, Where Are You? 50–1, *51*
Cardiff, Andrew 179, 186
Carey, Joyce 81
Carey, Ron 33
Cargill, Patrick 81, *82*, 113
Carling, Elizabeth 108
Carne, Judy 211
Carney, Art 122
Caroline in the City 51–2
Caron, Glenn Gordon 166
Carr, Robin 18
Carraher, Harlan 101
Carroll, Bob 20, 125
Carroll, Bob, Jr. 125
Carroll, Diahann 132
Carrott, Jasper 52
Carrott's Lib 52
Carry on Laughing 53
Carsey, Marcy 58, 61, 210
Carter, Dixie 65
Carvey, Dana 239
Casey, Peter 89
Cason, Barbara 130
Cassidy, David 192, *193*
Cassidy, Ted 15
Casson, Phil 196
Castellaneta, Dan 218, 235
Chambers, Ernest 221
Chapin, Lauren 83
Chaplin, Ben 97
Chapman, Graham 28, 69, 153, 164
Chappell, Eric 209
Charkham, Esta 182
Charles, Craig 202
Charles, Glen 53, 156, 229, 230

Charles, Les 53, 156, 229, 230
Charles, Tony 180
Chase, Chevy 214
Chatfield, Les 148, 150
Cheek, Molly 116, 130
Cheers 53–6, *54*, 230
Cherones, Tom 51, 75, 216
Cherry, Stanley Z 30, 67, 102, 152, 163
Chertok, Jack 177
Chesney, Ronald 188, 201
Chevillat, Dick 111
Childress, Alvin 24
Childs, Richard 225
Citizen Smith 56–7, *56*
Clark, Jacqueline 64
Clarke, Roy 134, 140, 191
Clary, Julian 231
Claver, Bob 169, 192, 205
Cleese, John 28, 69, 84, *85*, 96, 153, 164, *165*, 231, 235
Clement, Dick 29, 146, 184, 199
Cleveland, Carol 164
Clews, Colin 167
Climie, David 187
Clunes, Martin 161
Coffey, Vanessa 204
Cohen, Amy 51, 225
Cohen, Dan 44
Colasanto, Nicholas 53
Coleman, Gary 68
Colin, Sid 27, 150
Colleary, Bob 31
Collins, John D. 22
Collins, Pauline 148, 183
Coltrane, Robbie 57
Comic Strip Presents, The 57–8
Conn, Eileen 71
Connelly, Joe 143, 173
Conner, Betty 101
Connor, Kenneth 24, 218
Considine, Tim 178
Conway, Dick 143, 173
Conway, Tim 159
Coogan, Jackie 15
Coogan, Steve 64, 137, 225
Cook, Peter 184
Cooke, Brian 81, 97, 151, 209
Coolidge, Martha 220
Coons, Hannibal 15
Cooper, Bernie 29
Cooper, Hal 47, 76, 124, 158
Cooper, Jackie 155, 220
Cooper, Trevor 88
Cope, Kenneth 231
Coppage, Marc 132
Corbett, Harry H. 226, *227*
Corbett, Ronnie 96, 235
Corcoran, Noreen 30
Cornes, Lee 46
Cornwall, Judy 134
Correll, Charles 24
Cosby, Bill 58
Cosby Show, The 58–9, *59*
Cosby, William H., Jr. 58
Costello, Lou 12
Costello, Pat 12
Cotter, Tom 88
Cottle, Matthew 97
Coupland, Diana 43
Cousins, Bob 225
Cox, Courteney 95
Crabtree, Dave 178
Cragg, Steven 70
Craig, Wendy 50, 183
Cramer, Barbara Blachot 152
Crane, Bob 119, *119*
Crane, David 71, 95
Crane, Harry 122
Crapston Villas 60
Craven, Michael 225
Crawford, Michael 223
Crenna, Richard 25
Critic, The 60
Croft, David 22, 26, 61, 117, 127, 226, 233, 236
Croft, Mary Jane 17
Crosbie, Annette 188
Cryer, Barry 28, 53, 135
Csiki, Tony 19, 158
Csupo, Gabor 74
Curran, Kevin 152
Curtin, Jane 133
Curtis, Mark 220
Curtis, Richard 41, 171, 185
Cybill 61

Dad's Army 61–3, *62*
Daily, Bill 45, 124
Daily, E. G. 74
Dalton, Abby 33
Dames, Rob 36
Daneman, Paul 183
D'Angelo, William P 20
Daniel, Jay 61, 166
Daniels, Greg 136, 218
Daniels, Marc 125
Daniels, Stan 37, 153, 229, 230
Danson, Ted 53, 230
Dante, Joe 197
Dare, Bill 225
Daria 63–4
Darling, Joan 70, 155, 205
Dartland, Dottie 51, 110
Dauterive, Jim 137
Dave Allen at Large 64
Davenport, William 124
David, Larry 216
Davidson, Bruce 116
Davidson, Ian 49
Davies, Andrew 97
Davies, Geoffrey 69
Davies, John Howard 21, 77, 84, 106, 108, 164, 171, 226
Davies, Richard 46, 196
Davies, Windsor 127
Davis, Anne B. 48
Davis, Bernadette 97
Davis, David 45, 153, 205, 229, 230
Davis, Madelyn 20
Davis, Ned E. 175
Dawber, Pam 169
Day, Linda 133, 152
Day, Robert 31
Day, Simon 81
Day Today, The 64–5
De Caprio, Al 195
de la Tour, Frances 209
De Vito, Danny 230
Deayton, Angus 19, 139, 188
Debendictis, Lisa 75
DeCamp, Rosemary 145
DeCarlo, Yvonne *172*, 173
DeCordova, Fred 130, 178
DeFore, Don 17
DeGeneres, Ellen 75
D'Elia, Bill 70
Demetral, Chris 71
Dennis, Hugh 155, 225
Dennis, Martin 161
Denoff, Sam 67
Denver, Bob 102, 152
Derman, Lou 162
Designing Women 65–6
Desmond's 66
Deuel, Peter 101
Devaney, Pauline 21
Dey, Susan 192
Dhondy, Farukh 183
Diamond, Bill 175
Diamond, Lon 192
Diamond, Selma 181
Dick Van Dyke Show, The 67–8, *67*
Dieter, Susie 218
Diff'rent Strokes 68–9
Dillon, Denny 71
Dinner, Michael 240
Dixon, David 118
Dobie Gillis 152
Dobkin, Lawrence 173
Docherty, Jack 12
Doctor in the House 69
Dodson, Jack 25
Dolenz, Mickey 163, 183
Donahue, Elinor 25, 83
Donner, Richard 99
Doogie Howser, M.D. 70
Dotrice, Michele 223
Dougherty, Pat 76
Douglas, Donna 38
Douglas, Jack 53
Doumanian, Jean 214
Dow, Tony 182, 189
Downes, Johnny 187
Dr. Katz, Professional Therapist 70
Draeger, Justin 21
Dream On 71–2, *71*
Dreben, Stan 96
Driscoll, Mark 75
Driscoll, Robin 171
Driver, Harry 43, 98, 150, 179
Drop the Dead Donkey 72–4, *73*
Dubin, Charles 155, 220
Duckman 74–5
Dukane, Sy 89, 175
Duncan, Robert 72
Dungan, Frank 33
Dunn, Clive 61, 129
Dyall, Valentine 218
Dyson, Noel 81

East, Robert 64
Eastman, Brian 131
Eberhard, Leslie 89
Eberhardt, Thom 192
Ebersol, Dick 214
Ebsen, Buddy 38
Eddington, Paul 108, *109*, 242
Eden, Barbara 124
Edmondson, Adrian 46, *47*, 57, 86, 242
Edwards, Glynn 223
Edwards, Rob 92
Eichler, Glenn 34, 64
Eilbacner, Randy 178
Ellen 75–6, *75*
Elliot, Peggy 187
Ellis, James 182, *182*
Ellison, Bob 153
Elphick, Michael 29
Elson, Andrea 19
Elton, Ben 41, 86, 171, 215, 242
Emberg, Ella 35
Emery, Dick 27, 129
Empty Nest 76
Enfield, Harry 116, 161, 225
Eng, John 74
Engel, Stephen 71
English, Arthur 27
English, Diane 175
Erdman, Dennis 139
Eschley, Norman 97
Esmonde, John 100, 108, 196
Eton, Peter 27
Evans, Barry 69
Evans, Lissa 83
Evans, Marcus 18
Evans, Michael 110
Evening Shade 76–7
Evigan, Greg 179
Exton, Clive 131

F Troop 96–7
Fabrizi, Mario 27
Fairbank, Christopher 29
Fairfax, Ferdinand 131
Fairly Secret Army 77
Falcon, Ellen 65, 92, 210
Fall and Rise of Reginald Perrin 77–8
Family Affair 79
Family Ties 79
Fanaro, Barry 104
Fanelli, Alison 17
Fast Show, The *80*, 81
Father Dear Father 81–2, *82*
Father Knows Best 83
Father Ted 83–4, *84*
Fawlty Towers 84–6
Faye, Herbie 195
Faylen, Frank 152
Fedderson, Don 79, 178
Fegen, Richard 49
Fein, Bernard 119
Fein, Irving 130
Feiner, Ben 146
Feldman, Edward H. 119
Feldman, Marty 27, 28, 153
Feldon, Barbara 99
Felton, David 34
Fenton-Stevens, Michael 139
Ferber, Mel 114, 153
Ferguson, Jay R. 76
Fern, Sheila 97, 146
Ferrett, Eve 46
Field, Sally 101
Fields, Sid 12
Filthy Rich and Catflap 86
Fincham, Peter 64, 137
Finestra, Carmen 120
Finn, Herbert 87, 122
Fisher, Bob 124
Fisher, Gregor 201
Fisher, Joely 75
Fitzalan, Marsha 180
Flaherty, Paul 139
Fletcher, Diana 77
Fletcher, Mandie 50, 189
Fletcher, Mandy 41, 66
Flett, Anne 133
Flett-Giordano, Anne 89
Fleyming, Gordon 27
Flicker, Theodore J. 31, 124
Flintstones, The 87–8
Flippen, Ruth Brooks 101
Flower, Gilly 84
Fluck, Peter 225
Flynn, Joe 159
Ford, Faith 175
Ford, Paul 195
Fordyce, Ian 28
Forster, Brian 192
Forsythe, John 30
Foster, Warren 87
Fowlds, Derek 242
Fowler, Keith 15
Fox, Michael J. 79, 225
Francis, Stan 18
Frank, Sandy 92
Frank Stubbs Promotes 88
Frankau, Nicholas 22
Franklin, Jeff 130
Franklin, Jim 106, 206
Fraser, Bill 27
Fraser, Bob 36
Fraser, Liz 77
Frasier 89–91, *90*
Frawley, James 163
Frawley, William 125
Frazer-Jones, Peter 97, 151, 209
Frazier, Ronald E 37
Frears, Stephen 57
Frederick, Malcolm 183
Freeman, Dave 43, 209, 218
Freeman, Everett 30
Freinberg, Nina 104
French, Dawn 57, 91–2, *93*, 104
French and Saunders 91–2, *93*
Fresh Prince of Bel Air, The 92–5
Friday Night Live 215
Friedberg, Billy 195
Friendly, Ed 211
Friends *94*, 95–6
Fritzell, Jim 156
Front, Rebecca 64, 137
Frost, David 28, 96, 231, *232*
Frost Report, The 96
Frost, Steve 52
Fry, Stephen 131
Fryman, Pamela 51, 89, 95
Fuest, Robert 184
Fusco, Paul 19

Gable, June 33
Gabor, Eva 111
Gadenia, Vincent 21
Gail, Maxwell 33
Galton, Ray 112, 226
Game On 97
Gammon, James 31
Gard, Cheryl 92
Garden, Graeme 69, 106, *107*
Garefino, Anne 224
Garner, Anthony 29
Garrett, Betty 21
Garrett, Lila 178
Garrison, Greg 30
Gauberg, Joe 169
Gaughan, Shannon 92
Geeson, Sally 43
Gelbert, Larry 155, 156
Geldray, Max 218
Geller, Nancy 70
Gelwaks, Jeremy 192
Gene, Richard Benjamin 200
George and the Dragon 98–9
George and Mildred 97–8, *98*
Gerber, David 101, 200
Gernon, Christine 49
Gery, Brad 129
Get Smart 99–100, *100*
Get Some In 100–1
Gets, Malcolm 51
Getty, Estelle 76
Ghost and Mrs Muir, the 101
Gibson, Richard 22
Gidget 101–2
Gilbert, Colin 201
Gilbert, James 96, 140, 184, 235
Gilliam, Terry 164
Gilligan's Island 102, *103*
Gilman, Ian 64
Girls on Top 104
Glass, Ron 33
Gleason, Jackie 122, *123*, 145
Glennister, John 88
Glickman, Jennifer 51
Glover, John 225
Gold, Missy 36
Goldberg, Gary David 79, 225
Goldberg, Whoopi 31
Golden Girls, The 104–6, *104*
Goldstein, Josh 44
Gomer Pyle, USMC 106
Gomez, Jim 204
Gonshaw, Francesca 22
Gonzalez, Alvaro J. 64
Good Life, The 108, *109*
Good Times 110
Goodall, Howard 185
Goodies, The 106–8, *107*
Goodman, John 210
Goodnight Sweetheart 108–10
Goodwins, Leslie 96

Gordon, Andrew 71
Gordon, Colin 187
Gorton, Mark 173
Gosden, Freeman 24
Gosfield, Maurice 195
Gottlieb, Alex 12
Gould, Harold J. 206
Grace Under Fire 110–11
Grady, Don 178
Grady, Mike 56
Grafe, Judy 17
Grammer, Kelsey 89
Gran, Maurice 108, 180
Grandstaff, Tracy 34, 64
Grant, Bob 188
Grant, Merrill 133
Grant, Peggy 187
Grant, Rob 18, 52, 202, 225
Grau, Doris 60
Gray, Billy 83
Green Acres 111–12, *111*
Green, Katherine 152
Green, Sid 167
Greenbaum, Everett 156
Greene, John L. 177
Greenlaw, Verna 183
Greenstein, Jeff 71
Greenwood, Joan 104
Greenwood, Laurie 182
Gregory, Benji 19
Gregory, James 33
Gretchell, Robert 20
Grey, Brad 139
Griffith, Andy 25
Griffiths, Richard 240
Groening, Matt 218
Gross, Ayre 75
Gross, Michael 79
Grossman, Budd 68
Grossman, Terry 104
Guarnieri, Terri 58
Gugino, Carla 225
Guillaume, Robert 36, *36*
Gunther, Sherry 74
Gurman, Richard 152
Guyler, Deryck 229
Guzman, Claudio 67, 124, 192
Gwenlan, Gareth 50, 77, 189, 234
Gwynne, Fred 50, *51*, *172*, 173
Gwynne, Haydn 72
Haaland, Bret 60
Hagman, Larry 124
Haig, Jack 22
Hale, Alan, Jr. 102
Hale, Gareth 112
Hale and Pace 112
Hall, Andrew 50
Hall, Cheryl 56
Hall, Kevin Peter 116
Hall, Willis 209
Hamilton, Andy 72, 185, 240
Hamilton, Rex 199
Hampton, James 76
Hancock, Sheila 201
Hancock, Tony 113, *113*
Hancock's Half-Hour 112–14, *113*
Handle, Irene 113
Hanna, William 87
Hanner, Marilu 76
Hanson, Charlie 66, 112, 183
Happy Days 114–16, *114*, *142*
Hardie, Sean 184, 225
Hardwick, Johnny 137
Hare, Robertson 21
Hargrove, Brian 51
Harper, Graeme 180
Harper, Valerie 206
Harris, Jeff 68
Harris, Neil Patrick 70
Harris, Peter 225
Harris, Susan 36, 76, 104, 186, 222
Harry Enfield's Television Programme 116–17
Harry and the Hendersons 116
Hartman, Kim 22
Hartmann, Edmund 79
Hartnell, William 27
Hawn, Goldie 211
Hawthorne, Nigel 242
Hayes, Isaac 224
Hayes, Melvyn 127
Hayes, Patricia 35, 113
Hayter, James 27
Hayward, Chris 31
Haywood, Pippa 49
Healy, Tim 29
Heard, Daphne 234
Heisler, Eileen 75
Heline, Deanne 75
Helmond, Katherine 222
Hemsley, Sherman 21
Henderson, Florence 48
Hendries, James 202
Henner, Marilu 230
Henning, Carol 15
Henning, Linda Kaye 194
Henning, Paul 38, 111, 194
Henry, Buck 99, 200
Henry, Emmaline 127
Henry, Lenny 145, 215
Henson, Jim 174
Herskowitz, Brian 44
Hervey, Jason 241
Hervey, Winifred 104
Hesseman, Howard 241
Hey, Stan 145
Heydorn, Nancy 19
Hi-De-Hi 117–18
Hickman, Dwayne 152
Higgins, David Anthony 75
Higgins, Joel 37
Higson, Charles 81, 116
Hiken, Nat 50, 195
Hill, Benny 35
Hill, Rose 22
Hiller, Arthur 15
Hills, Dick 167
Hills, Julia 240
Hindman, Earl 120, *121*
Hines, Connie 162
Hines, Ronald 183
Hirsch, Judd 230
Hislop, Ian 52, 225
Hitchhiker's Guide to the Galaxy, The 118–19, *118*
Hoare, Ken 209
Hobbs, John B. 22, 50, 230
Hodge, Stephanie 186
Hodge, Sue 24
Hogan's Heroes 119–20, *119*
Holder, Ram John 66
Holiday, Polly 20
Holland, Todd 139
Holloway, Ann 81, *82*
Holloway, Jean 101
Holmes, Michelle 108
Holton, Gary 29
Home Improvement 120–22, *121*
Honeymooners, The 122–4, *123*
Hooley, Joan 66
Hoopes, Wendy 64
Hopper, Jerry 15
Horrigan, Sam 111
Horrocks, Jane 13, 60
Horsley, John 78
Horwitt, Arnold 152
Howard, Ron 25, 114, *114*
Howells, Ursula 81
Howerd, Frankie 236, *237*
Howland, Beth 20
Hubert-Whitten, Janet 92
Hughes, Nerys 148, *149*
Hughes, Terry 104, 186
Hunt, Peter H. 200
Hunt, Richard 175
Hunter, Moray 12, 225
Hurdle, Jack 122
Hurll, Michael 235
Hurran, Nick 88
Hurwitz, Mitchell 104
Huss, Toby 17
Hutton, Gunilla 194

I Dream of Jeannie 124–5, *124*
I Love Lucy 125–7, *126*
Iannucci, Armando 64, 137
Idels, Robb 71
Idelson, Ellen 51
Idle, Eric 96, 164, 213
Ilson, Saul 221
I'm Dickens, He's Fenster 127
In Sickness and in Health 234
Ingels, Marty 127
Inman, John 26
Innes, Neil 213
Insana, Tino 197
Isaacs, David 53
It Ain't Half Hot, Mum 127–9, *128*
It's Garry Shandling's Show 129–30
It's a Square World 129
Izzard, Bryan 188

Jack Benny Show, The 130–1
Jackson, Paul 52, 86, 104, 242
Jacob, Judith 183
Jacobs, Michael 179
Jacobs, Ronald 67, 106
Jacoby, Coleman 195
Jacques, Hattie 229
James, Polly 148, *149*

James, Sid 43, *44*, 53, 98, 113
Janis, Conrad 169
Janson, David 100
Janus, Samantha 97
Jaques, Hattie 113
Jason, David 189, *190*, 191
Jay, Anthony 242
Jayne, Billy 192
Jean, Al 60, 218, 220
Jeeves and Wooster 131
Jenkin, Guy 72, 185
Jenkinson, Philip 153
Jensen, Shelley 92
Jeup, Dan 60
John K. *see* Kricfalusi, John
John-Jules, Danny 202
Johnson, Arte 211
Johnson, Bruce 169, 200
Johnson, Douglas 65
Johnson, Sam 34
Johnson, Sandy 240
Johnstone, Bruce 169
Jones, Anissa 79
Jones, Carolyn 15
Jones, Davy 163
Jones, Gordon 12
Jones, Griff Rhys 18, 185
Jones, Hilary Bevan 88, 202
Jones, Peter 118, 201, 240
Jones, Quincy 92
Jones, Shirley 192
Jones, Simon 118
Jones, Terry 96, 153, 164, 206
Joyce, Yootha 97, *98*
Judge, Mike 34, 136, 137
Juhl, Jerry 174
Julia 132
Julian, Arthur 96
Jump, Gordon 241
Junge, Alexa 95
Junger, Gil 44, 75
Junkin, John 153

Kahn, Bernie 178
Kalish, Austin 96, 101
Kalish, Irma 96, 101
Kane, Joel 152, 163
Kane, John 148, 230
Kanter, Hal 132
Kaplan, Gabe 239
Kaplan, Vic 75
Karlin, Miriam 201
Karrell, Matia 70
Kate and Allie 132–134, *133*
Katz, Allan 44
Katz, Jonathan 70
Kauffman, Marta 71, 95
Kavner, Julie 206, 218
Kaye, Gordon 22, *23*
Kean, Jane 122
Keating, Bernie 74
Keating, Larry 162
Keating, Tracy 97
Keegan, Robert 148
Keenan, Mary Jo 186
Keeping up Appearances 134–135
Keill, Ian 213
Keith, Brian 79
Keith, Gerren 110
Keith, Penelope 108, *109*, 234
Keller, Sheldon 187
Kelley, David E. 70
Kellman, Barnet 175
Kelly, April 169
Kelly, Eamon 179
Kelly, Frank 83
Kelly, Sam 22
Kelton, Richard 200
Kendal, Felicity 108, *109*
Kennedy, Gordon 12
Kennedy, Sarah Anne 60
Kenny Everett Video Show, The 135–136, *135*
Kenny, Jack 51
Kern, James V 125
Kerr, Bill 113
Kessler, Bruce 163
Kessler, Peter 173
Keyes, Paul W. 211
Khan, Brigitte 29
Kilby, John 18, 117, 127, 139
Kimbrough, Charles 175
Kimpton, Lolli 57
Kinane, Terry 108
Kincaid, Aaron 30
King of the Hill 136–137, *136*
Kinon, Richard 192
Kirk, Joe 12
Kirkland, Dennis 35
Kirkland, Mark 218
Klasky, Arlene 74
Klein 181
Klein, Howard 136
Klemperer, Werner 119, *119*
Klugman, Jack 187
Knight, Ted 154
Knot, Gary 58
Knotts, Don 25
Knowing Me, Knowing You... with Alan Partridge 137–139, *138*
Kobin, Sherry 133
Kogen, Jay 218
Komack, James 99
Krasny, Paul 166, 197
Kreski, Chris 34
Kricfalusi, John 204
Kudrow, Lisa 95
Kukoff, Bernie 68
Kwapis, Ken 139
Kyan, Terry 49, 185
KYTV 139

La Frenais, Ian 29, 146, 199
La Marche, Maurice 60
Lachman, Mort 31, 133
Ladd, Diane 20
LaMotta, John 20
Lancashire, Geoffrey 150
Lander, David L. 141
Landesburg, Steve 33
Landis, John 71
Lane, Carla 43, 50, 148
Laneuville, Eric 70, 71
Lanfield, Sidney 15, 159
Langdon, Sue Anne 30
Lange, Hope 101
Langham, Chris 185
Langton, Simon 131
Lapidus, Adam I 218
Larbey, Bob 100, 108, 196
Larner, Elizabeth 236
Larrecq, Harry 173
Larroquette, John 181
Larry Sanders Show, The 139–140
Larsen, Regina Stewart 76
Last of the Summer Wine 140–141
Lathan, Stan 129
Laufenberg, Gene 74
Laurie, High 131
Laurie, John 61
Laver, Bob 101
Laverne and Shirley 141–143, *142*
Lavin, Linda 20, 33
Law, John 129, 184
Law, Roger 225
Lawrence, Bill 225
Lawrence, Joey 45
Lawrence, Scott 31
Lawrence, Vernon 209
Layton, George 69, 127, 188, 209
Lazer, David 174
Le Mesurier, John 61, 98
Lear, Norman 21, 110, 158
Leave It To Beaver 143–145, *143*
Leavitt, Ron 152
LeBeauf, Sabrina 58
LeBlanc, Karen 70
LeBlanc, Matt 95
LeBow, Will 70
Lederer, Helen *47*
Lee, Benny 129
Lee, David 53, 89
Lee, Joanna 87
Lee, Johnny 25
Leeds, Howard 47, 68, 101
Leeson, Michael 58
Leeves, Jane 89
Lehman, Michael 139
Leisure, David 76
Lembeck, Harvey 195
Lembeck, Michael 95
Lemon, Wayne 110
Lenny Henry Show, The 145
Leonard, Sheldon 25, 67, 106, 177
Leslie, Phil 15
Lessac, Michael 110
Lester, Dick 218
Levin, Bernard 231
Levine, Ken 53
Levy, David 15
Levy, Ralph 125, 130
Lewis, Al 173
Lewis, Albert E. 187
Lewis, Bill 17
Lewis, Clea 75
Lewis, Milo 27
Lewis, Patti 218
Lewis, Robert Lloyd 192
Lewis, Stephen 188
Life with Father 146

Life of Riley, The 145–146
Likely Lads, The 146–148, *147*
Linden, Hal 31, *32*, 33
Lindsay, Ian 161
Lindsay, Robert 56, *56*, 100, 182, *182*
Linehan, Graham 83
Lipp, Stacie 152
Little Bit of Wisdom, A 148
Little, Cleavon 31
Liver Birds 148–150, *149*
Livingston, Mary 130
Livingston, Stanley 178
Lloyd, Christopher 89
Lloyd, David 37, 153
Lloyd, Jeremy 22, 26
Lloyd, John 41, 184, 225
Lobue, J. J. 222
Lobue, John L. 179
London, Jerry 192
London, Marc 174
Long, Shelley 53
Loring, Lisa 15
Lorre, Chuck 61, 110
Lotterby, Sydney 50, 140, 148, 191, 199, 229, 242
Lotterstein, Rob 51
Louis-Dreyfus, Julia 216
Louise, Tina 102
Love Thy Neighbour 150–151
Lovenheime, Robert 220
Lovers, The 150
Lovitz, Jon 60
Lowe, Arthur 18, 61, *62*
Lowell, Jeff 225
Lowney, Declan 83
Lubin, Arthur 162
Lumley, Joanna 13, *14*
Lupino, G. B. 129
Lupino, Ida 101, 102
Lupus, Peter 199
Lurcuck, Len 209
Lutes, Eric 51
Lutler, Alfred 20
Lux, Ron 74
Lynch, Joe 179, *179*
Lyndhurst, Nicholas 50, 108, 189, *190*
Lynn, Jonathan 69, 188, 242
Lynn, Susie Lewis 64

M*A*S*H 155–158, *157*
McCarthy, Neil 148
McClanahan, Rue 104
McCormick, Maureen 48
Macdonald, Aimi 28
McDonald, Graeme 27
McDowell, Paul 64
McFadzean, David 120, 210
McGee, Henry 35
McGrath, Jeff 74
McGrath, Joe 129, 184
McGrath, Rory 18, 240
McHale's Navy 159–161, *160*
MacKay, Fulton 199
McKean, Michael 141
McKee, Gina 145
McKenna, Bernard 180, 209
Mackenzie, Will 51, 166
McKeown, Allan 29
Mackian, Doon 57
Mackichan, Doon 64, 137
MacLane, Roland 143
McLean, Ian 66
McLynn, Pauline 83
McMulen, Lauren 60
MacMurray, Fred 178
MacNaughton, Ian 164, 209
McNear, Howard 25
McNicol, Kirsty 76
McNight, Tom 145
MacRae, Sheila 122
McRaven, Dale 169
McRobb, Will 17, 204
Macy, Bill 158
Madden, Dave 20
Madoc, Ruth 117
Maffeo, Gayle S. 120
Mahoney, John 89
Makin, Paul 108, 182
Malick, Wendie 71
Mallett, David 135
Malone, Joe 235
Maltese, Mike 87
Man About the House 151
Mancuso, Gail 95, 210
Mandabach, Caryn 61
Mandan, Robert 222
Manoff, Dinah 76
Mansfield, Sally 30
Mansi, John Louis 24
Mantle, Clive 18
Manulis, Martin 152
Manusco, Gail 75
Many Loves of Dobie Gillis, The 152
Marber, Patrick 64, 137
Marcil, Chris 34
Marcus, Russell 192
Margolis, Jeff 210
Maria, Eve 166
Markle, Fletcher 146
Markowitz 74
Markowitz, Michael 74
Marks, Alan 238
Marks, Hilliard 130
Marks, Laurence 108, 180
Marks, Lawrence 119
Markus, John 58
Marlens, Neal 75, 240
Marner, Richard 22
Maronna, Mike 17
Marquette, Jack 173
Marr, Pati 173
Married... with Children 152–153
Marsh, Reginald 230
Marshall, Andrew 19, 185, 240
Marshall, Garry 114, 141, 169, 187
Marshall, Tony 169
Martin, Anne-Marie 220
Martin, Dick 45, 211
Martin, Jessica 225
Martin, Millicent 231
Martinson, Leslie H. 68
Marty 153
Marx, Marvin 122
Mary Tyler Moore Show, The 153–155, *154*
Mary Whitehouse Experience, The 155
Masters, Billy 51
Mastrogeorge, Harry 153
Mathers, Jerry 143
Mathie, Marion 18
Matthews, Arthur 83
Matthews, Larry 67
Matura, Mustapha 183
Maude 158–159, *159*
Maude, Mary 28
Mauldin, Nat 31
May, Juliet 145, 202
Mayall, Rik 46, *47*, 86, 180, *180*, 242
Mayberry, Russ 163, 192
Meadows, Audrey 122
Meara, Anne 20, 21
Medina, Benny 92
Medwin, Michael 27
Megahy, Francis 29
Mekka, Eddie 141
Melman, Jeff 89, 92
Melvin, Allan 21
Men Behaving Badly 161–2
Merrill, Howard 96
Merryfield, Buster 189, *190*
Mervyn, William 21
Metcalfe, Burt 155
Meyer, George 218
Meyers, Ari 133
Michaels, Lorne 214
Michelle, Vicki 22
Mikeon, Philip 20
Milkis, Edward K. 114, 141
Millan, Tony 19, 49
Miller, Didney 177
Miller, Gary H. 92
Miller, Harvey 187
Miller, Mary 153
Miller, Paul 129, 214
Miller, Sidney 39
Miller, Thomas L. 114, 141
Milligan, Spike 218, 235
Mills, Michael 18, 100, 153, 223, 236
Minster, Hilary 22
Misch, David 74
Mister Ed 162
Mitchell, Shirley 30
Mitchell, Warren 113, 233
Mockford, Jeanne 236
Moffat, Jordan 31
Moliarno, Al 187
Monkees, The 163–4, *163*
Monsoon, Edina 13
Montagne, Edward J. 159, 195
Montagu, Felicity 19
Monte, Eric 110
Montgomery, Belinda 70
Montgomery, Elizabeth 39
Monty Python's Flying Circus 164–6, *165*
Moonlighting 166–7
Moore, Del 30
Moore, Dudley 184
Moore, Mary Tyler 67, *67*, 153–155, *154*
Moore, Rich 60, 218
Moore, Tim 24
Moore, Tom 53, 61

Moorehead, Agnes 39
Mordente, Tony 79
Morecambe, Eric 167
Morecambe and Wise Show, The 167–8
Morgan, Dermot 83
Morgan, Harry 155
Morgan-Witts, Max 27
Mork and Mindy 169–70, *169*
Morris, Christopher 64
Morris, Howard 25
Morris, Linda 89
Morrisey, Neil 161
Morrow, Neil 130
Morse, Barry 240
Morse, Hollingsworth 96, 101
Mortimer, Bob 238
Mortimer, Johnnie 81, 97, 150, 151, 209
Mortimer, Marcus 19, 155
Mosher, Bob 143, 173
Moss, Denise 89, 175
Mount, Peggy 98
Moye, Michael G. 152
Mr Bean 171
Mrs Merton Show, The 173
Muir, Frank 69
Muir, Graeme 183, 226
Mula, Frank 218
Mulhare, Edward 101
Mullen, Marjorie 153
Mulligan, Richard 76
Mulville, Jimmy 18, 240
Mumford, Thad 156
Munroe, Carmen 66
Munsters, The *172*, 173–4
Muppet Show, The 174–5
Murdoch, George 33
Murphy, Brian 97, *98*
Murphy Brown 175–6, *176*
Murphy, Joey 61
Murray, Harry 110
Music, Lorenzo 45, 205
Musquiz, Raymie 74
My Favorite Martian 177–8, *177*
My Mother the Car 178
My Three Sons 178–9
My Two Dads 179
Myers, Mike 239
Myerson, Alan 45
Myerson, Peter 239
Mylod, Mark 81

Nabors, Jim 25, 106
Nader, Michelle 225
Nail, Jimmy 29
Najimy, Kathy 137
Nallon, Steve 225
Napier, Charles 60
Nash, Robin 108, 230
Nathan, Mort 104
Naylor, Doug 18, 52, 202, 225
Nedwell, Robin 69
Nelson, Dave 17
Nelson, Don 101
Nelson, Eric 17
Nelson, Gary 101
Nelson, Gene 124
Nelson, Harriet Hilliard 17
Nelson, Jerry 175
Nelson, Kris 17
Nelson, Ozzie 17
Nemec, Corin 192
Nesmith, Mike 163
Neufeld, Mace 200
Never Mind the Quality, Feel the Width 179–80, *179*
New Statesman, The 180–1, *180*
Newhart, Bob 45
Newland, John 30
Newman, Paul 70
Newman, Rob 155
Newman, Tracy 75
Nicholls, Sue 78
Nichols, Charles 87
Nichols, Dandy 233, *233*
Nichols, David 51
Nickerson, Charles 20
Nickolds, Andrew 145
Nieber, Linda 225
Nielsen, Leslie 199
Night Court 181
Nightingales 182–3, *182*
Nimmo, Derek 21, 187
Nixon, Alan 12
No Problem 183
No-Honestly 183
Nobbs, David 77
Noble, James 36
Nodella, Burt 99
Nolas, Lloyd 132
Normal, Henry 137
Norman, Christina 34
Norris, Pamela 65
Norriss, Andrew 49
North, Alan 199
Not in Front of the Children 183–4
Not the Nine O'Clock News 184–6, *185*
Not Only... But Also... 184
Nurses 186
Nyby, Christian I 166
Nye, Bud 152
Nye, Simon 88, 161

Oakley, Bill 218
O'Brian, Bob 162
O'Brien, Conan 218
O'Connor, Carroll 21
Odd Couple, The 187
Oddie, Bill 69, 106, *107*
O'Donnell, Steven 46
O'Donoghue, Denise 97, 116
O'Donoghue, Michael 214
Oh Brother! 187–8
O'Hanlon, Ardal 83
Oldroyd, Liddy 66, 72
Oliver, Lin 116
On the Buses 188–9, *189*
One Foot in the Grave 188
O'Neill, Ed 152
Only Fools and Horses 189–91, *190*
Open All Hours 191–2
Oppenheimer, Jess 99, 125
Orenstein, Bernie 133
O'Riordan, Shaun 98
Orkin, Harvey 195
Orlton, Peter 112
Orr, William T. 96
Orton, Peter 238
Osborn, Ron 74
O'Sullivan, Richard 151, 209
Owen, Bill 140
Owens, Gary 211
Oz, Frank 174, 175

Pace, Norman 112
Page, Harrison 220
Palin, Michael 96, 153, 164, 206, *207*
Palmer, Geoffrey 50, 77
Pardee, John 61
Paris, Jerry 67, 114, 187
Park, Nira 57
Parker, Anthony 150
Parker Lewis Can't Lose 192
Parker, Trey 224
Parsons, Nicholas 35
Partridge, Alan 137–139, *138*
Partridge Family, The 192–194, *193*
Pasquin, John 79, 120, 210
Passaris, Lex 104
Patchett, Tom 19
Paterson, Bill 29
Patterson, Hank 111
Patterson, Ray 87
Pattison, Ian 201
Paulsen, Pat 221
Peacock, Daniel 57
Pearce, Lennard 189, *190*
Penn, Leon 17
Pennette, Marco 51
Pentland, Bill 210
Percival, Lance 231
Periman, Rhea 230
Perkins, Geoffrey 83, 97, 116, 139, 215, 225
Perlman, Heide 53
Perrin, Nat 15
Perrin, Sam 130
Perry, Jimmy 61, 117, 127
Perry, Mathew 95
Persky, Bill 67, 133
Perzigan, Jerry 89, 152
Peterman, Steven 175
Petticoat Junction 194
Pevney, Joseph 173
Pew, Joseph de 38
Phil Silvers Show, The 195–196, *195*
Philbin, Jack 122
Phillips, Arthur 87
Phillips, Clyde 192
Phillips, Lee 101, 192
Phillips, Nic 66
Pierce, David Hyde 89
Pierce, Maggie 178
Pietz, Amy 51
Pilbrow, Giles 225
Pilsworth, Michael 180
Pitlik, Noam 31, 230
Planer, Nigel 57, 86, 185, 242
Plantin, Marcus 235
Plato, Dana 68

Platt, Edward 99
Please Sir! 196–197, *197*
Pleshette, Suzanne 45
Plowman, Jon 13, 19, 91
Poeti, Paolo 76
Police Squad! 197–199, *198*
Pollack, Jeff 92
Pomerantz, Earl 37
Pons, Beatrice 50
Pope, Philip 185, 240
Porridge 199–200
Porter, Don 101
Posner, Geoff 52, 116, 145, 215
Potter, Andy 145
Powell, Nosher 57
Powell, Vince 43, 46, 98, 150, 179
Prady, Bill 51
Prager, Stanley 50
Pratchett, Tom 45
Proft, Pat 197
Pugh, Madelyn 125
Punt, Steve 155, 225
Purcel, Richard 204
Pyl, Jean Vander 87
Pyne, Natasha 81, *82*

Quark 200–201
Quark, Adam 200
Quentin, Caroline 161
Quinn, Bill 21

Rab C. Nesbitt 201
Race, Roger 148, 153, 229
Radnitz, Brad 47
Rafelson, Bob 163
Rafkin, Alan 25, 39, 45, 124, 129, 177, 205
Rag Trade, The 201–202
Ranberg, Chuck 89, 133
Randall, Tony 187
Randell, Bob 133
Randolph, Joyce 122
Randolph, Lillian 25
Ransohoff, Martin 38
Rasche, David 220
Rashad, Phylicia 58
Raskin, Carolyn 211
Ratzenberger, John 53, *54*, 76
Rauseo, Vic 89
Ravens, Jan 19, 225
Rawis, Hardy 17
Rawle, Jeff 72
Ray, Leslie 92
Raymond, Jack 87
Raynis, Richard 60
Raznicka, Deborah 169
Read, Alan 87
Reardon, Jim 218
Reardon, John 240
Red Dwarf 202–204, *203*
Reding, Nick 88
Reed, Ralph 146
Reed, Robert 47, 48, 100
Reeves, Vic 238
Regalbuto, Joe 175
Reiner, Carl 67
Reiner, Rob 21, 114
Reiser, Paul 179
Reiss, Mike 60, 218
Ren and Stimpy 204–205
Renard, Gail 209
Reno, Jeff 74
Renwick, David 19, 188, 240
Reo, Don 44, 155
Revell, Nick 72
Reynolds, Burt 76
Reynolds, David 180
Reynolds, Gene 44, 101, 119, 155, 173, 178
Reynolds, Marjorie 145
Rhoda 205–206, *205*
Rhymer, Don 76
Riback, Billy 120
Rich, John 21, 31, 36, 47, 67, 102, 106
Richards, Michael 216
Richardson, David 76
Richardson, Donald 173
Richardson, Patricia 120
Richardson, Peter 57, 185
Richens, Pete 57
Riggi, John 139
Riley, Jeannine 194
Ripping Yarns 206–208, *207*
Rising Damp *208*, 209
Rix, Jamie 18, 139
Roach, Pat 29
Robbie, Seymour 96, 220
Robbins, John 35
Robbins, Michael 77
Roberts, Renee 84
Robertson, Sid 81
Robin's Nest 209–210
Robinson, Peter 77
Robinson, Tony 41, *42*, 240
Robolledo, Julian 64
Rocas, Cleo 135
Rock, Blossom 15
Rodger, Christine 28
Rodney, Eugene B 83
Rogers, Doug 153
Rogers, Peter 53
Rogers, Wayne 156
Rolle, Esther 110
Roman, Phil 60, 136
Romero, Victor 183
Rondeau, Charles 96, 173, 187
Roper, Tony 201
Rose, Adele 43, 209
Rose, Si 159
Roseanne 210–211
Rosen, Arnie 99, 195
Rosen, Sy 31
Rosenberg, Alan 61
Rosenthal, David 75
Rosenthal, Jack 150
Rosenthal, Lisa 92
Ross, Joe E. 50, *51*
Ross, Michael 21
Rossiter, Leonard 78, *208*, 209
Rotenberg, Michael 136
Rothwell, Talbot 236
Routledge, Patricia 134
Rowan, Dan 211
Rowan and Martin's Laugh-In 211–213, *212*
Rowe, Fanny 183
Rowland, Daryl 75
Rowley, Laurie 185
Ruben, Aaron 25, 38, 106
Rubin, Aaron 195
Rubin, Stanley 101
Ruddell, Kirk J. 225
Ruddy, Albert S. 119
Ruppenthal, Chris 220
Rushton, William 231, 236
Ruskin, Coby 106
Russell, Andy 122
Russell, William D. 79, 83
Rutland Weekend Television 213–214
Ryan, Christopher 46, 242
Ryan, Irene 38
Ryan, Terry 195
Ryder, Gerald 100
Sachs, Andrew 84, *85*
Sackheim, William 101
Sacks, David 218
Saffian, R. Allan 87
Sagal, Katey 152
Saint James, Susan 133
St John, Julia 49
Sakai, Richard 60, 218
Saks, Sol 39
Sallis, Peter 140
Sande, Walter 18
Sanderson, Joan 196
Sandrich, Jay 36, 58, 99, 101, 141, 153, 187, 222, 241
Sands, Billy 159
Sandy, Gary 241
Sanford, Arlene 51, 65
Sanford, Lee 163
Sanrich, Jay 104
Sapperstein, Frank 204
Sargent, Dick 39
Satenstein, Frank 122
Saturday Night Live 214–215
Saunders, Jennifer 13, *14*, 57, 91, *93*, 104
Saunders, Lori 194
Savage, Fred 241
Savel, Dava 110
Savel, Daval 75
Sawalha, Julia 13
Sax, Geoffery 180
Sayle, Alexei 19, 57, 242
Scales, Prunella 84, *85*
Scarpitta, Guy 152
Schaefer, Racelle Rosett 44
Schaffer, Jeff 216
Scharlach, Ed 169
Schedeen, Anne 19
Schell, Frank 106
Schiller, Bob 125
Schlamme, Thomas 95, 129, 139, 220, 225
Schmock, Jonothan 44
Schneider, Bert 163
Schneider, David 64, 137
Schreiber, Avery 178
Schwartz, Lew 148
Schwartz, Sherwood 47, 102
Schwarz, Lee 53
Schwarz, Lew 27
Schwatz, Elroy 47
Schwatz, Lloyd 47
Schwimmer, David 95

Scott, Evelyn 30
Scott, Joan 150
Scott, Sawan 116
Scott, Terry 230–1
Seeger, Susan 44
Segall, Pamela 137
Seinfeld 216–217, *217*
Seinfeld, Jerry 216
Selby, Sarah 83
Sellers, Peter 218
Sen Yung, Victor 30
Sessions, John 225
Shallat, Lee 79, 175, 225
Shandling, Garry 129, 130, 139
Shane, Paul 117
Shapiro, George 216
Shapiro, Julianne 70
Shaps, Cyril 179
Shardlow, Martin 18, 41, 189
Sharlach, Ed 187
Sharp, Bernie 43
Sharp, Phil 195
Shea, Jack 65, 110
Sheehan, Tony 31
Sheldon, James 79
Sheldon, Sidney 124
Shepherd, Cybill 61, 166
Sheridan, Liz 20
Sherrin, Ned 231
Shockley, William 31
Show Called Fred, A 218
Shuiovsky, Joel 175
Shulman, Max 152
Siegel, Don 89
Sierra, Gregory 33
Sikking, James B. 70
Sikowitz, Mike 95
Silla, Felix 15
Silver, Ron 36
Silvera, Carmen 22
Silverman, David 218
Silverman, Laura 70
Silverman, Treva 153
Silvers, Phil 195–196, *195*
Simms, Paul 139
Simon, Al 38, 162, 194
Simon, David Steven 92
Simon, Neil 195
Simon, Sam 53, 218
Simpson, Alan 112, 226
Simpsons, The 218–220, *219*
Siner, Guy 22
Singer, Alexander 163
Singletary, Tony 58, 152
Slade, Bernard 192
Slaten, Troy W. 192
Slatter, George 211
Sledge Hammer 220–221
Smack, Hilton 36
Smart, Jean 65
Smethurst, Jack 150
Smith, Elaine C. 201
Smith, Hal 25
Smith, Jim 204
Smith, Liz 60
Smith, Mel 18, 184, 185
Smith, Nicholas 27
Smith, Paul 49
Smith, Will 92
Smith, Yeardley 218
Smothers Brothers Comedy Hour 221
Smothers, Dick 221
Smothers, Tom 221
Snee, Dennis 76
Snoad, Harold 61, 134
Soap 222–223, *223*
Soklon, Sidney 15
Some Mothers Do 'Ave 'Em 223–224
Sommers, Jay 111
Soo, Jack 33
Sothern, Ann 178
South Park 224–225
Spall, Timothy 29, 88
Sparkes, John 12
Sparks, Robert 30
Spavia, Tam 47
Speer, Kathy 104
Speight, Johnny 229, 233
Spence, Peter 234
Spencer, Alan 220
Spicer, Bryan 192
Spiers, Bob 13, 19, 57, 61, 84, 91, 106, 127
Spin City 225
Spitting Image 225–226
Spriggs, Elizabeth 131
Sprung, Sandy 152
Staci, Keanan 179
Stallworth, Winifred Hervey 92
Standeven, Richard 88
Stanley, Florence 179
Stapleton, Jean 21, 31
Stark, Jonathan 75
Stark, Philip 224
Starr, Ben 47, 162
Steadman, Alison 60
Steele, Austin 64, 187
Steele, Brian 116
Steen, Nancy 197
Steen, Steven 60
Stein, Jeff 31
Steinberg, David 216
Stephens, Larry 27
Stephens, Mike 22, 49
Stephenson, Pamela 185, *185*
Steptoe and Son 226–227, *227*, 229
Sterling, Dan 224
Stern, Daniel 241
Stern, Elliot 120
Stern, Leonard 99, 122, 127, 195
Steuer, Jon Paul 110–11
Stevens, Ronnie 18
Stewart, Charles 194
Stewart, Horace 25
Stewart, Mel 21
Stewart, Robin 43, 88
Stewart, William G. 43, 81
Stillman, Joe 34
Stockridge, Sara 57
Stone, Ezra 173
Stone, Matt 224
Stone, Walter 122
Storch, Larry 96
Storm, Howard 37, 141, 169, 205
Strassman, Marcia 239
Strauss, Jeff 71
Street, John 35, 129, 184
Stringer, Nick 180
Stroud, John 97, 139, 225
Struthers, Sally 21
Stuart, Mark 35, 196
Stubbs, Una 233
Stuke, Neil 97
Sugden, Mollie 26
Sullivan, John 56, 189
Sullivan, Steven 76
Sultan, Arne 99
Summer, Geoffrey 27
Summers, Hope 25
Susskind, David 20
Sutton, Frank 106
Swackhamer, E. W. 101, 124, 192
Swartzelder, John 218
Sweeney, Bob 25
Swift, Clive 134
Swit, Loretta 156
Swope, Mel 192
Sykes 229
Sykes, Eric 229
Sylvester, Ward 163
Synder, Tom 70

Tabori, Kris 70
Tackaberry, John 130
Talbot, Lyle 17
Tambarelli, Danny 17
Tarrant, Alan 53, 98
Tarses, Jay 45
Tash, Max 192, 241
Taxi *228*, 229–30
Tayback, Vic 20
Taylor, Baz 29
Taylor, David 230
Taylor, Gwen 213
Taylor, Myra 43, 148
Taylor, Ronnie 148
Temple, Renny 76
Tennant, Andy 192
Tenowich, Tom 169
Terhule, Abby 34
Terrell, Steven 146
Terry and June 230–1
Tewksbury, Peter 83, 178
That Was The Week That Was 231–2, *232*
Thomas, Betty 71
Thomas, Danny 67
Thomas, Dave 110
Thomas, Ellen 145
Thomas, Gerald 53
Thomas, Janice 13
Thomas, Tony 36, 44, 76, 104, 222
Thomason, Harry 65
Thomerson, Jean Tim 200
Thompson, Bernard 140, 148
Thompson, Emma 52
Thompson, Lea 51
Thompson, Neil 197
Thompson, Rob 71
Thompson, Tommy 65, 76
Thomsett, Sally 151
Thorkelson, Peter H. 163
Thornton, Frank 26, 129
Thorpe, Harriet 19
Thorpe, Richard 38

Threlfall, David 182, *182*
Tibbles, George 15
Till Death Us Do Part 233–4, *233*
Tischler, Bob 76
To The Manor Born 234–5
Tobin, Julia 29
Todd, Bob 35
Todd, LaVerne 76
Tokar, Norman 143
Tolan, Peter 139
Tomlin, Lily 211
Tompkins, Steve 60
Tong, Sammee 30
Took, Barry 27, 153, 164
Tork, Peter 163
Torres, Liz 21
Tovey, Roberta 183
Tracey Ullman Show, The 235
Tracy, John 179
Travolta, John 239
Trogdon, Miriam 110
Troughton, Michael 180
Tucci, Michael 130
Tucker, Forrest 96
Tummings, Chris 183
Turner, Bill 69, 183
Turtletaub, Saul 133
Tuttle, Lurene 146
Tuttle, Mark 38
Two Ronnies, The 235–6
Tyler, David 12, 225

Uger, Alan 79
Ullman, Tracey 104, 215, 235
Up Pompeii! 236–8, *237*
Urecal, Minerva 18

Valley, Jim 104
Van Dyke, Dick 67, *67*
Van Dyke, Jerry 178
Vance, Vivian 125
Vanzo, Greg 204
Varney, Reg 188, *189*, 201
Vela, Norma Stafford 65
Vertue, Beryl 161
Vertue, Sue 171
Vic Reeves' Big Night Out 238–9, *238*
Vieller, Anthony 18
Vigoda, Abe 33
Vincent, Peter 49, 64
Virgien, Norton 74
Viscardi, Chris 17
Vitti, John 218
Vosburgh, Dick 53
Vosburgh, Marcy 152

Wade, Ernestine 25
Waldman, Frank 124
Walian, Werner 92
Walker, Arnetia 186
Walker, Jimmie 110
Walker, Nancy 206
Walker, William Lucas 89
Waller, Vincent 204
Wallerstein, Herb 192
Walling, Mike 49
Walston, Ray 177
Walton, Trevor 104
Ward, Preston 15
Waring, Richard 183, 209
Warren, Michael 192
Warrington, Don 209
Wass, Ted 44, 45
Watkins, Carlene 37
Watkins, Jon 148, 209, 230
Watson, Paul 64
Wax, Ruby 104
Wayne, John *212*
Wayne's World 239
Weatherwax, Ken 15
Webster, Donald 153
Webster, Tony 195
Weege, Reinhold 31, 181
Weiland, Paul 171
Weinberger, Ed 58, 153, 229, 230
Weinstein, Josh 218
Weis, Don 114, 155
Weiskopf, Bob 125
Weiskopf, Kim 152
Weisman, Sam 79, 166
Weiss, Bob 197
Weiss, Jonathan 61
Welcome Back, Kotter 239–40
Wendle, Kevin 92
Wendt, George 53, *54*
Werner, Peter 166
Werner, Tom 58, 210
Wesson, Dick 194
West, Billy 204
West, Howard 216
Weyman, Andrew 179, 210
Weyman, Andy 61
Whately, Kevin 29
Whelan, Geoff 34
Whipple, Randy 178
Whipple, Sam 31
Whitaker, Johnnie 79
Whitcomb, Dennis 173
White, Betty 104, *104*
White, Frances 148
White, Joshua 216
White, Michael 57
Whitehouse, Paul 81, 116
Whitemore, Peter 64
Whitesell, John 210
Whitfield, June 13, 113, 230–1
Whitmore, Peter 230, 235, 242
Who Dares Wins 240
Whoops Apocalypse 240
Whorf, Richard 38
Wilcox, Den 156
Wilcox, Paula 150, 151
Wiliam, Sioned 97
Williams, Cindy 141
Williams, Graham C. 12
Williams, Spencer, Jr. 24
Williams, Kate 150
Williams, Kenneth 113
Williams, Maiya 92
Williams, Matt 58, 120, 210
Williams, Samm-Art 92
Williamson, Malcolm 72
Willimas, Robin 169
Willis, Bruce 166
Wilson, Dave 214
Wilson, Dennis Main 56, 153, 201, 229, 233
Wilson, Hugh 241
Wilson, Paul 130
Wilson, Richard 188
Wimbush, Mary 131
Windsor, Barbara 53, 201
Wing-Davey, Mark 118, *118*
Wingreen, Jason 21
Winkler, Harry 15
Winkler, Henry 114, *114*
Wisdom, Norman 148
Wise, Ernie 167
Withers, Bernadette 30
Witt, Paul 36, 44, 76, 104, 192, 222
Woddell, Pat 194
Wolfe, Ronald 188, 201
Wolper, David 239
Wonder Years, The 240–1
Wood, Duncan 96, 112, 187, 226
Wood, Helen Atkinson 139
Woodey, Nick 112
Woody, Russ 175
Woolf, Henry 213
Wopat, Tom 61
Worrell, Trix 66
Wray, Bill 204
Wright, Max 19
WRKP in Cincinnati 241
Wuhl, Robert 197
Wyatt, Jane 83
Wyatt, Tessa 209

Yarborough, Jean 12, 15
Yates, Pauline 78
Yeager, Ed 110
Yes, Minister 242
York, Dick 39
Yorkin, Bud 21
Yothers, Tina 79
Young, Alan 162
Young Ones, The 242–4, *243*
Young, Robert 77, 83, 131

Zacharias, Steve 200
Zappa, Dweezil 74
Zelinka, Sydney 87, 122
Ziegler, Matilda 171
Ziegler, Ursula 76
Ziffren, John 44, 139
Zlotoff, Lee 175
Zucker, Danny 110
Zucker, David 197
Zucker, Jerry 197
Zuckerman, David 92
Zuckerman, Stephen 76, 95
Zweibel, Alan 129, 130
Zwick, Joel 141